PUBLICATIONS OF THE McMASTER UNIVERSITY
ASSOCIATION FOR 18TH-CENTURY STUDIES

VOLUME ONE
THE VARIED PATTERN:
STUDIES IN THE 18TH CENTURY

VOLUME TWO
THE TRIUMPH OF CULTURE:
18TH CENTURY PERSPECTIVES

VOLUME THREE
CITY & SOCIETY IN THE 18TH CENTURY

VOLUME FOUR
WOMAN IN THE 18TH CENTURY
AND OTHER ESSAYS

Woman

in the 18th Century

and Other Essays

EDITORS

PAUL FRITZ • RICHARD MORTON

SAMUEL STEVENS

HAKKERT & CO.

TORONTO AND SARASOTA

1976

International Standard Book Number: 0-88866-556-3

Printed in The United States of America

A. M. Hakkert Ltd.,
554 Spadina Crescent, Toronto, Canada M5S 2J9
3807 Bond Place, Sarasota, Florida 33580

Contents

Preface

The sixteen papers selected and edited for this volume were first presented to the McMaster Association for Eighteenth Century Studies. The editors hope that, as with the previous volumes in the series, this will provide a basis for yet further discussion and debate on the central themes. The first eight papers deal with women in the eighteenth century; the next four with the relationship between the illustrator and the poetic text. The remaining papers focus on aspects of philosophy, music and theatre in the century.

The editors wish to thank McMaster University for the encouragement and financial support that has been given to the Association during the past year. In addition we wish to thank all those members of the Association who have given so freely of their time and advice. In particular, we are grateful to James King, of the Department of English, for organizing the special symposium on "The Sister Arts" at which the papers on poetic illustration were read. Once again, we are deeply indebted to Alan Samuel and the staff of A. M. Hakkert for their efficiency in seeing this volume through the press.

Hamilton, 1974   P.S.F.
R.M.

List of Contributors

Editors

Paul Fritz, Department of History, McMaster University.
Richard Morton, Department of English, McMaster University.

Contributors

Miriam Benkovitz, Department of English, Skidmore College.
G.E. Bentley, Jr., Department of English, University of Toronto.
Ruth Graham, Department of History, Queen's College, CUNY.
Robert Halsband, Department of English, University of Illinois.
Jean E. Hunter, Department of History, Duquesne University.
Wilbert D. Jerome, Department of Music, Bryn Mawr College.
Lawrence Lipking, Department of English, Princeton University.
F.P. Lock, Department of English, University of Queensland.
Paul F. Marks, Department of Music, McGill University.
David Pears, Christ Church, Oxford.
Richard H. Popkin, Department of Philosophy, Washington University.
Katharine Rogers, Department of English, City University of New York
Edward J. Rose, Department of English, The University of Alberta.
Marie Laure Swiderski, Département de Lettres Françaises, Université d'Ottawa.
Irene Tayler, Department of English, City University of New York.
Arthur Wilson, Department of Government, Dartmouth College.

Woman

in the 18th Century

and Other Essays

The Feminism of Daniel Defoe

Daniel Defoe made clear his commitment to feminism from his first important book to his last, from *An Essay Upon Projects* in 1698 to *The Complete English Tradesman* in 1726. He constantly argued, directly in his journalism and indirectly in his novels, that women had the capacity to be independent and should be given educational and economic opportunities to become so. Proposing academies for women in the *Essay*, he declared that their apparent folly came from poor education rather than natural inferiority. Like his contemporary feminists, he did disclaim any intention of "exalting the Female Government in the least," saying "A Woman of Sense and Breeding" would "scorn as much to encroach upon the Preogative of the Man as a Man of Sense will scorn to oppress the Weakness of the Woman." However, he went on to question this assumption which justified masculine government, pointing out that once women were properly educated, they would no longer be weak in judgment: "Ignorance and Folly" would be no more common "among Women than Men."[1]

Defoe's journalism — his domestic commentary in *The Review* and other newspapers and his three manuals on famly life, *The Family Instructor*, *Religious Courtship*, and *Conjugal Lewdness* — expresses the same enlightened position — a remarkably enlightened position if we evaluate it in the light of conventional thought of his time. When most of Defoe's contemporaries wrote about marriage, they hammered on the wife's duties to be faithful and to submit. Works such as *The Ladies Calling*, Lord Halifax's

1. Daniel Defoe, *An Essay Upon Projects*, Menston, England, 1969, pp. 302-3.

3

The Lady's New Year's Gift, and Bishop Fleetwood's sermons on *The Relative Duties of Parents and Children, Husbands and Wives, Masters and Servants* instruct a woman that she owes her husband first of all absolute chastity. Indeed, she must deny "herself even the most innocent liberties, if she sees they dissatisfy him."[2] Secondly, she owes him obedience: she is to "obey without Dispute, and comply with Calmness and great Readiness, even under Doubt, Suspicion, and Uncertainty of what will follow."[3] She must not presume to judge her husband's decisions nor so much as to see his infirmities.[4] Indeed, the worse he is, the more need there is for her "to carry herself with that gentleness and sweetness that may be most likely to win him."[5] All these writers assumed that the wife was alone responsible for keeping her marriage harmonious.

In striking contrast, Defoe's voluminous discussion of the problems which can arise in marriage places little emphasis on chastity, which in itself shows that he saw marriage as more than a sexual arrangement and women as more than sexual objects. He also avoided references to the wife's duty to submit and obey, even though he fully endorsed the duties which were commonly classed with it in his time, those of obedience from children to parents and servants to masters. Most significantly, he constantly insisted that the responsibilities, duties, and rights of marriage are mutual. Throughout *Conjugal Lewdness* (which despite its title is not primarily concerned with sex) Defoe insisted upon the necessity for mutual respect in marriage, mutual forbearance, and natural compatibility between the partners. He recognized that women risk more than men in marriage, but nowhere suggested that this greater commitment meant that they should be the only ones to yield in order to make their marriages work. Both men and women, he said, should resolve before marriage "to disband all Humours and ill Tempers, and sacrifice every Inclination to their

2. [Richard Allestree], *The Ladies Calling*, Oxford, The Theater, 1673, Part II, p. 29.

3. William Fleetwood, *The Relative Duties of Parents and Children, Husbands and Wives, Masters and Servants*, London, John Hooke, 1716, p. 218.

4. Allestree, Ladies Calling, Part II, p. 34.

5. *The Ladies Library*, ed. Sir Richard Steele, London, W. Strahan et al., 1772, 7th ed., II, p. 54.

Family Peace. . . . to study each others Humours, and to endeavour so to match their Tempers, that the Marriage may Unite
their Souls as well as Bodies."[6]

Indeed, Defoe was "so little a Friend to that which they call
Government and Obedience between the Man and his Wife" that
he refused even to discuss subordination in marriage. "The great
Duty between" man and wife is love, and the only obedience is
obligingness on both sides: "Love knows no superior or inferior,
no imperious Command on one hand, no reluctant Subjection on
the other." Where his contemporaries complacently assumed that
the woman was created to be a helpmate to the man, Defoe
believed the two should constantly help one another; where they
assumed that womanly love involved submission, he insisted that
love could only be genuine and satisfying between equals. Without
loving friendship, Defoe maintained, neither virtue, nor fidelity,
nor "Conscience of the Conjugal Duty," nor religion, nor
"Goodness and Submission" on the part of the wife could create a
good marriage.[7]

Just as obligations are mutual in a good marriage, blame
usually is in a bad one. In contrast to the misogynistic tradition of
attacks on bad wives, Defoe maintained that "a man and his wife
never quarrel, but there are faults on both sidides . . . if one is to
blame for beginning it, the other is to blame for carrying it on . . .
if one is passionate, the other is provoking."[8] Moreover, he was
especially ready to question a husband who complained. When a
correspondent to *The Review* asked "for Directions what to do
with a bad Wife," Defoe gave him no sympathy whatever. "She is
a very bad Wife, that a kind good Husband cannot reclaim . . .
there are such Abundance of good Wives call'd bad ones, or made
bad Ones by bad Husbands, that" Defoe is "wonderful backward
to believe a Woman a bad Wife" on her husband's word. Possibly
the man's complaints of his wife's extravagance proceed from his
own stinginess; or perhaps he holds her responsible for the entire

6. Daniel Defoe, *Review*, ed. Arthur Secord, New York, 1938, Vol. V, p. 34.
(*Little Review*, No. 9.)

7. Daniel Defoe, *Conjugal Lewdness*, Gainesville, Fla., Scholars' Facsimiles, 1967,
pp. 25-26, 28; *Review*, Vol. III, p. 399.

8. Daniel Defoe, *The Family Instructor*, Bungay, Brightly and Childs, 1816, pp.
420-21.

expense of the household, while he squanders far greater sums on his private vices or follies.[9]

In *The Complete English Tradesman*, also, Defoe made a point of clearing wives of the traditional charge of extravagance. If a man marries before he is ready to support a family, he has no right to blame his wife for the inevitable household expenses. If he conceals his financial situation from her, he cannot blame her for spending beyond their income. However tradesmen may "endeavour to excuse themselves . . . by loading their wives with the blame of their miscarriage . . . as old father Adam in another case did before them," Defoe is confident that a woman will not reduce her family to poverty if her husband "truly and timely" shows her their financial position.[10]

Defoe did not condemn out of hand even the wife who committed the paramount sin of adultery. He declared it was a man's business "to preserve the Affection of his Wife entire," for "If she is once brought . . . to have an aversion to him . . . she must . . . be more a Christian than he ought to expect of her, if she does not single out some other Object of her Affection."[11] In a letter to *Applebee's Journal* Defoe had a husband complain bitterly of the wrongs which his adulterous wife was piling upon him, only to concede finally: "If I had not been a loose, cross, reprobate Fellow to my Wife, I believe she had never been drawn away to be so Wicked, and she makes me a fair Proposal, that if I will abate my Scandalous Living, she will convince me of her Fidelity for the Future." He is inclined to take her back, for he admits that "the best way to reclaim a Wife, is to reform the Husband." A husband's wickedness does not justify adultery in his wife, but it does stop "his Mouth very much."[12]

Defoe's sympathy with wives was sharpened by his recognition of their disadvantageous position under English law and economic conditions. In fact, his awareness of the oppression of women in marriage can be matched only by that of a woman, Mary Astell.

9. Defoe, *Review*, Vol. X, pp. 223-24.
10. Daniel Defoe, *The Complete English Tradesman*, in *The Novels and Miscellaneous Works*, ed. Sir Walter Scott, Oxford, D. A. Talboys, 1841, Vol. XVII, pp. 91-94.
11. Defoe, *Conjugal Lewdness*, p. 79.
12. William Lee, *Daniel Defoe: His Life, and Recently Discovered Writings*, London, J. C. Hotten, 1869, Vol. III, p. 295.

Defoe went to the length of questioning why a woman would marry at all except to have children: "take a married Life, with all its *Addenda* of Family Cares, the trouble of looking after a Household, the hazard of being subject to the Humours and Passions of a churlish Man," or possibly of "a Tyrant, and a Family-Brute; with still more the apparent hazard of being ruined in Fortune by his Disasters if a Tradesman, by his Immoralities if a Gentleman, and by his Vices if a Rake . . . she would be next to Lunatick to marry, to give up her Liberty, take a Man to call Master, and promise when she takes him to *Honour* and *Obey* him. What! give her self away for nothing! Mortgage the Mirth, the Freedom, the Liberty, and all the Pleasures of her Virgin-state, the Honour and Authority of being her own, and at her own dispose . . . to be . . . a Wife without Children."[13] Notice here the refreshing absence of sentimentality about the joys of submitting with love, or the bliss of sexual fulfillment, or the forlorn state of a woman without a man to look after her.

Defoe's discussion in *The Review* of "the worst sort of Husband a sober Woman can Marry" shows not only his vivid awareness of the difficulties of women in marriage but, indirectly, his respect for their intelligence. It strikingly contrasts with that in *The Lady's New Year's Gift*, where Halifax lists the various types of objectionable husbands his daughter might get, minimizes the sufferings produced by each, and concludes that it is her womanly duty to accept any afflictions with graceful resignation. Contrast, for example, Halifax's discussion of a drunkard with Defoe's. Halifax tells his daughter that, if her husband should prove to be a drunkard, she can console herself with the thought that this vice will obscure her faults in his eyes. When he comes home drunk she must receive him "without a storm or so much as a reproachful look," so that "the wine will naturally work out all in kindness, which a wife must encourage, let it be wrapped up in never so much impertinence." Defoe, on the other hand, passionately sympathizes with the woman who must put up with her husband's "Drunken Passions, his Drunken Humours, his Drunken Smell, his drunken Bed-Fellowships, and above all, his drunken Love."

13. Defoe, *Conjugal Lewdness*, p. 129.

Defoe's "Pen cannot bear the stench of relating" the intimacies between a modest wife and "an Amorous Drunkard, when he comes home, fully gorg'd and staggers into Bed." Defoe proceeds through the debauched husband, the fighting husband, the extravagant husband to, worst of all, the fool, who is *"in Good*, wavering; in *Mischief*, obstinate; in society, *empty*; in *Management*, unthinking; in *Manners*, sordid; in *Error*, Incorrigible; and *in every thing*, Ridiculous."[14]

The significance of Defoe's emphasis on the fool is his obvious assumption that a woman might be enough more intelligent than her husband to judge his stupidity, and that there is nothing improper in her doing so. When he dramatized such a situation in *Roxana*, he made us sympathize totally with Roxana's contempt for her pigheaded husband, fatuous in company and incapable in business. That this opinion was not conventional in the eighteenth century is shown by Fielding's presentation of his feminine ideal, Sophia, in *Tom Jones;* she primly states that she would never see defects of understanding in the man she married.[15] Fielding's rationale would seem to be that a right-thinking woman is too aware of the limitations of her sex to presume to judge the intelligence of any male; perhaps also he was disturbed because contempt for stupidity suggests superiority, while complaints of brutality would be appropriate from a victimized inferior. In any case, Defoe's discussion throughout implies that the bad husbands are offending their equals.

Defoe showed his respect for women in a more positive way through his presentation of the wife's role in *The Complete English Tradesman*. Believing women capable of business, he thought a wife should understand and participate in her husband's trade rather than passively consume his gains, and should be prepared to fend for herself in case of widowhood. Far from finding dependence attractive in women, he insisted that a tradesman's widow should understand his business and accounts,

14. Defoe, *Review*, Vol. X, pp. 403-4; H. C. Foxcroft, *The Life and Letters of Sir George Savile . . . First Marquis of Halifax, with . . . his works*, London, Longmans Green, 1898, Vol. II, p. 397.
15. Henry Fielding, *Tom Jones*, ed. R. P. C. Mutter, Baltimore, Penguin Books, 1966, p. 531.

lest she find herself at the mercy of lawyers or apprentices who might defraud her of everything. Women, like everyone else, should do all they can to avoid the role of passive victim. Although some women may be too foolish or proud to concern themselves with trade, the fault more commonly lies with the husband, who may be "foolishly vain" of keeping his wife an idle lady with nothing to do but make visits. Some husbands think the appearance of their wives in their shops would debase their trades by making them seem, "less masculine"; and some "unkind . . . imperious" men fear to make their wives "useful" lest they "value themselves upon it, and make themselves . . . as equal to their husbands." Finally, some wish to conceal from their wives that they are going bankrupt. "All these considerations are foolish and fraudulent," Defoe declared, "and in every one of them the husband is in the wrong."[16]

Defoe ended this section with an inspiring tale of a young woman, left by the sudden death of her husband with a flourishing business, five small children and another on the way. Far from passively desponding, the widow applied "her mind to carry on the trade herself," improved the knowledge which she had started to acquire during her husband's lifetime, and capably directed the employees. She built up the business steadily until her son grew up, then shared it equally with him and an apprentice whom she married to her daughter. How much better than if the family had merely divided what the father left, which would have barely kept them alive. Women, Defoe concluded, "when once they . . . think fit to rouse up themselves to their own relief, are not so helpless and shiftless creatures as some would make them appear."[17]

This resourceful heroine has something in common with Moll Flanders and Roxana, as Defoe's unsentimental insistence that a wife prepare herself for widowhood presages their preoccupation with comfortable survival in any eventuality. Defoe's awareness of the problems of marriage and the importance of its economic element, his belief that obligations are mutual in male-female as in other relationships, his recognition of women's strength and his

16. Defoe, *Complete English Tradesman*, pp. 216, 219-20.
17. *Ibid.*, pp. 221-23, 226.

belief that they should be active and independent in order to cope with the disadvantages society imposes on them, all appear in his novels. More significantly, in the novels he seemed to feel more free to pursue his feminism beyond the bounds of respectability. Assuming the personae of disreputable women, he suggested a truly radical criticism of marriage and accepted standards of feminine behavior. From insisting that the obligations of marriage are mutual and equal, he proceeded to look at women just as he looked at men. From sympathetic recognition of women's difficulties in marriage, he proceeded to raise the question of whether they should marry at all or would do better to lead an independent life. This in turn raised the question of whether women could be independent without casting off the moral restrictions placed on their sex. Defoe suggested an answer by presenting two heroines thriving without chastity or reputation.

Naturally, Defoe did not present opinions in his novels directly, as he did in his non-fiction. Instead, he created situations which could not be adequately dealt with in terms of conventional sexual morality. He presented heroines who must violate the most sacred laws laid on women, and made them sympathetic. He placed orthodox moral statements into situations which showed them to be irrelevant. For this reason, I do not believe we should accept Moll's or Roxana's expressions of guilt at face value; Defoe thought more deeply and boldly than his characters did.

The stories of *Moll* and *Roxana*, focusing relentlessly upon economic necessity, demonstrate that women were made helpless by Defoe's society and that it might often be impossible to reconcile proper feminine behavior with survival. When Moll as a child expresses her reasonable desire to make an independent living, she learns that she cannot possibly support herself no matter how industriously she sews or spins.[18] It soon becomes apparent that she will have to depend on a man; if one man leaves her, she must find another.

Yet women cannot rely on men to support them. The respectably married Roxana (married at fifteen to a fool her father

---

18. Daniel Defoe, *Moll Flanders*, ed. James Sutherland, Boston, Houghton Mifflin, 1959, p. 13.

mistakenly chose for her) can only watch while her inept, idle husband dissipates his business; she is helpless to prevent the financial ruin which she plainly sees coming. She cannot even inherit money, since her father will not leave her a legacy which would fall under her husband's control; instead, he leaves it under the care of her brother, who proceeds to lose it by going bankrupt. So much for the idea that women can depend on male protection.

When her husband deserts the family, Roxana is left with five small children to support. Their father, his relatives, and society at large leave them on her hands — "let her that brought them into the World, look after them if she will."Yet as a woman she is deprived of any means to do so. If she had one child or two she would have tried to support the family by needlework — provided people had kindly given her some to do — but for "one single Woman not bred to work, and at a Losse where to get Employment, to get the Bread of five Children" is, as she says, impossible.[19] All she can do is sell her possessions one by one and beg from relatives who regard her as a troublesome parasite — forced to these degrading expedients because she is a woman.

Thus Roxana must get rid of the children if any of them is to survive. It is only after they are gone that the kindly landlord comes forward to help her. As a respectable lady, conventionally brought up, Roxana is naturally horrified at the idea of prostituting herself to him "for Bread." But of course she has no other means of support, and — as Amy says — chastity "is out of the Question when Starvation is the Case." Since a woman's only source of support was a man, if marriage was impossible for her, she had to defy the law of chastity and become someone's mistress. Roxana's claim that she would have been happy if she had kept her chastity "tho' I had perished of meer Hunger; for, without question, a Woman ought rather to die, than to prostitute her Virtue and Honour" is surely to be read ironically.[20] Obviously it is better to become a man's mistress, especially if he is a nice congenial man like the landlord, than to starve.

Moll too repeatedly finds herself in a position where she must

19. Daniel Defoe, *The Fortunate Mistress (Roxana)*, Oxford, Basil Blackwell, 1927, Vol. I, pp. 13, 19.
20. *Ibid.*, Vol. I, pp. 28-30.

choose between morality and survival: she can starve as the deserted wife of the linen draper who has squandered her fortune, or she can marry another man bigamously; she can starve as the widow of the ruined banker, or she can take to stealing. Moll's professional attitude toward her thievery is incongruous of course, but it also brings out the point that only in crime could a woman exercise the skill, presence of mind, and application which would advance a man in honest trade. As a thief, also, she can make full use of her superior capacities by escaping the respectable woman's dependence on others: "I was seldom in any danger when I was by my self, or if I was, I got out of it with more dexterity than when I was entangled with the dull measures of other people."[21] In Defoe's society the average woman without a reliable husband — a woman who was single, widowed, deserted, or married to a spendthrift — could not support herself without breaking the laws of morality. As long as they live as respectable women, Moll and Roxana are passive victims.

Having revealed that a wife's position was not as honorable and secure as it was supposed to be, Defoe pushed on to the radical suggestion that a woman might actually be better off as a mistress. Roxana finds by experience that "a Wife is treated with Indifference, a Mistress with a strong Passion . . . a Wife must give up all she has; have every Reserve she makes for herself, be thought hard of, and be upbraided with her very *Pin-Money*; whereas the Mistress" can command her lover's property as well as her own; "the Wife bears a thousand Insults, and is forc'd to sit still and bear it, or part and be undone; a Mistress insulted, helps herself immediately, and takes another." Roxana immediately proceeds to disavow these "wicked Arguments for Whoring" but she cannot refute them,[22] so we are left with the feeling that, although women are unfairly treated in either case, in many significant ways the whore's lot is better than the wife's.

When the Dutch merchant argues that a woman should not object to giving up her liberty in marriage because in return she gets freedom from worldly cares, the fallacy is made apparent by

21. Defoe, *Moll*, pp. 191-92.
22. Defoe, *Roxana*, Vol. I, pp. 152-53.

the vivid picture of Roxana's marriage which opened the book. Far from taking care upon himself, her husband left her to face problems which she had no power to deal with. The experience of every one of the female characters in the book supports Roxana's argument and falsifies the merchant's. Roxana, miserable and helpless in her marriage, leads a satisfying life in her various relationships as a mistress. When Lord — "grew old, and fretful, and captious,"[23] she easily got rid of him; she could not have done so had he been her husband. Amy, too, has a more pleasant and profitable life as a mistress than as a poor man's wife. The virtuous Princess, on the other hand, is totally neglected by her husband and can exert persuasive power on him only by dying. The good, deserving Quaker also has a bad husband, who helps her not at all and does not trouble her only because he has abandoned her. When Roxana rewards the Quaker with an annuity, she must take pains to protect it from the woman's husband. The Quaker has the peace and dignity brought by self-respect and a clear conscience, but as the victim of a bad husband she lacks the dignity of independence.

Women's need to depend on a man for economic survival in part excuses the mercenary attitudes toward sex and marriage which repel us in Moll and Roxana. Moll's crass comparisons between marriage and prostitution — "a woman should never be kept for a mistress that had money to make herself a wife"[24] — point to the disconcerting parallel between the two states in a society where women had to depend on men for support. Moreover, men, who could support themselves and therefore had less excuse, also used marriage as a means for acquiring money. Our distaste for Moll's duplicity in making men believe she has a fortune is moderated by our knowledge that no one would consider marrying her without one. Moll's and Roxana's admittedly exploitative attitude toward men becomes less shocking when we consider men's attitudes toward them — the elder brother who taught Moll to see through "that cheat call'd love"[25]

23. *Ibid.*, Vol. II, p. 1.
24. Defoe, *Moll*, p. 54.
25. *Ibid.*, p. 53.

by exploiting the naiveté of her youth, the second husband who spent all her money and then walked out of the mess he had made, the fourth husband who married her expecting to live in style off her income for the rest of his life, Roxana's fool who squandered the family business and then left his wife and children to starve.

Yet, despite the crippling liabilities that society imposed upon women, Defoe had much faith in their natural capacity to defend themselves. This was easier if they had money, like Moll's friend who outmaneuvered the arrogant sea captain. But Defoe shows us through his heroines that a woman might have sufficient ability, strength, and unscrupulousness to make her life what she wanted, even without money to start with. Above all, his heroines have the same active enterprise that his heroes have; they never sit passively under their misfortunes, as Moll's otherwise estimable banker husband did. With his knowledge of business, Moll would have found some way to salvage the situation; and even without it, she survives. Too poor to be a wife and too old to be a mistress, she turns to the only profitable career still open and trains herself to be an expert thief.

More significant even than Defoe's belief that women could look after themselves was his belief that they should do so. He did not share the traditional view that dependence and helplessness are attractive qualities in women. Nor did he expect women to be free of the ego drives which are condoned if not approved in men. Although Moll and Roxana are driven by necessity into their first misdeeds, they are later motivated by a desire to gratify their egos. Moll begins to take pride in her professional skill and success: "I grew the greatest artist of my time."[26] Roxana embarks on her second affair because she enjoys being "courted by a Prince" and "call'd . . . the finest Woman in *France*." She refuses marriage to the Dutch merchant because she wants to gratify her ego with the same sort of independence that men have: she claims that a woman can enjoy "full Command of what she" has and "full Direction of what she" does just like a man; that a woman is "as fit to govern . . . her own Estate, without a Man, as a Man . . . without a Woman"; and — even more boldly — that a woman

26. *Ibid.*, p. 186.

"might entertain a Man, as a man does a Mistress."[27]

Although Defoe characteristically made Roxana undermine the sincerity of her argument, it stands as much more reasonable than the merchant's attempts to refute it. He can only say, first, that women gain ease and security by marriage, an argument disproved by events in the book; secondly, that marriage is customary; thirdly, that "where there was a mutual Love, there cou'd be no Bondage." Roxana effectively exposes this sentimentality: "the Pretence of Affection, takes from a Woman everything that can be call'd *herself*; she is to have no Interest; no Aim; no View; but all in the Interest, Aim and View of the Husband." This conception of love reduces the woman to a "passive Creature," who lives "by Faith (not in God, but) in her Husband."[28]

That Defoe agreed with Roxana's arguments is suggested first by the merchant's concession that she "was right in the Main";[29] secondly, by Defoe's own use of similar arguments in the passage I have quoted in which he questioned why a woman would marry unless for children; and finally by his characterization of Moll Flanders as a woman who could love without immolating herself. Though Moll loved Jemmy, her fourth husband, and treated him better than he deserved, she was never totally absorbed in him. When they parted, she gave him the smaller of her two bank bills, but concealed the larger one. When her son enthusiastically received her in Virginia, she "began almost to wish that" she had not brought Jemmy "from England at all". However, she immediately proceeded, "that wish was not hearty neither, for I lov'd" him "entirely, as I had ever done from the beginning."[30] The wish and the retraction are equally true to character, and compatible with realistic love. Moll's love is not total because love never is total. She contrasts strongly with a sentimentalized female character like Fielding's Amelia, who cannot wait to hand over all her money to a spendthrift husband and cannot even envisage the possibility of outliving him.[31]

27. Defoe, *Roxana*, Vol. I, pp. 72, 172-73.
28. *Ibid.*, Vol. I, pp. 171, 173-74.
29. *Ibid.*, Vol. I, p. 178.
30. Defoe, *Moll*, p. 291.
31. Henry Fielding, *Amelia*, Oxford, Basil Blackwell, 1926, Vol. I, p. 129.

While writers like Fielding unquestioningly applied different moral standards to men and women, Defoe assumed that they should be judged in the same way. He did not expect women to be any more delicate or selfless than men, nor did he condemn them for ambition. Roxana wants public acclaim and wealth, and prostitution happens to be the only field in which she can use her talents to pursue her aims. Defoe presents a woman fulfilling her ambition in the only way then open to a woman, and we wonder whether she is really more vicious than the man who fulfills his ambition by business deals or political maneuvering. Defoe's heroines have basically the same motivation as men. Yet, although they lack the conventional attributes of femininity – delicacy, weakness, emotionality – they have the essential ones – evidenced by their sexual attractiveness and symbolized by Moll's discomfort when she wears men's clothes.[32] Presenting women in the same terms as men, Defoe implied that they were equally capable and equally entitled to self-determination and self-fulfillment.

Defoe's ability to see women as he saw men is particularly striking in his presentation of their sex lives. Opposing the conventional assumption that woman is essentially a sexual being totally absorbed in romantic love, or sexual gratification, or preserving her chastity – he showed sexual motivation as comparatively unimportant in Moll and Roxana, despite their profession. Many critics have found the two characters strangely unfeminine on this account, but actually it is only that Defoe saw them as human beings who were not obsessed with sex any more than were their normal male counterparts. Although Moll does fall in love with her original seducer, she is motivated at least as much by greed and vanity as by sexual desire. Later she makes a point of telling us that she wouldn't think of having affairs out of lust, of coming "into the crime for the meer vice of it." Though she ultimately does feel desire for her Bath lover, this was not the case at first: "from the first hour I began to converse with him I resolv'd to let him lye with me, if he offered it; but it was because I wanted his help, and knew of no other way of securing him."[33]

32. Defoe, *Moll*, p. 186.
33. *Ibid.*, pp. 93-94, 104.

Her reasoning is realistic: all the men who help Moll and Roxana do so because they desire them sexually. Roxana too "had nothing of" lust in her constitution. It was "the Kindness and good Humour" of the landlord and her own poverty that brought her into her first affair. Later she is motivated by "Avarice . . . and . . . Vanity . . . not being able to resist the Flatteries" of a Prince and a King.[34]

Moll and Roxana, with their normal human motivation, are refreshingly different from the sentimental stereotype of the prostitute who offers perfect sexuality. Unlike their contemporary Fanny Hill, they do not live to have orgasms. On the other side, Defoe carefully avoided the misogynistic stereotype of the seductive, devouring whore. Though Moll and Roxana reproach themselves for their sexual sins, they neither seduce nor hurt other people. Thus the man who picked Moll up in Bartholomew Fair admitted that she "prompted me to nothing, she rather declin'd me."[35] Roxana did not injure anyone by becoming the Prince's mistress, for it is made clear that he would have been unfaithful to his wife in any case. In Defoe's novels, men bear full responsibility for persuading women to act as prostitutes. The only people who deserve sympathy are the only innocent parties in the affair, the wives whom their husband may infect with venereal disease.

Defoe's ability to view sexual affairs without excess emotionality also freed him from convention in dealing with the subject of female chastity. Where contemporary writers, even feminists like Richardson, made a woman's chastity the central concern of her life, Defoe sensibly showed that it is not all that important. In contrast to the emphasis placed by contemporary moralists on chastity as the supreme virtue for women, without which they are worthless, Defoe laid comparatively little stress on physical fidelity even in his works on marriage. In his novels Defoe repeatedly showed that a woman who lost her chastity was not necessarily ruined, and could in fact prove to be a very good wife. Moll may claim that having lost her virtue, meaning her chastity, she has "nothing of value left to recommend" her "either to God's

34. Defoe, *Roxana*, Vol. I, p. 44, Vol. II, p. 5.
35. Defoe, *Moll*, p. 202.

blessing, or man's assistance"; [36] but her story proves this conventional sentiment to be untrue. She has a full and satisfying life ahead of her, during which she will enjoy the assistance of other people, the sympathy of the reader, and many of God's blessings.

Moreover, despite their sexual lapses and mercenary attitudes, Moll and Roxana are both good wives, or mistresses as the case may be. They make their husbands and lovers happy; they are consistently obliging to them and faithful to them while the relationships last. Moll rightly claims that she "made the better wife for all the difficulties" she "had pass'd thro'." [37] One of Colonel Jack's two good wives had produced a bastard in her youth, but as she was "faithful, virtuous, [and] obliging" to him until she died, this information did not lessen his affectionate memories of her. [38] When he met the other, after a divorce for adultery and many years' separation, he found that she, like Moll, had been improved by the difficulties she had passed through; he remarried her, and she proved not only devoted but resourceful enough to save him his liberty. Defoe suggests that attractiveness, good-humor and intelligence amply outweigh the loss of chastity.

To show that an unchaste woman could be an excellent wife was unconventional; to imply that unchastity was necessary for freedom was subversive. That does seem to be the implication of *Moll Flanders* and *Roxana*. Moll is forced into her first, unwanted marriage "like a bear to the stake" [39] because, although she has lost her chastity, she is still trying to preserve her reputation. Roxana is a helpless victim as long as she remains faithful to her first husband. Only when she has cast off all concern for chastity and reputation is she completely free to direct her life as she sees fit. The Dutch merchant tries to coerce Roxana to marry him by getting to bed with her, expecting that she will then have to do so in order to patch up her reputation. But Roxana has no reputation to lose and, seeing she has nothing to gain by marrying him, refuses. "Thus his Project of coming to-Bed to me, was a Bite

---

36. *Ibid.*, p. 27.
37. *Ibid.*, p. 112.
38. Daniel Defoe, *The History ... of Colonel Jack*, Oxford, Basil Blackwell, 1927, Vol. II, pp. 80-81.
39. Defoe, *Moll*, p. 51

upon himself, while he intended it for a Bite upon me,"[40] for instead of forcing his will upon her, he merely relieved her of the obligation to repay him a large debt; she felt she had repaid him by giving herself to him sexually. The biter has been bitten, and it is pleasant to see the member of the dominant group foiled by the independent thinking of a member of the subordinate one.

Defoe agreed with Roxana that a woman should not allow cohabitation to force her into marriage. Where most of his contemporaries assumed that even a victim of rape would be eager to marry her attacker in order to salvage her reputation – for example, Fielding implied in *Tom Jones* that Sophia would have had to marry Lord Fellamar had he succeeded in raping her – Defoe said a rape victim should by no means marry the man. If she does, "she is abused daily, the Crime is renewed, and she is made unhappy to the End of her Life." – while if she leaves the man, she will ultimately recover.[41]

Defoe's insistence that women can survive the loss of their chastity, his demonstration that the whole course of their lives need not depend on their sexual status, shows his recognition of their full humanity and his wish to free them from sexual as well as economic dependence on men. Overemphasis on women's chastity has always diminished them, by making their sexual status the most important thing about them. It has also restricted their freedom, not only by keeping them from any activities which could possibly be construed as immodest, but by arbitrarily making their entire future hinge upon accidents which should not have to be fatal. Richardson's virtuous Clarissa keeps trying to control her own life, but she must necessarily fail because she cannot move freely lest she damage her reputation and she cannot deal effectively with Lovelace because direct speaking would be immodest; once Lovelace has deprived her of her virginity, life is over for her. Despite her intelligence and her will toward freedom, she remains a passive victim; like the Princess in *Roxana*, she can conquer only by dying. Defoe's heroines, early divested of their chastity, are free to adapt themselves to situations so as to survive

40. Defoe, *Roxana*, Vol. I, pp. 167-68.
41. Defoe, *Conjugal Lewdness*, pp. 171-72.

as well as possible, to choose whether or not they will have a man, and to remake their lives after any catastrophe. They resemble their real-life contemporary Mrs. Manley, who, having early lost her reputation by a fraudulent marriage, was thereafter free to choose congenial men to live with, make a career for herself, and advocate radical feminist views.

Defoe's relatively unemotional attitude toward sex perhaps contributed to his refusal to overemphasize romantic love. Not that Defoe undervalued love, which he considered the "one essential and absolutely necessary Part of" marriage, without which "I think [it is] hardly lawful, I am sure [it] is not rational, and . . . can never be happy."[42] But he insisted that love be solidly grounded on merit, compatibility, and mutual help; and that it could not dissolve all of life's problems. He assumed that a sensible woman would not marry without assurance that her suitor had an estate and would use it to provide for her: "you must have his Estate appear, your Part be settled, and the Land bound to you . . . you will have it under Hand and Seal, so that he shall not be able to go back."[43]

Defoe's preoccupation with the economic aspect of marriage is not uplifting, but it did help him to see more clearly than romantic contemporaries what each side owed the other in a marriage partnership. The economic exploitation of wives was a problem which the sentimentalist particularly wanted to smother in finer feelings. But Defoe, recognizing that marriage is a practical arrangement for living, was witheringly scornful of men who failed to support their families. If society deprives a woman of the opportunity to support herself, then the husband who does not support her is failing a vital responsibility. Defoe would never, like Fielding, present as a good husband a man like Captain Booth, who is incapable of supporting his family and gambles away the money they need to buy food.

It was Defoe's recognition that romantic love does not dissolve conflicts of interest that caused him to insist on the need for both husband and wife to put up with irritations. Those who see

42. *Ibid.*, p. 28.
43. Daniel Defoe, *Religious Courtship*, London, E. Matthews, 1722, p. 198.

marriage as potentially perfect bliss are those who look at it from the man's point of view and assume that a good wife will submerge her ego in the relationship. The connection between sentimentalizing marriage and exploiting women is very clear in Fielding's *Amelia*, where the Booth marriage is free of disharmony because the wife constantly gives up everything to her husband. All he has to do is love and admire her. It is true that Fielding is attractively idealistic about love and marriage, and Defoe is not. But idealism, especially in this area, is often unpleasantly close to a sentimental refusal to see the relevant facts. Fielding can idealize the Booth marriage only by slurring over its practical deficiencies, and he can idealize Amelia into an angel only by divesting her of the normal rights and claims of a human being. Charles Dickens sneered at Defoe's insensibility to romance, but it was Dickens, not Defoe, who was hostile and exploitative toward women. Defoe could see marriage as a mutual relationship in which both parties expected concrete gains because he could see women in the same terms as he saw men.

Defoe's personal experience, his lifelong struggle with practical problems, may have contributed to his rejection of high-flown ideals and refined sentiments. In any case, he retained through his life the tough-minded, plain-spoken attitudes of the Restoration period during which he grew up. He remained suspicious of ideals, cynical about human motives, and more concerned with ugly facts than tender feelings. Like the Restoration playwrights, he saw both men and women looking out for themselves even in courtship and marriage. He believed that women as well as men should be capable of defending their interests; that they should neither be weakly dependent nor heroically self-sacrificing.

With the reformation of manners in the early eighteenth century came a more sentimental attitude toward women, love, and marriage. Richard Steele, though only a few years younger than Defoe, was an outstanding spokesman for the new sensibility. As such, he shows sentimental ideals, however well-intentioned, diminish and limit women. Although in many ways a "friend" to women as he claimed, Steele never saw them as equals. For example, he recommended as appropriately feminine the helplessness which Defoe deplored in women. Steele's ideal woman had "gentle Softness, tender Fear, and all those parts of Life, which distinguish her from the other Sex; with some Subordination to it, but such an Inferiority that makes her still more lovely." Notice that femininity, however sweet, is connected with inferiority. Steele called himself a "Guardian to the Fair," but like so many self-styled protectors of women, he protected them to demonstrate their weakness, to boost his masculine ego at their expense. The eighteenth-century man of feeling rightly condemned the Restoration rake's heartless, predatory attitude toward women; but the Restoration rake at least credited them with sense and vigor to defend themselves, while the man of feeling saw them as passive victims, helpless and therefore inferior. Steel said of his ideal woman: "Kindness is all her Art, and Beauty all her Arms."[44]

Emphasis on the so-called natural differences between men and women is often used to justify a double standard of judgment — in practice, to justify denying women the opportunities which are offered to men. Steele deplored the least ambition in women on the grounds that it was undesirable for themselves as well as for men: "for their own Happiness and Comfort, as well as that of those for whom they were born" — that is, men — they ought to consider themselves "no other than an additional Part of the Species," made to adorn their fathers, husbands, brothers, or children. Defoe, who saw women existing in their own right, allowed them ego drives and did not expect them to submerge themselves in their emotional relationships any more than men do. Steele's ideal wife, on the other hand, has "no other Concern but to please the Man I love: he's the End of every Care I have; if I dress 'tis for him, if I read a Poem or a Play 'tis to qualify my self for a Conversation agreeable to his Taste: He's almost the End of my Devotions, half my Prayers are for his Happiness."[45] This, alas, became the ideal for good women in the novel, most shiningly exemplified by the heroines of Fielding.

Convinced that women were naturally weak, the sentimentalists saw little point in attempts to equalize their position by legal means. While Steele opposed conjugal tyranny, he deplored as

44. *The Spectator*, No. 144.
45. *Ibid.*, Nos. 254, 342.

mercenary any concern with legally establishing a wife's rights. He opposed a stipulated amount of pin money or any similar articles in a marriage contract on the ground that such articles "create a Diffidence; and intimate to the young People, that they are very soon to be in a State of War with each other ... Thus is Tenderness thrown out of the Question."[46] This attitude seems more appropriate to a marital relationship than Defoe's, but actually it shows complacent insensibility to the real economic problems of many women. In practice, wives were equally exploited under the new sentimentality and the old Biblical strictures. It is significant that Steele reprinted the harsh dicta I have quoted from Fleetwood and other moralists in his own anthology for women, *The Ladies Library*.

Although Defoe's presentation of women and women's relationships with men was unsentimental to the point of crudity, it was admirably fair-minded and actually opened up possibilities of freedom which anticipate those of modern times. When he exhorts wives to prepare themselves for widowhood or makes a heroine refuse a proposal on the grounds that she would lose money by the marriage, Defoe does show a shocking lack of proper feeling. He also shows his awareness of practical necessity and normal self-interest as they apply to women. Defoe's depressing lack of idealism does impoverish his picture of human relationships, but it also kept his mind free of many sentimental delusions which have traditionally served to inhibit and exploit women. Looking at women from the standpoint of observation instead of stereotyped ideals, Defoe was able to see them as human beings with the same rights and needs as other human beings. What most distinguishes all Defoe's writing about women is honesty; and what enabled him to write so honestly was his constant insistence upon reporting, not conventional morality, not refined sentiments, not stylized emotions, but the significant facts.

Mary Astell and Richardson suggested that a woman might have reason to prefer celibacy to marriage, but only Defoe created heroines who attained true independence — casting off the moral inhibitions laid on women in order to support themselves

46. *The Tatler*, No. 199.

economically and to control their relationships with men. By setting his female protagonists in situations where they had to fend for themselves, Defoe demonstrated his confidence that they could do so. His heroines remain exhilarating because they live with an independence unequaled in their own time and far from general even in our own.

Katharine Rogers

Astraea's "Vacant Throne": The Successors of Aphra Behn

Aphra Behn (1640-89) was the first woman to make a significant contribution to English drama. Woman dramatists before Mrs. Behn are few and unimportant: after her they are many and, with the exception of Mrs. Centlivre (1669-1723), unimportant. Before Mrs. Behn were the Duchess of Newcastle (1623-73) whose plays filled ample folios but never reached the public stage; Katherine Philips (1632-64), who translated two of Corneille's plays; and a Mrs. Frances Boothby (of whom nothing is known) whose tragedy *Marcelia* was performed in 1669. Between Mrs. Behn's death in 1689 and the production of Mrs. Centlivre's first play in 1700, a little-known group of women, Mary Manley (1663-1724), Mary Pix (1666-1709), and Catherine Trotter (1679-1749), consciously strove to fill the place vacated by Mrs. Behn. Although they were later eclipsed by Mrs. Centlivre, and the plays they wrote were soon forgotten, it is worth looking, through their dedications, prefaces, prologues, and epilogues, at the circumstances in which these plays were produced, for they reveal much about contemporary attitudes to female authors, and show how these pioneering literary ladies presented themselves to a sometimes hostile public.

Mrs. Behn's first play, *The Forc'd Marriage*, was produced in 1670, and between then and her death in 1689 she wrote about twenty more. She was a frankly commercial playwright who wrote for the public taste and usually accepted its verdict on her work. But she sometimes claimed that she was the victim of anti-feminist prejudice. A notable example is the epilogue to *Sir Patient Fancy* (1678):

> What has poor Woman done, that she must be
> Debarr'd from Sense, and Sacred Poetry?
> . . . . pray tell me then,
> Why Women should not write as well as Men.[1]

A different answer to Mrs. Behn's rhetorical question would have been given by many of her contemporaries. The case is succinctly put in the anonymous *Comparison between the Two Stages* (1702):

> What a Pox have the Women to do with the Muses? I grant you the Poets call the Nine Muses by the Names of Women, but why so? not because the Sex had any thing to do with Poetry, but because in that Sex they're much fitter for prostitution.[2]

The satiric portrait of the authoress Phoebe Clinket in *Three Hours after Marriage* (1717) shows the persistence of this attitude.

By showing that a woman could compete on equal terms in what had been a man's world, Mrs. Behn did the feminist cause a great service. This was recognised by Mary Astell, when in her *Essay in Defence of the Female Sex* (1696), she offered "the noble examples of the deservedly celebrated Mrs. *Philips*, and the incomparable Mrs. *Behn*."[3] It was perhaps unfortunate that Katherine Philips became the type of the poetess, and Aphra Behn the type of the female dramatist: for the bawdiness of the latter's plays, and the irregularities of her personal life, made it a disreputable type. The association of playwriting with immorality was unhappily reinforced by the careers of Mrs. Manley and Mrs. Centlivre. As a result John Duncombe could write in *The Feminiad* (1754):

> The modest Muse a veil with pity throws
> O'er Vices friends and Virtue's foes;

---

1. *Works*, ed. Montague Summers, London, 1915, vol. IV, pp. 115-16.
2. *A Comparison between the Two Stages*, ed. Staring B. Wells, Princeton, 1942, p. 17.
3. *An Essay in Defence of the Female Sex*, New York, 1970, p. 63. The authorship of the *Essay* is in doubt: see Florence M. Smith, *Mary Astell*, New York, 1916, pp. 173-82.

> Abash'd she views the bold unblushing mien
> Of modern Manley, Centlivre, and Behn;[4]

As a result of this association Fanny Burney shrank from the suggestion that she should write a comedy for the public stage.

When Mrs. Behn died in 1689 she had no immediate successor, and it is not until 1695-96 that we find women again actively occupied in dramatic authorship. *She Ventures and He Wins*, a comedy performed about September 1695, was the first play by a woman to challenge the male monopoly. The anonymous author-ess, who signs herself "Ariadne," apologises in her preface for "an infinite Number of Faults" which she candidly admits she is "not able to mend." Ariadne's is no "bold unblushing mien." She continues: "I believe the best Apology I can make for my Self and Play, is, that 'tis the Error of a weak Woman's Pen, one altogether unlearn'd, ignorant of any, but her Mother-Tongue, and very far from being a perfect Mistress of that too." It is instructive to compare this with Mary Astell's shrewd observation in her *Essay* that "I have often thought that the not teaching Women Latin and Greek, was an advantage to them, if it were rightly consider'd, and might be improve'd to a great height" (p. 63). This attitude to the lumber of classical learning is far ahead of its time.

Ariadne was not long alone. *Agnes de Castro*, a tragedy, was produced at Drury Lane about December 1695. It was published in January 1696 as "Written by a Young Lady," but unlike Ariadne, this writer did later drop her anonymity, and we know that *Agnes* was by Catherine Trotter. But the tone of the play's prologue and epilogue is close to that of Ariadne's apologies. The prologue pleads:

> They've oft the Breeches worn, why not the laurel too!
> . . . .
> She's Dead, if Try'd by strict Poetick Laws;
> But Men of Honour can't refuse a Woman's Cause.

A quite different note is struck in the commendatory verses addressed to the author by Mrs. Manley:

4. *The Feminiad: A Poem*, London, 1754.

> *Orinda*, and the Fair *Astrea* gone,
> Not one was found to fill the Vacant Throne:
> Aspiring Man had quite regain'd the Sway,
> Again had Taught us humbly to Obey;
> Till you (Natures third start, in favour of our kind)
> With stronger Arms, their Empire have disjoyn'd,
> And snatcht a Lawrel which they thought their Prize;
> Thus Conqu'ror, with your Wit, as with your Eyes.

Mrs. Manley breathes the defiant spirit of Mrs. Behn, not the modest apologetics of Ariadne and Catherine Trotter. Nor was Mrs. Manley content to be a spectator of the battle: "Fired by the bold Example" of *Agnes*," she announced her intention of joining it.

Before Mrs. Manley could translate this promise into a play, Mrs. Behn's posthumous *Younger Brother*, revised by Gildon, was produced (in February 1696) at Drury Lane. In the dedication to the printed edition, Gilden complains of the "unjust Sentence this play met with before very partial Judges." Contrasting this with the favourable reception generally accorded Mrs. Behn's plays in her own lifetime, Gildon concludes "that I may reasonably impute its miscarriage to some Faction that was made against it, which indeed was very Evident on the First day," and even more so on the third.[5] In view of the later references to claques formed against plays by women, it is tempting to interpret this posthumous opposition to Mrs. Behn in a like manner. Mrs. Manley's provocative verses had been published in *Agnes de Castro* the month before *The Younger Brother* was produced, and Mrs. Manley had (or fancied she had) her enemies: on the other hand, so did Gildon.

A clearer case is Mrs. Manley's own play, *The Lost Lover*, produced at Drury Lane about March 1696. In the prologue she hopes that the critics will "scorn to Arm against a Worthless Foe," but the tone of the preface, written after the play had been damned, is much closer to that of the earlier verses to Mrs. Trotter. It begins conventionally enough: only "the flattery of my Friends" persuaded her to have the play performed, and she was

---

5. *Works*, ed. Summers, vol. IV, pp. 316-17.

not surprised by its "little success." A bill of complaints is soon presented, however: "The better half was cut ... I am now convinc'd Writing for the Stage is no way proper for a Woman, to whom all Advantages but meer Nature, are refused." Most important is her charge that "the bare Name of being a Woman's Play damn'd it beyond its own want of Merit." Mrs. Manley's powerful sense of injured "want of Merit" was impotent against the town itself, but the Drury Lane management was made to suffer. She had a second play already in rehearsal there, but this was withdrawn and taken to Lincoln's Inn Fields, where it was performed in April or early May 1696. This was *The Royal Mischief*: later in the same year Drury Lane was revenged by burlesquing the play and its authoress in *The Female Wits*.

The *Royal Mischief* met with greater success than *The Lost Lover*. Sullen in *A Comparison between the Two Stages* admits grudgingly that "it made a shift to live half a dozen Days, and then expir'd" (p. 20). Six days, however, was a respectable run, and the *Comparison's* taunt that *The Royal Mischief* reached its sixth night with difficulty may be no more than its usual curmudgeonliness. That the play received a mixed reception is clear from Mrs. Manley's preface to the printed text, published early in June. These are some of her complaints:

> I shou'd not have given my self and the Town the trouble of a Preface if the aspersions of my Enemies had not made it necessary ... The principal Objection made against this Tragedy is the warmth of it, as they are pleas'd to call it ... as a Woman I thought it Policy to begin with the softest [passion] and which is easiest to our Sex ... I shou'd think it but an indifferent Commendation to have it said she writes like a Woman ...

She goes on to hope that when the play is read it will become obvious that only "prejudice against our Sex" could have damned it. This "warmth" — Lucyle Hook calls it the "hot surging sex"[6] — must have reinforced the idea that women's plays were unusually bawdy.

6. Introduction to *The Female Wits*, Los Angeles, 1967, p. viii (Augustan Reprint Society, Publication No. 124).

Apart from the combative preface, *The Royal Mischief* was printed with no less than three sets of commendatory verses: one by Mrs. Trotter, one by Mrs. Pix (a newcomer to the dramatic scene), and a third set sent by "an unknown Hand." Returning the favour that Mrs. Manley had done for *Agnes de Castro*, Mrs. Trotter used the same battle imagery:

> For us you've vanquisht, though the toyl was yours,
> You were our Champion, and the Glory ours.

Mrs. Pix, shortly to enter the poetic lists herself, took a softer line:

> Like *Sappho* Charming, like *Afra* Eloquent,
> Like Chast *Orinda*, sweetly Innocent . . .

With this less amazonian imagery, the tone of the verses is closer to Ariadne in feeling than to Mrs. Trotter or Mrs. Manley.

The less truculent attitude of Mrs. Pix's verses to Mrs. Manley is also characteristic of the preface, prologue, and epilogue to her own *Ibrahim*, which was produced at Drury Lane in May 1696. This was London's fourth play by a woman in as many months. In the preface Mrs. Pix expresses her fear that "those that will be so unkind to Criticize upon what falls from a Womans Pen, may soon find more faults than I am ever able to answer." This is what Ariadne had said in the preface to *She Ventures and He Wins*. Mrs. Pix's prologue appeals to the ladies to "protect one, harmless, modest play" and the epilogue disarmingly admits that:

> The Author on her weakness, not her strength relies,
> And from your Justice to your Mercy flies.

These defensive apologies confirm the evidence of *The Female Wits* that Mrs. Pix was a less tempestuous personality than Mrs. Manley, and the mental lightweight among the poetesses.

A second play by Mrs. Pix, this time a farce, *The Spanish Wives*, was produced at Dorset Garden about August 1696. Thus the season of 1695-96 was something of an *annus mirabilis*, for the women dramatists, with no less than seven of their plays presented on the London stages, about a third of the total number of new plays that season. This was probably the highest proportion ever: but the women were not to have it all their own way.

An anonymous burlesque, *The Female Wits: or, The Triumvirate of Poets at Rehearsal*, was produced at Drury Lane about October 1696. This play gave a dramatic version of the events of the previous spring leading to Mrs. Manley's withdrawal of her tragedy from Drury Lane. *The Female Wits* follows the pattern of *The Rehearsal*. Marsilia (Mrs. Manley) is joined at her house by Mrs. Wellfed (Mrs. Pix) and Calista (Mrs. Trotter). After exchanging strained compliments that only just conceal their mutual jealousy, they go to Drury Lane to see a rehearsal of Marsilia's new play. The rehearsal itself, which Marsilia constantly interrupts, exposes not only the absurdity and cheap theatricality of the play, but also the unbounded arrogance of its author. *The Female Wits* ends with Marsilia storming out, threatening never again to darken the doors of Drury Lane. Mrs. Wellfed and Calista are comparatively lightly treated: they are represented as (personally) less objectionable than Marsilia, but their scribbler's itch is ridiculed. Mrs. Wellfed's bulk and bibulousness, and Calista's classical erudition, are also derided.

The Female Wits enjoyed a run of six nights, but it was never revived and it was not printed until 1704. Unlike its obvious inspiration, *The Rehearsal*, it did not become a stock piece. There are several good reasons for this. It is decidedly inferior to *The Rehearsal*, and its chief target, *The Royal Mischief* was soon forgotten. Marsilia, unlike Bayes, could not become the type of the absurd poet, for *The Female Wits* ridicules her as much as an arrogant woman as in her capacity as dramatist, dealing as much with the events surrounding the abortive production of *The Royal Mischief* as with the play's own qualities. Thus *The Female Wits* could not easily be updated, as *The Rehearsal* could be and was,[7] and did not outlive the topicality of its subject. It seems therefore slightly surprising that after failing to get into print in 1696, the play should have been eventually published in 1704, or at all. The author of the preface (unsigned) to the printed edition describes *The Female Wits* as the work of a dead friend, "writ for his own Diversion," and explains the delay in printing it as the result of his

---

7. Cibber describes such an interpolated reference (to *Three Hours after Marriage*) in his *Letter from Mr. Cibber to Mr. Pope*, London, 1742, p. 18 (reprinted, Los Angeles, 1973, Augustan Reprint Society, Publication No. 158).

friend's reluctance to make his work public. This is hardly credible: no one would have written *The Female Wits* who did not want to expose Mrs. Manley to public ridicule. It is more probable that publication in 1704 was prompted by party reasons; that it was an attempt to discredit Mrs. Manley, by then an active Tory propagandist.[8]

The Female Wits show considerable back-stage knowledge of affairs at Drury Lane: its composition representing the collective outrage of the actors, whoever was the actual author. Since it is an obviously biased source, it is difficult to know how seriously to take its picture of the petty jealousies of the three poetesses. It is certainly tempting to accept it as an exposure of the reality behind the façade of the mutual admiration society exchanging complimentary verses. In *The Adventures of Rivella* (1714), her fictionalized and scandalmongering autobiography, Mrs. Manley smeared "Calista" as "most of *Prude* in her outward Professions, and least of it in her inward Practice."[9] But this was some years after the events that led up to *The Female Wits*.

Wider aspects of the feminist question than the propriety of female authorship were much discussed in the 1690s. Important works of radical tendencies were published: Mary Astell's *Serious Proposal to the Ladies* in 1694, and her *Essay in Defence of the Female Sex* (quoted above) in 1696. Like Mary Astell, Defoe in his *Essay upon Projects* (1697) proposed an academy for women. Mrs. Behn's *Younger Brother* and the anonymous *She Ventures and He Wins* show some emancipation in the sympathetic treatment of a heroine actively pursuing the husband of her choice: but there was nothing new about this theme except the treatment of it by a woman. The plays of the "triumvirate" are not notably radical, nor does *The Female Wits* raise any of the wider questions about the social position of women.

One result of the production of *The Female Wits* at Drury Lane was an estrangement of the play's victims from that theatre: between June 1697 and March 1700 all seven of the new plays by

---

8. For this aspect of Mrs. Manley's career, see Gwendolyn B. Needham, "Mary de la Rivière Manley, Tory Defender," *Huntington Library Quarterly* 12, 1948-49, pp. 253-88.

9. *The Adventures of Rivella*, reprinted, New York, 1972, p. 66.

women were produced at Lincoln's Inn Fields.[10] Mrs. Manley wrote no play for ten years after *The Female Wits*, but it would be rash to suggest that she had been laughed off the stage: she had, after all, to make a living, and her two plays had not met with any great financial success. But if *The Female Wits* did not silence its victims, the flood tide of plays by women ebbed somewhat after its production: there was no repetition of the furious activity of 1695-96.

A new comedy by Mrs. Pix, *The Innocent Mistress*, was produced at Lincoln's Inn Fields about June 1697. In the prologue (by Motteux) there is an interesting allusion to the women's reputation for smut: the speaker imagines a spectator exclaiming "No Bawdy, this can't be a Woman's Play." But this lack was apparently not to be imputed to Mrs. Pix, for the prologue goes on to assure us that a good deal had been cut out in production! The epilogue, also by Motteux, takes the same attitude that Mrs. Pix herself had adopted in her apologies for *Ibrahim*, trusting:

> you'll scorn to judge of Woman's wit;
> Tho' in Wit's Court the worst of Judges sit,
> Sure none dare try such puny Causes yet.

The following season saw two new plays by Mrs. Pix (now bidding fair to rival Mrs. Behn in fecundity), one by Mrs. Trotter, and one anonymous work. The anonymous play, *The Unnatural Mother*, "Written by a Young Lady," was the first to be produced, in September or October 1697. The prologue informs us that:

> A Woman now comes to reform the Stage,
> Who once has stood the Brunt of this unthinking Age;

This must be the re-appearance of Ariadne, authoress of *She Ventures and He Wins*. The prologue to this second play represents a serious attempt to clean up the image of women as dramatists, a task that Motteux began facetiously in his prologue to *The Innocent Mistress*.

Mrs. Trotter soon followed the lead of the "Young Lady" in

---

10. Mrs. Pix's *Deceiver Deceived,* however, was apparently offered to Drury Lane, although not produced there (this incident is discussed below).

moralizing her song. In the dedication to her next play, *The Fatal Friendship*, produced at Lincoln's Inn Fields about May 1698, she reiterated the old complaint that "when a Woman appears in the World under any distinguishing Character, she must expect to be the mark of ill Nature, but most one who seems desirous to recommend her Self by what the other Sex think their peculiar Prerogative." She struck a new note, however, when she claimed that her play's "End is the most noble, to discourage Vice, and recommend a firm and unshaken Virtue." The influence of Jeremy Collier is evident here. His *Short View of the Immorality and Profaneness of the English Stage* had been published in April 1698: the introduction begins with the assertion "The business of *Plays* is to recomend [sic] Virtue and discountenance Vice." Mrs. Trotter's echo of this formula was clearly intended to ally her with the reform movement, and the influence of Collier extends to the other prefatory matter published with *The Fatal Friendship*. There are four sets of commendatory verses, of which the last two (both unsigned) are the most interesting. One assures Mrs. Trotter that she has excelled both Orinda and Astraea, and that she has done so with "more just applause" because of her moral strain. The other writes in a vein of greater hyperbole that Mrs. Trotter has outshone Camilla, who lives only in Virgil's lines, by immortalizing herself through her own writings. The author is evidently a man:

> But you your Sexes Champion are come forth
> To fight their Quarrel, and assert their Worth.
> Our Salique Law of Wit you have destroy'd,
> Establish'd Female Claim, and Triumph'd o'er our Pride.

This writer, like the other, praises Mrs. Trotter as a moral author, and advised her not to descend to comedy.

Mrs. Pix's new plays of this season, *The Deceiver Deceived* and *Queen Catherine* are untouched by the reform movement. In the dedication to *The Deceiver Deceived*, however, there is an interesting hint of a claque against the play: "I look upon those that endeavoured to discountenance this Play as Enemys to me." In the prologue there is another complaint, this time about plagiarism: before it came out, she had apparently shown the play "To some, who, like true Wits, stole't half away." The play supposed to have been stolen from Mrs. Pix was George Powell's *The Imposture Defeated*, which was produced at Drury Lane about September 1697 (Mrs. Pix's play was brought out at Lincoln's Inn Fields about November of the same year). Powell defended himself in the preface to his *Imposture Defeated*: he claims that Mrs. Pix brought *The Deceiver Deceived* to him, and asked him to get it acted at Drury Lane. He agreed to do this, but then for unexplained reasons Mrs. Pix "very mannerly carry'd it to the other House." Powell had taken a prominent part in *The Female Wits:* he appears under his own name, and his attitude to the wits is distinctly unsympathetic. It is impossible to reconstruct the details of this new quarrel, but it probably was a re-opening of the old wounds associated with *The Female Wits*.

The next two seasons (1698-99 and 1699-1700) were comparatively barren of women's plays. Only Mrs. Pix kept the flag flying. The prologue to her *False Friend* (Lincoln's Inn Fields, about May 1699) announced that she has joined the Collier faction:

> Amongst Reformers of this Vitious Age,
> Who think it Duty to Refine the Stage:
> A Woman, to Contribute, does Intend,
> In Hopes a Moral Play your Lives will Mend.

Mrs. Pix must have hoped that her audience would not remember the prologue to her *Innocent Mistress*. Her next play, *The Beau Defeated* (Loncoln's Inn Fields, about March 1700), was the first attempt to present a woman's play as a man's. In the unsigned dedication to the Duchess of Bolton, she speaks of "my Charmed Eyes being lately bless'd with the sight of you," and more in a strain of gallantry intended to suggest male authorship. The prologue is also deceptive:

> But Hold — there's something I was begg'd to say,
> In favour of our modest Authors Play.
> He hop'd you'd like . . .

This trick was not immediately repeated, but it was used again several times in the years 1703-07, when women dramatists again faced serious opposition. The dedication to Mrs. Centlivre's *Love's*

Contrivance actually had the false initials "R. M." attached to the dedication.

Mrs. Pix and Mrs. Trotter are very inconsiderable figures in the history of English drama, and if Mrs. Manley is better known than her fellow wits it is chiefly for her *chroniques scandaleuses*. None of the trio proved themselves a worthy successor to Mrs. Behn. But in October 1700 a fourth woman entered the competition for the surely still "Vacant Throne." This was Mrs. Carroll (later Centlivre), whose first play, *The Perjur'd Husband*, was produced at Drury Lane that month. The play itself is a feeble tragedy (though not below the level of Mrs. Pix), but its comic scenes were a portent of greater things to come. With *The Gamester* (1705) and *The Busie Body* (1709) she scored the greatest popular successes by a woman since Mrs. Behn. Not that Mrs. Centlivre's career was an easy rise to fame: some of her earlier plays had to appear anonymously, some even masquerading as the work of a man.

But Mrs. Centlivre persevered as the other contenders dropped out of the race. Mrs. Pix wrote her last play in 1706 and, real success having eluded her, died in 1709; Mrs. Manley wrote only two plays after suffering from *The Female Wits*, turning her attention to politics and prose; Mrs. Trotter married a clergyman and turned to other intellectual pursuits. After 1706, Mrs. Centlivre was the only active woman dramatist: although none of her later plays were as successful in her own time as *The Busie Body* had been, *The Wonder* (1714) and *A Bold Stroke for a Wife* (1718) proved to have staying power. Together with *The Busie Body* they remained stock pieces through most of the nineteenth century, long after Mrs. Behn's plays had been relegated to the closet. *The Wonder* was successfully produced in New York as late as 1897. One reviewer was candid enough to admit that "comedy writing is one art which has not progressed in 200 years."[11] It was thus Mrs. Centlivre who proved the true successor to Astraea's "Vacant Throne."

F. P. Lock

11. *New York Dramatic Mirror*, 3 April 1897, p. 14.

Some Observations on Woman's Concept of Self in the 18th Century

The spirit of feminism in what is loosely called the eighteenth century, as in other centuries, was irrepressible. A tirade written to the Bishop of Salisbury in 1710 about the denigration of women and especially learned women, with its quotations from Erasmus, is only one feminist protest with which the remarkable Lady Mary Pierrepont, later Lady Mary Wortley Montagu, erupted.[1] Despite her distaste for women, as she made clear in her statement that her only "consolation" for being a member of the female "Gender" was the assurance it gave her of "never being marry'd to any one amongst them," and despite her opinion that "both good and ill husbands are their Wives' making" owing to the prevalence of greater folly in women than in men,[2] Lady Mary repeatedly brandished her pen in women's behalf. In 1714, in *Spectator* paper 573, she justified the members of the "Widow-Club" as described by Addison in an earlier number of the *Spectator*.[3] Lady Mary, writing as "Mrs. President," characterized the six poor husbands Mrs. President had already lost and thus demonstrated how little reason there was to grieve for any of them. Why not, then, follow her conviction that there was "as much Virtue in the Touch of a seventh Husband as of a seventh Son" and try once again? Later, Lady Mary adverted frequently to the question of marriage in her little essay sheet *The Nonsense of Common-Sense* and in her letters. Her attitude is epitomized in the remark that Lord Hervey

1. Cf. Lady Mary Wortley Montagu, *The Complete Letters of*, ed. Robert Halsband, 3 vols., Oxford, 1965, I, pp. 44-46.
2. Montagu, II, 33; I, p. 207.
3. *Spectator* 561.

lived with his wife "as well bred as if not married at all."[4] Of
course the question of marriage and the relationship between men
and women in courtship and marriage were not new with Lady
Mary. To look back brings Chaucer into view, and forward, George
Eliot, Gissing, Virginia Woolf, John Updike, and how many others,
whether feminist or not. In Lady Mary's own century, David
Garrick and George Colman made at least one comment in *The
Clandestine Marriage*. Samuel Johnson, who had something to say
about nearly everything else, compared the relative merits of
celibacy and marriage, only to find both wanting. The causes and
impediments in the making of marriages were, in part, Fanny
Burney's subject in both her published and unpublished works.

But feminism hardly confined itself to one aspect of women's
lives. In the sixth issue of *The Nonsense of Common-Sense*, in
particular, Lady Mary defended women as rational creatures,
long-suffering and courageous. In her letters she objected to the
contempt in which women were held, especially in England, and
found both the cause and the solution in their education.[5]
Furthermore she reminded the English clergy that in their "first
Creation" women were "designed a Help for the other Sex, and
nothing was ever made incapable of the End of its Creation." She
went on to say that although "the first Lady had so little
experience that she hearkened to the Persuasions of an imperti-
nant Dangler, . . . he succeeded by persuading her that she was not
so wise as she should be."[6] Mme du Châtelet, Voltaire's mistress,
also defended women's capacities in the introduction to her
translation of Mandeville's *Fable of the Bees*. She attacked the
opinion that women can write nothing more than comedies and
declared the situation ought to be changed by royal decree. "If I
were King," she said, "I would reform an abuse which curtails, so
to speak, half of human kind." Mme du Châtelet went on, "I
would cause women to participate in all the rights of humanity,
and above all, those of the spirit."[7] Thereby, men might gain a

---

4. In Robert Halsband, *The Life of Lady Mary Wortley Montagu*, Oxford, 1956,
p. 223.

5. Cf. Montagu, III, p. 40.

6. Lady Mary Wortley Montagu, *The Nonsense of Common-Sense* ed. Robert
Halsband, Evanston, 1947, p. 27.

7. In Ira O. Wade, *Voltaire and Madame du Châtelet*, Princeton, 1941, p. 231; cf.
p. 27. The translation from the French is mine.

new object for emulation. Mrs. Delany, friend of Swift and, at the end of her long life, a favorite of Queen Charlotte, was first attracted to Dr. Delany by his willingness to "converse with women and treat them like reasonable creatures." Eventually she went so far in a letter to Lady Andover as to attribute numerous advantages to women, over men, from both "nature and education."[8]

Obviously many words — and those recorded here are far from comprehensive — were spent on feminism by many people throughout the century. Much of it passed for social satire or incidental comment as in Johnson's *Rasselas*. In any case it was all only words. Almost no one did anything about feminism or suggested that anything ought to be done. Among the very few who did was Mary Astell, who, even before the century began, had a plan for a *"Religious Retirement,"* an academic sanctuary to which women weary with the "parade of the world" might escape for peace and study and self-improvement. But the *Tatler* and Bishop Burnet ridiculed the scheme out of existence.[9] Swift's implied advocacy in *Gulliver's Travels* of education for females equal with men's is only a half-measure. He proposed by education to make young ladies "as much ashamed of being cowards and fools as men" and to diminish their personal vanity by reliance on "decency and and cleanliness."[10] Swift's intent, however, was not to enlarge the lives of females but to provide wives who must prove agreeable and reasonable.

Perhaps the boldest action in the light of twentieth-century feminism was that of Miss Harriott Edwards, about whom *Thraliana* records that she "struck out for herself a new Plan of Happiness resolved to act the Man & the Libertine: She was a Young Person of large & independent fortune, who set Reputation at Nought & Scandal at Defiance."[11] Miss Edwards was "resolved to avoid Marriage, yet have a Son on whom to settle her Estate." Apparently she first chose John Salusbury, later Hester Lynch

8. Emily Morse Symonds, *Mrs. Delany A Memoir 1700-1788*, New York, 1900, p. 200.

9. Cf. [Mary Astell], *A Serious Proposal To Ladies*, London, 1694; *Tatler* 32.

10. Jonathan Swift, "A Voyage to Lilliput," *Gulliver's Travels*, Chapter 6.

11. Mrs. Hester Lynch Thrale (Later Mrs. Piozzi), *Thraliana*, ed. Katharine C. Balderston, 2 vols., Oxford, 1951, p. 277.

Thrale Piozzi's father, to father her child. Her judgment in that respect was bad inasmuch as together they failed to produce an offspring; and at last Miss Edwards grew weary of Mr. Salusbury, and she rid herself of him in favour of another handsome fellow. That Miss Edwards's behaviour, in the first place, was feminist can not be demonstrated. Her decision to play the *galante* may have been quixotic or it may just as well have been prompted by her appetites. The most that can be said is that she thought she knew what she wanted and that she could hardly get it within the limits of behaviour considered appropriate to women; so she broke free. Harriott Edwards's behaviour is significant not because it was unusual but because it was typical, extreme and flamboyant but typical. That is true because emotional and sexual awakening was the liberating factor in a woman's self-awareness, her self-evaluation. In some cases there went with it a second factor, as Mary Astell and Jonathon Swift both recognized, that is, education. Woman's urgency to be accepted as a rational, thinking creature was not for the sake of reason. If there was one lesson to be learned from the whole existence of Zélide it is that the life of reason whether for a man or a woman is an arid, empty one. Woman wanted to be called rational so that she might be accepted as a creature capable of the responsibility of freedom and thus of freedom of choice as to how she could best seek emotional fulfillment. The woman of the eighteenth century who liberated herself came to the realization that for self-development and self-fulfillment, she must first escape the narrow role assigned her by society, whether in the matter of education or in the making of marriages. She must have the right of choice in educational and sexual decisions, the right to define her own emotional needs and seek their satisfaction.

Education and its uses, according to Mme du Châtelet, expanded the spirit. Even so humble a literary performance as translation was a thing of the spirit. She proclaimed that she had happily renounced the frivolities on which most women, taught to think themselves born to beguile, spend their entire lives. In translating Mandeville and later Isaac Newton, Mme du Châtelet declared, she was cultivating her soul. On the other hand, Maria Agnesi, the Italian linguist and mathematician, found learning inadequate for her soul. After one publication, written in Latin when she was nine, defending the liberal arts as an appropriate study for females, and two publications of a mathematical nature, written as an adult, Signorina Agnesi turned her energies to the sick and the poor so that at last she founded a small hospital and helped administer a home for the aged poor. For Zélide and Mary Somerville, learning was an end in itself; and if it proved barren for one and for the other, Mrs. Somerville, the scientist, a beckoning light well into the nineteenth century, the reasons must lie in temperament and in the utmost privacy in which the thinking and feeling person, man or woman, lives his life.[12] These four women are judged here from the outside simply because there was no immediate access to an expression of their inner lives. Even so, that their educations helped shape their identities and sharpened their awareness of it is undeniable.

Fortunately there are women whose testimony allows a more searching view. When Lady Mary asked the Bishop of Salisbury to examine her translation of the *Enchiridion* of Epictetus, in 1710, she told him,

> My Sex is usually forbid studys of this Nature, and Folly reckon'd so much our proper sphere, we are sooner pardon'd any excesses of that, than the least pretentions to reading or good Sense. We are permitted no Books but such as tend to the weakening and Effeminating the Mind, our Natural Deffects are every way indulg'd, and tis look'd upon as in a degree Criminal to improve our Reason, or fancy we have any. We are taught to place all our Art in adorning our Outward Forms, and permitted, without reproach, to carry that Custom even to Extravagancy, while our Minds are entirely neglected and by disuse of Refflections, fill'd with nothing but the trifling objects our Eyes are daily entertain'd with.[13]

But Lady Mary considered herself wholly unlike most members of

---

12. Cf. Wade, p. 231; Sister Mary Thomas à Kempis, "The Walking Polyglot of Mary Gaetana Agnesi," *Scripta Mathematica* 6, 1938, pp. 211-17; Julian L. Coolidge, "Six Female Mathematicians," *Scripta Mathematica* 17, 1951, pp. 21-26; Geoffrey Scott, *The Portrait of Zélide*, New York, 1926, pp. 163-64 *et passim*.

13. Montagu, I, pp. 44-45.

her sex. She protested to Wortley at the "wrong notions" of Mr. Bickerstaff of the *Tatler*, declaring that many women and especially herself, contrary to his accusations, despised "charms of show, and all the pagenantry of Greatness, perhaps with more ease than any of the philosophers."[14] She believed herself more forthright, more honest than other women, unlike them incapable of dissembling, and unwilling to be coquettish. "I take more pains to approve my conduct to my self than to the world," she insisted and was pleased not to have to accuse herself "of a minute's deceit." To be true to herself was important, although she made little of it. In 1709 she told Wortley's sister Anne that, fully aware of the fact that "Nature is seldom in the wrong, custom always," Lady Mary compiled with it in the trivial matter of dress but she was amazed that "people of good sense in other things" could make their happiness consist in the opinions of others, and sacrifice everything in the desire of appearing in fashion." Despite such declarations, Lady Mary's attitude was sometimes ambivalent. On the one hand she was dependent on her father and admitted knowing no more of her "own Affairs than a perfect stranger." And yet, although she quailed before her father's wrath, Lady Mary refused to marry the man of her father's choice. Indeed, she refused to marry "but for *Love*." She took the initiative in her pursuit of the dour, quarrelsome Wortley Montagu and ran him to ground, at the same time demanding that he travel with her after their marriage as the "most likely way to make a Solitude agreeable and not tiresome." Then she added, "'Tis something Odd for a Woman that brings nothing, to expect any thing, but after the way of my Education I dare not pretend to live but in some degree suitable to [it]." Of all the women whose names occur in this paper, to none, not even to Mary Somerville, who was forced to teach herself mathematics from her brothers' texts or not to learn it at all, was education as essential a part of a sense of personality as it was to Lady Mary. Her advice in 1755 to Lady Bute on the education of daughters insisted that "Learning is necessary to the happiness of Women, and ignorance the common foundation of their Errors, both in Morals and Conduct." All

14. Montagu, I, p. 24; cf. *Tatler* 143.

young women, Lady Mary thought, should learn to "confine their desires to probabillitys, to be as useful as is possible to themselves, and to think privacy (as it is) the happiest state of Life." She emphasized, as well, knowledge of mankind as the most useful of all knowledge and suggested that above all it is wise to recognize that "Civility costs nothing and buys everything."[15] Lady Mary's education was not academic as Maria Agensi's, not specialized as Mrs. Somerville's, but rather a mixture of learning, cultivated taste, and cynical practicality. At each stage of its development, it was central to Lady Mary's view of herself.

By comparison, Mrs. Thrale, that connoisseur of trivia, took different views of education at different times. Like Lady Mary, she conventionally disparaged the customary education of women. "Every female," she said, "is harrassed with Masters she disregards, and heaped with Accomplishments which She ought to disdain, when she reflects that her Mother only loads her with Allurements, as a Rustic lays Bird Lime on Twigs, to decoy & catch the unwary Traveller." In the same breath Mrs. Thrale explained why she found education admirable. "Whoever has not been bred to Science," she declared, "considers his early Life as a Source of future Misery; whatever may be his Talents, his Fortune, or his Reception in the World, he never ceases to lament his *Loss* of *Learning* with a seriousness that makes those wonder who have all their lives been taught to consider it not as an End, but a means."[16] Yet Mrs. Thrale had written for *Thraliana* an account of her life in which she viewed her childish precociousness as only a rewarding form of entertainment. She found that education served her little in time of crisis. In 1782 when an estrangement with Dr. Johnson threatened, Mrs. Thrale said she had thought he could not exist without her conversation but presently concluded he "cared more for her roast Beef & plum Pudden." More than a year later when she was unwillingly at Bath with her daughters, she complained that she was forced to "live a Life of Vigilance & Constraint, ill suiting a liberal & expanded Mind; which conscious of no Ill *ought* to fear no Inspection."[17]

15. Montagu, I, pp. 25, 6, 162; III, pp. 83, 106, 107; II, p. 450.
16. Thrale, pp. 590-91.
17. Thrale, pp. 541 n. 1, 572; cf. pp. 281-87 *et passim*.

The years 1782 and 1783 in which Mrs. Thrale made those last two statements were those in which her self-awareness was heightened by her passion for Gabriel Mario Piozzi, a passion which both forced and allowed her to choose between him and £800 per year along with her daughters and her dearest friends, Dr. Johnson and Fanny Burney. Mrs. Thrale probably met Gabriel Piozzi for the first time in 1778 at one of the Burneys' evening parties, when she stood behind him and mimicked his gestures as he played the harpsichord and sang; after which Piozzi, while some of the other members of the company played a duet, "regaled himself with a short nap." By August 1780, Mrs. Thrale confessed a regard for him, and by October 1782, he had become the only man "she ever could have loved." By that date, October 1782, Henry Thrale, her husband, had been dead about a year and a half.[18] Within a few months, the question of Mrs. Thrale's taking her daughters to Italy, with Piozzi to follow, or of marrying him over the objection of friends, advisers, and her daughters, especially the eldest, Hester or Queeney, reached a crux. Mrs. Thrale sent him away. After great agony set down in florid terms, she recalled him and on 23 July 1784, Piozzi and Mrs. Thrale were married.

Over Mrs. Thrale's passion for Piozzi and the course of their romance, Fanny Burney expended thousands of words, most of them disapproving or pleading. Miss Burney believed in marriage for love or at least one in which each principal found the other agreeable. That is a conviction which pervades much of her fiction, published and unpublished. *Evelina*, "The Witlings," *Cecila* and "Love and Fashion" are a few indications of her faith in the necessity for individual decision. And she could only regret that Mrs. Thrale's marriage to Henry Thrale had been made, as Mrs. Thrale herself put it, "to please her mother." Miss Burney was convinced that such a marriage was responsible for her friend's present "ungovernable passions." She urged Mrs. Thrale's daughter to "live single forever, rather than *first* marry with that conscious indifference for which your poor Mother pays so dearly & so

18. Cf. Thrale, pp. 546, 448 *n.* 7, 452; Charlotte Burney, "Some Letters and Fragments . . .," in *The Early Diary of Frances Burney*, ed. Annie Raine Ellis, 2 vols., London, 1913, II, pp. 284-87.

late."[19] To Mrs. Thrale, on the eve of her decision to send Piozzi away, Miss Burney wrote in part,

> I tremble at the Final answer you are to give — ah, *think* a little before you utter it! — you will say you have been thinking all this Time, no dear Madam, you have *never* thought, — you have distressed & harrassed yourself not about changing your plan, but merely in a wild anxiety to obtain *approbation* for it. That approbation will *forever* be withheld! The Mother of 5 children . . . will never be forgiven for showing so great an ascendance of passion over reason.[20]

Of course Fanny Burney talked and wrote in the jargon of her time, and her talk of reason and passion may have had various meanings. But in this case she more than likely was opposing duty and obligation to sexual desire. In a few years — in 1798 to be exact — Miss Burney expressed not condemnation but pity when her oldest brother James and her half-sister Sarah Harriet Burney eloped. "Poor James!" Fanny said, " — his heart is not made to be callous long to the daring offence he has both given & influenced. . . . My Heart aches for him often . . ." As for his companion, Fanny lamented the "lot" Sarah Harriet had "dealt herself" and added, "What has the life she has chosen that can repay her, when its novelty & wilfulness are past, for the life she has relinquished?"[21] Indeed, Dr. Burney made more of a fuss about the fact that James and Sarah Harriet attempted to lure his servant away. That act, he said, "did mortify and chagrine" him "to the quick." And he added that it was "so completely Jacobinical & selfish" that he could never "forget such a barbarous piece of egotism."[22] Now, in 1783, the talk caused by servants who reported numerous long and private interviews between Piozzi and Mrs. Thrale proved "too humiliating" for Miss Burney to repeat.

19. *The Queeney Letters* . . ., ed. The Marquis of Lansdowne, London, 1934, p. 70.

20. Frances Burney to Hester Lynch Thrale, n.p., n.d. (All MS material herein cited is a part of the Henry W. and Albert A. Berg Collection, The New York Public Library, the Astor, Lenox and Tilden Foundations, and is quoted with their permission.)

21. Frances Burney to Esther Burney [West Hamble], 5 October 1798 (Berg).

22. Charles Burney to Frances Burney, [Chelsea], 26 October 1798 (Berg).

More outrageous was the advice of Mrs. Thrale's physician, Matthew Dobson, that her "Health required a *Man*." Fanny Burney asked again, "How can she suffer herself, noble-minded as she is, to be thus duped by ungovernable passions?"[23]

Fanny Burney might have been even more aghast had she observed the change and development in concept of self under the influence of her love for Piozzi which Mrs. Thrale exposed in her *Thraliana*. She moved from a conventional mask which both she and her social environment accepted to an honest admission of helplessness before her sexual desire. In April 1782, she evaluated herself as a "Woman of passable Person, ancient Family, respectable Character, uncommon Talents and three Thousand a Year" with the "Right to think herself any Man's equal; & . . . nothing to seek but return of Affection from whatever Partner She pitches on." She concluded that to marry for love would be rational and determined not to marry until she was in love, if she did so at all. Even then she saw herself with the right to choose, as she made clear in pondering love and friendship as "distinct things." She declared that she would "go through Fire to serve many a Man, whom nothing less than Fire would force" her "to go to Bed to." By September 1782, she had reached a crossroads in her view of self. One way led to a confirmation of an identity between the world's and her own view; the other, to an affirmation of independent choice as a distinct thinking creature. Mrs. Thrale decided first that, however "worthly" or "lovely" Piozzi might be, he was below her and thus she must sacrifice her own choice. Then she went on,

> But why? Oh because I am a Woman of superior understanding, & must not for the World degrade my self from my Situation in Life, but if I *have* superior Understanding, let me at least make use of it for once; & rise to the rank of a human Being conscious of its own power to discern Good from Ill — the person who has uniformly acted by the Will of others has hardly that Dignity to boast.[24]

23. *Queeney Letters*, pp. 171, 70; cf. Madame d'Arblay, *Diary and Letters of,* ed. Austin Dobson, 6 vols. London, 1904, II, pp. 283, 267.
24. Thrale, pp. 531, 544-45.

Two months later she could enumerate with tenderness her reasons for loving Piozzi and less than a year had passed when her love for Piozzi and her pain at his absence had conquered her social self and she prayed, "Oh return, my Love! and bless me with your Sight once more; I cannot bear these Agonies of Absence, what Madness to part when our Souls were so fondly united! to hope Happiness from future Union, and delay the hour of Bliss." Love had it two to one over pride. As the next year, 1784, opened Mrs. Thrale, who had lived forty-three years and had countless pregnancies, indulged in a dream of still another one by Piozzi. She wrote,

> Oh might I hope to be once more in that State [of pregnancy] by the Man my Heart doats on — how little would I value Death or Danger! — but such favours from Heaven, how have I merited? impatient under God's fatherly & gentle Corrections — can I hope to be blest to the full Accomplishment of all desired Felicity? What! die in my Piozzi's Arms, & leave him a Pledge of my unbounded, my true Affection![25]

And why not? Was she different from women before her and those who followed? There was Mrs. Kenneth Grahame who wrote to Mrs. Hardy in bewilderment during the early days of marriage and asked whether she had expected too much. Or there was Nancy Cunard who reminisced happily about her life with Henry Crowder in the 1920s and 30s: "Honey, what love we did have!"

But Fanny Burney in 1783 or 84 could not condone Mrs. Thrale's middle-aged passion. Despite her talk of passion and reason, Fanny Burney was prompted partly by commonsense and partly by expediency. She declared that as long as she possessed her reason, nothing could cause her to approve what reason must condemn, "that Children, Religion, Situation, Country & Character — besides the Diminution of Fortune by the certain loss of 800£ a Year were too much to sacrifice to any One Man." More important was her regret that "such a Woman" as Mrs. Thrale could be "blind to all sense of propriety."[26] Propriety was a

25. Thrale, pp. 573, 583.
26. Thrale, p. 550; *Queeney Letters*, p. 84.

serious consideration for Miss Burney. Her reluctance to acknow-
ledge her authorship of *Evelina* is too familiar to repeat here.
About her next venture, a play called "The Witlings," she said she
would "a Thousand times" rather forfeit "her reputation as a
writer than risk ridicule or censure as a female." She added, "I
have never set my heart on fame, and therefore would not, if I
could, purchase it at the expense of all my own ideas of
propriety." Miss Burney's ideas of decorum were so strict that she
suffered unduly from the "doubts, suspicions or reports" which
attended her romance with the clergyman George Cambridge. Her
behaviour offended him, but she was sensitive enough to the
inquisitiveness of their friends to relinquish "all the pleasure of an
evening merely from a watchful eye or a curious glance."[27]
Frequently, moreover, Miss Burney's father dictated her behaviour. Dr. Charles Burney had the highest respect for "the World"
and Fanny had the greatest reverence for her father. "Every virtue
under the sun is his," she said and willingly allowed him to make
decisions for her, sometimes against her wishes and her own
judgment. When Burney decreed that the Latin lessons which Dr.
Johnson wanted to give Fanny were "too Masculine for Misses,"
she ended the lessons. "I have more fear of the malignity which
will follow its being known," she said "than delight in what
advantages it may afford." At Dr. Burney's insistence, she ended a
rewarding friendship with Mme du Staël, who had come to
England in 1793 as an emigrée from the French Revolution. Dr.
Burney feared that Mme de Staël's political position might
endanger his daughter's pension from Queen Charlotte. Furthermore the talk was that Mme de Staël had neither emigrated nor
suffered banishment from France but that Narbonne had seduced
her from her husband and children. Fanny Burney awkwardly
withdrew from Mme de Staël, while wishing the "world would
take more care of itself and less of its neighbors."[28]

The one time Fanny Burney risked her father's disapproval
and neglected public opinion was in working out her own

27. d'Arblay, I, p. 162; Burney, MS Diary [c. 22 March 1786] (Berg).
28. Burney, *Early Diary*, I, p. 189; d'Arblay, I, p. 216; Burney, MS Diary
Concerning her Courtship Written to Susan Burney Phillips, 8-19 April and 3-9 May
1793, p. [44] (Berg).

middle-aged passion. In this instance she showed more personal dignity, more honesty, and more maturity than at any other time of her life. The object of her passion was General Alexander d'Arblay, who had come to England with Narbonne and Mme de Staël. They lived with other emigrés at Juniper Hall in Surrey, a residence near that of Fanny's sister Susan. Miss Burney met them on a visit to her sister in late January 1793 and at once thought d'Arblay one of the "most delightful characters" she had ever met. Before long she was correcting themes which d'Arblay wrote in English in return for his instruction in French. They fell in love and meant to have each other although there was almost nothing to encourage their marriage. D'Arblay had neither income nor expectations and his political views were anathema to the English court on which Fanny was dependent. Indeed Fanny Burney's sole income was from Queen Charlotte, who had arranged for a pension amounting to £100 a year. As for Dr. Burney, he was no more than coldly civil when d'Arblay came to call in June or July 1793; and Burney took pains to explain his disapproval in a letter written to d'Arblay in July. Fanny confessed to her sister Susan that although she could look forward to a marriage with a "mutual freedom from ambition," the loss of the pension was "too serious in its consequences" to risk. Nevertheless, Fanny Burney managed. On 28 July 1793, without the presence of her father, she married General d'Arblay at Mickleham Church in Surrey.[29] Thereafter Miss Burney settled back once more into a limited view of woman's proper behaviour and called on nature to justify it. But at least once she had asserted the right of choice in human relations, possibly the most important decision she made throughout her life. Unfortunately, ten years earlier, unaware of the fact that passion is usually stronger than reason, she found it difficult to sympathize with Mrs. Thrale's grief for Piozzi or to advocate the choice Mrs. Thrale made.

If any proof is wanting that passion is very likely to dominate reason or that high romance intensifies woman's sense of self, then Lady Mary Wortley Montagu provides it in her own poetic passion

29. Cf. Joyce Hemlow, *The History of Fanny Burney*, London, 1958, p. 241 *et passim*; cf. Charles Burney to Alexandre d'Arblay, Chelsea, 11 July 1793 (Berg).

of middle age. When compared with the experiences of Fanny Burney and Mrs. Thrale, Lady Mary's was the most generous (she gave more than she got), the most aristocratic (there was no talk of pensions and incomes for her, no demands except sincerity), and the most doomed to failure because the most exotic (the object of her devotion was Francesco Algarotti, Italian poet and opportunist more often excited sexually by men than by women). Algarotti came to London in March 1736 after a visit of six weeks with Voltaire and Mme du Châtelet. He was twenty-four years old, educated, brilliant in a facile way, handsome, ambitious, and self-seeking. By April, Lady Mary, who was forty-seven years old, was writing light graceful notes to the young man. She must surely have suspected his homosexual inclinations if for no other reason than that she knew the emotions he had fostered in Lord Hervey. Yet by August of that same year she had come to recognize his "merit and graces" which she enumerated as "the most lively taste, the most refined sentiments, the most delicate imagination."[30] With these characteristics, he made such a contrast with Wortley. And so Lady Mary declared herself to Algarotti, describing her feelings as too ardent to explain or to hide. When he left England in September, after lying to Lord Hervey in order to dine on his last night in London with Lady Mary, she wrote again,

> I am so foolish about everything that concerns you that I am not sure of my own thoughts. My reason complains very softly of the stupidities of my heart without having the strength to destroy them. . . . All that is certain is that I shall love you all my life in spite of your whims and my reason.[31]

To rehearse the details of this affair, here, is impossible. In any case to do so is unnecessary because Lady Mary, like Mrs. Thrale and Fanny Burney, has had a gifted biographer. But to understand the extent of Lady Mary's passion, it must be stated that in July 1739 she abandoned her country, her home, and a marriage (which had gone stale) for the purpose of meeting Algarotti in Venice. She awaited him there and elsewhere on the Continent

30. Montagu, II, p. 514 (This and the following references are to Halsband's translations from French, in which Lady Mary wrote to Algarotti).
31. Montagu, II, p. 501.

while he bettered his fortunes or satisfied his whims first through one man and then another: Lord Baltimore, Lord Burlington, a young man named Firmaçon, Crown Prince Frederick, later Frederick II, King of Prussia, and someone by whom he was infected with the "pox" in 1741. And throughout these years she fashioned poetry for him and wrote him adoring letters.

Each confirms her sense of self, a self which Lady Mary put forward in a spirit of generosity, of giving the best she had, exactly as she had years before with Wortley. As she had done with him, she took the offensive with Algarotti, suggesting that she leave England for him and naming Venice for their rendezvous because she thought it would please him. Repeatedly when he failed to reply to her letters, she pleaded for an answer and almost as often assured him of her willingness to settle anywhere he chose except Paris or Holland. Once more she asserted her difference from other women as when she compared herself with the "sad Dido." Lady Mary wrote, "I have thrown myself at the head of a foreigner just as she did, but instead of crying perjurer and villain when my little Aeneas shows that he wants to leave me, I consent to it through a feeling of Generosity which Virgil did not think women capable of." Her faith in her own honesty (while she deceived Wortley or he allowed her to) is in these words written in September 1736 when she promised Algarotti a certain pleasure from her letters:

> You will see (what has never been seen till now) the faithful picture of a woman's Heart without evasion or disguises, drawn to the life, who presents herself for what she is, and who neither hides nor glosses over anything from you. My weakness and my outbursts ought at least to attract your curiosity, in presenting to you the accurate dissection of a female Soul.

Two years later she assured him again of her constancy and integrity, so steadfast, she said, they must take the place of "charms and graces." And in 1739, she wrote once more, confirming her sincerity. "To make up for the charms that you will not find," Lady Mary said, "you will always find the rarest and most perfect good faith."[32]

32. Montagu, II, pp. 501, 503, 506; cf. p. 505.

There is something at once sad and ludicrous in an older woman's pursuit of a young man, and Lady Mary knew it. "My reason," she wrote "complains very softly of the stupidities of my heart without having the strength to destroy them." Three years later, she was still protesting that she no longer wished "to feed on chimeras." Yet, that was what she did, and Lady Mary knew that, too. "Feeble Reason!" she complained, "which battles with my passion and does not destroy it, and which vainly makes me see all the folly of loving to the degree that I love without hope of return."[33] Lady Mary was right when she declared that she herself carried the serpent which poisoned her paradise. After expending such a wealth of passion and loving sentiments, she was reduced to telling Algarotti that mere friendship and conversation would "make the delights" of her life. She explained to him how they might live, not in the same house but close enough to see each other every day. But that failed, too. For two months in 1741, both Algarotti and Lady Mary lived in Turin, whether side by side, whether in intellectual communion, is impossible to say. But by May 1741 she had had enough and she told him,

> I have begun to scorn your scorn. . . . In the time (of foolish memory) when I had a frantic passion for you, the desire to please you (although I understood its entire impossibility) and the fear of boring you almost stifled my hand five hundred times a day when I took up my pen to write to you. At present it is no longer that. I have studied you, and studied so well, that Sir [Isaac] Newton did not dissect the rays of the Sun with more exactness than I have deciphered the sentiments of your soul. . . . I saw that your soul is filled with a thousand beautiful fancies but all together makes up only indifference.

With rare magnanimity, Lady Mary then blamed only herself. After listing the "beautiful fancies" of his soul she asked why she found only "churlishness and indifference" and answered sadly that she was "dull enough to arouse nothing better."[34] And

33. Montagu, II, pp. 501, 506, 502.
34. Montagu, II, pp. 513-14; cf. p. 509.

thereafter, for Lady Mary, Algarotti and his words were no more than a sop to the vanity which she had long cultivated as one of the chief qualities (the other being credulity) to which she declared she owed all the pleasure of life.

There is no escape from the suspicion that credulity and vanity played a considerable part in Lady Mary's pursuit of Algarotti. Certainly she was not following the dictates of feminism. Nor were Mrs. Thrale and Fanny Burney. However often these three women mouthed feminist platitudes and however sincere they were in doing so, feminism had little part in establishing a sense of identity in any one of them, or indeed, as far as is known, in those others mentioned here, Mme du Châtelet, Maria Agnesi, Mrs. Somerville. Rather, they arrived at a sense of self by way of education or a grand passion. What else was there? Certainly there were no careers for these women to follow and almost no women filling roles on which to model a career. In Lady Mary's younger days, there was Queen Anne, of course, but she occupied a position which school girls might dream about but no women aspired to. Her presence on the throne appears to have had no influence on the position of women. They hardly mattered in the twelve years of her reign, filled with war and fractious party politics. No woman held an official position outside the Queen's bedchamber. If there were influential women at Queen Anne's court, such as the Duchess of Marlborough, they held no office. When the Hanovers came to the throne, the women who counted were their mistresses, and these women were hardly career models. Nor was Maria Skerrit, Lady Mary's friend and Robert Walpole's mistress and then his wife. Lady Mary might have made a career for herself with her pen, and in another time she would have. But in the eighteenth century, she refused. Nothing was published in her lifetime to which she signed her name. No person "of Quality," she declared, should "turn Author," but instead "confine himself to the Applause of his Friends."[35] When the females in the Burney household wanted to escape the unpleasantness of the "odious" Mrs. Burney, the Doctor's second wife, they made bad marriages. That includes her own daughter, Maria, the offspring of Mrs.

35. Montagu, III, p. 37; cf. Halsband, pp. 50-51.

Burney's first marriage. Not even a poor marriage had presented itself to Fanny when she received an invitation to serve as dresser to Queen Charlotte. Thus Fanny had no choice. She regarded the position as "the saddest lot that Destiny without positive calamity could frame for her!" But she knew that "to have disdained such a proposal would ... have been thought madness & folly." She knew, too, that she would not "have been permitted to decline it, without exciting a displeasure," — that of her father — which would have made her "quite unhappy." Even if it had paid enough, an open career as a writer was out of the question. Miss Burney published *Evelina* to help her brother Charles and she kept at her writing because she needed whatever money it brought. Yet she thought it necessary to justify the writing of novels on the grounds that they gave to "juvenile credulity knowledge of the world, without ruin, or repentance; and the lessons of experience, without its tears."[36] And she never signed her books. After *Evelina*, her authorship was no secret, but her name appears on none of her novels.

To assert their uniqueness of personality and its rights, then, these women — Lady Mary, Mrs. Thrale, Fanny Burney — turned either to the mind or the emotions, and for them apparently love was the greatest of human emotions. It was well worth all the risk and defiance it required. It enriched their worlds and sharpened their perceptions of self. Thereby they were fully women and fully themselves.

Miriam J. Benkovitz

36. Burney, MS Diary [1787 or early 1788]; Fanny Burney to Esther Burney, n.p. [June or July 1786] (Berg); [Fanny Burney], *The Wanderer*, 5 vols., London, 1814, I, p. xvi.

Women and Literature
in 18th Century England

"Women and Literature in 18th-century England": what an ambitious and grandiloquent title! It should serve also as a warning that I can only sketch in the most cursory way a few aspects of the relationship between women and literature in that century. Obviously, such a connection can be investigated and discussed for any historical period in which literature and women existed, but I believe that their relationship in the 18th century sets up an exceptional, I might even say unique, pattern.

In that period, as in no preceding or succeeding one, two particular and connected phenomena took place. Women became professional writers and journalists; that is, they were for the first time able to earn their living through the sale of their writing. Like men they exploited all available ways: these were private patronage (mainly derived from dedications), subscription publication, journalism, and (through publishers) sale of their books to libraries and the general reading public. Women as authors became so numerous and so prolific, in fact, that during the second half of the century they actually produced the majority of all the novels that were published. The other phenomenon is that during this century women constituted for the first time an important sector of the reading public — a consumer group, one might say, whose appetites all writers had to satisfy. This can be seen at the beginning of the century in the *Tatler* and then in the *Spectator* essays when Mr. Spectator declares that his paper is intended to be useful to "the female World"; and it can be seen later in the growth of lending (or circulating) libraries, which catered so largely to women readers. These two phenomena — women's emergence as writers and as readers — arose simultaneously.

The prominence and activity of women in the literary life of the 18th century coincided, of course, with the rise of the feminist movement. That movement has always aroused controversy, and its prominence today need not be underlined. I daresay that is why its ramifications in 18th century literature and life are being discussed here. Feminist attitudes in that century covered a wide spectrum. At one extreme is the point of view neatly set forth in a late 17th century pamphlet translated from the French: "A Discourse of women, shewing their imperfections alphabetically." But more characteristic of the modern point of view is another pamphlet, also anonymous, published in England in 1751: "Beauty's triumph: or, The superiority of the fair sex invincibly proved. Wherein the arguments for the natural right of man to a sovereign authority over the woman are fairly urged and undeniably refuted."

The chronological span of feminism's steep rise is almost exactly the limits of the century: its standard signposts are Mary Astell's *Serious Proposal to the Ladies* in 1694 and Mary Wollstonecraft's *Vindication of the Rights of Women* in 1792. Worth noting, too, is that unlike previous champions these are not men — whose advocacy, however enlightened, cannot help having a patronizing tinge — but articulate and vigorous women. Compared to the feminists of today they made demands that seem timid, even maidenly; in their own day these were revolutionary.

It is an oversimplification to speak of 18th-century women writers as though they were a homogeneous group. For, as I pointed out in a published lecture a few years ago, in the earlier part of the century women who wrote for money, who made writing their profession, were regarded as social outcasts. Their mercenary motives also directed their choice of genres; they wrote fiction and drama rather than poetry. When (in 1733) Alexander Pope pointed to four "remarkable poetesses and scribblers" famous for their scandalous lives he named two who wrote for the stage, and two who wrote mainly prose fiction. One of these, Eliza Haywood, is grotesquely portrayed in *The Dunciad;* and Swift, although he had not read any of her writings, calls her "a stupid, infamous, scribbling woman." The pious Earl of Egmont, when he heard a premature report of Mrs. Haywood's death, neatly summed up her moral and fiscal reputation; "a whore in her youth, a bawd in her elder years, and a writer of lewd novels, wherein she succeeded tolerably well. By the use of these several means she had amassed, 'tis said, near 10,000 £." Her financial success as a writer certainly did not sweeten her reputation. In general the low repute of fiction and the low repute of the women who wrote it reinforced each other. It was not until the novel had been raised to respectability by Richardson (in 1740) and not until respectable woman novelists achieved fame − Sarah Fielding, Charlotte Lennox, and Fanny Burney − that the two respectabilities were joined.

Before the rise of a reading public large enough to support them, authors of either sex had several paths open to them by which they could earn some money, even if not enough to provide their living. They could dedicate their books to patrons. This practise, venerable enough to be traced back to Augustan Rome, obviously appealed to women since it was more genteel and less tainted by commercialism. Its advantage was that the author received immediate payment, albeit a modest one; but she could hope for further rewards if the dedicatee exerted any power or influence. In 1703 Lady Chudleigh dedicated her *Poems on Several Occasions* to Queen Anne, who had ascended the throne the previous year. In 1710, when it was clear where the dynastic succession lay, Lady Chudleigh dedicated her *Essays Upon Several Occasions* to Sophia, Electress of Hanover. Royalty generally attracted dedications; a daughter of George II was thus honored in 1750 (by Mary Jones in her *Miscellanies in Prose and Verse*), sixteen years after the Princess had sailed to Holland as consort to the Prince of Orange.

Ladies of less stringent respectability also benefited by private patronage. Mary de la Rivière Manley, after her heyday as a writer of scandalous *romans à clef*, wrote a poem in praise of the Earl of Bristol's family; and that genial peer − father of the more famous Lord Hervey − gallantly accepted her tribute, and then rewarded her with 20 guineas when it was published in 1719. Some years later Laetitia Pilkington, whose raffish career extended from Dublin to London, attempted a similar scheme. Since she was obliged to live by her wits, she states, she determined to write a panegyric on Lord Hardwicke, newly appointed Lord Chancellor. Instead of using a poem that, like a bishop's pastoral letter, had already been sent to many prospective patrons, she composed a fine new one for him; and after sending it she was invited to call one Sunday, that being his only leisure time. Her account of the interview is remarkably vivid: "Accordingly, I waited on him at Eight o'Clock on *Sunday* Morning; the House had rather the Appearance of Desolation and Poverty, than that of the L—d Ch—ll—r of Br——n; He had Complaisance enough to send his Mace-Bearer to keep me Company, till such time as a Pair of Folding-doors flew open, and my Lord appeared in his Robes, ready to go to Church; he bowed down to the Ground to me, and asked me if I would drink a Dish of Chocolate with him? which you may not doubt I accepted of; and was surprized to find myself, though sunk in the most abject Poverty, sitting with so great a Man! So, for my Labour, I got a Dish of Chocolate, which I now return, with the utmost Humility, to his L—d—p again." How many parallel episodes would the history of patronage yield if all unlucky claimants recorded their memoirs!

At best, private literary patronage for men was bleak and frustrating; but how much bleaker for women since government appointments and sinecures could not as easily be awarded to them. One can think of lucrative appointments, sinecures or not, given to men as a reward (or as an inducement) for their writing, but how many to women? As for the appointment of poet laureate: is it even conceivable that that honor should ever go to a woman?

Women writers, like men, had recourse to another method of raising money, publication by subscription. This practice, though begun before the 18th-century, flourished during that period, serving as an intermediate stage between support from private patrons on one hand, and on the other from the unknown, anonymous reading public for whom the bookseller served as intermediary. The pioneer woman scholar Elizabeth Elstob published her *English-Saxon Homily* in 1709 by subscription; but the number of subscribers — about 260 — is relatively small. Almost half of them were women, a tribute (one suspects) to friendship rather than to love of Anglo-Saxon. Other women writers issued their works by this method — one of the most successful was Elizabeth Carter's translation of the works of Epictetus in 1758. Its list of subscribers is impressive: twelve double-columned pages headed by the Prince of Wales and his mother, the Dowager; a multitude of peers and bishops, the libraries of several Cambridge colleges but only one in Oxford — perhaps Oxford preferred to read Epictetus in Greek — and literary men including Samuel Johnson, who was a great admirer of Miss Carter. His remark about Miss Carter is too well known to resist quoting: "[She] could make a pudding, as well as translate Epictetus."

Given the advantage of many friends who were prosperous a writer could amass a large sum by subscription; and women writers took advantage of this method. Fanny Burney, after her marriage to an impecunious French emigré, deliberately set about to raise a sum large enough to buy a house. In 1796 she issued by subscription *Camilla*, her long, didactic novel; and although the list adds up to only 300, some subscribed for more than a single copy (Edmund Burke for 15, Elizabeth Montagu for 10); and altogether with general sales, the edition of 4,000 copies was sold out so that Mme D'Arblay was able to buy a house that she gratefully named Camilla Cottage.

One of the more bizarre cases of women's connection with literature and subscription publication in the 18th-century is that of Anne Yearsley, the milkwoman of Bristol. In her brief career we see several strands of the literary fabric — a simple woman who educated herself to some literary distinction, private patronage from the charitable Hannah More, and subscription publication. Mrs. Yearsley was not the first of those whom Robert Southey called "Our Uneducated Poets" but she was the first notable woman among them. (The best known was Stephen Duck, the thresher poet; patronized by Queen Caroline, he later became a clergyman and ended a suicide in 1756.) Mrs. Yearsley's first book, *Poems, on Several Occasions*, was published by subscription in 1785; and in its list of over 1,000 names more than half are women's. When a new edition was issued, Mrs. Yearsley enrolled new subscribers, whose names are printed after the original list. But she then quarreled bitterly with Miss More, for she evidently wanted a patron but she did not want (in another sense) to be patronized. Her next publication, two years later, was also issued by subscription, but with only about half the number she had gathered for her first book. It is evidence of the close connection between private patronage and subscription publication.

A rich vein of information about women's activity as magazine editors and contributors has been uncovered recently in a book by Alison Adburgham, whose impressive roll-call stretches from Mrs. Manley to Miss Mitford. Along the way she praises *The Nonsense of Common-Sense* by Lady Mary Wortley Montagu, who (she says) established "a milestone in the history of women's journalism by writing a weekly essay paper for political purposes." Unlike most other journalists, of either sex, Lady Mary retained her amateur status by writing out of conviction and not for profit. Those 18th century women who labored for money won the feminist praise of Virginia Woolf. At the same time Miss Woolf condemns the amateurs, whom she describes thus: "shut up in their parks among their folios, those solitary great ladies . . . wrote without audience or criticism, for their own delight alone." (She must have been thinking of the eccentric Duchess of Newcastle.) There were other ladies, neither great nor shut up in their parks, who wrote for their own delight. It was a harmless enough pastime, even in their own day, yet they had to endure ridicule and discouragement. In one of his later papers Mr. Spectator recommends that the best way for a woman to show her "fine genius" is — needlework. "I cannot forbear wishing," he continues, "that several Writers of that Sex had chosen to apply themselves rather to Tapestry than Rhime. Your Pastoral Poetesses may vent their Fancy in Rural Landskips, and place despairing Shepherds under silken Willows, or drown them in a Stream of Mohair. The Heroick Writers may work up Battels as successfully, and inflame them with Gold or stain them with Crimson. Even those who have only a Turn to a Song or an Epigram, may put many valuable Stitches into a Purse, and crowd a thousand Graces into a Pair of Garters." This gentle mockery of women's aspiration tells them plainly enough that their proper concerns are domestic and not literary.

If the *Tatler*'s and *Spectator*'s attitude toward women seems enlightened for its time it does not for ours. The notion that

woman could receive a serious education was scoffed at in the
Tatler paper that ridiculed Mary Astell's proposal to establish a
college for women where — the *Tatler* remarked — "instead of
scissors, needles, and sampler" their whole time will be taken up
by "pens, compasses, quadrants, books, manuscripts, Greek, Latin,
and Hebrew." Just as the male *bel esprit* disapproved of learning
for women, so did he look askance at their activity as writers.
Women writers are among the objects of Pope's satiric targets in
The Rape of the Lock. You will recall how the gnome descends to
the Cave of Spleen and addresses the wayward Queen, who rules
the sex from fifty to fifteen:

> Parent of Vapours and of Female Wit,
> Who give th'*Hysteric* or *Poetic* Fit,
> On various Tempers act by various ways,
> Make some take Physick, others scribble Plays.

If Pope meant this passage to apply to the eminently respectable
Lady Winchilsea, which is at least possible, then a few years later
he may have again honored her in the farce *Three Hours After
Marriage* as Phoebe Clinket, a scribbling playwright. In his great
epic on dullness he chose two ladies of impeachable respectability
— Mrs. Hayward and Mrs. Centlivre; "two slipshod Muses," he calls
them, the "Glories of their race." He treats them with such
contempt, it must be said, not so much because they are women
writers as because they inhabit Grub Street.

This picture of women writers condemned and ridiculed is
more typical of the earlier part of the century, for later in the
century they were given recognition, praised, and encouraged. In
1752 George Ballard published by subscription a large handsome
book he called *Memoirs of Several Ladies of Great Britain* —
several in this instance equals 64 — ... *Celebrated for Their
Writings or Skill in the Learned Languages, Arts, and Sciences*. He
began as far back as Juliana, the 15th century Anchoret of
Norwich, and continued down to his own day. Two years after
Ballard's book another champion stepped forth in verse, John
Duncombe, who issued a poem with a title to invest his theme
with epic dignity: *The Feminiad: or, Female Genius*.

> Shall lordly Man, the Theme of every Lay,
> Usurp the Muses's tributary Bay?

he begins; and his poem names twenty female geniuses, beginning with Catherine Philips, the "Matchless Orinda." But he carefully distinguishes the respectable ladies from the shameful ones, and of these six shameful ones four were professional writers.

For further evidence of women's emergence into the practice and profession of authorship we can look at biographical dictionaries. As early as 1720, Giles Jacob published *An Historical Account of the Lives and Writings of Our most Considerable English Poets, whether Epick, Lyrick, Elegiac, Epigramatists, &c..* This industrious compiler, immortalized by Pope in the *Dunciad*, treats 216 poets altogether, and of these only 7 are women. In 1753 Theophilus Cibber, in his four-volume *Lives of the Poets* (which begins with Chaucer), found 203 poets worthy of inclusion, of whom 15 were women. These compilers seem to be willing to grant women a small corner in the world of literature. In the listing of Horace Walpole's exclusive *Catalogue of Royal and Noble Authors* a few years later (1758) 3 queens and 14 peeresses find places. But privately, Walpole hardly approved of uncrowned or uncorneted women writers, for he remarked — after abusing poor Mrs. Yearsley, the milkwoman of Bristol — "We have hen-novelists and poetesses in every parish."

When we turn to Samuel Johnson's *Lives of the Poets*, published in 1779 and 1781, we find that of the 52 lives in that collection, although they include such obscure writers as Richard Duke and Edmund Smith, not a single one is a woman. This was evidently the decision of the booksellers who commissioned Johnson, yet if he had wished to include a woman poet no doubt he would have been permitted to, since his suggestion for including five men was accepted. He evidently thought that no woman poet was worthy of inclusion in his collection.

Yet Johnson was certainly aware of the fact that woman writers were becoming more numerous and more prolific. He thought it a remarkably striking development. In one of his essays (in 1753) he reflects: "In former times, the pen, like the sword, was considered as consigned by nature to the hands of men . . . a female writer, like a female warrior, was considered as a kind of excentric being, that deviated, however illustriously, from her due sphere of motion, and was, therefore, rather to be gazed at with wonder, than countenanced by imitatio . . . the revolution of years has now produced a generation of Amazons of the pen, who with the spirit of their predecessors have set masculine tyranny at defiance, asserted their claim to the regions of science, and seem resolved to contest the usurpation of virility. . . . To what cause this universal eagerness of writing can be properly ascribed, I have not yet been able to discover. . . . The cause, therefore, of this epidemical conspiracy for the destruction of paper, must remain a secret. . . ." The cause of women's proliferation as writers is not too mysterious a secret. Perhaps it can be revealed by invoking Henry Fielding's jest that "to the composition of novels and romances, *nothing is necessary but paper, pens, and ink, with the manual capacity of using them.*" And what Johnson himself said of Richard Savage can be paraphrased to apply to women: "having no profession, they become by necessity authors." In later years Johnson was still "astonished" at the "amazing progress made . . . in literature by the women," for he well remembered "when a woman who could spell a common letter was regarded as all accomplished."

However astonished he may have been by the progress of women writers Johnson did not suffer the foolish ones gladly. He was once approached by a woman playwright who importuned him to read her new play before it was acted. When pressed, he actually refused, telling her that by carefully looking it over herself she could see, as well as he could, if anything was amiss. "But, sir," said she, "I have not time. I have already so many irons in the fire." "Why then, Madam," he said (quite out of patience,) "the best thing I can advise you to do is to put your tragedy along with your irons."

There is, we must remember, this comic side to the proliferation of women writers. Some of them, swollen with the pride of female accomplishment, exhibited a kind of overstrain. "How the Women do shine of late!" exclaimed the irrepressible Mrs. Thrale, and she then continues: "Miss Williams's Ode on Otaheite, Madame Krumpholtz' Tasteful Performance on the Harp, Madame Gautherot's wonderful Execution on the Fiddle; — but say the

Critics a Violin is not an Instrument for *Ladies* to manage, very likely! I remember when they said the same Thing of a *Pen*." Far from saying that women could not manage a pen, critics might more justly say that they refused to put their pens down.

It has been estimated that the majority of novels published in the 18th century were written by women. From only 1760 to 1800 about 2,000 novels by women appeared. Sometimes the author put her name on the title page, sometimes demurely at the end of the preface, and sometimes she shielded herself with "By a Lady" on the title-page. Was there a pattern? Evidently not. And in the following century Jane Austen put no name on her title pages, the Brontës used a name ambiguous as to sex, and Mary Anne Evans hid her sex behind a man's name.

Yet in the latter half of the 18th century by a curious paradox, novels were sometimes dishonestly attributed to women authors because a book by a woman was regarded as more salable than one by a man. As early as 1759, when Oliver Goldsmith reviewed an epistolary novel "By a Lady," he complained that although the ladies carried off the glory of this sort "it is plain by the stile, and a nameless somewhat in the manner, that pretty fellows, coffee critics, and dirty-shirted dunces, have sometimes a share in the atchievement." He promises in the future to regard every publication "ascribed to a lady, as the work of one of this amphibious fraternity." A writer in the *Monthly Review* (in 1774) — probably John Cleland — went further in reviewing a novel entitled *The School for Husbands. Written by a Lady*: "As ladies are generally acknowledged to be superior to our sex in all works of imagination and fancy, we doubt not this is deemed a sufficient reason for placing their names in the title-page of many a dull, lifeless story which contains not one single female idea, but has been hammered out of the brainless head of a Grubstreet hireling." In this novel, he continues, many of the scenes convince him of "the *femality* of its Author."

This practice of "literary fraud," as the *Gentleman's Magazine* called it (in 1770), remained widespread. It was sometimes used, according to one reviewer (in 1774), "to preclude the severity of criticism"; but, he added, since reviewers are generally such "churls and greybeards" the deception was rarely effective.

One of its effects was to encourage critics to define what they regarded as feminine qualities in literature, to analyze what was distinctive in the mind and art of women writers. In the *Gentleman's Magazine* the reviewer of *Sermons Written by a Lady* believed it to be authentic because it had "a strain of native sense, and elegant simplicity, which a writer of the other sex would have found it very difficult to imitate." The commonplace observation, like that by the youthful editors of an anthology called *Poems by Eminent Ladies* (in 1755), was that poems by "the Fair Sex" prove that compared to men's "their genius often glows with equal warmth, and perhaps with more delicacy." Henry Fielding was more specific in defining the "delicacy" of women writers when, in 1747, he contributed a preface to a book written by his sister. He stresses here the advantage women have in "that great and important Business of their Lives, the Affair of Love." Unlike men, he continues, women's education in this regard is directly opposed to truth and nature; hence sensible women writers can, when dealing with this subject, inject more humor into their characters than men are capable of doing.

In similar fashion, when the argument was continued into the next century William Hazlitt believed that women's social conditioning encourages in them "a quicker perception of any oddity or singularity of character than men," and that the "intuitive perception of their minds is less disturbed by any abstruse reasonings on causes or consequences." Ian Watt implies the same when he invokes Fanny Burney and Jane Austin to suggest "that the feminine sensibility was in some ways better equipped to reveal the intricacies of personal relationships."

The problem of how women's writing differs from men's has erupted in our own day with particular vehemence because of the Women's Liberation Movement. That discussion takes as its starting point the remark of Coleridge: "The truth is, a great mind must be androgynous." Virginia Woolf dealt with this subject in *A Room of One's Own*, where she wrote ". . . in each of us two powers preside, one male one female"; and that in the man's mind the man predominates, and in the woman the woman's. When Virginia Woolf applies the litmus paper of androgyny to ten English writers to test whether they color blue or pink, she names only two 18th-century writers as androgynous — Sterne and Cowper. Yet if we look at the important 18th-century novelists, should we not enroll the creator of Pamela and Clarissa? I hesitate to name John Cleland in the same breath, the creator of a very different kind of heroine, Fanny Hill. And if a woman writer were sought who could march under the banner of androgyny I would nominate Lady Mary Wortley Montagu. For she wrote, in some verse addressed to the homosexual she fell in love with:

> Why was my haughty Soul to Woman joyn'd?
> Why this soft sex impos'd upon my Mind?

Leaving aside as vague and inchoate such matters as womanly literary characteristics and of androgyny I wonder whether another result of women's role is the emergence of women as heroines in realistic fiction. The courtly prose romances of the previous century had depicted heroines, of course; and although these elaborate narratives continued to be read and even, by some, to be imitated they were essentially outmoded. The 18th-century heroines who have remained alive begin with Roxana and Moll Flanders. These picaresque accounts of a prostitute and a thief were probably too coarse for middle-class reading, and it is unlikely that these novels were as widely read by women readers as were Richardson's. In Ian Watt's phrase, Pamela "may be regarded as the culture-heroine of a very powerful sisterhood of literate and leisured writing-maids." And Clarissa's appeal to readers of higher station is strikingly demonstrated by the ordinarily tough-minded Lady Mary, who confessed that she "was such an old Fool as to weep over Clarissa Harlowe like any milk maid of sixteen over the Ballad of the Ladie's Fall." And from Richardson's Pamela and Clarissa through Fielding's Amelia to Fanny Burney and Jane Austin the heroine seems to dominate the novel.

The question of whether the subject matter of fiction was affected by the emergence of women writers is as speculative a venture as the parallel question of whether it was affected by the growth of a feminine reading public. But there is ample certainty in the fact — as stated in the opening of this paper — that in 18th-century England women readers needed to be served by all writers. With the rising rate of literacy, particularly in the lower economic classes — who were educated in charity schools and dissenting academies — more women were able to read. In 1694 one publisher appealed to this new readership with *The Ladies' Dictionary*, which claimed to be the first compendium of its kind attempted in English. The more durable *Ladies' Diary* was the first magazine (it claimed) "designed for the Sole Use of the Female Sex." This annual, begun in 1704, continued to appear until 1840 — a hardy annual, one might say. Magazines for women continued to flourish throughout the century; in the 1770's two very similar ones — *The Lady's Magazine* and *The New Lady's Magazine* — were able to run simultaneously for nine years, so great was their readership.

If we examine the women readers through the distorting lense of satire we see them separated into two divergent groups: on the one hand, women as pretentious pedants, and on the other, women as frivolous novel-readers, who not only wasted their time but corrupted their minds. Pedantry in general was a popular satiric target — one need only recall how important a part it had in Pope's and Swift's writings. The force of this ridicule is more evident in the latter part of the century, with the rise of the blue-stockings, who were analagous to the *précieuses* in the salons of Paris the previous century, when they served as the butt of Molière's satiric comedy.

In England the satire on learned women was gentler, as in Joseph Addison's *Guardian* essay (of 1713) suggesting that women combine intellectual uplift with domestic duties. Lady Lizard and her daughter, we are told, have in one summer completed the needlework coverings of a set of chairs and couches while hearing Tillotson's sermons read over twice; they have preserved fruit while listening to Fontenelle's *Plurality of Worlds*, thus dividing their speculations between jellies and stars, and making a sudden transition from the sun to an apricot, or from the Copernican system to the figure of a cheesecake.

It is doubtful that many women were so high-minded as to combine domesticity with such serious reading. Obviously their inferior educational training put classical and learned literature out of their reach. We can see evidence of this (as well as of their increasing importance as readers) in this episode. When (in 1743) Conyers Middleton was about to publish a learned work on monument inscriptions Horace Walpole offered him the same advice. "If you design your work in Latin," Walpole cautioned him, "I am entirely against its being published by subscription, as the language excluding the women, would reduce the number too much to make it worth your while." Two years earlier Middleton had made a tremendous profit by issuing his subscription edition of the *Life of Cicero* in English; he now took Walpole's advice, and his *Monumenta* was published in 1745 in Latin, without the patronage of subscribers, many of whom should have been women.

These subscription lists not only tell us something of how authors could gain support but also — and this is unexpected — of the relatively large number of women who subscribed to publications by men as well as by women. This can be said only tentatively now; when more research has been done on subscription publication we may discover that women played a more influential role than has hitherto been recognized in supporting and reading these books.

Women's taste for more frivolous reading is easier to document. From Biddy Tipkin in Richard Steele's *Tender Husband* to Catherine Morland in Jane Austen's *Northanger Abbey* they are frequently depicted as readers of silly fiction. Biddy Tipkin, who has spent all her solitary time reading romances about shepherds, knights, flowery meads, groves, and streams, has traveled widely in the fairyland of the French romances. In describing the reading of upper-class girls Steele was literally accurate, for the reading list of Lady Mary Pierrepont (later Wortly Montagu) is almost precisely the same as Biddy Tipkin's. And after *Pamela* set the vogue for realistic and sentimental fiction, the French romances were displaced as reading for the fashionable young woman. It is curious though, that by a kind of cultural lag, the heroine of Charlotte Lennox's *Female Quixote* in 1752 is addicted to reading and believing the old romances.

George Colman (in 1760) is more up to date. In the prologue to *Polly Honeycombe* — which is tellingly subtitled "A Dramatick Novel of One Act" — he explains:

'Tis not alone the Small-Talk and the Smart,
'Tis NOVEL mostly beguiles the Female Heart.
Miss reads — she melts — she sighs — Love steals upon her —
And then — Alas, poor Girl! — good night, poor Honour!

Novel-reading by women was regarded not merely a waste of time but a positive threat to morality. While Polly Honeycombe believes that novel-reading is the "only thing to teach a girl life," her father is convinced that "a man might as well turn his Daughter loose in Covent-garden [haunt of the prostitutes], as trust the cultivation of her mind to" — and here he mentioned with upper-case emphasis the source of her nefarious reading — "A CIRCULATING LIBRARY."

The circulating library, which has its origin in the 18th century, enabled women, particularly the omniverous consumers of fiction, to read the many books that they could not afford to buy, or would have considered an extravagance. The close connection between circulating libraries and women's leisure-reading is evident when we note that the earliest known library was opened in Bath in 1725, and flourished in that fashionable resort for thirty years. Edinburgh and Bristol (at that time a popular spa) were the next cities where circulating libraries were set up. In Samuel Foote's *The Author*, Mr. Vamp the bookseller orders his hackwriter to produce some novels, which are "pretty light Summer reading, and do very well at *Tumbridge, Bristol*, and the other watering Places." Not until about 1740 was a lending library established in London, and between 1725 and 1760 no fewer than fifteen were set up in England and Scotland. Although some were of short duration, one of them — in Birmingham — flourished from 1750 to 1815.

You will remember Lydia Languish in Sheridan's *Rivals*, the young lady whose imagination is so distorted by her reading of romantic fiction. Her maid has been to every circulating library in Bath to satisfy Lydia's insatiable appetite for novels. In the earth-bound opinion of Sir Anthony Absolute the effect of novel-reading is summed up in his remark to Mrs. Malaprop: "Madame, a circulating library in a town is as an evergreen tree of diabolical knowledge! It blossoms through the year! And depend on it, Mrs. Malaprop, that they who are so fond of handling the leaves, will long for the fruit at last." The moral objection to fiction, which has existed as long as fiction has, was easily transferred to the lending libraries that disseminated it.

Even in the rural areas, where ladies imitated the sophisticated pastimes of the city, they could borrow novels from country circulating libraries, which — according to one estimate in 1760 — consisted of about 100 volumes. I doubt that many of these were books of religious devotion or domestic economy. Perhaps women's avidity for fiction has been exaggerated, Ian Watt cautions as he suggests that religious literature appealed to them. We do have some idea of the sort of books that were stocked by circulating libraries. One pamphlet on how to set up such libraries suggested that 80 per cent of their stock be fiction; and while this may have been true of the smaller ones, large libraries contained more serious non-fiction, and catered to men as well as to women readers. And the increasing number of such libraries that were opened during the century indicates their increasing popularity.

In treating the connection between women and literature in 18th-century England I have not yet exhausted the catalogue of their activities. For in one branch of literary production which one would think is intrinsically men's province women played a small but visible role. I speak of their activity in the book trade. Here, in the tough world of business — a sector of society which even today they have hardly penetrated — they vigorously pursued careers as printers who issued books, pamphlets, and newspapers, and as booksellers who published and sold what came off the press. In London, in the latter part of the century, there were numerous pamphlet shops that sold newspapers and journals, almanacks, parliamentary speeches, plays, and pamphlets of all sorts; and these shops were almost invariably kept by women. A Mrs. Green, who kept a stationer's shop in Fleet Street until her death in 1783, had also enjoyed the appointment of "pencutter to His Majesty."

To what extent women played a part as printers and booksellers can be more exhaustively calculated in H. R. Plomer's dictionary of printers and booksellers — the volume covering the years from 1726 to 1775. During this fifty-year period no fewer than eighty-seven women were active in the book trade. The total number is probably greater since a good many names show only a first initial. Some of the women in the book trade worked with their husbands, and then when left widows continued to carry on the businesses they inherited. One valiant woman printer named Elizabeth Blackwell, after seeing her husband sent to prison for debt, published by subscription a two-volume work in folio, thereby raising enough money to have him released. The printer who issued the first edition of Locke's *Essay on Human Understanding* (1690), that seminal 18th-century work, was a widow. Not all women entered the trade on their husband's coattails. In the large provincial town of Ipswich a spinster bookseller printed and sold books from 1728 to 1776, a span of almost fifty years.

When we compare the activity of 18th-century women in publishing, printing, and selling books with their activity today we are struck by the regression. In this aspect of their connection with literature 18th-century women are easily ahead of our contemporaries.

But this is relatively unimportant compared to the other advances 18th-century women made that affected the literature of their time. They emerged into the profession of authorship, sustained (as men were) by patrons, subscription, and the reading public; their activity as writers and readers stimulated a mode of criticism that tried to identify the womanly element in literature; and they grew to be a significant part of the reading public, perhaps the dominant group of readers, as they were the writers, of fiction.

Robert Halsband

The 18th-Century Englishwoman: According to the Gentleman's Magazine

The eighteenth-century Englishwoman has largely been ignored by scholars working in the newly popular field of women's history. While a great deal of work has been done answering questions about the Victorian woman, no one has as yet even asked most of the questions about her predecessors in the previous century. There are a few scattered chapters here and there, and a few old specialized monographs,[1] but little historical research is currently in progress which deals with eighteenth-century women. And yet, this was the century which began with Mary Astell and ended with Mary Woolstonecraft, the century which saw momentous if subtle changes in the political, social, and economic life of Great Britain, which must have had a considerable impact on women. And noting the tremendous changes that occurred in the status of women in the nineteenth century, surely some of the groundwork must have been laid during the eighteenth.

1. Among the books which have chapters on 18th century Englishwomen, the following are particularly useful: Mary Beard, *Woman as Force in History*, New York, 1946; Walter Lyon Blease, *The Emancipation of English Woman*, London, 1913; George Edwin Fussell, *The English Country Woman*, London, 1953; Ida B. O'Malley, *Women in Subjection*, London, 1933; Katherine Rogers, *The Troublesome Helpmate*, Seattle, 1969; Doris Mary Stenton, *The English Woman in History*, London, 1957; Frederick William Tuckner, *Women in English Economic History*, New York, 1923. Books which deal in some detail with 18th century English women are: Jean Gagen, *The New Woman: Her Emergence in English Drama, 1600-1730*, New York, 1954; E. and J. de Goncourt, *The Woman of the Eighteenth Century*, New York, 1927; Florence Hoagland, *The Woman of Steele and Addison*, Ithaca, 1933; Margaret Phillips, *English Women in Life and Letters*, London, 1926; Myra Reynolds, *The Learned Lady in England, 1650-1750*, New York, 1920; Robert P. Utter, *Pamela's Daughters*, New York, 1936; UCLA-William Andrews Clark Library, *The Lady of Letters in the Eighteenth Century*, Los Angeles, 1969; Ada Wallas, *Before the Bluestockings*, London, 1929; Ethel Rolt Wheeler, *Famous Blue Stockings*, New York, 1910.

One reason for this neglect of the eighteenth century by historians of women is the attraction that many of them feel to the nineteenth century, when the women's rights movement really got under way, and when the social forces and mores which still retain such force today had their origin. In addition, there is not the same kind of data readily available and easily accessible for the student of eighteenth-century women. There are no census reports, no social surveys to give clues as to how the majority of women lived. Moreover, periodicals were in their infancy, and were both fewer in number and harder to use, as they did not necessarily reflect anything except the prejudices of their editors.[2] The pamphlet literature on women — although extensive — is scattered. Nor is it easy to discern any obvious trends in reading such material.[3] All in all, the eighteenth-century woman is more remote, less accessible, more difficult to study.

And yet studied she must be if we are to gain a coherent picture of the origins of the modern woman, for clearly during the eighteenth century several important changes occurred in the status of women. First of all, there was a tremendous increase in female literacy, first apparent around the turn of the century. A debate followed over exactly how much education a woman needed. Such debates were new; in the past anything but the most basic knowledge of reading and writing was simply unavailable to the vast majority of women. Learning in a woman, while not unknown before about 1660, had been limited to the higher ranks of society. That a controversy was raging during the eighteenth

2. Among the magazines for women, I have looked at the following: *The Female Spectator, The Ladies' Magazine, The Lady's Magazine, The Lady's Museum, The Old Maid, The Royal Female Museum.*

3. Of the books and pamphlets published after 1660, the following are basically pro-woman: Mary Astell, *A Serious proposal to the Ladies for the Advancement of their Sex*, London, 1697; Mary Astell, *Some Reflections upon Marriage*, 2nd edition, London, 1704; Judith Drake, *An essay in Defense of the Female Sex*, London, 1697; George Ballard, *Memoirs of several Ladies of Great Britain*, Oxford, 1752; Laetitia Matilda Hawkins, *Letters on the Female Mind*, London, 1793; "Sophia," *Woman Not Inferior to Man*, London, 1740; Antoine Thomas, *Essay on the Character, Manners and Genius of Women*, Philadelphia, 1774.

Some more traditional views are: M. Alexander, *History of Woman*, London, 1769; J. Bennet, *Strictures on Female Education*, London, 1788; Thoman Gisborne, *An enquiry into the Duties of the Female Sex*, London, 1799; Dr. Gregory, *Legacy to his Daughters*, London, 1784; William Kenrick, *The Whole Duty of Women*, London, 1753; Timothy Rogers, *The Character of a Good Woman*, London, 1697.

century over what kind of education a woman should receive, indicates that it had become an issue that mattered to a large number of people, which in turn indicates that more women were receiving some kind of education.[4]

Another sign of increased literacy among women was the growing number of journals directed to a female audience. The first such periodical appeared during the 1690s, and for the first seven decades of the century, there were frequent if short-lived attempts to create a woman's magazine. All these early "Good Housekeepings" and "Cosmopolitans" were designed to "instruct and amuse" their readers; all bore the imprint of their very idiosyncratic editors, and all had short but exciting careers. In 1770, with the appearance of the *Lady's Magazine*, publishing for women came of age. This periodical survived for seventy years, bringing a varied diet of instruction, amusement, and household hints to the women of the upper and middle classes.[5]

The eighteenth century saw another important change in the status of women: the appearance of the professional woman writer. Aphra Behn during the Restoration, had been the first Englishwoman to earn her living with her pen. She was less than respectable. But by the middle of the century, it had become respectable for women to publish books, and publish they did in increasing numbers.[6]

Still, only a small minority of women ever thought of publishing a book, so this change had little impact on their lives. Of much more importance to many women were new attitudes towards marriage which became current in eighteenth-century England. In the past marriage had been a family affair, and a young woman accepted her parents' choice without demur. But now, the opinion grew more and more prevalent that love should accompany marriage, that a young lady should have a say in whom

---

4. Reynolds, *The Learned Lady*, pp. 258-315 has a rambling but complete discussion both of the kind of education available and of the debate on the kind of education that should be available.

5. Two recent books have studied the first women's magazines: Cynthia L. White, *Women's Magazines, 1693-1968*, London, 1970; and Alison Adburgham, *Women in Print*, London, 1972.

6. Ada Wallas, *Before the Bluestockings* describes the growing respectability of literary efforts on the part of women.

she married, and that parents should not force their daughters to marry men they could not esteem. Of course, men and women still married for financial advantage, but such marriages met with increasing attack in novels, plays, and journals. Eighteenth-century marriage, even with love, could and did pose serious problems for women. But, the new insistence on marital love and freedom of choice was a step forward for women, since marriage remained the only career open to most of them.[7]

This brief summary indicates that the eighteenth century was an era of considerable change in the status of women. But what kind of change? Some students of the period have concluded that much of the change that was occurring was detrimental to women. They have posited that the so-called "trivialization of women" became increasingly apparent after about 1660, reaching its height in the Victorian era. The argument goes something like this — in the seventeenth century, women remained real economic assets to their husbands. Upper class women managed large households and often ran the family estate. Middle class women were their husbands' business partners and played an important role in shop or workshop as well as in the home. But, late in the seventeenth century, the growth of capitalistic organization, both in business and in agriculture, divorced the woman from any share in the husband's productive life, while the growth of "luxury" and the servant class limited her contribution to the family's economy. Shunted aside, she became merely an object, a toy, an attractive plaything. As a result, men's opinions of the capacities and capabilities of the female sex diminished. Women became the "fair sex," the "gentle sex," the "soft sex," the "weaker sex," incapable of any labor and existing only to be pampered and protected by men. This view of the incapable, helpless female became standard in the eighteenth century. Women sought to fit themselves into this mould, and men looked

---

7. For earlier views on marriage, see Louis B. Wright, *Middle Class Culture in Elizabeth England*, Chapel Hill, 1935, pp. 208-11. Chilton Powell, *English Domestic Relations*, New York, 1917, discusses the genesis of change. Gagan, *New Woman*, pp. 119-28, discusses the changing attitudes as reflected in drama. Samuel Richardson, *Clarissa Harlowe*, is of course, the most famous literary work opposing property marriages. For the forces influencing marriage for property, see H. J. Habakkuk, "Marriage Settlements in the 18th century," *Trans, R.H.S.*, 1950, pp. 15-27.

with horror on any woman who demonstrated any self-awareness or self-confidence. Women existed only for man, to serve his needs and care for his children.[8]

There are numerous indications in books and pamphlets that this poor creature was indeed the ideal woman of the eighteenth century. But there are also numerous indications in books and pamphlets that many women and men found this ideal totally unrealistic and unacceptable. One valuable source of information about popular attitudes about women is the *Gentleman's Magazine*, the age's most successful periodical. What was the "Lady according to the Gentleman"? What did the *Gentleman's Magazine* have to say about eighteenth-century Englishwomen? How prevalent was this ideal of the helpless, useless female in this journal's pages? How much opposition was there to such a conception of womanhood?

Among the articles in the *Gentleman's Magazine* which deal with women, their status, their education, their good points and their bad, there is a rather startling division. Only one-quarter seem to support the supposedly traditional ideas. For the most part, these were excerpts of essays first published elsewhere and condensed for the readers of the *Gentleman's Magazine*. For example, the journal *Common Sense* not infrequently includes in its pages diatribes against women. *Common Sense* was a journal that thrived on controversy, and when parliament was recessed and there were no politicains to attack, the author turned to other targets, just to keep interest alive. The female sex was his frequent victim. In 1737 the *Gentleman's Magazine* re-published one such attack, "On affectation, In Women." The author considered the "Weaknesses and Vanities" of the female sex, particularly objecting to women who tried to assume those prerogatives which belonged to men. This was unnatural. "Women are not form'd for great cares themselves, but to sooth and soften ours. They are confined within the narrow Limits of Domestick Offices, and when they stray beyond them, they move eccentrically, and

---

8. Perhaps the most influential and complete statement of this theory is to be found in Alice Clark, *Working Life of Women in the Seventeenth Century,* London, 1919, but authors like Blease, *Emancipation,* de Goncourt, *Woman in 18th Century,* J. M. S. Thomdkins, *The Polite Marriage,* Cambridge, 1938, and Morton Hunt, *The Natural History of Love,* New York, 1959 all suggests the trivialization of women.

consequently without Grace." The chief object of this attack was the learned woman or the woman who affected learning. Such a woman should forget her pretensions, and

> confine herself to her natural Talents, play at Cards, make Tea and Visits, talk to her Dog often and to her Company, sometimes.

These women should not seek to understand metaphysics or politics, male concerns at which no woman could excell. The author was forced to admit that Queen Elizabeth for one, excelled at politics, but he avoided the problem that she posed by simply denying that Elizabeth was a woman at all. Should some "Lady of Spirit" object to these restrictions and ask,

> What province I leave to their Sex? I answer, that I leave 'em whatever has not been peculiarly assign'd by Nature to ours. I leave 'em a mighty empire of Love. There they reign absolute, and by unquestioned right, while Beauty supports their throne.

The perfect woman kept strictly within her character, and, without affectation, had "a natural Cheerfulness of Mind, Tenderness and Benignity of Heart, which justly endears them to us, either to animate our Joys or sooth our Sorrows."

By insisting that women must not appear learned, i.e. affect wisdom, the author of *Common Sense* did not however imply that women were the intellectual inferiors of men. He admitted freely that women could be as wise or wiser than men. But the truly wise woman did not parade her knowledge:

> She conceals the Superiority she has with as much care as others take to display the Superiority they have not: She conforms herself to the company she is in, but in a way of rather avoiding to be silenced, than desiring to take the Lead: are they merry; she is chearful; are they grave; she is serious; are they absurd; she is silent: Tho' she thinks and speaks as a Man would do, still it is as a woman ought to do; she effeminates . . . whatever she says, and gives all the Graces of her own Sex to the Strength of ours.

Women then, were not inferior or unlearned, nor necessarily should they be. But they were to hide their superiority and learning by always behaving in a manner acceptable to society. The need for women to hide whatever knowledge they possessed was a commonplace in the eighteenth century.[9]

Other essays in the *Gentleman's Magazine* also complained of women who did not know their place. In July, 1732, the Universal Spectator wrote of "Female Extravagancies," complaining that women were seeking to supplant men in some of their prerogatives. They were wearing breeches, riding astride, shaking hands, ordering men to get the coffee rather than serving them as they should, carrying pistols, and even taking the initiative in love affairs. All these accusations were patently nonsensical. Women were doing no such things. This article was the work of a typical social conservative who was using the technique of exaggeration to satirize what he felt to be unwholesome changes in society. His peroration indicated that his basic concern was what he held to be an increasing neglect on the part of women of their domestic responsibilities:

> But is it not a melancholy reflection that our Females are Women at 12 or 13, Men at 18, and very Girls at 50 or 60? That Virtue, Religion, and Economy are now turn'd to Ridicule! and this not only in the Town but amongst our Country Ladies! Where the double entendre, a thorough Disregard for their Husbands and Children is so much the Mode, that I fear if it gets among the lower Class of Females, the Farmers will have Care of the Dairy as well as Husbandry thrown on their Hands.

Of course, opponents of female education and equality had always warned that they would lead women to neglect their family responsibilities. Defenders of women had to continually re-assure the public that, indeed, a woman who possessed knowledge would

9. The *Gentleman's Magazine*, vii, pp. 553-55. One of the most famous quotations reflecting this view was that of Lady Mary Wortley Montagu, who, after advising that her granddaughter be well educated, warned, "The second caution to be given her and which is absolutely necessary is to conceal whatever learning she attains with as much solicitude as she would hide crookedness or lameness; the parade of it can only serve to draw on her the envy and consequently the most inveterate hatred of all he-and she-fools, which will certainly be at least three parts in four of all her acquaintance."

be a better wife and mother.[10]

Other articles did not attack women, as such, but merely tried to explain and enlarge on their subordinate place in society. An essay on physiology explained that women are what they are because of a deficiency in body heat. But the author held that this defect had positive advantages for women. It gave them whiter and softer skin, as well as gentler manners. It also exempted them from labor. Woman's temperament was not inferior to man's, but merely finer and gentler, and thus women were freed from many of the cares and vexations of men. Men, in turn, were forced to serve and please and love the fair sex, and all because of a deficiency in body heat. This early attempt to prove a biological cause for the differences between men and women was even less successful than its successors. Still, the image offered of women — gentler, softer, whiter, finer — was highly traditional.[11]

At times the *Gentleman's Magazine* excerpted books and pamphlets which discussed the nature and duties of women. In 1752, in "Extracts from a Pamphlet entitled 'The Whole Duty of Women'" supposedly written by a lady of quality, but actually the work of a male hack journalist, a highly traditional view of women was put forth. This book, in a nauseating parody of biblical style, offered such pearls of wisdom as:

> Discover not the knowledge of things it is not expected thou shouldst understand; for as the experience of a matron ill becometh the lips of a virgin, a pretended ignorance is often better than a shew of real knowledge. (Or) Art thou letter'd, let not the difficulty of thy speech puzzle the ignorant; lest, instead of admiring thy knowledge, they condemn thee for pride and affectation. (Or) Perspicuity will never force thee to be indelicate or to forget thou shouldst support the elegance of a woman.[12]

But the pages of the *Gentleman's Magazine* were remarkably free from such effusions and, indeed, from such conventional views of womanhood. Most articles that dealt with the female sex were

10. *Gent. Mag.* ii, pp. 850-51.
11. *Gent. Mag.* xvii, pp. 230-31.
12. *Gent. Mag.* xxiii, pp. 133-34.

sympathetic to the problems women faced in the society of eighteenth-century England.

Articles on the woman-problem approached the question in four ways. They discussed (1) lack of educational opportunities; (2) lack of career opportunities outside of marriage; (3) the inequities of the married state; and (4) the equality of the sexes. Clearly, these four were closely related to each other, and together, formed the basic substance of most of the essays concerning women in the *Gentleman's Magazine*, as well as that of other such literature published in eighteenth-century England. Lack of educational opportunities headed the list of the grievances of the female sex in almost every case. Since the days of Bathsua Makin and Mary Astell in the seventeenth century, all perceptive women reformers believed that better education for women was the key to improving their position in society. They recognized that women were caught in a double bind. As long as they were poorly educated, women would appear unfit for responsible positions, and indeed, unworthy of men's esteem and respect. As long as men did not respect women, they would not make education available to them. Women, thus, could not demonstrate their capabilities, and could not earn men's respect. Every author who sympathized with women complained that the education given to women was unsatisfactory and was, more than any other factor, the cause of their unhappy lot and subordinate position in society. Moreover, it was noted that the typical education received by most women, consisting as it did mostly of useless accomplishments, did not even prepare her to be the wife of a man of sense.[13] A most interesting exposition of this idea was a supposed letter to the editor which was given two titles, "Delicate Education of a Young Lady," and "Triumph of Beauty Short and Fading." This letter told the story of a lovely young lady, Victoria, whose mother raised her only to be beautiful. She was never allowed any activity that might impair her looks; she was instructed in every

---

13. This was the complaint of both social reformers like Bathsua Makin (*An Essay to Revive the Ancient Education of Gentlewomen*, London, 1673) and social conservatives like Hannah More (*Stricture on Female Education*, London, 1789). Almost everyone agreed that women should be able to converse with their husbands, and most agreed that their present education did not prepare them adequately for this task.

fashionable accomplishment; but she was allowed no real education for her mother believed, "that nothing so much hindered the advancement of a woman as literature and wit, which generally frightened away those that could make the best settlements . . ." Victoria was a success when introduced into society, but though she had many admirers, no one sought to marry her. She soon discovered why:

> I felt in myself the want of some power to diversity, amusement, and enliven conversation, and could not but suspect that my mind failed in performing the promises of my face. This opinion was soon confirmed by one of my lovers, who married Lavinia, with less beauty and fortune than mine, because he thought a wife ought to have qualities which might make her amiable when her bloom was past.

Victoria's mother refused to worry, merely counseled patience, and advised her daughter "to improve my minuet step with a new French dancing master." Then, tragedy intervened. Victoria caught small pox and lost her beauty. Her mother, rather than offering comfort, "grieved that I had not lost my life together with my beauty." She lost all interest in her child. But Victoria was made of sterner stuff. Left alone, she improved her mind, and by her wisdom, attracted a most eligible suitor — and of course, they lived happily ever after.[14] This cautionary tale was clearly designed as a warning that learning and wisdom without beauty could succeed where beauty alone had failed in the all important task of catching a husband. Stories like this were designed to promote better education for girls.

Similarly, another letter the following year, "Modish Accomplishments and Employments of a Young Lady," also sought to warn women of the dangers of depending on beauty alone. This heroine, Bellaria, had been well taught, and had been instructed in the value of learning. But her head turned by flattery, she chose to ignore the advice of her mother, and was clearly heading for trouble.[15]

14. *Gent. Mag.* xxi, pp. 225-27.
15. *Gent. Mag.* xxii, pp. 20-22.

Many reasons were given why girls should receive a better education. As Victoria's tale implied, women should be educated to be better companions to their husbands. They should be trained to handle money so that they would be better household managers while their husbands lived, and less likely to fall prey to swindlers and fortune hunters if they should become widows. Women should be educated because nature and society had given them control over morals and manners, and they must be prepared to exercise this important function. And they should be so educated as to be able to support themselves if that dread need arose.[16]

Observers recognized the unhappy plight of gentlewomen who never married and who were left destitute or with miniscule fixed incomes. Once it was suggested that a home for such women be established where, in return for modest food and lodging, the women would undertake such tasks as lace-making, spinning, knitting, and embroidering. The gentlewomen would have been expected to produce one-half as much as an ordinary working woman.[17] But such a solution was clearly impractical; nor would it have offered the poor gentlewoman a very genteel life. In 1739, an essay dealt with this problem, what to do about spinster gentlewomen without fortunes. This author went right to the heart of the matter. She blamed their plight on their parents, who, while knowing that they could only leave their daughters small fortunes, still persisted in giving them useless educations:

> Miss is taught to work a Cushion, or a Picture in seven years, a little Dancing and French with English and Writing which she is never made perfect in. In short, her time is for the most part employ'd in Trifles, whilst the useful and becoming Part of her Education is wholly neglected.

Moreover, she was trained only to catch a husband, not to be a wife, for she was never trained in household management. The author had another program which she thought would serve women's needs better. Parents should see that their daughters were taught "the most useful Part of Needlework, all the Arts of

16. *Gent. Mag.* lviii, pp. 864, 961.
17. *Gent. Mag.* viii, p. 85.

Economy, Writing, and Bookkeeping, with enough Dancing and French to give them a graceful and easy Freedom both of Discourse and Behavior." Then, at the age of 15 or 16, parents should apprentice them to "genteel and easy trades, such as Linnen or Woollen Drapers, Haberdashers, Mercers, Glovers, Perfumers, Grocers, Confectioners, Retailers of Gold and Silver Lace, Buttons, etc."

These trades were as suitable for women as for men, and a woman with a trade would be economically independent; she would not be forced to marry or left to starve. Moreover, experience in trade would make her a better and more attractive wife, since her insight into business would make her economical and more useful. To those who doubted the competency of women to engage in business, the author insisted that women were in no way inferior to men and with the proper training, would equal or excell their male competitors.[18]

One motive for proposing such a scheme was to save unfortunate women from being "deluded into a Marriage, which lays the Foundation for irremediable Misery and Distress." Many observers recognized that, for a women, eighteenth-century marriage could be a very unhappy state. In 1738, Arabella answered the attacks on her sex in *Common Sense* with an article entitled "The Disadvantages of the Female Sex in a Marry'd State." She lamented the delusions of young girls about marriage. During her courtship, a girl was the center of attention and received promises of eternal love and felicity. But how quickly she was disabused of her illusions, once the marriage vows were taken!

> ... the same Woman, that just now personated a Lady is anon to be a Waiting Woman, a Cook, and a Nurse: And well it is, if, after all, she can gain the applause and approbation of her Proprietor.

If only the bridegroom had been honest with his bride, how different the outcome would have been.

> If a Man would in so many plain Words tell a Woman, that, when she has entirely given up her Fortune, her Liberty and

18. *Gent. Mag.* ix, pp. 525-26.

her person into his Keeping, she is immediately to become Slave to his Humor, his Convenience, or even his Pleasure, and that she is to expect no more Favour from him, than he in great Condescension thinks fit to grant: I believe there would be few Women, in this case, however young or weak that would accept the offer.

Arabella complained that the wife lost her liberty, while her husband retained the right to do as he pleased. He excluded his wife from his life, spending as little time at home as possible. The husband cared nothing about his wife's happiness, but "viewed all her Actions with so cold an Indifference as neither to be pleased when she is cheerful nor concerned when she is sinking under Pain and Sorrow."[19] Such was marriage *à la mode.*

Another correspondent offered the following lines to sum up women's unhappy lot:

> How hard is the Condition of our Sex
> Thro' every state of Life a Slave to Men,
> In all the dear, delightful Days of Youth,
> A rigid Father dictates to our Will,
> And deals out Pleasure with a scanty Hand;
> To his the tyrant Husband next succeeds,
> Proud with Opinion of superior Reason,
> He holds domestick Business and Devotion,
> All we are capable to know, and shuts us
> Like cloistered Ideots, from the World's Acquaintance,
> And the Joys of Freedom. Wherefore are we
> Born with high Souls, but to assert ourselves?
> Shake off this vile Obedience they exact
> And claim an equal Empire o'er the World.[20]

To "claim an equal Empire o'er the World." This, of course, was the crux of the matter. Were men and women equal? The *Gentleman's Magazine* almost always answered this question in the affirmative. In an article entitled "Female Virtue," the author insisted that neither the soul nor the intellect knew any difference because of sex. This, however, did not imply that women should

19. *Gent. Mag.* viii, pp. 85-87.
20. *Gent. Mag.* vi, p. 75.

seek to be men's social and political equals, for even if the existing system of subordination was not the result of any defect in the female nature, it was woman's punishment for her role in the fall and not to be tampered with.[21]

Other writers had no hesitation in claiming for women real equality, without any reservations. In an essay entitled "The Female Sex not the Weakest," Climene defended her sex against the attack of the fop, Cento. She hinted not merely at equality, but at superiority. She insisted that women were inferior to men in nothing but brute strength, and excelled the male sex in such attributes as beauty, constancy, friendship, and love. She concluded her argument by declaiming:

> I know not by what barbarous Policy we were first debarred the Improvements of our Mind by study, and our time employ'd about Trifles, while your Sex has all the Advantages of this Kind; but I can impute it to your jealousy only: It is to this Injustice of your Sex that you ought to attribute the greater part of us being pleased with Follies and accustomed to utter them ... Had we the same Pains and Cares taken of us, we should find, I fancy, more excellent Philosophers among the Women than among the Men.

Climene clearly won her battle with Cento, for he left the room in a huff, to the laughter of the assembled company.[22]

Calidore, writing in 1788, carried the demand for "equal Empire" to its logical conclusion. She argued that women should be admitted into parliament itself. The introductory reasons offered made the essay appear satiric. Women, Calidore stated, would improve the quality of the debates in parliament with the "musical modulations and natural melody of feminine eloquence." But then the author became deadly serious. She argued that women had a natural right to representation, a potent argument in the eighteenth century. Men could claim only superior strength; by nature, both sexes were equal, and each had a similar right to a share in the government. Calidore also pointed to the mess which men had made of political affairs when "uncontrolled by the

21. *Gent. Mag.* vi, p. 75.
22. *Gent. Mag.* v, pp. 588-89.

superior discernment of the female mind." When women have ruled, they have excelled, and the author asked, why deny England the benefit of female wisdom?[23]

What conclusions can be drawn from this excursion into the pages of the *Gentleman's Magazine*? What new insights can this study offer about the status of the eighteenth-century Englishwoman? This particular magazine is a fertile source for popular ideas about women for two important reasons. This was not a woman's magazine. Although clearly read by women and although using contributions by women, it was directed to the general, literate public. It sought a wide audience, and thus included articles of general interest. It was therefore more likely to reflect the ideas of both sexes. Secondly, the *Gentleman's Magazine* was the most popular, most widely read, and most successful eighteenth-century journal. From its inception in 1731, and throughout the century, it succeeded in catching and keeping an ever increasing audience. Eclectic, all inclusive, often mundane, sometimes fascinating, it mirrored as closely as any single source the ideas, ideals and way of life of the English upper and middle classes. Therefore, what it had to say about women was particularly instructive.

And what does it say? The *Gentleman's Magazine* seems to be saying that there was a considerable awareness of the women-problem in the eighteenth century. It says that the problem was perceived in a fourfold manner: lack of educational opportunities, lack of career opportunities for unmarried gentlewomen, the inequities of marriage, and finally, the whole question of sexual equality. None of this is all that surprising. What is surprising is that the articles in the *Gentleman's Magazine* seem to indicate that there was a great deal of sympathy with non-traditional, non-ideal views of womanhood. If three out of every four writers who touched on the woman question bemoaned the plight of women, and suggested concrete reform measures, perhaps the traditional, conservative ideal of woman had less widespread support and more opposition in the eighteenth century than has been thought.

What can be concluded from this study of the eighteenth-

23. *Gent. Mag.* lviii, pp. 222-24.

century Englishwoman as portrayed in the pages of the *Gentleman's Magazine*? Is seems very possible that the eighteenth century has had a bad press from the writers of women's history. They have too often seen it as a time of decline in the status and stature of women, particularly in the upper and middle classes, as women lost their economic value and role. They have posited that the trivialization of women, all too evident in the Victorian age, had its roots in the eighteenth century. They have thus concluded that this century was a bad time to be an Englishwoman. The evidence for such ideas seemed very persuasive at first. But this excursion into the pages of the *Gentleman's Magazine* raises serious doubts about the validity of this thesis. The pages of the age's most popular journal demonstrate that the problems women faced were recognized and sympathetically explored, and that practical solutions were offered to the age old "woman question." This recognition was a necessary pre-condition for any kind of social reform. Perhaps in eighteenth-century England, women were painfully and slowly taking the first steps that would lead to personal autonomy and individual self-respect. Perhaps conservative books like Dr. Gregory's *Letter to his Daughters* were weapons in defense of an embattled status quo. Perhaps Mary Wollstonecraft's work was not a *cri de coeur* in the face of a deteriorating situation, but rather a call to revolution, a revolution only possible if conditions were improving. The *Gentleman's Magazine* offers convincing evidence that such improvement was under way.

If the eighteenth century was an era of continuing if gradual improvement in the status and position of women, why was such a promising beginning so long in coming to fruition? What forces postponed the revolution Mary Wollstonecraft dreamed of for more than a century? These are questions that must be answered. But they can only be answered in a meaningful way after we gain a working knowledge of what it was like to be a woman in the eighteenth century, a task which has scarcely begun.

Jean E. Hunter

"Treated Like Imbecile Children" (Diderot): The Enlightenment and the Status of Women

One of the most characteristic and most popular of the books published during the Enlightenment was Montesquieu's *Lettres persanes*. It appeared early, only six years after the death of Louis XIV. In form it was delightfully exotic, purporting to be the letters exchanged ten years earlier between two Persian noblemen traveling in France and their friends, eunuchs, and some of their wives back home. Monogamous societies always seem to find reading about polygamous ones, with their multiple wives, eunuchs, and all the other apparatus of the seraglio, absolutely irresistible. Moreover, Montesquieu's device of the exchange of letters between foreigners, made more credible by his having mastered the Mohammedan calendar, so that he appended to each letter a most impressive date line, allowed its French author to shelter himself behind a Persian mask Thus he was able to comment with great frankness upon almost all aspects of French life.

The *Lettres persanes* was characteristic of the Enlightenment in numerous ways. For one thing, the book tried to broaden man's intellectual outlook, free it from being parochial, and allow it to become more cosmopolitan. In the course of the Enlightenment, the previous century's interest in travels, in the customs of savage tribes and of other civilized nations, easily led to a familiarity with the comparative method, as Montesquieu himself later demonstrated in his *Esprit des lois*. This study of other cultures rather quickly resulted in subjecting one's own society to a critique, which the writers of the Enlightenment learned to do with great effect. Attempts to control them by means of censorship or intimidation taught these critics how to make their points in roundabout and indirect ways, and the *Letters persanes* was again characteristic of the Enlightenment in its employment of pretense and of ruse. The *Encyclopédie* utilized these devious methods very successfully. But such daring had its risks. It should be remembered that Voltaire once spent time in prison as an unwilling guest of the King of France; Diderot was a hundred days in Vincennes in 1749, and was not incarcerated in the Bastille at that time only because it was already full up. Rousseau fled from Montmorency to Switzerland in 1762 because he had been too plainspoken. A highly placed judge was alleged to have said *en plein Parlement* in 1766 that no progress could be made in preventing the expression of free thought so long as the public executioner burned only books.[1] A Persian mask for the writer of the *Lettres persanes* was therefore very practical.

The most poignant and indeed tragic character in the *Lettres persanes* is Usbek's favorite wife, Roxane. Roxane, whom Usbek regarded as the soul of virtue, hated her condition and in reality hated her husband. She managed to be unfaithful to him and, when discovered, committed suicide. "How could you imagine," she wrote in her letter of farewell, "that I was credulous enough to suppose that the reason I was put here on earth was simply to dote upon your whims? that while you allowed yourself to do anything, you had the right to frustrate all my desires? No, I was able to live in slavery, but I have always been free. . . . My spirit always maintained itself in independence." Roxane knew that she was the victim of a system which in the most extreme form treated her as an object and not a person.

The fate of Roxane in Ispahan no doubt caused the shedding of many tears in Paris. Moreover, her plight must certainly have led to multitudinous discussions throughout Western society regarding the status of women. The *Lettres persanes* was a widely read book, for, besides the numerous editions in French, there were at least two editions in German, the second in 1760, and English translations in 1722, 1730, 1731, and 1760. I speak here

1. Denis-Louis Pasquier; see Delisle de Sales to Voltaire, 26 Feb. 1776 (Besterman, No. 18821). Arthur M. Wilson, *Diderot*, New York, 1972, pp. 505, 813 n. 68.

of the status of women rather than the rights of women, because it must be admitted that their rights were not very visible to the naked eye.

The history of the movement for greater rights for women has been a sequel of the history of civilized man's moving from status to contract. This old-fashioned but illuminating formulation was devised by Sir Henry Maine in his book *Ancient Law* to describe the process, usually a slow and painful one, of the evolution of human rights.[2] It is a way of visualizing progress from a juridical point of view. People were born into a status; eventually, more or less completely, their standing in the eyes of public and private law became a more nearly contractual one. Becoming contractual, status thereby became actionable in law. The twentieth century has witnessed some dramatic developments from status to contract in respect to women, as for example in the pending Equal Rights Amendment to the United States Constitution. And the Enlightenment, though its gains were only moderate, nevertheless played a part in nudging public opinion towards a greater awareness of woman's social and legal handicaps, and in suggesting the desirability of proceeding from status to a more contractual conception of women's place in society.

From the abject position of the wives of peasants and day-laborers, women who were many of them really beasts of burden, to the women of the bourgeoisie and the aristocracy, traditionalism governed the status of women in eighteenth-century life. Arthur Young, traveling in the east of France, made this entry in his journal on July 12, 1789: "Walking up a long hill, to ease my mare, I was joined by a poor woman, who complained of the times, and that it was a sad country. . . . This woman, at no great distance, might have been taken for sixty or seventy, her figure was so bent, and her face so furrowed and hardened by labor; but she said she was only twenty-eight." The status of woman, based on old folkways and hallowed by time, was deeply entrenched legally. And in the last analysis, woman's position went back to money, as such things usually do — dowries, dower rights, the legalistic safeguarding of family estates. In England the legal

2. Sir Henry Maine, *Ancient Law*, ch. v.

position of a wife was really one of being a permanent minor. English common law, as can readily be seen by peering into Blackstone, the first volume of whose *Commentaries* was published in 1765, had developed the legal fiction of the unity of person, i.e., that by marriage the husband and wife are one person. "By marriage," wrote Blackstone, "the husband and wife are one person in law; that is, the very being or legal existence of the woman is suspended during the marriage, or at least is incorporated and consilidated into that of the husband . . ."[3] What this boiled down to in fact was that the husband could alienate his wife's property without her having any redress by common law. Actually redress was possible by Chancery proceedings, that is to say by equity law, but these actions were expensive, restricted, and only the wealthiest and the most strong-minded would have recourse to them.[4]

In France, too, the doctrine of the unity of person prevailed. This may be seen in a treatise published in 1770 by Robert-Joseph Pothier, whom the *Grand Larousse* calls "the greatest jurisconsult of the eighteenth century," entitled *Traité de la puissance du mari sur la personne et les biens de la femme.* "The parties to a marriage should regard themselves as being in a certain way only one person," wrote Pothier. It is true, however, that in France the possibility of a husband's appropriating his wife's property was somewhat less than in England, especially in that half of France that was called the *pays de droit écrit* (as distinguished from the other half, the *pays de droit coutumier*). In the *pays de droit écrit*, dowries, if explicitly itemized and specified, were inalienable by the husband. But then, they were inalienable by the wife too. Consequently the rights of families were better safeguarded in France than in England. Nevertheless the personal subjection of women in matrimony was about the same.

French official doctrine held that the powers of the husband over the wife were authorized by natural law. According to

---

3. Sir William Blackstone, *Commentaries on the Laws of England*, Book I, ch. xv, iii.

4. These legal aspects have been excellently delineated by Dr. Janelle Greenberg (Chatham College), "The Legal Status of Women in the First Half of the Eighteenth Century," a paper read to the American Society for Eighteenth-Century Studies meeting at McMaster University, 8 May 1973.

Pothier, "La puissance du mari sur la personne de la femme, consiste, par le droit naturel, dans le droit qu'a le mari d'exiger d'elle tous les devoirs de soumission qui sont dus à un supérieur."[5] Moreover, in France there were enormous economic and social pressures on families to provide dowries for their girls and get them married off. Unmarried women were not very common in eighteenth-century France, and the unmarried state was looked upon as somewhat unnatural. If they had small dowries, too small to attract husbands of their own social class, they were likely to be hustled off to convents. In Protestant England, maiden aunts were more common. Providing a dowry for his daughter became an obsession even with Diderot, at some grave cost to his integrity. And he detected, just barely in the nick of time in the marriage negotiations, that his intended son-in-law proposed a settlement whereby, if he should pre-decease his wife, her dowry should revert to his brothers, so that his wife, Diderot's daughter, would be left penniless. No wonder Diderot remarked that a marriage contract is the most important legal transaction in one's whole life, and that it is impossible to remedy it if it is made wrong in the first place.[6]

The subjection of women was of course reenforced by, indeed largely caused by, religious sanctions and authority of the most august kind. The teachings of the Old Testament, and also of St. Paul in the New, inculcated the subjection of women. It is very likely — though I have not yet seen this specifically studied — that the Enlightenment's criticism of the Bible, undertaken for the purpose of discrediting bigotry and promoting religious tolerance, had the side effect of tending to discredit also that subjection of women inculcated by Scripture.

Another subject for reasearch that I should like to see explored is the influence in the eighteenth century of Plato's ideas, as expressed in *The Republic*, regarding women's proper role in society, for he advocated for the guardian class equality of women intellectually and politically. Women too were to be

5. Robert-Joseph Pothier, *Oeuvres,* 10 vols, Paris, 1861, vii, p. 1. See also Léon Abensour, *La Femme et le féminisme avant la Révolution,* Paris, 1923, pp. 7, 8, 14.

6. Denis Diderot, *Correspondance,* ed. Georges Roth and Jean Varloot, 16 vols, Paris, 1955-1970, XI, pp. 138, 143.

guardians of the republic, and receive the education of guardians. Moreover, there was to be equality in the social and work functions of men and women. Most commentators have interpreted the sexual commonalty of women advocated in *The Republic* as though this would increase the subjection of women, and make them more exposed than ever to *machismo*. But when one comes to think about it, the sexual relationships that Socrates is shown by Plato as defending in *The Republic* imply not sexual subjection of women but rather a greater and freer choice of mates. (Socrates was perhaps inspired by his esteem for Aspasia, the celebrated Athenian *hetaira*). I suspect that the social, political, and sexual position of women in *The Republic* comes very close to fulfilling the specifications demanded for women by Women's Liberationists today.

Of no less authority in the culture of the West, though, is Aristotle, and he it was who strongly criticized the equality of women advocated in *The Republic*. In his *Politics* Aristotle affirmed that there was a natural inequality between the sexes, thus becoming one of the earliest and certainly one of the greatest of male chauvinists. It would be an interesting reasearch project to study the traces of the syncopated beat, first of Plato and then of Aristotle, in the thought of the West in regard to women's rights. In the eighteenth century, for instance, Dom Deschamps in *Le Vrai système* refers to Plato and *The Republic*, and D'Holbach, in his *Système social*, published anonymously in 1773, remarked that "Plato calls women to the governance of states and even to the command of armies; . . . he stipulates that their education should be the same as that of men."[7] The Neo-Platonists of the Italian Renaissance and of seventeenth-century England can be shown to have had a special regard for the greater equality of women. Aristotle, on the other hand, could always be made to be the apologist for women's subjection, as he was made, in the United States ante-bellum South, the apologist for slavery. He asserted flat out that "the male is by nature superior, and the female

---

7. Paul Thiry d'Holbach, *Système social*, London, 1773, 3e partie, p. 129; Dom Deschamps, *Le Vrai système*, ed. Jean Thomas and Franco Venturi, Paris, 1939, p. 126. D'Holbach: "Platon appelle les femmes au Gouvernement des Etats, & même au commandement des armées; mais il veut que leur éducation soit la même que celle des hommes."

inferior; and the one rules, and the other is ruled; this principle, of necessity,extends to all mankind."[8]

The first faint traces of a challenge to the traditionalism of Ancien Régime societies in respect to the status of women is to be found in the emergence of that most interesting social phenomenon, the *salon*. Salons were expensive to run. Prerequisites were a liberal budget and a superior chef, and consequently *salons* were not numerous. But the fact that there were any at all signified that the men guests were willing to accept women as being interested in ideas. And sure enough, within the tight traditional society of the France of Louis XIV, conservatives looked upon these *salons* − those of Mme de Rambouillet, of Mlle de Scudéry, of the duchesse de Maine and of Mme de Lambert, for instance − askance. The *salon*, with its promise of greater social and intellectual freedom for women, was savagely satirized in Molière's *Les Femmes savantes*. As an eighteenth-century critic remarked of this play, "this was setting the clock back two hundred years."[9] Moreover, one of the most famous educational foundations in Ancien Régime France, established in 1686 by the morganatic wife of Louis XIV, had a traditionalistic purpose. Mme de Maintenon's School for Noble Girls at St. Cyr seems to have had for its principal intention the reenforcement of the conventional female virtues, *Kirche, Küche, und Kinder*, topped off with ′a slight frosting of literacy.

In the eighteenth century, *salons* became one of the principal engines of the Enlightenment. Most famous of all was Mme Geoffrin's, at her house (still standing) on the Rue Saint-Honoré, where she gave dinners for artists on Mondays and for men of letters on Wednesdays. Mme Geoffrin was a woman of independent spirit. Diderot once recorded of her, "I received a visit from Mme Geoffrin who treated me like a ninny and counseled my wife to do the same."[10] Also very famous, especially because they too were favorite haunts of the *philosophes*, were the salons of Mlle de

8. Aristotle, *Politics*, Book I, ch. v, 7. See also *ibid.*, Book I, ch. xii and xiii. For comments on the Plato-Aristotle "syncopation," see A. R. Humphreys, "The 'Rights of Woman' in the Age of Reason," *Modern Language Review*, XLI, 1946, pp. 257, 263.

9. "C'était remonter à deux cens ans" (Antoine-Léonard Thomas, *Essai sur le caractère, les moeurs et l'esprit des femmes dans les différens siècles*, Paris, 1772, p. 176.

10. Diderot, *Correspondance*, VII, p. 132: "Je reçus la visite de Made Geoffrin, qui me traita comme une bête et qui conseilla à ma femme d'en faire autant."

Lespinasse and of Mme Necker, the wife of the famous Swiss banker and the mother of Mme de Staël. But there were many other lesser ones as well, reverberating the ideas of the *philosophes*. The *salons* were invaluable for the *philosophes*. There they found a forum, whence their ideas were carried away and circulated with a rapidity characteristic of a leisured aristocratic society slowly stifling from ennui and eager for any diversion. The success of the *salons* testified to the intellecutal capacity of the women who presided over them. It took a great deal of skill and tact as well as intelligence to run a *salon* successfully, to gain the respect of temperamental intellectuals and authors, to make them want to come again, to be able to steer a conversation without seeming to do so, to govern discussions so adroitly that they became neither anarchical nor contentious, to draw out the timid and circumvent the bores.

Another indication of the changing attitude towards women during the eighteenth century was the growing conviction of leading Enlightenment thinkers that respect for women, and especially for the intellectual capacity of women, was an infallible mark of an advanced civilization. Literary examples of this esteem may be observed on almost every hand, foreshadowed in Fontenelle's *Entretiens sur la pluralité des mondes*. The point is made by Goethe in *Torquato Tasso*; indeed, there is a mulititude of instances, becoming more numerous as the century draws on. Conversely, the subjection of women became the mark of a barbarous or even savage society in the estimation of some Enlightenment thinkers. Thus, in an eloquent passage in Raynal's *Histoire philosophique des établissements . . . des Européens dans les deux Indes* (a passage supplied by Diderot), the author has a native woman "from the banks of the Oronoco" recount all the burdens she carries because of her sex, lament that she ever was born, and justify the infanticide of her own daughter.[11] It can readily be seen that the momentum of such literary and rhetorical manifestations during the Enlightenment was in the direction of an ever-increasing confidence in the intellectual capacities of

11. *Op. cit.*, 5 vols, Geneva, 1780, II, pp. 183-84. This passage is also found in Diderot's *Sur les femmes* (Denis Diderot, *Oeuvres complètes*, ed. Jules Assézat and Maurice Tourneux, 20 vols, Paris, 1875-77, II, pp. 258-59).

women and, implicitly though perhaps unconsciously, a disposition to accept their equality.

Yet not all of the leading writers in France were conspicuous in desiring more nearly equal rights for women. Voltaire, surprisingly enough, was, as David Williams points out, "somewhat ambivalent on the issue. . . ." He, however, "by virtue of his position, gave the whole debate plenty of valuable publicity, even if he added little that was at all original or even sympathetic."[12] Rousseau — though it is hard to say whether he was a part of the Enlightenment or counter to it — revealed his feelings about women and about *salons* in an astonishing passage in his *Lettre à Mr. D'Alembert sur les spectacles*, where he speaks of "every woman in Paris assembling in her apartment a seraglio of men more womanish than she."[13] And Rousseau, of course, devoted a section of *Emile* to a discussion of female education, that is to say, the upbringing of Sophie, the girl who was to become Emile's wife. Sophie, however, was scarcely a feminist. In many respects her intelligence seems to resemble that of Rousseau's dim-witted mistress, Thérèse Levasseur. Rousseau's views on women, which were severly criticized in his own century by Mary Wollstonecraft in *A Vindication of the Rights of Woman* still make him the bugaboo of Women's Liberationists today.

I do not include the celebrated Marquis de Sade among the writers of the Enlightenment, even though he was born in 1740. Granted that he certainly bespoke a greater sexual freedom, his doctrines really went against the grain of the Enlightenment, which was very humanistic and humanitarian in character. The teachings of Sade, in effect, end up in the dehumanization of people, who do indeed get treated as things rather than persons. And this, psychologists and psychiatrists are beginning to say, is (if I may use a feeble pun) the saddest thing that can be said of pornography.

12. David Williams, "The Politics of Feminism in the French Enlightenment," in *The Varied Pattern: Studies in the 18th Century*, ed. Peter Hughes and David Williams, Toronto, 1971, pp. 338-39. Similar conclusions have been reached by Madeleine Rousseau Raaphorst, "Voltaire et féminisme: un examen du théâtre et des contes," *Studies on Voltaire and the Eighteenth Century*, LXXXIX, 1972, pp. 1325-35.

13. Jean-Jacques Rousseau, *Lettre à Mr. D'Alembert sur les spectacles*, ed. M. Fuchs, Geneva, 1948, p. 136: "et chaque femme de Paris rassemble dans son appartement un serrail d'hommes plus femmes qu'elle . . ."

Of all the leading writers of the French Enlightenment – and here I have in mind Voltaire, Rousseau, Montesquieu,[14] and Diderot – the latter was the one who showed himself most concerned by the subjection of women in European society. This concern manifested itself at numerous places in his writings, but nowhere more so than in the brief essay *Sur les femmes*. This was written in 1772, when he was 59 years old, and came at a time when he was much absorbed by problems involving the status of women, partly because of his daughter's impending marriage (which occurred on 9 September 1772), and partly because of an autumnal but vivid love affair of his own. Some of the most interesting of his writings, most of them in the dialogue form that he was so skilful in employing, came just during these years, and were concerned with the nature of love, sexuality, and the sociology of sexual relationships. There was his *Supplément au Voyage de Bougainville* about Tahiti, a subject of inexhaustible attraction to people with sex fantasies. There was *Le Rêve de d'Alembert*, and there were two short stories about the misery and inscrutability of love, *Madame de La Carlière* and *Ceci n'est pas un conte*.

The immediate occasion for Diderot's *Sur les femmes* was the publication by Antoine-Léonard Thomas in 1772 of his *Essai sur le caractère, les moeurs et l'esprit des femmes dans les différens siécles*. Thomas' opinions are very representative of the most liberal and advanced school of Enlightenment thought. He was a member of the circles that met at D'Holbach's house and at Mme Necker's; he was also a member of the French Academy, a man whose views would be both typical of the changing social thought of his time and also influential.

Thomas began well, though some critics declare that the best paragraphs in his book were the first ones:

If we take a survey of ages and of countries, we will find the women – almost without exception – at all times, and in all places, adored and oppressed. Man, who has never neglected an opportunity of exerting his power, in paying homage to

14. See Robert F. O'Reilly, "Montesquieu: Anti-Feminist," *Studies on Voltarie and the Eighteenth Century*, CII, 1973, pp. 143-56.

their beauty, has always availed himself of their weakness. He has been at once their tyrant and their slave.

In another of his introductory pages Thomas demonstrated most convincingly that the Enlightenment was aware of the problem:

In the temperate latitudes ... the women have not been deprived of their liberty; but a severe legislation has at all times kept them in a state of dependence. ... even in countries where they may be esteemed most happy, [they are] constrained in their desires, in the disposal of their goods, robbed of freedom of will by the laws, the slaves of opinion, which rules them with absolute sway, and construes the slightest appearance into guilt; surrounded on all sides by judges who are at once their tyrants and their seducers, and who, after having prepared their faults, punish every lapse with dishonour − nay, usurp the right of degrading them on suspicion; ... [such] is the lot of women over the whole earth.[15]

These views are very similar to those of D'Holbach, who, at just this time, wrote of women that "Le Gouvernement ne les compte pour rien dans la Société. Dans toutes les contrées de la terre, le sort des femmes est d'être tyrannisées." And D'Alembert, in an essay published in 1762, had remarked upon "l'esclavage et l'espèce d'avilissement où nous avons mis les femmes."[16]

Diderot's reason for writing a supplement to Thomas' work

15. Thomas, *op. cit.*, pp. 1, 4-5. The original of these passages: "Si l'on parcourt les pays & les siècles, on verra presque par-tout les femmes adorées & opprimées. L'homme qui jamais n'a manqué une occasion d'abuser de sa force, en rendant hommage à leur beauté, s'est par-tout prévalu de leur faiblesse. Il a été tout à la fois leur tyran & leur esclave." The second: "Dans les pays tempérés ... les femmes n'ont pas été privées de leur liberté; mais la législation sévère les a mises par-tout dans la dépendance. ... dans les pays où elles sont les plus heureuses, [les femmes ont été] gênées dans leurs désirs, gênées dans la disposition de leur bien, privées de leur volonté même dont la loi les dépouille, esclaves de l'opinion qui les domine avec empire, & leur fait un crime de l'apparence même; environnées de toute part de juges qui sont en même temps leurs Séducteurs & leurs tyrans, & qui après avoir préparé leurs fautes, les en punissent par le déshonneur, ou ont usurpé le droit de les flétrir sur des soupçons; tel est à-peu-près le sort des femmes sur toute la terre." My quotations are from the English translation, *Essay on the Character, Manners, and Genius of Women in Different Ages*, 2 vols, Philadelphia, 1774, I, pp. 1, 6-7.

16. D'Holbach, *Système social*, 3ᵉ Partie, p. 122. Jean Le Rond d'Alembert, *Oeuvres philosophiques, historiques et littéraires*, 5 vols, Paris, 1805, V, p. 349.

was not that he objected to such views. On the contrary, he shared them. It was what he regarded as deficiencies in Thomas' essay that caused Diderot to write his own. "I like Thomas," Diderot began. "I respect the uprightness of his soul and the nobility of his character"; but in this book "he has thought a great deal but he has not felt enough. His head was agitated but his heart remained unmoved." Diderot thought, transparently, that he could do better. "When one writes of women," he remarked, "one should dip one's pen in the rainbow and blot the lines with the dust of butterfly wings."[17]

In fact, a twentieth-century Women's Liberationist would emphatically inform me that anyone who could use language like this is a male chauvinist. In his essay Diderot emphasized the biological differences between men and women, and he did so with the assurance that came from his being fully abreast of the best medical information of the time. Thus he spoke of the effects of menstruation, pregnancy, child-bearing and lactation, the menopause, sexual frigidity, and even discussed whether or how frequently women experience orgasm. He also emphasized (as did all medical opinion in his day) that women were greatly subject to sexual hysteria. To this clinical approach he added some views regarding women's psychology that would not endear him to feminists. For instance, he stated that practically all women lack logic. Also, "the symbol of women in general is that of the Apocalypse, on the forehead of which is written MYSTERY. . . . More civilized than we are in externals, they [women] have remained true savages inside, all of them Machiavellians more or less." "O women, you are very extraordinary children."[18] Is this what is meant by dipping one's pen in the rainbow and blotting the lines with the dust of butterfly wings?

Just the same, the weight of Diderot's thought was for a greater freedom than a lesser. For example, he strongly favored the legalization of divorce, though here he was thinking of the social and personal benefits that would accrue therefrom for both sexes, and very likely he was thinking particularly of himself. I am sure that had he been able, he would have divorced his wife and

17. Diderot, *Oeuvres complètes*, II, pp. 251, 260.
18. *Ibid.*, pp. 260, 257.

married Sophie Volland. (Had he done so, he would not have had to write all those incomparable letters to her, and posterity would have been the loser.) Diderot did not live to see marriage become a civil contract, as it did in 1792. Divorce became legal at that time too.

Whatever his deficiencies from the point of view of a militant Women's Liberationist, Diderot shows in his writings as in his life that he gladly accepts women as his moral equals, respects female intelligence (though he does not regard it the equal of male), and traverses in his career the trajectory between depicting women as objects, as he did in his early and somewhat pornographic novel, *Les Bijoux indiscrets*, to women as persons, as in his very fine novel, recently made into a remarkably good film, *La Religieuse*. Throughout his works Diderot shows that he is compassionate in regard to women. He deplores injustices. He laments that the education of women is defective, that girls are more restrained and more neglected in their education than boys.[19] He was an editor and perhaps almost co-author of a book, *De l'Education publique*, published in 1762, which called for the public education of girls on a national basis. He believed in sex education for women, and, somewhat appalled by his own temerity, himself imparted to his fifteen-year-old daughter a broad range of sex information and then sent her to a private course in anatomy conducted by Mlle. Biheron, famous in the eighteenth century for her skilful construction of wax models of the human body.[20] Writing in 1774-1775, Diderot referred in the *Réfutation d'Helvétius* to the "servitude" of women. And of women's legal disabilities he wrote in *Sur les femmes*, "In almost all countries, the cruelty of the civil law has combined with the cruelty of nature, against women. They have been treated like imbecile children. There is no kind of vexation which in civilized nations a husband may not exercise with impunity against his wife."[21] Although *Sur les femmes* was not published during Diderot's lifetime, it expresses his considered views, which probably had great currency in that volatile and communicative world of the Paris *salons*. For Diderot liked to talk

19. *Ibid.*, p. 257.
20. Wilson, *Diderot*, pp. 447-48, 549, 594-95.
21. Diderot, *Oeuvres complètes*, Vol II, pp. 294, 258.

– Horace Walpole described him as "a very lively old man, and great talker"[22] – and one can readily imagine Diderot's remarks putting their stamp upon contemporary opinion just as they have done with posterity.

A person surveying the status of women during the Enlightenment naturally becomes aware of promising topics that invite further research. It would be helpful to have an analysis of the eighteenth-century novel from the point of view of woman's status and of women's rights. Was there a development corresponding to that in the thought of the *philosophes?* Or did the eighteenth-century novel remain relatively static in this regard? Can one make a feminist of Marivaux? It can be demonstrated that a whole continent mourned the fate of Clarissa, but were they not more aware of her wrongs than they were of her rights? It is true that Mme de Merteuil, the repellent antiheroine of *Les Liaisons dangereuses*, was an emancipated woman who declared that she had been born to avenge my sex and dominate yours." But she can scarcely be said to be, if we remember how she treated other women, a Women's Liberationist.

Another tempting area of research would be the utopias of the century.[23] If one cannot find a vivid awareness of woman's disabilities and inequalities among utopian writers, then one can scarcely say of the eighteenth century as a whole that it displayed deep concern for women's rights. I suspect that, very surprisingly, the evidence may prove quite negative. Certainly, there is nothing about women in the best-known utopia of the century, Morelly's *Code de la nature.* And though Dom Deschamps does mention women briefly in *Le Vrai système*, the point of view seems to me to be more with reference to male advantage than it is from women's point of view.

In this day of the refinements and sophistication of the techniques of social history, there seem to me to be great opportunities for the social historians to explore the economic

22. "Horace Walpole's Paris Journals" (Horace Walpole, *Correspondence,* ed. Wilmarth S. Lewis, VII, New Haven, 1939, p. 262.

23. See Leslie C. Tihany, "Utopia in Modern Western Thought: The Metamorphosis of an Idea," in Richard Herr and Harold T. Parker, eds., *Ideas in History: Essays Presented to Louis Gottschalk by his Former Students,* Durham (N.C.), 1965, pp. 20-38.

status of women in the eighteenth century. What employments were open to them? Were the opportunities for women in commerce and industry increasing, allowing them to be truly independent and to lead autonomous lives? Léon Abensour, in his *La Femme et le féminisme avant la Révolution*, has an excellent and extended section about women and the guilds in France, both before Turgot's suppression of them in 1776 and after their subsequent reconstitution, but his monograph is now a half-century old and the whole subject cries for the exhaustive statistics and graphs of the social historians. As Abensour wisely said, already in 1923, monographs are needed studying women's economic activity in each province and each guild, and the materials for this search lie at hand in the *archives départementales et communales*.[24]

Nevertheless, the push of Enlightenment thought in the direction of greater equality for women can be measured. Its force can be gauged by what Condorcet, the disciple of D'Alembert and probably the greatest *philosophe* of the generation following Voltaire and Diderot, tried to bring about during the Revolution. Already in 1787, in his *Lettres d'un bourgeois de New-Haven*, he argued that women should be eligible for elective office. He repeated these arguments in 1790 in *Sur l'admission des femmes au droit de cité*. And in preparing his famous *Rapport sur l'organisation générale de l'instruction publique*, which he presented to the Legislative Assembly on 20 and 21 April 1792, he wrote a *mémoire*, "Nature et objet de l'instruction publique," in which he declared that "les femmes ont le même droit que les hommes à l'instruction publique."[25] In respect to woman's social and political status, Condorcet's writings sought to move significantly from status to contract. His views regarding women's rights – and notice that he called them "rights" – are a high-water mark in eighteenth-century French thought, just as Mary Wollstonecraft's publication, in this same year, of *A Vindication of the Rights of*

24. Abensour, *op, cit.*, 194 n.; cf. *ibid.*, pp. 181-227.

25. *Lettres d'un bourgeois de New-Haven* (*Oeuvres de Condorcet*, ed. A. Condorcet O'Connor and F. Arago, 12 vols. [Paris, 1847-49], IX, 3-93, esp. 15-20; *Sur l'admission des femmes au droit de cité* (ibid., X, 121-30; "Nature et objet de l'instruction publique" (*ibid.*, VII, 169-229, esp. 215-26. This quotation, 220).

Woman, is a bench-mark for England. Together they constitute the culmination of the Enlightenment's contributions to feminism.

Arthur M. Wilson

La condition de la femme française au XVIIIe siècle d'après les romans

"Le roman est pour nous, historiens, la seule façon correcte de connaître la vie réelle, publique ou privée des hommes du passé, leur sensibilité, leur représentation du monde."

Pensée de Seignobos, citée par M. Zeraffa, in *Roman et Société*.

Voilà qui peut rassurer un peu la littéraire que je suis d'oser parler devant des historiens! Pour me donner encore meilleure conscience, sur ce plan, je prendrai mes exemples, pour la plupart, chez un romancier dont l'oeuvre doit beaucoup à son expérience d'avocat au Parlement de Paris, Robert Challe, auteur des *Illustres Françaises* (1713).[1] Chaque fois que ce sera possible, je corroborerai par des rapprochements avec d'autres oeuvres romanesques du temps, choisies en général dans la première moitié du siècle. Il s'agit de *Gil Blas* de Lesage, de la *Vie de Donami* et du *Paysan Parvenu* de Marivaux et pour la deuxième moitié des *Liaisons dangereuses* de Laclos.

Avant d'entrer dans le vif du sujet, une mise au point reste à faire. Le titre général de cette communication ne doit pas faire illusion sur sa portée réelle. Il ne sera pas question ici de la condition de toutes les femmes. Même si le roman du 18e siècle élargit l'éventail social, nous en tirerons peu de renseignements sur la femme du peuple, la paysanne, l'ouvrière, bien que de tels

---

1. *Robert Chasles* (sic), *Les Illustres Françaises*, édition par F. Deloffre, Les Belles Lettres, Paris, 1967. Tous les exemples pris dans cette oeuvre seront suivis de l'abréviation, *I.F.* et de la page de référence.

personnages se rencontrent maintenant dans le roman, mais rarement à titre de protagonistes. Dans *Gil Blas* de Lesage, par exemple, on trouvera des aubergistes, des duègnes, des servantes, de même d'ailleurs que le monde interlope des entremetteuses et des actrices. Dans certaines autres parties de cette même oeuvre, nous rencontrerons, au contraire, des femmes de sang royal ou de la plus haute qualité.

Cet exemple nous fait constater un autre phénomène influant sur la peinture de la condition féminine. La femme sera évoquée différemment selon le type de roman dont se réclame l'auteur. Les personnages princiers se font alors plus rares, contrairement au grand roman classique; par contre l'influence du picaresque et de l'"histoire," sorte de fait-divers du temps, faît apparaître les aventurières en tout genre, déclassées, immorales bien souvent, dont Manon Lescaut restera l'incarnation. Par ailleurs, le besoin des romanciers de donner au genre sa dignité. en même temps que leur volonté de témoigner de leur temps, explique que le gros des personnages romanesques féminins se recrute en général dans ce que l'on appelle la "bonne société." Celle-ce comprend la noblesse, mais aussi la haute et bientôt même la moyenne bourgeoisie.[2] Enfin, le sort de la femme varie considérablement selon la place exacte qu'elle occupe dans l'échelle sociale, étant donné l'importance du rang à l'époque.

Ces réserves faites, le roman du 18e siècle apparaît la source rêvée d'informations sur le sort de la femme sous l'Ancien Régime, puisqu'en dépit de ses limitations, il offre du personnage féminin un éventail d'une variété jamais encore atteinte. En outre, la prétention affichée des romanciers de compléter l'histoire de leur temps ou d'en être les témoins privilégiés semble nous promettre à l'avance la vérification de la pensée de Seignobos citée en exergue.

Voyons donc maintenant comment apparaît le sort féminin dans le roman du 18e siècle.

I. La Condition Sociale

Importance du Rang

Qu'il s'agisse du début ou de la fin du siècle, de *Gil Blas* ou des

2. La présence de ces dernières catégories vérifie, ce dont témoigne aussi l'histoire, la montée croissante de la classe bourgeoise et son insertion de plus en plus fréquente dans les rangs de la noblesse par le mariage et surtout l'argent.

Liaisons Dangereuses, il faut se rappeler, nous avons déjà mentionné l'importance de cette constatation, que c'est dans le monde hiérarchisé de l'Ancien Régime qu'évoluent les héroines de roman. Dans ce monde, tous les personnages, quel que soit leur sexe, se définissent d'abord par la place qu'ils occupent dans l'échelle sociale. Nous verrons que cet assujettissement se fait plus lourdement sentir encore dans le cas des femmes.

C'était vrai déjà pour la *Princesse de Clèves*. Son destin n'est-il pas d'abord d'être princesse, ne la condamne-t-il pas ainsi fatalement au mariage sans amour, et donc à la passion illégitime ainsi qu'à l'écrasement et à la dépersonnalisation des bienséances?[3]

Tout se joue donc, dès la naissance. Si l'on est "née," si, en outre, l'on a du bien, le destin est fixé d'avance par la société. On n'aurait presque pas besoin d'être belle. Mais, en vertu de la formule qui domine encore le roman, l'héroine aura tout sans doute, titre, fortune, beauté et toutes les qualités de l'esprit et du coeur. L'absence de rang ou une naissance illégitime pèse bien plus lourd, dans le roman comme dans la vie, sur le destin de la jeune fille que du jeune homme. A l'époque où les Paysans parviennent, où Gil Blas, simple bachelier, devient favori du premier ministre, il faut bien de la beauté et de la vertu chez une héroine pour compenser ce handicap, comme le montrent Marianne, Angélique ou Silvie.

L'Education

Il n'en est pas toujours question. C'est sans doute que l'héroine a reçu l'éducation traditionnelle de l'époque: celle que dispensent un certain nombre d'établissements religieux, se réclament tous du modèle fameux que leur a fourni le 17e siècle: le Saint-Cyr de Mme de Maintenon, où l'on tentait non seulement de meubler l'esprit mais plus encore, en développant la piété et l'obéissance, de préparer les jeunes filles à leur vie. Loin d'avoir les ambitions de Fénelon dans *De l'Education des Filles,* il semble que les couvents n'aient conservé que la seconde partie de ce programme. Aussi, le reproche qu'on leur adresse le plus souvent, outre la piètre qualité de leur enseignement, est de maintenir les jeunes filles dans l'ignorance du monde la plus préjudiciable à leur avenir. Ainsi,

---

3. Et Mme de La Fayette savait de quoi elle parlait, vivant à Versailles, etant de plus familière de l'infortunée Madame, Henriette d'Angleterre.

dans les *Illustres Françaises,* sortent du couvent les héroïnes qui acceptent le plus passivement leur sort.[4] A la fin du siècle, de même, dans les *Liaisons Dangereuses,* les deux victimes de Valmont, Cécile et la présidente, sortent également du couvent et ont la même ignorance de la vie et du danger des fréquentations. Pourtant la présidente âgée de 22 ans est déjà mariée tandis que Cécile est dans toute l'innocence de ses quinze ans. A l'opposé, l'âme damnée du livre, maîtresse d'elle-même comme de l'action, Mme de Merteuil, est une autodidacte et proclame orgueilleusement qu'elle est son propre ouvrage. Sans avoir sa perversion, les *Illustres Françaises* qui ont fait leur éducation dans le monde se révèlent les plus autonomes, les plus hardies dans la recherche du bonheur au mépris, s'il le faut, des conventions sociales. Dans deux cas, il s'agit de jeunes filles qui n'ont pas dans la société une situation normale. Silvie, enfant illégitime de grande maison, est recueillie par sa tante qui lui fait donner l'éducation de son rang, sans rien révéler pourtant de celui-ci; quant à Angélique, jeune fille noble très pauvre, sa grande intelligence lui permet de tirer plus de profit que sa maîtresse de l'instruction dispensée à cette dernière. La nécessité d'affronter seules les réalités de la vie, l'autonomie dont elles se trouvent gratifiées ainsi que la conscience de leur infériorité sociale expliquent le rôle déterminant que joue leur éducation dans l'évolution de leur caractère et de leur vie.[5] Babet Fenouil, la seule des *Illustres Françaises* qui osera braver la société en se donnant à son amant nous est présentée comme "plus savante qu'une fille ne doit l'être" (*I.F.,* p. 175). Cet exemple nous montre, qu'en ce début du 18e siècle, les femmes savantes ne sont toujours pas appréciées; ne pourrait-on en conclure que l'éducation traditionnelle du couvent est précisément censée fabriquer en série des jeunes filles dociles, prêtes ainsi à se soumettre au sort qui les attend?[6] Une telle éducation reste, malgré tout, le meilleur critère de l'appartenance à l'élite sociale. Nous en avons un

---

4. C'est le cas, entre autres, de Manon Dupuis, dans la première histoire.

5. Dans la *Princesse de Clèves,* déjà, Mme de La Fayette avait éprouvé le besoin de justifier l'originalité de la princesse par la formation morale que lui avait donnée sa mère.

6. Au fur et à mesure que l'accent est mis davantage sur les droits de l'individu, la méfiance à l'égard du couvent niveleur s'accroît et les individualités les plus marquées se voient gratifiées par les romanciers d'une éducation soignée, à laquelle les parents eux-mêmes ont veillé.

exemple frappant avec l'héroine de Marivaux, Marianne. La perte dramatique de ses parents la prive définitivement de la preuve de sa naissance illustre. Elle sera donc élevée en province par la soeur d'un curé qui la prépare, avec réalisme, à un avenir qu'on ne peut attendre que modeste. La répugnance et le peu d'aptitude au métier manuel qu'elle doit exercer, son refus indigné de "servir," fût-ce pour échapper à la misère, sont autant de preuves aux yeux de l'héroine, comme de ses protecteurs, de sa "qualité." Aussi, trouve-t-elle, bientôt, une mère adoptive noble qui s'empresse de faire compléter au couvent l'éducation dont elle est digne.[7]

Si l'instruction et la formation morale ont pu sembler varier d'un genre d'éducation à l'autre, il est un domaine où les exigences sont les mêmes pour toutes. Même au couvent, on insiste beaucoup sur le développement des talents de société. Tout ce qui permet d'être agréable en société (et en tête-à-tête), et d'occuper décemment ses loisirs est fort prisé. Les plus douées sauront tout aussi bien danser, chanter, jouer d'un instrument (la harpe de Cécile Volanges), peindre même et bien sûr s'adonner aux divers ouvrages de dames. On insiste bien plus sur ces talents que sur le savoir; il est un point cependant qui semble n'avoir pas été négligé: à en juger par les *Illustres Françaises*; les unes sont orphelines, une autre avec un père impotent; elles doivent tenir elles-mêmes le budget; toutes, après le mariage, prennent en main les intérêts de leur mari, et témoignent ainsi qu'on les a très bien préparées à gérer une fortune.[8] C'est important puisque l'alternative où se trouve placée la jeune fille est la suivante: le mariage ou le couvent.

Mariée ou Nonne?

On a vu l'importance accordée dans l'éducation aux talents sociaux. La beauté est également cultivée. Il n'est pas d'auteurs de cette période qui ne soulignent l'importance de la coquetterie

---

7. Nous avons là une preuve entre autres du mépris qui s'attache dans le roman au travail, surtout féminin, ce qui est la marque de l'allégeance persistante de ce genre à une idéologie aristocratique qui interdit aux nobles le travail, cause de dérogation.

8. Tant Manon Dupuis que Silvie de Buringes, Angélique tout comme Babet connaissent la valeur de l'argent et s'occupent d'assurer la position sociale de leur époux par l'achat d'une charge.

féminine, élevée par certaines, prétendent-ils au rang d'un véritable génie. On le comprend mieux quand on songe que le manque de ces qualités peut vous condamner au célibat et donc au couvent.

Laissons de côté celles qui y demeurent par vocation. Pour les autres, comme les goncourt l'expliquent très bien dans leur livre,[9] il faut voir que le couvent se retrouve à toutes les étapes de la vie féminine. Ecole dans la jeunesse, refuge pour les moins fortunées et pour les laides, punition des dévergondées, abri des veuves et des femmes séparées, dernier séjour des favorites repenties, on le trouve dans la plupart des romans comme dans nombre de vies de femmes à l'époque. Mais, surtout, bien avant la *Religieuse*, le roman abonde en vocations forcées. Le thème immortalisé par Diderot est aussi fréquent dans la littérature du temps que celui du mariage de convenances. Peut-être plus fréquent encore, étant donné la propagande anti-cléricale.[10] Même chez des romanciers chrétiens il est traité. Marivaux, par exemple, dont la fille unique entre au couvent en 1745, semble avoir été obsédé par ce thème. Dans la seule *Vie de Marianne*, on le trouve, selon une structure compliquée, à trois niveaux différents; pour défendre Marianne contre les séductions des religieuses et la tentation de fuir la vie en devenant nonne, Tervire, elle-même voilée, évoque comment dans sa jeunesse les confidences d'une religieuse malgré elle l'empêchèrent de tomber elle-même dans un complot semblable. Pour Clémence de Bernay, des *Illustres Françaises*, il ne faudra rien moins que la fougue soldatesque de Terny, venu l'enlever audacieusement en pleine cérémonie de prise de voile, pour la soustraire *in extremis* à la claustration (*I.F.*, p. 165).[11] Le mépris où est tenu le couvent dans la littérature, tout comme dans l'opinion d'alors, est manifeste. Il ne semble bon qu'à recevoir le rebut du monde, comme l'affirme crûment Terny (*I.F.*, p. 130), comme le montre Cécile Volanges en allant y terminer sa jeune vie brisée, comme en témoignent aussi tant de conversions "tardives"

9. *Les Goncourt*, La Femme au 18e siècle, Paris, 1862, p. 8.

10. C'est que le 18e siècle tout entier, avec sa hantise de la "nature" est hostile à la vie monastique profondément "anti-naturelle." En outre, tout comme le mariage forcé, la vocation forcée est dénoncée comme une violation de la liberté de l'individu.

11. Et c'est, l'on s'en souvient, pour éviter le même sort à Manon, condamnée au couvent par sa famille effrayée de son penchant au plaisir, que Des Grieux, enflammé au premier regard, l'enlève aussitôt.

des plus célèbres belles repenties du temps, Adrienne Lecouvreur, par exemple.

On comprend alors que le mariage attire davantage. Il semble, par opposition à la prison du couvent, le commencement de la vie libre. Si l'on a la fortune ou le rang, le mariage sera facile, mais le bonheur n'est pas sûr pour autant.

Ce sont les parents, en effet, qui décident du choix du conjoint. De la *Princesse de Clèves* aux *Liaisons Dangereuses*, quel que soit le rang social des personnages, il en est toujours ainsi. Plus même on est élevé socialement, moins on a de chances d'échapper au mariage convenu. Le roman abonde, comme la réalité que nous révèlent les mémoires et autres documents d'époque, en jeunes filles qu'on ne tire du couvent que pour les marier avec un étranger, comme la Cécile des *Liaisons Dangereuses* qui ignore jusqu'au nom de son futur mari. Les parents sont d'autant plus sûrs d'être obéis que l'enfant est plus jeune. Dans un texte qui n'est pas un roman,[12] Mme d'Epinay raconte la rapidité incroyable du mariage de sa cousine, Sophie d'Houdetot, qui inspirera à Rousseau sa Julie.[13] Cette façon de faire semble s'être maintenue pendant tout le siècle, malgré l'opposition des Encyclopédistes, après celle de Molière et de Marivaux. L'un des buts de Challe dans son oeuvre est justement de proposer un moyen terme entre la pratique en usage et les exigences du coeur. De nombreux exemples montrent, d'ailleurs, que les jeunes filles trouvaient un moyen d'échapper à cette contrainte, en faisant elles-mêmes un choix qui puisse satisfaire les exigences parentales.

L'évolution des idées se manifeste aussi dans l'attitude des prétendants eux-mêmes. Non contents d'avoir obtenu le consentement des parents, ils veulent être sûrs d'être agréés de leur future épouse.[14] Par contre, celui qui profite de l'appui des parents pour

---

12. Mémoires de Mme d'Epinay, Volume I, cité par Goncourt, op. cit., p. 23.

13. Quand l'initiative vient de la société elle-même, marier une fille malgré elle peut être un moyen de prévenir une mésalliance qui bouleverserait l'ordre social; ainsi tente-t-on de réduire Marianne en lui faisant épouser l'insignifiant Villot pour empêcher Valville de se mésallier.

14. M. de Clèves se disait ainsi opposé, déjà, à l'idée d'épouser Mlle de Chartres sans son aveu. A l'autre bout de l'échelle sociale, un demi-siècle plus tard, le roturier anobli, Gil Blas, fait preuve des mêmes scrupules, alors qu'il s'apprête à épouser Antonia, la fille de son fermier.

faire fi des sentiments d'une jeune fille est tenu désormais pour un malhonnête homme.

La solution est souvent de l'ordre du compromis. Les héroïnes de Challe y sont passées maîtresses. Face à l'opposition de leur famille, elles font de leur vertu le garant de la réussite du coeur. Ce n'est pas par conformisme, ni pour suivre une éthique qu'elles résistent à l'amour, mais pour entretenir la passion de leur amant et s'en faire un allié avec lequel elles triomphent finalement de la résistance paternelle ou sociale. L'histoire d'Angélique présente certainement le cas limite de cette valeur sociale qu'on peut donner à la vertu.[15] D'autres héroïnes de Challe recourent au mariage secret. L'abondance de cette solution dans les romans ne doit pas faire croire qu'ils aient été aussi nombreux dans la réalité mais l'existence d'un certain nombre d'édits les concernant et la mention de certains scandales importants montrent qu'ils ont aussi existé réellement. Challe s'attache à nous en montrer les dangers, ainsi que de toute solution qui brave l'ordre social. L'histoire de Babet Fenouil (*I.F.*, pp. 189-190) est là pour montrer que l'enlèvement n'est pas sans risques, surtout quand le jeune homme, inférieur socialement, peut être accusé de rapt, alors puni de la peine capitale. Enfin, plusieurs épisodes, surtout dans l'histoire de Dupuis, prouve tout l'abus qu'un scélérat peut faire d'une promesse de mariage pour débaucher une fille crédule. Tandis que l'homme peut facilement violer sa promesse, en volant le document écrit, la jeune fille séduite, par ce moyen, ne dispose d'aucun recours. Quand elle est de rang inférieur, on pourrait même la faire poursuivre pour subornation (Des Ronais). Il ne lui reste donc, en cas de grossesse, qu'à faire comme Célénie: dissimuler de son mieux, se rendre à pied chez la sage-femme et en revenir de même.[16]

C'est là encore s'en tirer à bon compte, car pour celles qui bravent ouvertement les convenances, trompées par l'amour ou égarées par leurs appétits, la société a une punition toute prête: le déshonneur qui, si elles sont pauvres, les mènera, en les privant du

---

15. C'est par la constance de sa vertu, pendant quatre années, qu'Angélique gagne en effet le droit de devenir malgré sa pauvreté l'illustre Mme de Contamine.

16. Si, ensuite, elle a la chance d'attraper un mari, le "marchand d'illusions" peut l'aider à se refaire une virginité!

mariage, à la débauche, puis à la prostitution, faute de métier honnête. Sans doute Manon aurait-elle pu finir ainsi, sans l'amour prodigieux qui poussait Des Grieux à l'épouser malgré tout et sans la miséricorde du romancier qui la fait mourir avant cette déchéance. Quant à Babet, la seule illustre à avoir vécu l'amour en dehors du mariage, elle n'en meurt pas et sauve même son amant de la mort. Il est vrai qu'elle est très riche, et il lui faut tout de même expier, de sept ans de chasteté exemplaire et de fidélité, les libertés qu'elle a prises avec la morale sociale (*I.F.*, p. 196).

A quoi s'attendre alors pour celles qui osent s'opposer ouvertement à la volonté paternelle. Mlle Grandet, bafouée volontairement, pendant le dîner de fiançailles par Jussy qui veut échapper à ce mariage, ose timidement annoncer à ses parents qu'elle préférerait rester fille. Comme cette union était une bonne affaire, les parents se vengent d'une telle inconduite, en la mariant prestement au plus affreux barbon, qui la rendra horriblement malheureuse avant que le sort ne vienne enfin l'en délivrer. Clémence de Bernay ose aussi refuser l'affreux prétendant que ses parents voulaient lui imposer. Pour pénitence, elle sera enfermée de nouveau au couvent.[17]

Le roman manifeste donc, ce qui ressort aussi des documents historiques, que la norme reste encore le mariage de convenances arrangé par les parents. Cette contrainte pèse, il faut le reconnaître, sur les deux sexes, mais il semble bien qu'il soit plus difficile encore aux jeunes filles d'y échapper. Tout comme l'éducation s'est peu souciée de la développer personnellement mais plutôt de la conditionner pour sa vie ultérieure, c'est généralement sans tenir compte de ses goûts qu'on l'a mise au couvent ou mariée au gré de ses parents. Une fois mariée, du moins, a-t-elle une chance de pouvoir devenir elle-même?

La Femme Mariée

Le roman ne s'intéresse pas bien sûr aux vies conjugales sans histoires. On trouve pourtant, chez Challe, l'évocation de quelques couples heureux. Remarquons, cependant, qu'il s'agit de jeunes

---

17. Le même sort attend Marianne, si elle ne renonce pas à Valville, pour épouser l'incolore Villot.

mariés de quelques mois, quelques années tout au plus.[18] Le plus heureux des maris, Contamine, ne craint pas de dire franchement que tout ce bonheur lui donne parfois la nausée, et lui fait regretter la liberté et la solitude (*I.F.*, pp. 277-78). Enfin, l'amour le plus vivant reste celui des maris dont la femme est morte. Encore, l'un des deux, Des Frans, s'apprête-t-il, à la fin du livre, à convoler avec une femme qu'il n'aime pas mais dont il est aimé. "C'est le plus sûr moyen d'être heureux," lui affirme son meilleur ami. Curieux paradoxe qui souligne une fois de plus la répugnance de l'époque à mêler l'amour au mariage!

Depuis la *Princesse de Clèves*, le coeur de la femme mariée constitue un bon sujet de roman et l'on trouve déjà dans cette oeuvre tous les éléments qui formeront les composantes du malheur féminin à l'époque: l'éducation et l'absence d'amour dans le mariage, l'importance de la galanterie dans le monde. La situation même de la princesse suffisait à faire le malheur d'une femme vertueuse et sincère. Elle se trouve en effet déchirée entre deux exigences inconciliables de son être: la passion qu'elle éprouve pour Nemours qu'elle n'estime pas lui fait découvrir et redouter en elle-même un être sauvage et sensuel que son mari qu'elle estime et n'aime pas n'a pas su éveiller.

Challe, dont l'oeuvre constitue, pour l'époque, le tableau romanesque le plus complet de la condition féminine, adapte cette situation au niveau de la bourgeoisie. Dans la 7e histoire des *Illustres Françaises*, Mme de Londé, qui aime secrètement Dupuis, depuis sa jeunesse, est frigide avec son mari. Celui-ci est trop honnête homme pour la forcer (comme l'y autoriserait la législation du temps qui oblige la femme à se soumettre aux désirs de son époux).[19] Ils vivent donc comme frère et soeur; lui, prend ailleurs quelques compensations, ce dont elle souffre, tout en le comprenant.

A l'époque, c'est pourtant la situation inverse qui est la plus fréquente. Dans un mariage arrangé, comme ils le sont presque tous, on comprend aisément que, dépassé le plaisir de jouer les initiateurs pour la petite oie blanche, fraîche émoulue du couvent,

---

18. C'est le cas de tous les couples de l'oeuvre dont l'expérience conjugale ne dépasse jamais trois ou quatre ans.

19. L. Abensour, *La Femme et le féminisme avant la Révolution*, Paris, 1923, p. 8.

les maris préfèrent retourner à des divertissements plus croustillants, d'ailleurs à la mode et que la société multiplie à plaisir. Il n'est pas courant, en effet, qu'un mari tombe alors amoureux de sa femme.[20]!. Avec le naturel du paysan fraîchement débarqué au sein de la corruption parisienne, Jacob dresse, chez ses premiers maîtres, le constat de ce qui semble être la norme de la vie conjugale dans les milieux aisés. On vit sous le même toit, chacun des conjoints mène sa vie de son côté, elle a ses amants, lui, ses maîtresses, on envoie prendre des nouvelles l'un de l'autre chaque matin et voilà tout. Dans Gil Blas, même tableau, ou dans Manon, où Des Grieux justifie sa débauche, devant son père, par des exemples fameux de ducs et autres nobles entretenant, au su de tous, une ou plusieurs maîtresses en titre. D'ailleurs, on le sait, l'exemple vient de haut. Qui est véritablement reine de France de Marie Leczinska ou de la Pompadour?

On ne s'étonnera donc pas de voir l'infidélité masculine figurer au nombre des expériences de la vie d'une femme, condamnée en général au mariage de raison. L'inconstance cesse d'être un défaut, chez un homme, avant de devenir pour les roués la plus grande des qualités. Challe est trop réaliste pour y soustraire ses héroïnes; aussi, les confidences de la veuve et sa soeur sont-elles là pour nous renseigner sur ce qui attend la femme (*I.F.*, pp. 475 sq). Mariée par amour ou par convenance, elle sera toujours trompée finalement.

Or, la loi faite par et pour les hommes ne lui laisse aucune possibilité d'échapper à son infortune. Seuls, les sévices graves autorisent la demande de séparation de corps, celle des biens est plus difficile encore à obtenir.[21] Là encore, les *Mémoires* de Mme d'Epinay, rapportant son expérience de jeune mariée, bafouée, à moitié ruinée par un époux volage et inconséquent, et ne disposant à peu près d'aucun moyen de sauvegarder l'avenir matériel de ses enfants, viennent corroborer ce qu'évoquent les romans et montrer que tout cela n'est pas seulement "littéraire."

Passe encore si le mari ne fait que tromper sa femme! Challe, dans l'histoire de Dupuis, soulève un autre problème, lié à la propagation incroyable des maladies vénériennes pendant le 18e'

20. M. de Clèves, déjà, croyait devoir s'excuser, auprès de sa femme, d'éprouver une passion si inattendue et déplacée chez un mari.
21. Abensour, op. cit., p. 12.

siècle. Que peut faire une épouse saine contaminée par les mauvaises fréquentations de son mari? La veuve des *Illustres Françaises* a vécu ce cauchemar, en a dérobé à l'opinion le scandale et en est sortie finalement seule, bien résolue à ne jamais tenter une seconde expérience du mariage.[22]

Aliénée, dépendant d'un indifférent sinon d'un ennemi, qui la bafoue bien souvent, la femme peut-elle se risquer du moins à rendre au mari infidèle la monnaie de sa pièce? D'après les mémoires du temps, il semble que beaucoup ne s'en soient pas fait faute.[23]

Il est compréhensible que les romanciers, se protégeant par des préfaces moralisantes contre les attaques d'une critique bien pensante et assez réactionnaire, se soient montrés prudents sur ce sujet. Ainsi, Challe nous peint-il une seule adultère (*I.F.*, 6e nouvelle). Non content de la faire atrocement punir par son mari (elle en mourra finalement), il l'innocente ensuite en prouvant qu'elle fut vaincue grâce à un charme magique![24] Lesage ou Marivaux n'ont pas de tels scrupules et pourtant les nobles initiatrices de Jacob sont des veuves, affectant même la dévotion. Par contre, chez Laclos, très "fin de siècle," les femmes n'ont plus rien à envier aux roués mâles de l'oeuvre, qu'il s'agisse des "trois inséparables," ou de la vicomtesse qui, pour le plaisir d'un "réchauffé" avec Valmont, trompe la même nuit, à la fois, son mari et son amant.

Une constatation s'impose cependant. Même s'ils se veulent fidèles témoins du vécu de leur temps, les romanciers ne parlent pas sur le même ton des infidélités masculines ou féminines. Ce qui va de soi pour un homme, est plus difficilement admis pour la femme. L'exemple le plus intéressant est ici encore Challe. Les commentaires qui suivent l'histoire de l'adultère de Silvie voient s'affronter les maris de l'auditoire dans des positions fortement opposées. Des Frans, l'intéressé, n'a pas tué son épouse sur le coup, résistant à son premier mouvement de fureur. Il s'en est

22. Problème mentionné également par Abensour, op. cit., p. 12.
23. Abensour peut même dresser une curieuse carte de l'adultère, selon l'audace plus ou moins grande des femmes et l'endurance variable des maris, pp. 135-36.
24. Il est bien fait dans l'oeuvre d'autres mentions à l'infidélité féminine, mais il s'agit alors de personnages fort épisodiques (dans l'histoire de la Récard, par exemple), ou bien Challe laisse le lecteur conclure lui-même sur l'ambiguité d'un cas (la femme du vieux Dupuis).

lentement et cruellement vengé pendant trois mois de séquestra-
tion et de sévices divers, avant de s'en séparer définitivement.
Silvie, qui a choisi le couvent,' y est morte assez rapidement du
chagrin d'être répudiée par un mari qu'elle n'avait pas cessé
d'aimer. Or, si l'un des maris présents dit qu'il aurait pardonné,
l'autre affirme au contraire qu'il aurait tué sur-le-champ sa femme,
son amant et sa suivante en même temps pour être sûr du secret et
qu'ainsi il n'aurait pas craint d'être inquiété (*I.F.*, p. 401). Ceci est
tout à fait conforme à la loi du temps qui absout aisément le mari
assassin de sa femme adultère surprise en flagrant délit.[25]

Même si l'on doit à la vérité historique de mentionner que peu
de maris à l'époque usaient de la rigueur des lois en leur faveur,
force est de remarquer que, pour le même délit, l'homme a la loi
pour lui, la femme, rien. C'est ce que souligne la veuve des *Illustres
Françaises*, en disant spirituellement que les hommes ont bien
raison de céder à leurs caprices, puisqu'ils ont la loi avec eux, ce
que les femmes, elles, ne peuvent, bien entendu, pas se permettre
(p. 480).

Pour les romanciers de l'époque, le mariage paraît donc être
non une panacée, mais plutôt un mal nécessaire. C'est la veuve,
encore une fois, chez Challe, qui souligne son caractère social:
c'est, dit-elle, l'assemblage de deux êtres voulu par la société pour
prévenir les désordres (p. 477); et aussi, ajouterait le légiste, pour
protéger la propriété dont la famille est le garant. Ainsi, la femme,
éternelle mineure, doit-elle passer d'une domination à l'autre, des
parents, au mari, aux enfants, sans jamais être maîtresse d'elle-
même.

La Mère

Aux yeux de la société, c'est dans le maintien de la race que la
femme trouve sa raison d'être. Dans le roman, ce rôle reste la
plupart du temps sous-entendu, puisqu'il est normal.

Avant Rousseau, les joies de la maternité n'existent pas, non
plus en tant que thème romanesque. L'enfant n'intéresse guère la

---

25. Abensour, p. 9. S'il opte pour une autre solution, il peut la faire enfermer à vie,
sur simple lettre de cachet, et ses biens seront redistribués. Silvie, donnant ainsi une
dernière preuve d'amour, satisfait de son plein gré à cette dernière exigence en acceptant
de se dépouiller de toute sa fortune en faveur de son époux inflexible.

société du 18e siècle, avant l'*Emile*, et dans le roman, il n'est généralement qu'un accident. Les *Illustres Françaises* comportent plusieurs cas de filles-mères,[26] ainsi que des naissances illégitimes.[27] Comme dans la vie, Challe montre les mères aimant l'enfant qu'elles ont eu d'un homme aimé; l'enfant-accident, au contraire, n'est guère prisé et le romancier s'empresse généralement de le faire mourir.

La véritable importance de la mère va se révéler dans son rôle d'éducatrice. L'influence de la mère sur l'avenir de ses enfants par l'éducation est un thème romanesque traditionnel. Les rapports entre les enfants et leur mère sont la preuve de sa réussite ou de son échec. Tous les types de mères sont représentés, bien que certaines constantes se dégagent parfois, renvoyant peut-être à l'expérience personnelle du romancier. Chez Challe, le noeud de la 2e histoire est le lien tout-à-fait remarquable qui existe entre une mère veuve, qui s'est consacrée entièrement à l'éducation de son enfant, et son fils, timide et respectueux, nous dirions maintenant surprotégé. A l'opposé, l'amour déçu de Dupuis pour sa mère qui favorise visiblement son aîné, amour qui se tourne en haine explique, sans doute, en partie, la conduite immorale de Dupuis envers les femmes. Or, Challe s'est beaucoup mis en Dupuis. Le rôle de la mère peut être parfois entièrement négatif, comme dans les *Liaisons* où l'aveuglement de Mme de Volanges, son manque d'intimité avec sa fille sont une des causes indirectes de la perte de la jeune fille.

Le rapport des enfants avec leur mère varie en fonction du rôle social de cette dernière. Ainsi, dans *Gil Blas*, le héros, devenu favori du premier ministre, abandonne ses parents, n'aimant pas se rappeler qu'il est fils d'une simple duègne. A l'opposé, chez Marivaux, Tervire abandonnée par sa mère dans son enfance la retrouve pour la secourir quand elle est vieille et délaissée des enfants qu'elle a avantagés. Dans les *Illustres Françaises*, Angélique, qui veut parvenir au sommet de la réussite sociale, grâce à l'amour du riche et puissant Contamine, a honte du manque de distinction

---

26. La jeune fille séduite par Des Ronais. Célinie etc....
27. Idem.

de sa mère, pauvre femme qui a dû travailler pour l'élever et que sa fille meprise justement à cause de cela (*I.F.*, 2e nouvelle). Plus dramatique est le cas de Marie-Madeleine de l'Epine, dont la mère dépendant socialement du terrible, juge Des Prez, croira devoir, pour se ménager sa protection, se faire l'auxiliaire de sa vengeance et persécuter son propre sang, causant ainsi la mort de sa fille et de l'enfant qu'elle portait (*I.F.*, 3e nouvelle). On ne pouvait souligner plus fortement les effets de l'aliénation sociale.

A l'opposé, se trouve la mère idéale, généralement adoptive, comme Mme de Cranves pour Silvie, dans les *Illustres Françaises*, et Mme de Miran pour Marianne. Son importance réside dans le fait qu'elle incarne, par son rang social, la société et rend possible l'insertion normale à la place qui légitimement devrait lui revenir d'un être en porte-à-faux du fait de sa naissance (illégitime pour Silvie, noble mais invérifiable pour Marianne).

Ces mères sont souvent des veuves. Elles disposent donc, nous le verrons bientôt, d'une certaine autonomie dans la société, parfois même, elles sont chefs de famille, en attendant la majorité de leur enfant. D'un certain âge, elles incarnent avec douceur et largeur d'idées, comme Mme de Miran, la famille. Soucieuses, la plupart du temps, d'assurer à leurs enfants un bonheur qu'elles n'ont peut-être pas eu, elles ne sont pas prêtes à faire entendre, avec toute la rigueur voulue, la voix de la raison contre celle du coeur. Même quand elles semblent tenir aux prérogatives de leur rang, ou n'être qu'un instrument entre les mains de la famille toute puissante et fermée aux élans du coeur, leur fils joue rarement en vain auprès d'elles la carte du tendre. Peut-être, l'amour maternel les pousse-t-il à oser faire, pour leur enfant, ce qu'elles n'ont pas fait pour elles-mêmes: se rebeller contre l'ingérence de la société dans leur vie privée.

Que les romanciers souscrivent par là au préjugé qui montre la femme plus sensible aux élans de sa sensibilité, qu'ils traduisent peut-être aussi l'attitude de la loi du temps qui empêche une mère de faire obstacle à la volonté de ses enfants sans justification, alors que le père peut le faire en tout arbitraire, le fait demeure.[28]

---

28. Abensour, p. 24.

La Veuve

Nous venons de voir des mères veuves. Il est bien des sortes de veuves dans cette société, qui repose sur le mariage arrangé où la disproportion des âges est fort courante. Cet état paraît normal, dans la vie de la femme et, en outre, comparé aux autres que nous avons déjà étudiés, il semble que celui-ci n'ait que des avantages. Libérée par le mariage de la tutelle des parents, par le veuvage de celle du mari, au courant des réalités de la vie, très jeune encore bien souvent, et donc en possession de tous ses charmes, bien nantie, enfin, par la fortune du défunt, que pourrait encore souhaiter la veuve? Nombreuses semblent, d'ailleurs, celles qui comprennent les charmes de cet état. surtout quand elles viennent juste d'échapper aux contraintes d'un mariage malheureux. Qu'elles aient eu, en effet, le malheur ou le bonheur de devenir veuves, on en voit peu qui cherchent ensuite à changer d'état.[29] Celles qui le font se donnent ainsi, après parfois un long temps d'épreuve, la joie de satisfaire leur coeur. Ainsi, Mme de Londé, qui va enfin épouser Dupuis (*I.F.*, 7e nouvelle), ou Mme de Mongey, qui aime Des Frans en secret depuis si longtemps.

Pour les autres, il faut mettre à part les quelques exceptions qui resteront dans le veuvage fidèles à un cher disparu. La plupart du temps, une telle conduite a de tout autres motifs. Challe, avocat, connaissant bien les femmes et les lois, est tout à fait conscient des servitudes du mariage pour la femme; aussi comprend-il très bien, que celle qui a la chance d'y échapper, ne soit guère pressée de se jeter à nouveau dans l'esclavage. S'il a peint une Mme de Contemine, restée fidèle a la mémoire d'un mari aimé et se consacrant dans son veuvage à l'éducation de son fils, il a aussi présenté le personnage de veuve le plus révolutionnaire de son temps. Après un premier mariage très malheureux, elle s'en est détournée pour jamais et a opté définitivement pour la liberté et l'autonomie. Respectueuse, en apparence, des exigences de la société dont elle connait les rigueurs, surtout pour les faiblesses des veuves,[30] elle évite la débauche et le scandale. Amoureuse de

---

29. Il semble, en particulier, que les veuves de rang inférieur (Mme Dutour, Mme d'Alain chez Marivaux) se montrent plus respectueuses à l'égard de la répugnance du temps face au remariage des veuves.

30. Un épisode à l'intérieur de sa propre histoire illustre ce thème du sort ignominieux frappant la veuve qui s'est "abandonnée" sur la foi d'une promesse de mariage (cf. *I.F.*, p. 489 sq.).

Dupuis, elle mènera avec lui pendant cinq ans une vie d'amour et de fidélité, au sacrement près qu'elle refusera malgré les enfants et les supplications de son amant (*I.F.*, pp. 500-89).

C'est une conduite semblable, en apparence, mais avec des motivations et surtout des conséquences toutes différentes que mène l'inquiétante Mme de Merteuil. Elle a attendu puis traversé l'expérience de mariage de raison comme une des épreuves nécessaires à l'éducation qu'elle entend se donner à elle-même. Elle voit, ensuite, dans le veuvage la délivrance et surtout la situation idéale pour mettre ses théories en pratique. Dans son personnage de veuve respectable mais sensible qui désarme les autres femmes, coquettes ou dévotes, elle peut désormais jusqu'à la tombée finale des masques, mener à sa guise le programme de domination et d'exaltation d'elle-même dont elle a toujours rêvé. Conduisant avec une prudence jamais prise en défaut[31] une vie de débauche qui surpasse en audace celle des pires roués de son temps, elle s'arrange pour ne jamais donner prise aux autres tandis qu'elle-même recueille toujours de quoi perdre ou annihiler ses partenaires d'un moment. Parfaitement libre, parfaitement immorale, sans coeur et sans pitié, elle se grise de destruction et de noirceurs.

Voilà, imaginé par un cerveau d'homme féministe, le produit ultime de l'aliénation que la société hypocrite et misogyne fait subir aux femmes du 18e siècle. Bien sûr, à la fin de l'oeuvre, la Merteuil est démasquée, ruinée, défigurée, punie enfin. Mais la question est posée et ce n'est pas la morale expéditive du dénouement qui peut suffire comme réponse.

Faisant écho en fin de siècle aux interrogations et au témoignage de Challe à son début, elle révèle la mauvaise conscience de l'époque qui a, sans doute, le plus aimé mais aussi le plus maltraité la femme.

II. Ambiguité de la Condition Féminine

Ce rapide tour d'horizon sur une vie de femme nous l'a montrée, passant d'une domination à l'autre, en butte à tous les stades de sa vie aux conditionnements que la société lui impose, comme si elle ne pouvait remplir adéquatement son rôle qu'à

---

31. Sauf son faible incompréhensible pour Valmont, concession aux exigences du dénouement moral.

condition que son être fût nié dans ses aspirations les plus profondes. Par ailleurs, outre des cas nombreux et frappants de révolte contre cette situation, l'abondance même des exemples que nous ont fournis les romans montre quelle place y tiennent les personnages féminins et quel rôle, parfois capital, ils y jouent.

Une fois ce paradoxe posé, il est facile de trouver dans la réalité historique des équivalents de ce double visage féminin, présent dans le roman. D'ailleurs, ce n'est pas au 18e siècle seulement que la littérature, comme la vie sociale, témoigne de ce contraste étonnant. La femme, vivante incarnation du démon pour les Pères de l'Eglise, tenue par le droit romain, repris ensuite par le code Napoléon, pour le "sexe imbécile," ne cesse pourtant de hanter poètes et écrivains dont elle est la principale inspiration et la thème essentiel, en même temps qu'elle joue un rôle dans la société qui la nie en tant que personne.

Jamais peut-être le paradoxe du sort féminin n'a eu un tel relief qu'au 18e siècle. On comprend alors les Goncourt qui, dans le livre qu'ils consacraient à la femme de cette époque, ne craignaient pas de voir en elle le ressort caché mais bien réel de toute la vie du siècle.[32] Hypothèse séduisante que la première partie de cet exposé ne permet pas d'accepter sans réserves, mais que confirme en grande partie l'examen de la vie politique, littéraire et sociale du temps.

On sait quel rôle capital jouèrent les favorites du roi, les membres féminins des différentes coteries de la cour et plus encore, le véritable ministère qu'exerça la Pompadour pendant vingt ans auprès de Louis XV.

Dans les circonstances les plus importantes de la vie littéraire et sociale de ce siècle, c'est la même prédominance féminine qui s'affirme. Derrière chaque grand écrivain se dessine l'ombre d'une ou plusieurs Egéries: Voltaire et Mme du Châtelet, Mme d'Epinay, Sophie d'Houdetot et Rousseau, Diderot et Sophie Volland, pour ne citer que les plus célèbres. Les salons, où vie sociale et littéraire se retrouvent pour s'enrichir mutuellement, sont aussi animés par des femmes: Mme de Lambert, qui influence toute une génération

32. Les *Goncourt*, op. cit., p. 321. "La femme au 18e siècle est la cause universelle et fatale, l'origine des événements, la source des choses etc."

d'écrivains (Marivaux, Montesquieu), Julie de L'Espinasse et Mme Geoffrin auprès des Encyclopédistes. Non contentes d'inspirer le génie, elles créent à leur tour et l'on ne compte plus, à l'époque, les romancières de talent.[33]

Comment s'étonner que le roman reflète un phénomène aussi manifeste? Vivant dans un monde où l'emprise féminine se fait jour dans tous les domaines, les romanciers laissent transparaître cette expérience dans leur oeuvre. Découvrant dans leur vie privée comme dans les salons, les qualités intellectuelles et morales de leur compagne, ils s'intéressent à son sort autant qu'à son être. Aussi la femme que nous montrent ces romans n'est nullement seconde. En effet, comme l'annonce souvent le prénom féminin qui sert de titre au livre, elle est le ressort de l'action (Manon) tout autant que le personnage principal (Marianne). Même dans les romans à protagoniste masculin, on retrouve une femme à chaque étape importante de la vie du héros. C'est vrai dans *Gil Blas*, et plus encore dans le *Paysan Parvenu* ou dans les romans de Crébillon.[34] Dans les *Liaisons Dangereuses* enfin, Valmont apparaît le grand vaincu, doublement défait, sur son propre terrain de roué par sa rivale féminine, la Merteuil, et transformé par sa victime, la Présidente, qui lui a fait découvrir le véritable amour. Pourtant, lui seul aura une mort honorable, tandis que la marquise reçoit le châtiment qu'on a vu et que la présidente agonise dans des tourments inexprimables.

L'ambiguité demeure donc. Les romanciers du temps, qui affirment constamment ne vouloir dire que la vérité, vérifient la pensée de Seignobos citée en commençant. Ils témoignent de leur société. Marqués, qu'ils le veuillent ou non, par une vision du monde où la femme n'a pas de place dans la vie publique, ils expriment le paradoxe qui oppose la condition et le rôle de la femme. Ainsi, chez Challe, les *Illustres Françaises* ont assez d'intelligence et d'autonomie pour se faire une vie heureuse. A l'exception de la veuve, elles ne conçoivent celle-ci que dans le mariage. Une fois parvenues à ce but, elles s'empressent de se

33. Par exemple, Mme de Tencin ou Riccoboni, entre autres, à l'époque que concerne cet exposé.

34. Un type important, dans ce genre de roman, est celui de l'initiatrice dans le domaine sexuel et social à la fois.

soumettre à l'homme de leur choix. A lui l'action sociale, dont elles seront seulement les inspiratrices intelligentes et discrètes. Tout comme elles ont triomphé par des moyens féminins: la souplesse, la ruse et surtout la vertu, elles incarnent, face à l'activité mâle, l'équilibre de la vie intérieure, de la nature, plus proche des valeurs. Elles peuvent être heureuses, donc, parce qu'elles ne remettent pas en cause l'ordre social. Par contre, la veuve, qui veut vivre en homme, doit disparaître (*I.F.*, 7e nouvelle, p. 502).

Outre les exemples de la première partie, de nombreux épisodes de roman témoignent 'de la dureté du sort féminin: les actrices bafouées dans *Gil Blas*,[35] la veuve, Mme Dutour, lingère qui vit à peine de son travail,[36] Mme de l'Epine qui doit laisser mourir sa fille pour ne pas perdre son procès (*I.F.*, 5e nouvelle), autant d'exemples de l'injustice sociale envers les femmes. Et Manon, qui se vend parce qu'à défaut de naissance, l'argent est la seule valeur qui lui donne l'être dans la société corrompue de la Régence. Pourtant comme elle est roturière et femme, elle paiera de la déportation et de la mort ses errements, tandis que le jeune noble Des Grieux pourra se racheter et rentrer dans le droit chemin moral et social! La mort pour celles qui ne jouent pas le jeu. Mortes, les adultères, Silvie ou la présidente, même si la magie ou les sombres machinations du vice les ont seules vaincues, morte socialement, Mme de Merteuil, qui a surpassé les hommes dans l'art de tromper et de vaincre à tout prix!

Mais le roman n'est pas un reportage. Aussi, Challe peut-il faire épouser Contemine à Angélique par le pouvoir de sa seule vertu, malgré l'énorme distance sociale (*I.F.*, 2e nouvelle); de même Marivaux fait retrouver à Marianne la position sociale qui lui revient, à grand renfort d'heureux hasards. Les deux romanciers ont exprimé ce qu'ils auraient souhaité tout en témoignant que cela n'était pas possible dans la réalité. L'heureux dénouement est pour le roman, les énormes difficultés rencontrées par les héroïnes pour la réalité.

La place de la femme dans le roman du 18e siècle ne

---

35. Voir dans *Gil Blas* le récit de Lucinde ou de Laure.
36. *Vie de Marianne.*

pourrait-elle, alors, apparaître comme une sorte de compensation offerte à son infériorité réelle dans la société? En l'exaltant dans leur oeuvre les romanciers ne cherchent-ils pas à libérer leur mauvaise conscience de membres d'un système injuste?

L'hypothèse paraît plausible, quand on constate, que dans le roman comme dans l'histoire, le triomphe féminin reste limité à quelques individualités remarquables qui se détachent sur une masse assez ignorante, soucieuse surtout de son charme, se laissant facilement réduire au rôle d'utilité que lui offre la société. La plupart des romancières, d'ailleurs, semblent souscrire, plus que leurs confrères, aux images traditionnelles de l'être et du rôle féminins, imposées par la société.

Ainsi la peinture de la condition féminine se révèle, au 18e siècle, un autre dilemne du roman que les auteurs n'ont pas pu résoudre. Ils ont eu du moins le mérite de le faire apparaître, souvent avec une acuité remarquable. Aussi rencontre-t-on, dans les oeuvres de ce temps, des images très contrastées de la femme, qui reflètent la perplexité des auteurs. Qu'ils en fassent la personnification de l'amour (Manon) ou le Mal absolu (La Merteuil), elles incarnent toute la difficulté d'être femme. Seul, Challe a peint des êtres humains, aux mêmes aspirations que les hommes, prenant lentement conscience de leur identité, faisant leur bonheur par les moyens que la société avait prévus pour les en priver et méritant bien pour cela leur titre: Les *Illustres Françaises*.

Marie Laure Swiderski

Rousseau's Sexism Revolutionized

Women in the French Revolution were born anew, cleansed of the corruption of the ancien regime; they were seen as both strong and feminine, powerful enough to defend *la Patrie*. First and foremost, they were the virtuous mothers of the French people regenerated by revolution. The pamphlets so stating were written by women in the early years of the revolution; they provide considerable evidence that their inspiration derived from Jean-Jacques Rousseau.[1]

To twentieth century feminists, Rousseau is the *bête noire*, the founding father of male sexism in the western world. According to them, some of the *philosophes* had a good word about women, provided they were privileged to an education; but Rousseau, it is said, led the counter-revolution against enlightened feminism.[2] This may be the case. Nevertheless, Rousseau's *Émile* was devoured by women readers before the French Revolution. Unless we conclude that all those women moved to tears by Rousseau were idiots — a very sexist conclusion — we must reexamine what there was in *Émile* that appealed to them. Although *Émile's*

1. The author thanks Prof. James Leith of Queen's University, Ontario, and Beatrice F. Hyslop, Professor emeritus of Hunter College, New York, for calling attention to these women's pamphlets. The size of this paper ruled out the use of women's newspapers, educational tracts, memoirs, accounts of societies and civic fêtes during the French Revolution to assess Rousseau's influence on women. The author is aware that some women's pamphlets might be satirical "put-ons" but, nevertheless, they are worthwhile.
2. Simone de Beauvoir, *The Second Sex*, New York, 1970, p. 99; Eva Figes, *Patriarchal Attitudes*, London, 1970, pp. 94-103; David Williams, "Aspects of Feminism in the Enlightenment," pp. 12, 15 (paper read to 2nd annual Inter-University Seminar for Eighteenth Century Studies, November 1968).

Sophie was undeniably a submissive creature, we find Rousseau's women were "beautiful people" whose moral ascendancy over men made them necessary for man's happiness; they were man's natural companion, and not his slave.

The historian, Jules Michelet, who placed women in the vanguard of the French Revolution, claimed that Rousseau's *Émile* a generation earlier fired their hearts with two sparks: Humanity and Maternity.[3] We are not here to reassess Rousseau's sexist ideas but to show how Rousseau influenced the women who wrote pamphlets during the French Revolution to ask for social and political rights. No doubt the rights demanded by these women would have turned Rousseau who was then in his grave, but so would have the Committee of Public Safety's implementation of Rousseau's concept of the general will.

On the eve of the French Revolution women of the Third Estate or *roturier* or common class, and sometimes of the *noblesse*, presented pamphlets addressed to the King, or to the Estates-General — the assembly of the three orders of clergy, nobility and commoners called by Louis XVI to meet in Versailles in May 1789. Sometimes these women's pamphlets were entitled "cahiers" or "cahiers de doléance," after the notebook of grievances officially drawn up by electoral assemblies throughout France to instruct their deputies in Versailles. The women's "cahiers" were unofficial but the very name reminded readers that women were excluded from the Estates-General. Most, but not all, women's pamphlets supported the Third Estate which wanted voting by head, and not by separate order, so as to provide France with a constitution based on equality of the law, to end the privileges of the nobility and the clergy.

France in 1789 was in acute, economic distress; society was turned upside down and the women advocated one cure: Rousseau's regeneration of *moeurs* or morality. Turning on their own sex as corrupted by luxury and devoted to frivolity, the women blamed the ancien regime and looked toward the constitution to regain their natural role. Almost unanimously they called for better education for women so as to become better

3. Jules Michelet, *Les Femmes de la Révolution*, Paris, 1855, p. 12.

wives and mothers, whose natural task was to educate the children of both sexes. Sometimes their pamphlets called for an education for poor girls so they could find decent work and not be led astray. Vice was unanimously condemned; prostitutes were to be rounded up, segregated, treated perhaps with compassion, but always to be distinguished from virtuous women.

Reading the women's pamphlets of 1789 and 1790, we sense their marriages were not happy. They wanted to be respected companions of their husbands, as Rousseau had promised, but now they asked for laws to protect them from marital abuse and give them some control over family property and their children. Far from believing they were insignificant because they were "naturally" the weaker sex, women claimed from Rousseau a moral superiority to men. From this, they concluded they were entitled to rights which were undreamed of by Rousseau.

One pamphlet early in 1789 on the influence of women on civil and political order quoted Rousseau for its epigraph: "Les hommes feront toujours ce qu'il plaira aux femmes. L'ascendant que les femmes ont sur les hommes, n'est pas un mal; c'est un présent que leur a fait la nature, pour le bonheur du genre humain."[4] Therefore, claimed this anonymous writer, women with their fertile genius (a Rousseauist attribute), had the power to defend liberty. Mothers of families should convert their homes to schools of patriotism, for it was in the midst of peaceful, domestic life that the foundations of liberty were assured. Under despotism women's charms were objects of luxury and commerce; love was unknown. Now women could influence their husbands to renounce all odious privileges, to regard each other as brothers, to carry to the nation's assembly this patriotic unselfishness.

Other women's pamphlets complained of their neglected or vicious education.[5] Not that they wished an education to usurp the authority of men. The sciences would make women "mixed beings" who were rarely faithful wives or good mothers of

---

4. De l'Influence des femmes dans l'order civil et politique, Eleathéropolis, 1789.
5. Pétition des femmes du Tiers-Etat au Roi. 1er Jan. 1789; Requête des femmes pour leur admission aux Etats-Généraux, 1788; Remontrances, plaintes et doléances des dames françoises à l'occasion de l'assemblée des Etats-Généraux, M.L.P.P.D.St.L. 1789.

families. This was what Rousseau had told them, but now the women begged the King to establish free schools for girls, so they could learn their language as well as principles of morality. An angrier woman's pamphlet reproached men for giving them a narrow education which was the basis for men's prejudice and responsible for extinguishing women's talent.

Does the happiness of men depend on that of women, asked one woman's pamphlet later in 1789 of the gentlemen in the National Assembly.[6] The answer she provided was yes, because the most sacred of man's duties was to make happy the companion which nature had destined to complete *his* happiness. This much was from Rousseau, but then the writer added that the idea of a companion excluded the idea of man's authority. Why were women born to strew flowers in man's private life and receive in recompense only chains, torments, injustices? The writer asked the National Assembly for a decree to oblige men to marry women without dowries. She resorted to another of Rousseau's tenets, that man should choose his companion by following only his heart. The writer (who added in a footnote that she was a wife and a mother of boys) claimed that the dowry was responsible for the deplorable lot of women whose husbands dissipated it and then abandoned them. Society owed these women some means of existence; she recommended that some of the better positions held only by men be given to capable women. The unfortunate girls who were unable to buy a husband and vegetated in poverty should be placed according to their talents.[7]

Decent work for women was a frequent concern in these pamphlets. It was thought that men should not be allowed to exercise trades which by nature belonged to women, such as women's fashions or sewing, while women, with a Rousseauist regard for the "natural" separation of the sexes, were not to

6. *Motions adressées a l'Assemblée nationale en faveur du sexe*, chez l'auteur, rue des Poitevins, no. 20, Paris, 1789.

7. *Ibid.*, pp. 7-9. A third class of more miserable women were in the cloisters where the author of the pamphlet remained until she was twenty-five years old. They were innocent victims of their passions or their families. Religion should come freely from the heart (Rousseau's idea). Women who wished to remain in convents should stay there in peace, but those who were forced to enter would thank the National Assembly for their freedom.

intrude on masculine occupations, "... que l'on nous laisse au moins l'aiguille & le fuseau nous nous engageons à ne manier jamais le compas ni l'équerre."[8] Work for poor girls was the antidote for vice on the streets. Furious that some prostitutes did so well they were mistaken in their carriages for duchesses, one women's pamphlet called for the confiscation of their property.[9]

Bachelors were scorned in these pamphlets as social parasites who should pay double in taxes and be denied positions belonging to fathers of families.[10] Because the true wealth of the country was its population — an idea generally held in the eighteenth century — celibacy should be taxed, men obliged to marry girls without dowries, and married women made happy.

For women were at least half if not the greater part of the nation. Sometimes the pamphlets added to describe this half, "la plus saine," and sometimes, "la plus intéressante," and once, "la plus aimable, la plus douce et quelquefois la plus sensée."[11] These superlatives were Rousseauist. According to these pamphlets, women's moral ascendancy over men, a gift of nature, entitled them to *political* rights, which was not what Rousseau had in mind.

One modest pamphlet from women of the Third Estate denied wanting to send deputies to the Estates-General, and admitted a Rousseauist weakness of the sex for being personally influenced in political matters. Other pamphlets expressed rage that their political exclusion was a violation of nature.[12] Demanding the *restoration* of natural rights, which Rousseau intended for men but not for women, they claimed that women throughout history had played significant political roles; biblical, Homeric, noble Roman ladies from Plutarch and German women from Tacitus

8. *Pétition des femmes du Tiers-Etat au Roi; Motion de la pauvre Javotte, deputée des pauvres femmes,* Paris, 1790.

9. *Cahier des représentations & doléances du beau sexe, adressé au Roi au moment de la tenue des Etats-Généraux,* 1789.

10. *Requête des femmes pour leur admission aux Etats-Généraux.*

11. *Cahier des représentations & doléances du beau sexe . . .;* Requête des dames à l'Assemblée nationale, 1789.

12. *Pétitions des femmes du Tiers-Etats au Roi; Protestations des dames françoises, contre la tenue des Etats prétendus Généraux; convoques a Versailles, pour le 27 Avril 1789; Requête des dames à l'Assemblée nationale.*

served as examples. Women had lost their natural political rights in the more modern age of monarchical despotism when vile, nocturnal political intrigues degraded them. It was suggested to the Estates-General that capable abbesses could represent the clergy, noble women who held fiefs, and many respectable women of the Third Estate could serve as deputies. Another writer agreed, but she proposed as an alternative a fourth estate for women, equal in numbers to all the men. Later in the year a pamphlet reminded the gentlemen of the National Assembly that in the last resort their decisions were to be brought back to women's tribunals to be annulled or confirmed according to the interests of the general welfare.[13]

On October 5 and 6, 1789, Parisian women exercised their rights during one of the most famous *journées* or events of the revolution. The women of the markets, desperate from the shortage of bread, led other women (some of them middle-class) to the palace at Versailles.[14] They were followed by the National Guards who marched to avenge the insult to the national tricolors at a royal banquet. The King and the National Assembly listened to delegations of these women. On October 6th the women escorted in triumph the royal family to Paris where they would be removed from aristocratic intrigues.

How political were the market women in the October days? And how did they think of themselves as women? Certainly these women never read Rousseau, nor was it likely they were influenced by his ideas, even in diluted form. Earlier in the year the women of the markets addressed to the Estates-General a pamphlet, dictated in colloquial French to a scribe.[15] Their demands were naively couched to disguise political awareness. They complained of the conditions of their trade, the lack of protection from the winds in the open market; they hated the tax

13. *Requête des femmes pour leur admission aux Etats-Généraux; Remontrances . . . des dames françoises; Protestations des dames françoises.*

14. George Rudé, *The Crowd in the French Revolution*, Oxford, 1959, pp. 73-75. According to the March 1790 police enquiry, *Procedure criminelle au Châtelet de Paris sur la journée du 6 octobre*, more than 6,000 women, some armed and some bourgeois *femmes à chapeau*, took part or were compelled to march to Versailles.

15. *Cahier des plaintes & doléances des Dames de la halle & des marchés de Paris, redigé au grand sallon des Porcherons*, le premier dimanche de Mai, pour être présenté à Messieux les Etats généraux.

collectors at the city's barriers; they hated the king's ministers who had deceived the good King; they hated the bishops for their selfish, luxurious lives, but thought that the poor priests should marry because they were flesh and bones like themselves. They complained of the hospitals with four dying in a bed, and the children who contracted diseases there and learned vices. The rich, they thought, who speculated in grain should be punished for having caused the death of so many poor people. Unpolitical, perhaps not, but this pamphlet was not concerned with women's rights. Yet on October 5th they organized other women to march to Versailles. The reality of French life among all classes validated Rousseau. In a pre-industrial society women's work was not too far from home, but activities outside the home were separate from men's.

By 1790 the considerable presence of women was manifest in the galleries of the National Assembly. A woman's legislative viewpoint based on, or rather using Rousseau's ideas, was written by Mlle Jodin at Angers.[16] In answer to some anti-feminist remarks concerning divorce which appeared on February 6th in the *Mercure de France*, she reminded her readers that women were also citizens, and as the essential half of society they must participate in the promulgation of a legislative code to restore morality. Morals were for the body politic, as for the physical body, the source of strength and energy. Quoting Rousseau who had thought Parisian women mixed too freely with men, and assumed the boldness of men and even their walk, she criticized him for not adding that women also had the virtue of men and their talent. Women were not on this earth as another species than man, and one sex was not meant to be the oppressor of the other. She refuted a ridiculous claim of male superiority — that women were incapable of grasping political ideas but excelled in domestic economy. Such debates, she thought, were injurious to nature, for men were born to be friends of women, and not rivals. In France, women's natural role was to legislate morality which could not be regulated as other laws — and here Rousseau was quoted again —

16. *Vues législatives pour les femmes adressées à l'Assemblée nationale par Mlle Jodin, fille d'un citoyen de Genève*, Angers, 1790.

because laws influenced morals only when they were backed by them. To make women the legislators of morals would be to *restore* their natural rights which had been wrongly appropriated; history proved that women's jurisdiction was not an innovation.

Mlle Jodin, in this eighty-six page tract, outlined a project for a tribunal composed of women only of high moral character — fifty women sitting in Paris in a Chamber of Conciliation and eighty in a Civil Chamber. The Chamber of Conciliation would examine causes of separation in marriages, listen to complaints of widows, of daughters entering convents or forced into marriages, of breach of promises. The Civil Chamber would have jurisdiction over disturbances and women's conduct in public places. In addition, the women's tribunals would provide asylum for needy, old women, workshops for idle women, and hospitals for sick women.

In regulating the laws, good morals or, as she cited, Rousseau's "l'esprit social" would preside over the institution. Women were to legislate public morality with the same authority as a mother had over private morality in the bosom of her family. But marriage as an indissoluble tie, she claimed, was unnatural. All institutions, and here she used Rousseau's *Contrat social*, which placed man in contradiction with himself, were worth nothing. If a union of two sexes were contrary to nature in the duration of affections, the union must be dissolved. As Jean-Jacques observed, she wrote, man in a state of savagery thought all women were good; during the progress of civilization he departed from natural ways to become a tyrant. Mlle Jodin looked forward to a return to simplicity, where marriage was not contracted for estates and fortune, but woman would be man's loving companion, sheltered by his strength in her feeble old age. A proper Rousseauist conclusion, but what had Rousseau thought of divorce?

In 1791 the *Cercle social* was an enlightened group sponsored by the *Amis de la Vérité*, a society concerned with women's education. A Dutch woman, Etta Paln d'Aelders, had addressed the society on November 26, 1790, itself a daring act, and organized women's branches affiliated to the society throughout France. A woman's pamphlet printed by the *Cercle social* in 1791 complained that in the twenty-six months that the legislature assembled, half the human race was still denied natural rights.[17] These rights, which were a moral force given women by nature, had been taken away in past centuries by the artifice of priests. (1791 was an anti-clerical year, the year of the oath of the clergy to the Constitution.) Deprived of these rights, women devoted themselves to degrading frivolity. Rousseau had charmed the women into returning to their more gentle functions, wrote this author, but he himself did not understand that a general system was needed to rehabilitate women, or perhaps the times did not permit him this understanding. In the new constitution, she asked, what recompense was provided for the most sacred of duties, the caring for children? Women were still without rights, without property, without power. It was the moment for France to declare that the two sexes were equal.

In September 1791, when the National Assembly disbanded upon completing the constitution, the feminist Olympe de Gouges wrote a *Déclaration des Droits de la Femme et de la Citoyenne*. It closely parallelled in form and content the seventeen articles in the Declaration of the Rights of Man decreed by the National Assembly in 1789. Olympe de Gouges was an unusual woman, a woman of letters although virtually illiterate, daughter of humble parents, though hinting at noble but illegitimate birth. She had come to Paris at eighteen and by 1785 had written thirty plays which were dictated at great speed.[18] With the coming of the French Revolution she wrote many political tracts with strong monarchist sentiments. She sympathized with the miseries of the poor, and urged taxes on luxuries; she wanted French women to make heroic sacrifices by emulating the women of Rome who gave their jewels to aid their country. In *Le bonheur primitif de l'homme* she attacked luxury and vice among women and revealed

17. *Du Sort actuel des femmes.* De l'imprimerie du Cercle Social, rue du Théâtre François, no. 4, 1791.

18. For a recent account of Mme de Gouges, see Paule-Marie Duhet, *Les Femmes et la Révolution, 1789-1794,* Paris, Julliard, 1971, pp. 67-75, 83-86; older works: Michelet, *Les Femmes de la Révolution,* pp. 104-107; E. Boursin and A. Challamel, *Dictionnaire de la Révolution française,* Paris, 1893, pp. 559-60; Ch. L. Chassin, La Génie de la Révolution, Paris, 1865, I; Léon Abensour, *Histoire du féminisme,* Paris, 1921: Léopold Lacour, *Trois femmes de la Révolution,* Paris, 1900: Winifred Stephens, *Women of the French Revolution,* London, 1922: Marc de Villiers, *Histoire des clubs de femmes et des légions d'Amazones,* Paris, 1910.

the influence of Rousseau.[19]

Her Declaration of the Rights of Women was dedicated to the Queen — an odd dedication late in 1791 when Marie Antoinette was detested for conspiring with foreign powers and for influencing the King recently to attempt flight. In the dedication Olympe de Gouges came to her real message: unless women's rights were restored, the revolution was not going to work. The preamble to the Declaration stated that the sex superior in heart as in courage declared under the auspices of the Supreme Being the seventeen rights which followed. Article X provided her a famous and, what was later, a prophetic quotation: "La femme a le droit de monter sur l'échafaud; elle doit avoir également celui de monter à la tribune."[20] Article XI guaranteed free thought for women. In article XIII women were to contribute equally to meet public expenditures but they were to have the same rights of public employment as men. In article XVII property was a right of both sexes, married or single.

In the postamble to the Declaration she exhorted women to assert their rights, full equality under the law. However, her thinking was Rousseauist. Women must become a moral force. Legislators must include women in their plans for a national education. Under the ancien regime, marriage had become vicious, the tomb of confidence. Inhuman laws refused the children of unmarried women rights to the property of the fathers. Prejudice must fall, morals be purified and nature regain its rights. This Rousseauist problem had a revolutionary solution. Olympe de Gouges wanted to join the rights of women to all the rights of men.

Attached to her Declaration was what she called a *Contrat social*, or marriage contract that would have sent Rousseau reeling. We, so and so, by our own wish are united during our life for the duration of our mutual affections under the following conditions: our fortunes are held in common, reserving, if we are separated, our property in favor of our children, or in case of a private

19. Some early pamphlets by Olympe de Gouges: *Rémarques patriotiques*, 1788; *Le Bonheur primitif de l'homme ou les rêveries patriotiques*, 1789; *Action héroïque d'une françoise, ou la France sauvée par les femmes*, 1789.
20. *Les Droits de la femme. . .*, p. 9.

inclination, children from whatever bed they came from; all children had the right to the names of the mothers and fathers who avowed them. This might be open marriage based on the rights of nature, but was it ever acknowledged by Rousseau?

Such was what Olympe de Gouges thought in September 1791. On September 20, 1792, two days before the National Convention declared France a Republic, important laws concerning marriage and the right of divorce were decreed.[21] The women who had used Rousseau's ideas earlier in the revolution won some of their demands. Marriage became a civil contract which like any other could be dissolved. Children born of the dissolved marriage were generally entrusted to the mother if they were girls, so were boys less than seven years old; above that age the boys were handed over to the father. The parents, however, could make other arrangements. The children would retain their right of inheritance; boys and girls were to inherit in equal proportions.

The National Convention on December 19, 1793 passed a decree for national education, both public and coeducational. Schoolmasters and schoolmistresses (indicating a separation of sexes in the primary grades) were placed under the supervision of municipalities where they could be denounced for violations of public morality.[22]

Would Rousseau have been pleased? We cannot know if Olympe de Gouges was pleased; she was guillotined on November 4, 1793. Some writers today conclude she died because she was a feminist.[23] However, her *Testament politique*, written on June 4 of that year, a few weeks before her arrest, provides the cause of

21. These laws are translated in *A Documentary Survey of the French Revolution*, ed. John Hall Stewart, New York, 1966, pp. 322-40. The preamble to the decree for divorce referred to "a consequence of individual liberty, which would be doomed by indissoluble engagements. . . ," phrases similar to Mlle Jodin's *Vues législatives. . .*in 1790. According to Henri Gregoire, at the time constitutional bishop of Blois, in the first twenty-seven months of this law, there were 5,994 divorces in Paris, of which more than half were requested by women. *Histoire des sectes religieuses*, Paris, 1828, I, 188.

22. Stewart, *A Documentary Survey. .*, pp. 515-19. It is questionable whether this law was fully implemented during the French Revolution. A decree on November 17, 1794 provided for primary instruction of both sexes. The practical and moral influence of Rousseau's *Emile* on this decree is obvious. Stewart, pp. 616-19.

23. This opinion is expressed by Jacques Godechot in his preface to *Histoire de la presse féminine en France des origines à 1848*, by Evelyne Sullerot, Paris, A. Colin, 1966, Duhet, p. 86.

her downfall — lack of political understanding. Certainly her offer the year before to defend the King on trial was a political blunder. Her condemnation of the sans-culottes who had purged the Convention, and of Robespierre and the Jacobins who were in power, led to the guillotine.[24]

A reaction had set in against women in politics after Charlotte Corday assassinated Marat in July 1793. On October 16, Marie Antoinette mounted the scaffold; on November 8, so did Mme Roland, leader and wife of the minister of the defeated faction. Chaumette, the procureur of the Paris Commune, condemned them as unnatural women, as monsters. In this radical period of the French Republic, societies of women, such as the *Femmes républicaines révolutionnaries*, were suppressed by decree. The reasons given by the deputy Amar of the Committee of General Security on the 9th of brumaire, year II of the revolutionary calendar (October 30, 1793) derived from Rousseau's sexism. Women, according to Amar, did not have abilities for political life: their natural vocation was the care of children and family.[25]

The few women who sought to exercise political rights were condemned as unnatural and counter-revolutionary. These women, it is true, were either exceptional or marginal to the mainstream of women during the French Revolution. Robespierre praised the women of the October days, as well as the heroic sacrifices of mothers who gave their sons to the revolution. However, he wrote of the society of *Femmes républicaines révolutionnaires*:

Elles sont chargées d'apprendre à l'univers que la pudeur est un préjugé, que la distinction des talens, et des occupations

24. *Testament politique d'Olympe de Gouges,* le 4 Juin, 1793; *Avis pressant à la Convention, par une vraie Republicaine.* Olympe de Gouge, le 15 Dèc. 1792.

25. For Amar's speech, *Journal de la Montagne,* no. 151 (Oct. 31, 1793), p. 1018; on the society, *les Républicaines revolutionnaires, Journal de la Montagne,* no. 108 (18 Sept. 1793), no. 117 (27 Sept. 1793), no. 122 (2 Oct. 1793), no. 128 (8 Oct. 1793), no. 129 (8 Oct. 1793), no. 150 (30 Oct. 1793). Also, *Rapport fait par la citoyenne Lacombe a la société des républicaines revolutionnaires* de ce qui s'est passé le 16 Septembre a la Société des Jacobins. A recent secondary work, Marie Cerati, *Le Club des citoyennes républicaines révolutionnaires,* Paris. Editions sociales, 1966. sociales, 1966.

des deux sexes, n'est autre chose qu'un invention de l'aristocratie; que les hommes doivent abandonner aux femmes la tribune et les sièges du senat; et tous les clubs masculins doivent ressortir au tribunal des présidentes révolutionnaires. . . . Elles sont stériles comme le vice; mais en revanche, elles déclameront contre les fondateurs de la république, et calomnieront les représentans du peuple. . .[26]

Robespierre, the leading disciple of Rousseau's morality during the French Revolution, denied women their political rights because they could be used by factions to destroy the general will of the people, Rousseau's concept in the *Contrat social*. Therefore, women were granted only social rights which would revolutionize social morality.

It would be tempting, but a mistake, to conclude that Rousseau was interpreted to fit whatever was needed. In the early years of the revolution, women correctly interpreted Rousseau to ask for rights based on their moral ascendance. This moral regeneration was impossible in the corruption of the ancien regime. Women looked to the French nation regenerated by revolution to gain their rights based on morality. The political rights refused women during the French Revolution were further removed from Rousseau's ideas.

Ruth Graham

26. *Pièces trouvées dans les papiers de Robespierre et complices*, Brumaire, l'an III, pp. 95-96.

The Reform of Subject and Style in Ballet-Pantomime at Vienna between 1740-1767

We shall be dealing in this paper with developments of music and dance that took place around the middle of the eighteenth century. Of necessity we shall deal only with some sharply defined details in the vast complex of questions connected with the change from theatrically staged dance as spectacle (an extention of the court dance as social participation) to the dance as an art of story-telling through the combined forms of the traditional dance and mime: ballet-pantomime. It should be stated here that the choice of particular events for emphasis may be explained by the term *plausible interpretation* (as used by Louis Gottschalk in his interpretation of the French *Philosophes*).[1] As Mr. Gottschalk puts it, "this contention is based on the principle that whereas the evaluation of evidence in the historiographical process is as scientific as any other process that examines a recognizeable object for data that may be credited, debated, or discredited for a larger context," the choice of a particular viewpoint is a subjective and imaginative decision that depends not so much on general acceptance as it must on a version of structural logic.

The period from 1740 to 1770 has often been characterized as embracing critical years in European musical history, with the implication that the greater change or more decisive change took place during this thirty year span than in others, say 1720-1750 or 1760-1790. The assumption behind this hypothesis, often only

1. Louis Gottschalk, "A Plausible Interpretation of the French *Philosophes?*" *Studies in Eighteenth Century Culture,* Volume 2, *Irrationalism in the Eighteenth Century,* edited by Harold E. Pagliaro, (Cleveland and London: The Press of Case Western Reserve University, 1972). p. 4.

stated in the absence of another approach, is that the decades between 1740 and 1770 witnessed the change from the so-called "baroque" period to the so-called "classical" period. There are two more hypotheses that become involved as well. "Every man that purports to express the nature or the quality of a period is already prejudicial," as Jan Huizinga stated in his *Tasks of Cultural History*.[2] Historians, musical or otherwise, have often warned about becoming entrapped by the terminological crutches handed down by the past. Yet, in too many cases what was yesterday's convenient construction is promoted into today's donnée. The strongest temptation of all is the will to close whatever subject has been put into a system. Unfortunately, for all attempts at final systematization, the constant historical fact is an elusive element; it changes according to distance and perspective. The issues raised by periodization and sub-periodization are never settled. The periods we deal with so lovingly in music history are at best conveniences, possible explanations for the groupings and relationships of events. As with any explanation, these possibilities must be ever tested against others, and when necessary modified and replaced.

It has been held that the baroque-classic dichotomy, as well as the classic-romantic, no longer serves to illuminate the main issues in eighteenth-century music: that, in fact, it has been obscuring some issues, and is out of step with recent historiography in other fields. The main issue here is what was called the *modern* musical style of the eighteenth century. Before going further it might be helpful to consider several negative propositions. These take the form of five events that did not happen until after 1770.

1. The *Basso Continuo* practise was not abandoned — it continued to form an independent part of most concerted music with large forces throughout the century. The harpsichord continued to flourish along with it, especially in theater music.

2. *Crescendi* and *diminuendi*, contrast dynamics and an elaborately nuanced tone production were not *discovered*. They formed an essential part of Italian singing technique, accounted by eighteenth century critics to have reached its peak about 1730.

2. Jan Huizinga, *Wege der Kulturgeschichte*, (Munich: Drei Masken Verlag, 1930) pg. 3.

3. Finely nuanced orchestral effects along the same lines were not *first* introduced (although commentators of the late eighteenth century such as Charles Burney and Christian Friederich Daniel Schubart, were impressed enough by what they heard of European orchestras at Mannheim and other centers, to believe they were). De Brosses wrote from Italy marvelling at the chiaroscuro effects commonly produced by large orchestras in great theaters, and mentioning a dynamic range from pianissimo to fortissimo.

4. The symphony was not invented. Like the symphony orchestra, its framework came from the *Sinfonia avanti l'opera*, while much of its content, in particular its mixture of the serious with low comic effects, which certainly annoyed musicians and critics in northern Europe, derived from *opera buffa*.

5. There was certainly no sudden emergence of a prevalence of simple melody, supported by chordal accompaniments, and static, repeated-note basses. This trend, along with a simpler and broader approach to harmonic rhythm, had already prevailed in the operatic arias of a generation earlier.

The place to look, then, for the movement toward the progressive style of mid-century is in the musical theater as represented by opera and dance; and by this should be understood what the first half of the century meant by opera: not comic opera, a vast and vitally important subject, nor *Tragèdie lyrique*, also vast in extent. "Opera," unqualified, meant the serious "opera in musica" — the most demanding art form of the eighteenth century.

The question is how critical were these three decades after 1740? The stylistic turns of the period manifested themselves in ballet and pantomime during these years, just as they were in *opera seria*. The overlapping of the old and new (Baroque Classic) traditions applied not only to so obvious an example as Johann Sebastian Bach's last instrumental works, but also, by logical extention, to those theories of reform in the musical stage which led to the Viennese reforms of opera by Gluck. In response to the same years of crisis and change an active part was taken by ballet and ballet-pantomime in Vienna.

The sudden closing of the Vienna opera under Maria Theresa after the death of Josef I, created a situation that allowed for an emphasis upon and a development of a completely different medium – the tragic element in narrative dance, based on classic themes. This particular tendency had begun to develop gradually in the dances provided for opera scenes and intemezzi from the beginning of the century: however, Vienna became a particularly appropriate place for a surge in this development during the theatrical leadership of Count Giacomo Durazzo (1717-1794). In fact, Vienna took over the complete leadership in European dance from Stuttgart, especially after Jean-Georg Noverre (1727-1810) had made his first major choreographic successes in Vienna at the end of the period in question, 1767.

The esteem in which the dance theater of the German-speaking world was held toward the end of the century is due, though, to the developments in Vienna prior to the international successes of Noverre. An example of the contemporaneous realization of the actual situation in Vienna is in a work by the Jesuit priest Stephan Arteaga's *Le Rivoluzioni del Teatro Musicale* (Bologna, 1783).

The dance has reached an unheretofore approachable fullness in Europe, something supposedly only previously reached by the Romans ... which perfection is evidenced in the presentation of entire tragedies and comedies with the strictest dramatic rigour, with full theatrical resources – and all without the help of any words. The honour of bringing this art to its present peak belongs to a nation that one generally associates with creativity, studiousness, and a serious, scientific and rigorous attempt to build charm and taste into all the arts. The Germans prove this with their Klopstock, Haller, Gassner, Zacharia, Gleim, and other no less acclaimed poets, just as by means of Handel, Stamitz, Bach (Carl Phillip Emmanuel, ed.) Naumann, Gluck, Haydn, Graun and many other composers famous over all Europe. - ... In 1740 Hilverding presented for the first time on the stage at Dresden (others say at Vienna), for the pleasure of the entire court, *Britannicus* by Racine. Afterwards he followed with *Idomeneus* by Crebillon and *Alzire* by Voltaire.[3]

3. Stefano Arteaga, *Le Rivoluzioni del Teatro Musicale Italiano*, (Bologna, 1783)

It is one of the aims of this paper to place in the correct perspective the development of the theory of the so-called *Ballet-d'Action*, that is the ballet-pantomime, which was experimented with and under constant discussion in the Viennese circle round Franz Hilverding (1710-1768) and his even more important pupil and protege Domenico Maria Gasparo Angiolini (1731-1803); these dates are the result of archival investigations by Walter Toscanini[4], yet *Grove's Dictionary* still lists Angiolini's dates as 1723-1796[5]). In the main, history ascribes the lion's share of the credit for the infusion of dramatic, narrative, and pantomimic qualities into the too often sterile court ballet to Noverre (as well as his part in the development of modern ballet techniques.) Yet, the critical change in ballet style during the careers of Hilverding and Angiolini at Vienna provides ample evidence of an equally creative, and in most respects, independent development. The unique quality of the Viennese school lay in its emphasis upon what Johann Mattheson had called "silent Music" in describing pantomime (*Ehren-pforte*, Hamburg: 1740) and what both Hilverding and Angiolini wrote of as *danza parlante*. This so-called speaking quality was the ideal of Angiolini's style, a unity of choreography and music through the medium of pantomime. In comparing the written pronouncements of the two rival dancer-choreographers, Noverre and Angiolini, the latter appears in a considerably more modern light. For Noverre, the author of the *Lettres sur la Danse et les Ballets*[6] (1760), prime importance is

Second expanded and revised edition, Venice 1785. 3 volumes. Translated into German by Johann Nicolai Forkel as *Geschichte der itlaienischen Oper*, Leipzig, 1789). p. 202 ff (vol. 3, 2nd edition). The translation given is from vol. 2, p. 463 of the Forkel German edition.

4. The correct dates first appear in an article by Robert Haas, "Die Wiener Bühnentanz von 1740 bis 1767", *Jahrbuch der Bibliothek Peters, 1937*, (Leipzig: Peters, 1938) pg. 82. Toscanini's archival work, to have been used in a biography of Angiolini, never materialized.

5. *Musik in Geschichte und Gegenwart* (Basel, Kassel: Barenreiter, 1951-68) doesn't even mention Angiolini in a separate article. The *Enciclopedia dela Spettacolo* (Rome: La Maschere, 1954-62), *Dictionare de Musique* (Bordas, 1970), and the *Enciclopedia della Musica* (Milan: Ricordi, 1963) all list the correct dates.

6. The *Lettres* were published in Lyon and Stuttgart. They were translated by Cyril Beaumont from a revised Russian edition of 1803. The original edition served as the basis for the modern edition of André Levison (Paris, 1927).

given to the furtherance of choreographic dance. For Angiolini, as we shall investigate further, choreography is a cross-section of the workings of the music; music holds first place. Ideally, for Angiolini, the music should contain all the latent possibilities for expression in pantomime, so that a detailed programme was superfluous.[7]

Noverre's work, an eloquent plea for realism in staging, owes much to treatises of 1757 and 1758 by Denis Diderot (1713-84). As an augury of the Romantic view of artistic creation, Diderot's article "Genie" in the seventh volume of the *Encyclopédie*, (1757) represents the key to both Noverre's and Angiolini's departure from the aesthetics of imitation. A short excerpt from the article stresses the change of attitude at mid-century:

> Taste is often distinct from genius. Genius is a pure gift of nature: what it produces is the work of an instant; taste is the product of study and time and depends upon the knowledge of a multitude of rules, either established or supposed. In order for something to be beautiful according to the rules of taste it must be elegant, finished and studied, without appearing to be so. To be genial, it is necessary sometimes that the work be rough, craggy and savage. Genius and the sublime shine forth like lighting in a dark night in Shakespeare, and Racine is always *beau*; Homer is full of genius, and Virgil of elegance. The rules and laws of taste impose fetters upon the genius. He breaks them to fly toward the sublime, the pathetic and the grand. Love of the external beauty of nature and the passion for creating his works after an indefinable image within himself that forms his ideas of beauty and expression — these are the ways of the man of genius.

The inspiration of nature is stressed, but the artist does more than merely imitate nature: he draws from within himself. This view, that art is the creation of the individual imagination, was expanded and refined by Diderot throughout his life. In 1757 Diderot's domestic tragedy *Le Fils natural* was published, with

7. The forward to the ballet-pantomime *Don Juan* by Angiolini, music by Gluck. (Vienna: Trattnern, 1762).

three appended 'Entretiens,' subtitled *Dorval et Moi*. The conversations dealt with the future of the arts, with Dorval, the melancholy hero of the play, holding that the stage must be enriched by a great variety of new subjects by taking advantage of what is uniquely theatrical. Much of the conversational debate between Dorval and his interlocutor *Moi* hinged upon the differences between the tableau, meaning gesture raised to the level of the whole stage action, and the contrived and trite *coup de théâtre à la* Crebillon. We are told that the plastic should often relieve the verbal. Ballet and opera need revitalization from the source of the ancient playwrights — not for their rules, but their simplicity, force and grandeur.

Another landmark appeared in 1758 with Diderot's second play, *La Père de Famille,* accompanied by a wide-ranging essay of 22 chapters, *De la Poésie dramatique.* Diderot considers everything theatrical from the poetic subject to the physical conditions of theaters. The penultimate chapter, "On Pantomime," brings together as exemplary models antique legend and the English novel. Diderot writes of a Richardsonian character, "whether he talks or not, I see him, and his actions affect me more than his words."

Noverre adopts the same attitudes in his *Lettres.* Again we are told that the great painters provided the example that could liberate the stage from symmetry and frippery; again, that gesture and poetic subjects were the means of transforming ballet from a decorative to a dramatic art. Tragic pantomime was Noverre's chief interest, and like Diderot he associated it with classical antiquity. Of two other sources acknowledged by Noverre, the theoretical work by Cahusac, *La Danse ancienne et moderne* (1754) was, along with the *Encyclopédistes*, the source for Angiolini's practical application of theory, independent of Noverre's writings. Another admitted source for Noverre was the English actor David Garrick, for whom he worked at Drury Lane in 1755. The ninth letter proposes ways of forming a new breed of pantominists:

Mr. Garrick, the celebrated English actor, is the model I wish to put forward. . . . He was so natural, his expression so lifelike, his gestures, features and glances were so eloquent and so convincing, that he made the action clear even to those who did not understand a word of English. It was easy to follow his meaning; his pathos was touching; in tragedy he terrified with the successive movements with which he represented the most violent passions . . . he lacerated the spectator's feelings, tore his heart, pierced his soul, and made him shed tears of blood.

In his last Letter Noverre explicitly pays homage to Diderot:

this philosopher and friend of nature, that is to say of simple truth and beauty, who would substitute pantomime affectation, a natural voice for the stilted diction or art, simple dress for the false luxury, truth for fable, wit and common sense for involved dialogue and for all ill-painted portraits which caricature and distort nature.

While Noverre was putting his ideas into practice at the Stuttgart opera, reformist works for the stage, spoken, lyric and dance, were emerging in other centers, one of the most vital of which for ballet-pantomime was Vienna. Vienna had acquired a French repertory company in 1752 and for twenty years without interruption witnessed Molière, Racine and Voltaire sharing the stage with the latest *opéras comiques* and ballets from Paris. There was no permanent company for Italian opera between 1752 and 1765; Count Durazzo became sole intendant in 1754. With the aid of the Chancellor, Prince Kaunitz, he began to encourage original efforts from the repertory companies at both the *Burghtheater* and the *Kärtnertortheater*. Gluck arrived in Vienna in 1755 as musical arranger for the *opéras comiques*, and was given a free hand to compose his own music. On to the same scene, during the winter of 1760-61, appeared Ranieri Calzabigi (1714-1795), direct from a decade of operatic battles in Paris.[8] The first artistic event involving his work was the dramatic ballet-pantomime *Le Festin de Pierre ou Don Juan* presented by the French troupe in October of 1761, with sets by Giovanni Maria Guaglio, choreography by

8. See Robert Haas', *Gluck und Durazzo im Burgtheater (Die Opéra Comique in Wien)* (Leipzig: Peters, 1925). The best general account of the background to the Viennese reform movement remains that of Herta Michel, "Ranieri Calzabigi als Dichter von Musikdramen und als Kritiker", *Gluck-Jahrbuch*, 4 (1918), pp. 99-171.

Angiolini and music by Gluck; Calzabigi wrote the scenario. A year later operatic history was made when the same forces brought forth *Orfeo ed Euridice*, by coincidence on the birthday of Diderot, 5 October.

We shall have more to say about Angiolini's work for *Don Juan*, as it was the peak of Angiolini's applications of the new dramatic theories for dance. Though he had several other successes, Angiolini was unable to compete with Noverre once the latter had arrived in Vienna. However, it is first necessary to consider the prime source of Angiolini's style, Hilverding, in order to show that Angiolini was not merely an emulator and rival (though he certainly was a rival) of Noverre. Hilverding had begun to put into action the theories of Luis de Cahusac,[9] Rameau's librettist and a theoretical pioneer, on the return to an inspiration from Classic Greek and Roman dance. The work being done in Vienna was something that Cahusac obviously did not know in his work of 1754. Cahusac specifically points to the famous Parisian dancer Mlle. Antionette Salle who made a great and dramatic success in London during the season of 1752, with two ballet dramas, *Ariadne* and *Pygmalion*.

An even earlier example of an adoption of Greek legend to ballet, dates from 1724 with a pair of dances with music by Mourets using the story of Horatius. The transformation of these concepts of ballet into pantomimic scenes with short, independent choreographic and musical motifs by Hilverding is alluded to by several of his contemporaries; the writings of Angiolini, J.H.F. Müller, Johann Sulzer,[10] and Arteaga attribute to Hilverding a sensitivity and especial genius for combining and understanding contemporary aesthetic theories on poetry, painting and music and applying these to dance. Unfortunately, the ballets alluded to by Arteaga, *Brittanicus* and *Alzire* are no longer extant. We also only know of the dances Hilverding created for Ignaz Jacob Holzbauer's (1711-1783) opera *Ipermestra* of 1743 for a last great performance at the court opera house. The music for both the

9. Lusis de Cahusac. *La Danse ancienne et moderne ou traite historique sur la danse,* à la Haye (1754).

10. Johann Georg Sulzer, *Allgemeine Theorie der Schönen Kunst.* (Leipzig: Wiedmann'sche Buchhandlung, 1771-1774; 1792-1794) 5 volumes. = Mitiegleid der Königlichen Akademie in Berlin.

ballets and the opera were in this instance written by Holzbauer. Holzbauer and Hilverding collaborated again for the ballet scenes used in Hasse's *Armino* in 1747. The association of Holzbauer with Viennese ballet and with Hilverding was short-lived however, as by 1750 he had been called to Mannheim to take charge of the opera and conduct the most famous orchestra in Europe. The archives of the Kärtnertortheater show that Hilverding had written three ballet scenes, *Abenteur in Serail* as early as 1742 for the opera *La Fedelta sin alla Morte* by a composer named Franz or Francesco Holzbauer — but this is probably only an error and that Ignaz was the composer. In any case, the ballet for *Ipermestra* and *La Fedelta sin alla Morte* were part of a distinct pattern of "Turkish" entertainments.

From 1737 Hilverding was court dancer (Ballarino di Corte) under the dance master Alexander Phillebois.[11] At this time, and since 1728, the court ballet in Vienna had been under the direction of Borosini-Silliers. Interestingly, Eva Marie Viegel, another product of the court ballet contemporary with Hilverding, became the wife of David Garrick. The son of Alexander Phillebois (who had been the leading dancer at court under Karl VI), Anton, became another of the leading choreographers in Vienna, and a colleague of Hilverding at the Kärtnertortheater. We know from contemporary sources that Phillebois the younger — perhaps following the example of Hilverding — created miniature mythological scenes which were used many times in various operas. Prime examples of his work are *Daphnis et Cynthia* of 1746, which was used as the third scene in Catel's opera *Semiramis*, and *Pygmalion*, of the same year, for Holzbauer's opera *La Clemenza di Tito*. The first ballet scene in this latter opera was set by Hilverding to a version of Molière's *Geizigen*. Phillebois also choreographed ballets for the French theater's productions of Molière's plays. In 1746 he wrote the dance scenes for *L'Avare*. In 1747 the archives show that another work, *Dido*, was supplied with dances by one Joseph Salomone and Phillebois. Phillebois at this period, as well as did Hilverding, retained some element of

---

11. Alexander Phillebois became ballet master in 1737. His 13 dancers were Peter Rigler, Tobias Gumpenhuber, Andreas Bruno, Niklas Buch, Simon Sack, Josef Sellier, Franz Tamm, Kajetan della Mota, Philip Gumpenhuber, Franz Anton Phillebois, Josef Bruno, Hilverding, and Niklas Scio.

Baroque allegory in his work; his ballet scenes for Handel's *Ariodante* is entitled "The Form of the Danube Uniting with the Spirit of the City of Vienna."

The archives for the "Repetoire des Theatre de la ville de Vienne" were begun at the time of the first performances of the French Hebert troupe at the Bürgtheater. The category of ballets seems little more than a catalogue of the titles of Hilverding's works. It is these works that provide the evidence for judging the trend in Hilverding's choice of content, and the basis for his reputation as an intelligent choreographer of unified and emotionally successful works. Hilverding's first work using a mythological plot was *La Generosita trionfante* (*Sfonisba*) for an opera-ballet, the music again provided by Ignaz Holzbauer in 1745. Other works from the same repetoire include *Orpheus et Euridice*, *Acis et Galatea*, *Ariadne et Bacchus*, *Amor et Psyche*, and *Ulisses et Circe*. All of these pantomimic ballets used intricate stage machinery.

During the 1752 season at the Kärtnertortheater facial expression for mythological epics became important enough to necessitate the use of masks. This innovation in Vienna was particularly the work of Hilverding. The Kärtnertortheater had already used masks in the main for German comedy, as did the Hebert Society for French works at the Bürgtheater.

From the time that Hilverding became a leading court dancer and ballet master in 1737 he received a salary of 600 florins, with an additional 200 florins for each new choreography. He soon came into complete domination of the dance at both theaters in Vienna with ballet corps: the Kartnertor and the Civic (Bürg) Theaters. In so doing, he became a constant and direct influence upon his colleagues and students: Anton Pirot, from Dresden, who came to Vienna in 1750: Josef Salomone (Giospetto di Vienna): Franz Salomone, who worked at the Bernardi theater: Pierre and Bernardo Lodi, and of course Angiolini. As early as 1748 Hilverding was ballet master for the Lopresti Society opera, where he had presented his first ballet as part of Hasse's opera *Leucippo*, the allegorical "The Awakening of Aurora."

Though allegory had all but disappeared in Vienna by 1752, the lighter entertainments continued alongside the more serious pantomimes. Many of the ballets presented were group *divertissments*, especially at the Kärtnertortheater, of sailors, farmers, hunters, soldiers, workers, Tyroleans, lumbermen, Netherlanders, Spaniards, Hungarians, Turks, and Americans. Color ballets, all in blue or red, with songs were frequently used. A favorite subject for many of these so-called *Groteskballets* was Don Quixote. The harem scene became popular as well, along with the pyramids of Egypt. Of course, these *divertissments* and *Groteskballets* retained the tableaux format of an unconnected series of traditional dances of the previous century.

By the mid-eighteenth century the construction of the ballet corps at the German and French theaters were somewhat different: the German theaters, led by the Kärtnertortheater, used five prima ballerinas and six premier danseurs, with six and four respectively as the *corps de ballet*; the French theatrical group at the Bürgtheater used only three prima ballerinas, three premier danseurs and four and six female and male tutti dancers.[12]

In 1758, the turning point in the development of ballet-pantomime (the *ballet d'action*) in Vienna, three composers were dominantly active in connection with the dance theaters: Josef Starzer (ca. 1726-1787), Franz Asplmayr (1728-1786), and Christoph Willibald (Ritter von) Gluck (1714-1787). Josef Starzer, a violinist as well as a composer, began his career as concertmaster of the Vienna Court Chapel and for the French theater. Though he wrote a good deal of interesting chamber and orchestral music, it was his ballets that made his greatest success. His earlier compositions for Hilverding's choreography consisted mainly of loose dance successions, of the type of *divertissments* described above. It was not until 1768, after his return to Vienna from a ten year stay in Russia, and he began to compose music for Noverre, that his music took on a more serious tone. Asplmayr, ballet composer for the German theater, earned less than Hilverding (400 florins) and one-third the salary of Gluck at the French theater. However, despite his economic insignificance (compared to his contemporaries) several of his ballets are still extant, such as

---

12. The prima ballerinas at the *Bürg Theater* included Louise Bodin, née Jefroi, who also performed in the opéra comique, and the great Italian favorites Theresa Fogliazzi (one of Casanova's attempted conquests, who became Angiolini's wife) and Theresa Morelli. The leading soloist at the Kärtnertortheater was Onorato Viganò.

"Agamemnon," "Ipheginia," "Flora," "Acis and Galatea," and "Alexander." Unlike his colleagues, he seems to have spent his entire life in Vienna.

In November of 1758, after some twenty years of increasing dominance over the dance theater in Vienna, and taking the important initial steps toward dance reform, Hilverding accepted the post of ballet master at the court in St. Petersburg under Catherine II. Josef Starzer accompanied Hilverding, and both composer and choreographer remained for ten years before returning to Vienna, in that interval creating some important works in Russia, and certainly contributing toward the development of modern Russian classical ballet. However, when Hilverding leaves Vienna he also moves outside the scope and intentions of this paper.

Hilverding's successor at the Civic theater was Angiolini, while his position at the Kärntnertortheater was given to Bernardo Lodi. As late as 1923 Angiolini was said to have been born in Milan in 1723;[13] however, within a few years both his birth and death dates were revised to the later years of 1731 and 1803.[14] Angiolini is the personality most closely associated with the extention and the spirit of a purposeful effort toward a new decisive meaning in Viennese ballet-pantomime, especially in his association with the Gluck circle.

There is some conjecture that Angiolini began his work as a dancer in Florence, the city of his birth, but the first records show him as a member of the ballet chorus at the Teatro Giustian di San Moise in Venice from 1747 until 1750. Angiolini relates[15] that he choreographed works for the theater in Innsbruck also during this period before moving to Turin. He remained in Turin until 1756, at which time he moved on to Vienna to become associated with Hilverding. In Turin Angiolini prepared several works of import to the development of his aesthetic attitudes, alongside "The Discovery of America by Columbus," and "Diana and Endimion."

13. Robert Haas, "Wiener Ballet-Pantomime im 18 Jahrhundert und Glucks Don Juan", *Studien zur Musikwissenschaft*, vol. 10 (Vienna: Universal Edition, 1923) pp. 6-36.
14. These dates are certainly more reasonable than the earlier ones, considering that Angiolini would still have been an active dancer in his seventies if he were born in 1723.
15. *Lettere di Gasoaro Angiolini à Monsieur Noverre sopra i Balli Pantomimi* In Milano MDCCLXXIII. Appresso Gio. Batista Bîanchi. p. 20.

Angiolini's first choreographies in Vienna were the simpler types of *divertissments* of the previous decade. Count Zinzendorf's *Wiener Diarum* for 1760 refers to the three ballet scenes interpolated into Hasse's festival opera, *Alcide al Bivo* (1760). The ballet scenes are titled: "La Promenade," L'Amour Venge," and "La Foire de Lyon." Hasse himself supplied the music for the ballet scenes in the way of a refrain-chorus.[16] The same fourvoiced chorus serves as the music through all three ballets. The final ballet appears at the end of the opera, after the end of the Alcidian tragedy, with a rejoicing by the Olympian heros.

The critical Zinzendorf refers to several other works in the same vaudeville manner: a Chinese divertissment in 1761, and in the same year works called "les amusements Champêtres" (for which the critics complained of the poor stage lighting), "des Cosaques," "Retour de Printemps" and others. As late as 1762, after Angiolini had begun his important association with Gluck, Angiolini created a ballet using marionette figures to represent Posenaas' army in Hasse's opera *Il Trionfo de Clelia.*[17] There is no indication with the manuscript or the original announcement as to the composer of the dance music; however, the same music was used in the ballet scenes attached to Scarlatti's *Ataserse* in a production of 1763, and Josef Starzer is indicated as the composer, with Angiolini as the choreographer. The latter work has two distinct dance scenes, one centered around Apollo and Daphne, the other various tableaux of joyous Dutch winters.

It was with the entrance of Angiolini into the rigorous world of the intellect surrounding Gluck and his circle, that the former turned to a considerably more serious approach to ballet, based on the contention of building on Hilverding's innovations to create in one ballet a variegated *gesamstkunstwerk* founded on pantomime. The six year association of Angiolini and Gluck was one more major step in the change from the smiling world of the rococo to the complexities of the tragic stance. In a programme note, actually an addendum, to the scenario for his first attempt at this new style, *Don Juan* or *Le Festin de Pierre*, Angiolini develops his intentions, in the main, from Luis de Cahusac's *Treatise* of 1754,

16. The libretto is in the music section of the Wiener National Bibliothek. 396.431 B.M:S.

17. Robert Haas, "Wiener Ballet-Pantomime im 18 Jahrhundert . . ." p. 26.

though brought to a new depth of purpose. Angiolini credits his knowledge of Molière's drama, probably seen by Angiolini during the first year of his arrival in Vienna, as the direct inspiration for the choreography.

Cahusac's theories centered upon a revival of what Cahusac thought to be the ancient Roman art of pantomime, which represented the deeds, emotions and passions of heroes and gods through strictly organized rhythmic movement, in a dumb show that he called "silent speech."[18] The dance, then, was a two-fold means of communication: a dumb declamation, of course meant only for the eyes, but the character of which was reinforced and underscored by music that shifted to fit the expressive content of the action. Unlike the spoken or sung theater, communication must be centered in the visual aspect. And, unlike the Neo-Classic theater, unity of place, as well as time, is in a practical sense impossible, while a flowing action through time and place is everything. Action, covering a wide range of time and place, had to be compressed into much smaller theatrical time span than in the spoken or sung theater. The more successfully the music aids in the communication of the visual content, the more complete is the unity between the two elements of the drama, dance and music.

Angiolini incorporated these dicta by several means, though he mentions only two. For Angiolini expressiveness was possible in two ways: through intense facial expressiveness — without the use of masks — especially through the eyes, and, following Cahusac, by an explicit change of mood in the music to follow the ballet scenario. The immediate result of Angiolini's style change in *Don Juan* was considerably more stage movement, and the practical eradication of tableaux. In his exchange of theories with Noverre in 1773,[19] Angiolini writes about his innovations in the Viennese dance theater of the previous decade, and in mentioning Hilver-

18. The equation of speech with the arts, especially music, became one of the important characteristics of the growth of nineteenth century romanticism in the second half of the eighteenth century. Both Rationalists, through the doctrines of "imitation" and the writers of the German *Sturm und Drang*: Gerstenberg, Hamann, Herder, Goethe, and Heinse all made a direct relationship between the speech of ancient (Greek and Hebrew) sense-perceptive peoples (a term used by Hamann, Herder and Heinse) and their music.

19. *Lettere . . . à Monsieur Noverre . . .*, 1773. p. 25.

ding's pantomimes *Psyche*, *Pygmalion* and *Circe*, states, "It is unfortunately the case with our theaters and even the pantomimes of my master, the famous F. Hilverding, but one has the pain of saying that until then we were only cognizant of the simplest forms of dance expression. . . ."

Catastrophic, intense tragedy became the order of the day in the Gluck circle, with all its members: Gluck, Angiolini, Calzabigi, and Johann Maria Quaglio, subscribing to the general reform movement. The historical comparisons with melodrama and *singspiel* (particularly the melodrama in Germany, in the main produced at the courts of Gotha and Bückeburg[20]) are obvious. There is a cross-fertilization of means in the advance of the anti-rational, the reaction against the superficialities of the Rococo, and the impetus these forms gave to the general European malaise of the 1770s we have come to label the *Sturm und Drang*. This early or pre-Romantic surge has been the topic of much scholarly and definitive work in the areas of the spoken theater, aesthetics and philosophy. The musical arts have not been so fortunate. Pre-Romanticism has not been as clear cut an historical phenomenon in the second half of the eighteenth century for musicologists. In any event, though the 1770s certainly provide a peak of dramatically intense instrumental music for Haydn, and to some extent Mozart, the instrumental recitatives of Carl Phillip Emanuel Bach (1714-1788) appear as early as 1740 in his *Prussian Sonatas*, and the dramatic reforms of the Gluck circle belong to the 1760s.

One consistent element in these dramatic surges throughout the century, was the alternation of various emotional levels by quick changes of most of the elements of music: in the main, though, this meant quick change of dynamics, range and tempi, along with the alternation of non-metrical with measured rhythm and of a monodic-like melodic bareness with full-throated harmonies. Both the so-called *Empfindsamkeit* of North Germany, and

20. The *melodrama*, another musical manifestation of the growing elements of Romanticism, was developed in Germany during the eighteenth century most consistently by Georg Benda (Jiri Antonin; 1722-1795) working at the court of Gotha with the Seyler Troupe. Johann Christoph Friedrich Bach and Johann Gottfried Herder working at Bückeburg from 1770-1775 produced several melodramas, the most important of which was *Brutus*.

its popularization in the 1770s through the upsurge of the minor mode and the injection of imitative polyphony — that is, the *Sturm und Drang* were based on the fragmentation of active and passive content rather than on the fragmentation of the articulated phrase alone, as had been the case with music of the rational Rococo, the *Stile Galante*.

Angiolini complemented Gluck's spun-out melodic unity through a set of free character variations, and, for Gluck, a rich working out of polyphonic detail, by making *Don Juan* into a series of short, intense character pieces. According to Zinzendorf in the *Wiener Diarum*,[21] writing about the first performance of *Don Juan* at the Bürgtheater on October 17, 1761, presented together with the five-act comedy *Le Joueur* by Regnard, the audience was, in the main alienated by the tragic intensity, the frightening and melancholy atmosphere — which, of course, was not what they had come to expect as the normal course of affairs in an evening of ballet. The critical commentary on the technical side of the performance and about Gluck's music was favourable. An especially impressive scene was said to have been the judgement pronounced upon Don Juan by the stone guest.

Don Juan consisted of a one movement *sinfonia*, followed by thirty short scenes, and a long closing number, a Chaconne. Gluck's use of pithy motivic style, approaching a kind of *Leitmotiv* usage, and his comparatively rich use of polyphony were certainly influential elements of *Don Juan*. The dramatic rushing passages of the closing scene partakes of a musical language that became the common property of the Viennese Classical period. Certainly Gluck's use of the trombones in the final scene, in connection with the appearance of the statue, is clearly echoed in Mozart. Gluck and Angiolini employ the traditional social dances, especially in the festive middle act, in more or less traditional shape: minuet, gavotte, sarabande, gigue, and finally the chaconne.

21. Count Zinzendorf (1739-1813) who seems to have been present at every First Night throughout the century, is best remembered for the blasé entries in his diary about Mozart's operas. He continues, . . . (in the end) "the ghost vanishes and suddenly Hell appears, furies dance with lighted torches and torment Don Juan, in the background a beautiful firework representing hell-fire. One sees some devils flying . . . the devils carry Don Juan away and leap with him into the flaming pit. All this was excellently done, the music being very lovely."

Number nineteen of the dances is a Fandango (Mozart used the Fandango again in *The Marriage of Figaro*) which is another manifestation of Hilverding and Angiolini's penchant for the folk and national element. Especially noteworthy is the fact that Gluck uses a predominantly four-measure balanced phrase structure (differently than in the opéra comique *La recontre imprevue*, 1764). The closing Dance of the Furies becomes quite far removed from the ideal chaconne of Rameau; the form is free from the restrictions of the ostinato. The two closing numbers, in fact, in their freedom, characterize the whole ballet.

A shorter version of the ballet was performed on November 2nd and 3rd at the Kärtnertortheater, using only fifteen of the numbers. The same short version appeared the following year in Darmstadt. The manuscript scores in both cities attest to the abridged version. The choreography and the stage directions are appended to the full score in the library of the Paris Conservatoire.[22] Later performances of the ballet in Vienna were cut even more. In a performance of June, 1772, directed by Vincenzo Rossi, four more scenes were cut, and the character of the valet made infinitely more comic. A performance of *Don Juan* in Frankfurt in 1781, was directed by the ballet master of the Bohemian Society of the city, Peter Vogt, (a student of Noverre's). The work was now in five acts. Donna Anna is now called Amarillis, and inexplicably does not appear until the second act. Two additions of note, Leporello's recitation of Don Juan's conquests and the peasant wedding seemed to have been cribbed by Da Ponte.[23]

It would seem, that while normative performance practice for the dance theater did not view these shortened and altered versions of *Don Juan* as out of the ordinary, there certainly also appears to be a relationship between the eventual destruction of Angiolini's dramatic intent and the influence of Noverre's professional rivalry with Angiolini. In any case, *Don Juan* remained in the repetoire in Vienna while Angiolini worked with

22. Manuscript No. 20.

23. This more than conjecture. Mozart's *Don Giovanni* was written and performed in Vienna and Prague in 1787. Both the Vogtian scenario and Gluck's music were known to Mozart. The second scene of the Vogt version of *Don Juan* opens with the same peasant wedding as the Da Ponte libretto.

Gluck, in most cases with Angiolini dancing the title role.

It would seem that one explanation for the reaction to the dramatic intent of *Don Juan* lay in the attitude of society toward both the dance and its dual role in eighteenth century culture. The dances of the *ballet de cour* were fully decorous because they were designed to represent the summation of standards of social behavior familiar to the seventeenth 'century and the first half of the eighteenth century. It fitted the ideals of the nobiliar classes. Certainly, much of the eighteenth century was a period tending toward heightened politeness and formality in the interrelations of men and women. The minuet, for instance, demonstrated this restricted sense of freedom in man/woman relations: it was an open couple dance, involving only fingertip physical contact. Even modesty of gaze between partners was encouraged as being in the best taste: it would not do to regard one's partner too forthrightly or for any length of time. The stylized dance forms were, like the minuet, in fact an extended series of decorous behaviors strung together and danced to music, as it were art applied to life. The spirit of the Rococo is evident in the design and shapes of the floor plans for court dances that made up the ballets prior to mid-century. The curling motif of decoration characterizes the general spacing of the dancers.

Yet, the separation between dance for spectators as distinct from dance for general participation was not inflexibly determined. There continued through the mid-century a rich exchange of influence between "professional" and "amateur" dancing, and as a result stage dancing resembled court dancing to a very striking degree. The confusion between dance as spectacle and as a participatory activity persisted even in the ballroom, with those in attendance wearing the two hats of performing artist and audience interchangeably. Dances such as the social minuet certainly provided a ready made technical apparatus for the ballet-pantomime: turned out positions of the feet, a penchant for dancing on the toes, erect posture with an emphasis upon gesture as a restrained means of expression, and several basic steps, as the *coupe, chasse, tonlie, plie*, and *pas de bourée*.

It becomes evident, then, that it was difficult for the aristocratic audiences in Vienna to view the dances of *Don Juan*, dance forms they themselves performed socially, with equanimity when these same dances were turned into vehicles for stronger passions then they cared to admit to.

Angiolini's commentary for the ballet is important enough to be quoted here in its entirety.

Le Festin de Pierre,
ballet pantomime, composé par Mr Angiolini, Maître des Ballets du Théâtre près de la Cour a Vienne, et representé pour la première fois sur ce théâtre le . . . Octobre 1761.
"Sergius irritant animos demissa per aures, quam quae sunt oculis subjecta fiselibus." (Horat: "De Arte Poetica").

Ce qui ne frappe que l'oreille fait moins d'impression sur les esprits, que ce qui frappe les yeux. Traduction du Père Tarteron.

A Vienne, chez Jean Thomas Tratner, Libraire et Imprimeur de la Cour. M.D.CC.LXI.

Le spectacle que je présente au Public est un Ballet Pantomime dans le goût des Anciens. Ceux qui ont lû les auteurs Grecs ou Latins, qui, soit en Original, soit en Traduction, sont dans les mains de tout le monde; connoissent les noms célèbres de Pylade & de Bathylle qui vivoient sous le Regne d'Auguste. Les merveilles de leur Art sont immortalisées par les Historiens, les Orateurs & les Poètes. Lucien nous a même laissé un Tarité de cet Art célébre, qu'on peut regarder comme une espéce de Poétique des Dances Pantomimimes, quoi qu'il soit imparfait.

Le sublime de l'ancienne Danse étoit la Pantomime, & celle-ci étoit l'art d'imiter les moeurs, les passions, les actions des Dieux, des Heros, des hommes, par des mouvemens & des signes faits en cadence & propres à esprimer ce qu'on avoit dessein de representer. Ces gestes devoient former, pour ainsi dire, un dicours suivi: c'étoit une espèce de Déclamation, faite pour les yeux, dont on rendoit l'intelligence plus aisée aux spectateurs par le moien de la Musique qui varioit les sons, suivant que l'Acteur Pantomime avoit, dessein d'exprimer l'amour ou la haine, la fureur ou le désespoir.

Tout cela étoit appelle *Saltation*. Ce nom ne lui renoit pas de Saltare qui signifie Sauter, mais d'un certain Salius, qui, le premier, avoit enseigné cet Art aux Romains & tous les auteurs conviennent qu'on l'exécutoit par des gestes parlans, par des signes expressifs & par des mouvemens de la tête, des yeux, de la main, des bras & des jambes.

Les Pantomimes étoient donc des imitateurs de tout, pour me servir de l'expression de l'Abbe du Bos: ils jouoient des fables et des histoires, quelquefois par parties détachés, quelquefois entières. Ils contrafaisoient la colère d'Achille, la fueur d'Ajax, l'orgueil d'Agamemmnon. Ovide nous apprend que ses vers avoient été dansés sur le Théâtre: quelqu'auteurs ont cru qu'il a voulu parler de ses Metamorphoses, d'autres de sa Tragédie de Médée. Apulée nous a laissé la description d'un Ballet Pantomime qui représentoit le jugement de Paris.

C'est le fameux Pylade qui inventa de danser ainsi des Pieces entières. Les Pantomimes appellerent cette nouvelle manière de danser la Danse Italique. Elle embrassoit tous les genres de Spectacles, & jouoit la Tragédie, la Comédie, la Satyre & la Farce.

Je ne m'etentrai pas davantage sur ces recherches, ce ne seroit pas ici leur place. J'ajouterai simplement que cet Art est perdu. Il a ou la sort de bein d'autres qu'on n'a endin fait revivre que par des efforts & des travaux pénibles. Le notions abrégées que j'en donne pour le présent suffisient pour le justifier d'avoir entrepris de mettre une Piéce entière en Danse Pantomime. C'est le friot de mes études que je présente au Public, & j'ouvre une novelle carrière aux Maîtres de Ballets qui auront les connoissances & les talens nécessaires pour y entrer.

J'ai choisi pour mon coup d'essai une Tragicomédie Espagnole qui a réuni les suffrages des toutes les Nations: c'est le Festin de Pierre. Cette Pièce a réussi sur tous les Théâtres quoiqu'elle ne soit pas dans les règles. Les unitées du tems & du lieu n'y sont pas observées, mais l'invention en est sublime, la catastrophe terrible, & dans notre croiance elle est vraisemblence. Ces qualités sont plus que suffisantes pour la traiter en Ballet Pantomime.

La Danse n'a pas de Recits. Nous ne pouvons pas raconter aux Spectateur qu'on Heros a été tué ou qu'il s'est donné la mort. Ils n'ont que des yeux pour nous entendre, les oreilles leur sont inutiles il faut que nous leur fassions voir toute l'action. L'unité du lieu n'est donc pas compatible avec Saltation; & comme il ne nous est pas permis non plus de nous arrêter à dialoguer, & que nous devons toujour agir et suivre des mouvemens qui nous lassent nous sommes forcés de resserrer dans un espace de quelques minutes, les sujets les plus étendus, & l'unité du tems, dans ces bornes étroites, est impossible à conserver. Lucien, en nous donnant des préceptes sur la danse-Pantomime, n'a pas dit un seul mot des unités; & nous n'avons pas d'autre Maître. Notre règle certaine est le vraisemblable: exiger de nous l'observation scrupuleuse des Règles dramatiques, c'est nous demander l'impossible.

Au surplus nous ne pouvons pas entendre de corriger les Pièces que nous traitons en Danse Pantomime. Le Festin de Pierre, avec tous ses defauts, a été bien reçu par-tout en recit, pourquoi ne réussira-t-il pas, de même en Danse. Le mot d'Horace que j'ai place a la tête de cet écrit, me le fait espérer.

Le sujet en est triste, je l'avoue, mais ceux la plus-part des Tragédies sont ils rians? Les comédiens plaisent par le terrible ainsi que par l'agréable; la variété qu'on demande dans les Spectacles exige que nous traitions alternativement les deux Genres. Nous seroit-il défendu d'epouvanter en dansant ainsi qu'en déclamant? La terreur nous fait plaisir aux Tragédies, nous y pleurons avec une espèce de sensibilité douce qui nous charme. Si nous pouvons exciter toutes les passions par un jeu muet pourqoui nous seroit-il interdit de le tenter? Si le Public ne veut pas se priver des plus grandes beautés de notre Art, il doit s'accoutumer à s'attendrir & à pleurer à nos Ballets.

Il n'en a pas été ainsi jusqu'à présent; si l'on en excepte notre

Théâtre & les Pantomimes qui y ont été donrées par mon Maître, le célèbre M. Hilverding. Mais on peut assurer hardiment, qu'en général nous n'avons connû, pour ainsi dire, que le simple Alphabet de la Danse. Nous n'avons fait que bégaier comme les enfans, sans pouvoir mettre deux phrases ensemble. Des spectateurs froids & tranquilles ont admiré nos pas, nos attitudes, nos mouvemens, notre cadence, notre à plomb, avec la même indifférence qu'on admire des yeux, des bouches, des nez, des mains artistement craionés. Qu'il y a loin de là à l'assemblage d'un beau portrait vivant du Titien, ou de d'un grand tableau de Raphael ou de Rubens qui nous ravit, qui secoue notre ame avec violence! Quel est celui d'entre nous qui s'est jamais vanté de pouvoir représenter en Danse un seul personage célebre, comme Hercule, Thésée, Alexandre, dans sa dignité & dans la verité de leurs caracteres? Et cependent quelle distance encore entre ce portraits isolés & l'ensemble d'une grande histoire, telle que le Sacrifice d'Iphigenie, l'Entrevue de Coriolan avec sa Mêre, Medée qui dechire ses enfans, au Clytremnestre qui fait assassiner Agamemnon! Quelle puisse être la prêsomption que nous avons de nousmêmes, un sentiment intérieur nous forcera toujours d'avouer notre pauvreté actuelle & la richesse des anciens.

Cette richesse m'a ébl
oui: je l'ai ambitionée avec transport. C'est elle qui m'a donné la hardiesse de mettre en pratique ce que j'ai recuelli, par un travail assidu, touchant les Pantomimes de l'antiquité. Si mes efforts ne sont pas couronnés par le succès, je n'en serai pas rebuté. L'Art n'est pas résponsable des fautes de l'Artiste. Je réusserai peut-être mieux lorsque j'aurai ajouté l'expérience à l'etude; & le Public me fera certainment un mérite de l'avoir entrepris dans la vue de lui plaire, & me tiendra compte du défaut des moiens: nous manquons de tout ce qui seroit nécessaire pour de tels Spectacles.

J'ai divisé le Ballet en trois actes. Le premier représente une rue publique. La maison du Commandeur est d'un coté, celle de Don Juan de l'autre. L'Action commence par une Sérénade que Don Juan donne à Donna Elvire sa Maîtresse, fille du Commandeur. Il obtient l'entrée dans la maison, où il est

surpris par le Père, il se bat contre lui; le Commandeur est
tué: on l'emporte.

Dans le second Acte Don Juan donne chez lui un grand repas,
précedé d'un bal, à ses amis & à ses Maitresses. Lorsque'on a
danse on se met à table. Au plus fort de la joie, le Commandeur, en statue, frappe rudement à la porte. On a ouvrir; il
entre dans la salle; les conviés sont épouvantés, ils prennent la
fuite. Don Juan reste seul avec la statue. Il la prie, par
dérision de manger. Elle refuse, & convie, à son tour, Don
Juan à manger à son tombeau. Don Juan accepte, & reconduit le Commandeur. Le bruit cesse; les conviés, un peu
rassurés reviennent dans la sale, mais la fraieur les accompagne, ce qui donne lieu à une entrée de Trembleurs. Don
Juan revient. Il tâche de les rassuer; ils l'abandonnent. Il reste
seul avec son laquáis, il donne des ordres, & sort.

Le triosième Acte se passe dans un endroit destine à la
sépulture de personnes de distinction. Le Mausolée du Commandeur nouvellement achevé est au milieu. Il est lui même
debout devant son tombeau. Don Juan est un peu étonné en
le voient. In prend cependent un air assuré, & s'approche du
Commandeur. Celuici le saisit par les bras, & l'exhorte à
changer de vie. Don Juan paroit obstiné, & malgré les
menaces du Commandeur & les prodiges dont il est temoin, il
persiste dans son impénitence. Alors le centre de la terre
s'ents'ouvre vomis sant des flammes. Il sort de ce Volcan
caucoup de spectres, & de Furies qui tourmentent Don Juan.
Il est enchainé par elles, dans son affreux désespoir il est
englouti avec tous les monstres; & un tremblement de terre
couvre le lieu d'un monceau de ruines.

Les Décorations de ce Ballet ont été faites avec beaucoup
d'intelligence par le S. Quaglio. M. Gluck en a composé la
Musique. Il a saisi parfaitement le terrible de l'Action. Il a
tache d'exprimer les passions qui y jouent, & l'épouvante qui
regne dans la catastrophe. La musique est essentielle aux
Pantomimes: c'est elle qui parle, nous ne faisons que les
gestes; semblables aux anciens Acteurs des Tragédies & des
Comédies qui faisoient déclamer les vers de la Pièce, & se

bornoient eux mêmes à la partie de la gesticulation. Il nous seroit presque impossible de nous faire entendre sans la Musique, & plus elle est appropriée à ce que nous voulons‛ exprimer, plus nous nous rendons intelligibles. J'en parlerai plus emplement dans une autre occasion.

Gaspar Angiolini[24]

Because of Angiolini's rational approach to dance, through Cahusac and Lucian's Roman style, he was led to tirades against the one-sidedly dilletantish approach to dance: "No one amongst us will believe that it is actually necessary or important for an orderly [that is, rationalistic] approach to a knowledge of dance that this is necessary to be a dancer." Angiolini's commentary to *Don Juan* goes on to demand a scientific-rationalist approach to the technique of ballet, as an aesthetic form of communication, in opposition to the *divertissment* and its Viennese counterpart, the *Groteskballet*, the "hopping and springing of farmers and swineherds in various national costumes . . . the lowest of forms. . . ." In fact, there had grown up a sort of half-way house between Angiolini's intense style and the *Groteskballet* – the so-called *Halbcharaktertanz*, consisting of shepherd's stories, gypsies, and anacreontic poetry, or as Angiolini stated, ". . . indeed all that the French opera had brought forth!"

For Angiolini, the dancer had to be capable of the same high acting ability for tragedy as the dramatic actor.

Just as the actors of antiquity based the expression of his role on the verse which he declaimed, so we apply the dance step (Pas), the expression, the attitude, the expressivity of the role performed, to the music. It is as difficult to compose such music as it is to write a tragedy in verse. *Everything must speak*: [emphasis added] it must help one to understand us as dancers.

Angiolini made a calculated differentiation between the effect of spoken dialogue and declamation, and the same mood, atti-

24. Unicum, Wiener National Bibliothek. B.E. 8. V. 72 (4). There are certain inconsistencies to be noted in Angiolini's French. The programme presented here is as in the original. One must assume a certain weakness in the Italian's command of French.

tude and expression in Dance. Angiolini applied a ratio of three to one in the telescoping of time, action and proportion of characters in a ballet, as compared to an equivalent theatrical piece. The most important source of subjects remains for Angiolini, however, Greek mythological tragedy.

The commentary for *Don Juan* appears under Angiolini's name, and surely he put these ideals into action; however, there is at least one thread of thought that runs through the words that lends credence to the strong possibility that the work was either styled after Calzabigi or actually written by the latter, who was in Vienna from February of 1761. Angiolini puts an inordinately strong emphasis on rationalistic attitudes for the choreographer and the composer, to the point where his romantic intensity seems a bit out of place.

Ghino Lazzeru, in his biography of Calzabigi[25] of 1918, quotes the poet from his *Lettera al S. Conte Alfieri*:

> Nel 1762 [sic] quando gia a Stougard erano stato fatti da Noverre i Balli Pantomimi di Medea, della Morte d'Ercole ed altri che sorpresero, e furono ammirati, fu rappresentato a Vienna, di composizione dell'Angiloini il Convitato di Pietra. L'immortale Gluck ne scrisse la musica; lo il programma francese, in cui diede delle preliminari abreviate notizie dell'Arte Pantominica degli Antichi.

Only the first edition of Calzabigi's work has this section; it was deleted from subsequent editions.

The 1765 edition of Angiolini's *Dissertation sur les Ballet Pantomimes des Anciens* and the forword to the scenario for the ballet *Semiramis* are both very likely to have been combined efforts of Angiolini and Calzabigi, as well as both of Angiolini's *Lettre al Sr. Noverre sugli Pantomimi & Riflessioni sopra l'uso de Programmi ne'Balli Pantomimi*, (published in Milan in 1773). The latter two works were probably written while Angiolini was still in Vienna, and with the aid of Calzabigi. Noverre doesn't miss an opportunity to make an allusion to the combined authorship in his answer to Angiolini.

25. Ghino Lazzeru, *La Vita e l'opera letteraria di Ranieri Calzabigi.* (Citta di Castella, 1907), p. 213. See also Hertha Michel, "Ranieri Calzabigi als Dichter ...", *Gluck-Jahrbuch,* (1918).

The Paris Conservatoire library contains another edition of the choreography for *Don Juan*, a version that was put together in 1850 by George Trautwein in Berlin, and published as a piano reduction in several volumes. The version comes from an actual performance with three rather than the four acts of the first performance. Elvira, here the daughter of the Commander, for some unknown reason, doesn't appear until the ball scene of the second act. There are two other versions, seemingly based on the Trautwein reduction, in the British Museum. All of these versions have only the reduced number of set dances, fifteen, which jibes with the score in the library at Darmstadt, and with the keyboard reduction in Vienna.

The tie between Gluck and Angiolini continued to produce ballets of the same dramatic fervor as *Don Juan*. The following year Angiolini provided the ballets for the performance of Gluck's opera *Orfeo*. The report in the *Wiener Diarium* for the 6th of October goes thus:

> Herr Caspar Angiolini has provided a work of individuality in the new production, bound together with choruses and fables as to provide a very informative evening.[26]

It was mainly the pantomime for the scenes of mourning and the "Dance of the Furies" that created the most lasting impression. Other works of the same year, 1762, are a ballet titled *Cleopatra* (used by Angiolini again some years later in Milan), a marionette ballet for a performance of Hasse's opera *Clelia*, and for Giuseppe Scarlatti's (1718-1770; this Scarlatti was the grandson of Alessandro, though his father is not known) *Issipile*, a ballet titled *Les aventures de Serail*.

For his opera *Ezio* of 1763, Gluck continued to collaborate with Angiolini for the ballet scenes, one of which used the story of *Thetis and Peleus*, and another scene of a vaudeville nature, concerning certain Spanish gentlemen buying wives from a harem in Algeria — and buying Spanish ladies at that! In 1764 the two worked together on the four dance intermezzi for Gluck's comic

26. "Herr Casp. Angiolini hat die ihm eigene Geschicklichkeit in Ausarbeitung der Tänze dadurch auf das neue bewahnt dass er dieselben mit den Chören und mit der Fabel auf eine solche Art verbunden, welche der Vorstellung ein nicht minder prachtiges als lerreiches Ansehen gibt."

opera. *La recontre imprevue*, and then in the same year went on to produce an autonomous pantomime, *Alessandro*. Like *Don Juan*, *Alessandro* contained a one movement *sinfonia* and a series of short dance pieces, in this instance eight numbers, and a closing longer dance, a Chaconne. Angiolini typically retained the premises of the work for further use, as he was obviously referring back to *Alessandro* in 1780 at the Teatro Filarmonico at Verona for a production of his *Ballo eroico pantomimo: Alessandro trionfante nelle India*.

In 1765 Angiolini created a series of dance works that showed an increase in the tone of dramatic intensity, and probably for this reason went beyond the acceptable standards of the Viennese audience and led to an increasing and continuous loss of popularity in the Austrian capitol. The first hints of dissatisfaction appear because of an act of omission rather than commission — and most likely has more to do with Gluck than Angiolini. On January 30, 1765 Gluck's *Telemaco* was given with no ballet, something that seems to have disturbed the audience and Khevenhüller a good deal. However, the most serious disturbance was created by the ballet pantomime written for a festival performance, *Semiramis* with a libretto by Calzabigi and music by Gluck. Khevenhüller provides some explanation of how the ballet's unrelieved austerity was received by the Viennese court when he described it as "much too pathetic and sad . . . and that the audience had been both frightened and shocked." The title page of the programme for *Semiramis* reads as follows:

Dissertation/ sur les Ballets pantomimes/ des Anciens,/ pour serir de Programme/ au Ballet Pantomime tragique/ de/ Semiramis(.) Composé par Mr. Angiolini Maître des des Ballets/ du Théâtre près de la Cour à Vienne, &/ représenté pour la premièr fois sur ce/ Théâtre le 31 Janvier 1765./ A l'occasion des fêtes/ pour le/ Mariage de Sa Majeste/ le Roi des Romains./ Vienne, chez Jean-Thomas de Trattnern,/ Imprimeur de la Cour./ 1766./[27]

27. The title page contains a dystich by Horace in French translation by Père Sanadon. *Semiramis* is truly a "pantomime without dance. What in *Don Juan* had been traditional dance forms, were here turned into abstract, intellectual situations. Hymns, marches, etc., were to be expressed through bodily motion. All were to react to the rhetorical in mime and become sensitized to its "secret whisperings."

The basis of Angiolini's Pantomime was Voltaire's tragedy, set by Angiolini in three acts, and pervaded by the guiding force of the ghostly character Ninus. "The ghost served greatly as a focus of my understanding and made my tragedy truly terrible and catastrophic." In the first act Ninias, the son of Ninus, is tormented by the Shakespearean-like ghost, both in dreams and in hallucination; however, the peak of terror in the act, a true paroxysm of fear, occurs at the appearance of a hand writing upon a wall: "My son, avenge me! Faithless woman, tremble!" The second act, as in *Don Juan*, is a magnificent mass scene, with Semiramis taking Ninias as her husband in the high temple, in spite of the protests of the high priest Oröes. As Semiramis approaches the altar a storm erupts during which the statue of the god Belus is struck and destroyed by lightning. The third act takes place at the court of the Assyrian kings, before the tomb of Ninus, in the midst of a great sacrifice to Belus. Semiramis is present, but not Ninias. At a point early in the act the mausoleum opens. Ninus' spirit rushes out to grab the new queen and returns into the tomb with her, the doorway shutting again. Ninias is at first unaware of what has happened after arriving on the scene; however, he at one point drops a dagger and at the point of its contact with the tomb the same words appear . . . "Go! Avenge your father.!" Upon this command by his father and because of the need to placate Belus, Ninias enters the tomb in order to kill Semiramis. The Ballet ends with the death of Semiramis and the suicide of Ninias. The work succeeds in maintaining an unrelieved intensity and austerity of purpose, in keeping with the main concern of most *Sturm und Drang* drama, that of the battle of man against inexorable fate.

Angiolini again provides a commentary to support his intentions in *Semiramis*, a commentary which continues the ideals presented in the forword to *Don Juan*. Angiolini again complains that dance had been deprived of any real art for too long a time. There was no attempt at executing *entrechats* or other steps in time with the music, nor to carry oneself well, to be in command of the hands, nor to understand what was fine and artistic. "One is usually powerless to bend, or to hold one's balance, since the dances are normally set to very gay and fast melodies. Not once could one dance the slow and dignified steps of the *passacaglia.*"

Therefore, it is not difficult to make the next logical step and to see ballet pantomime as the vehicle for the greatest tragic dramas. In these pantomimes, the content is centered in the rhetoric of the dance, and to achieve these heights of intensity the dancers must approach the art of the spoken stage. The music becomes the poetry of the ballet, just as unable to be dispensed with as an actor can do without words.

Certainly Gluck encouraged Angiolini in this trend toward the severe and austere, and was abetted in turn by his colleagues, Angiolini, Quaglio and Calzabigi. They agreed that the dance, which had to telescope the events of the spoken theater, showed its true nature in a focus on the miniature. The most varied sensations were to be depicted and exposed by the most restricted expression. The "silent language" was to be able to communicate an entire set of concepts in one moment.

Angiolino felt that it would be astonishing for the uninitiated to be exposed to a thoroughly tragic ballet-pantomime, correctly presented, severely restricted, but intensely "catastrophic": one of Angiolini's favorite expressions. Angiolini felt that Semiramis was a successful attempt in this direction, ". . . appropriately, as my ballet is no longer than twenty minutes." The ballet librettist normally will have only two or three solo dancers to work with, so that he cannot insert extraneous episodes. Five or six actors, relieving each other, can easily keep going for three hours or more, while one cannot dance at full strength for more than a minute or so at a time . . . so, it is obviously more difficult to dance than to act. If the librettist should attempt to overcome these restrictions by using a stage full of dancers, Angiolini felt strongly that he would fail, despite the fact that Angiolini obviously felt that the use of the ballet corps, particularly as a point of contrast for the opening of the second act, was very important. Angiolini's reasoning, in keeping with his general tone toward ballet, was more pragmatic: he only states that the ballet corps is there to give a respite to the solo dancers. The focal point of Angiolini's fanatic feeling toward the meaning of his art hangs just on this element: that it is far more costly physically to be a successful pantomimist and dancer than to act, let alone to write plays. The interesting element here is the analogy with the spoken word, a recurring facet of Angiolini's philosophy.

As stated previously, Angiolini gave priority for subject matter to Greek tragedy, in explicit contrast with the procedures of the French opera, with its confusion of episodes and emphasis on fantasy. Allegory seemed no longer to interest Angiolini. Greek tragedy, then, expressed in a kind of dumb declamation, but nevertheless set forth in a visual medium. To quote Angiolini again, ". . . the subject that we handle must be thought of as being put through a glass that centers all the sun's rays upon one point."

Gluck's music is also more bare-boned than that for *Don Juan*. There is certainly a greater avoidance of a *bel-canto* melodic style. The elements of musical *Sturm und Drang*: unison entries for the strings, large melodic leaps, an orchestra dominated by wind color but in the main of a monochrome character, syncopation, and the emphasis upon the minor mode make up the style of the music. The format is again that of a one-movement *sinfonia* and fifteen short dance pieces. Semiramis was danced in Vienna by Noverre's pupil Nancy Trancard. The work was quickly referred to as a *Pantomime without Dance*, a musical character-language made up of the most tightly knit techniques, bound together by the qualities of the *Sturm und Drang*.

Gluck's music for *Semiramis* is incorrectly catalogued in the appendix of Alfred Wotequenne's *Verzeichnis* of Gluck's music.

On the 19th of May, 1765 another ballet of Angiolini's was produced in Vienna, based on another Greek tragedy, *Iphegenie*. The problem in this instance is that the programme gives no information as to who composed the music. Aside from the possibility that it was again the work of Gluck, the music could have been written either by Angiolini himself (as he did for the ballet *Cleopatra* mentioned above), or by Florian Gassmann (1729-1774) who began writing music for the ballet in 1763 and then succeeded Gluck at Civic Theater in 1764. The ballet was given along with a comedy by Rochon de Chabannes, *La Manie des Arts*. Khevenhüller pronounced *Iphegeie* as a more successful work than *Semiramis*, rather a typically terse understatement.

Probably the best example we have of Angiolini's composing ability is in his score for the pantomime in praise of Josef, performed for the coronation festivities upon Josef becoming Holy Roman Emperor. The pantomime-ballet is called *La Muse protette dal Genio d'Austria.*[28] The work is a rather conventional, uninteresting handling of the allegorical subject. In spite of the turn to the use of allegory (however justified by the purpose of the performance) the music more than holds its own as a substantial contribution to the genre of that period. The technique is smooth and flowing, with good handling of motivic writing, with a unified style. The score, in the Vienna National Library, shows a *sinfonia* and nine sections. The one movement form of the *sinfonia*, obviously adopted from Gluck in this case, is a well structured and fully developed sonata-allegro form. The work indicates that Angiolini had developed an interest in irregular rhythmic patterns, with sections in which no two instruments playing have the same rhythmic pattern. Of the nine sections, six are dances and marches, the remaining three numbers being entrance musics. The orchestration has a point of interest in its use of two English horns in the first two dance numbers. The dark quality was probably an influence of Angiolini's knowledge of Starzer's scores for Hilverding. Starzer also made use of the special quality of the English horn.

There are five other *Sinfonias* written by Angiolini still extant: to the ballets *Telmaco*, *La Didone abbandonata*, *Pittore o Natura*, *Ariana e Bacco*, and *Alescandro*. In several instances the manuscripts for these works lists the composer as Angullini or Angiulini.

The winter of the year 1764 saw the first of several events that helped change the situation for dance in Vienna in a drastic manner. On February 2, 1765 Hilverding returned to Vienna. With Hilverding came Josef Starzer and a protegé of Hilverding's, the Russian dancer Timofey Bublikov, known as *Tomoschka*. Bublikov remained in Vienna for several years, dancing with the ballet of the court opera.

On January 24, 1765 another festival ballet was produced for the royal family, on the occasion of the marriage of Josef with Maria Theresa of Bavaria, presented in the *Salon des Battailles* at Schönbrunn Palace. The choreography for this *Intendente di Machine, Pitura e Ballo* was Hilverding. The pantomime is titled *Le Triomphe de l'Amour*, quite appropriately. The solo dancers were

---

28. Mss. 18.781, Music Section, Wiener National Bibliothek. The body of the work is in manuscript, but the title and dedication are printed.

members of the royal family, including the Archduchess Marie Antoinette, and the Archdukes Ferdinand and Maximillian; this was an occasion that Marie Antoinette took with her to Paris as a childhood memory.

The music for this ballet-pantomime cum cantata was by Leopold Gassmann. The latter also set the music for Hilverding's heroic ballet *Eneo in Italia,* danced for a presentation of Hasse's opera *Remolo e Ersilia* at Innsbruck for the marriage of Archduke Leopold. Up to this point Hilverding's work had yet to appear before the public; however, on February 2, 1765 Hilverding choreographed a ballet for the comedy presented at the Civic Theater, *Les Amans proteges par l'Amour,* in a very successful, though conventional performance. The trend, then, was to a reversal of the romantic movement in Viennese dance. Angiolini's master, who had set the stage for his successor, remained a conventional hack for the remainder of his years, who emphasized just those qualities that Angiolini had riled against.

It was the next event, however, that was even more critical in bringing a halt to the work of the Gluck-circle. The death of the Emperor resulted in the closing of the theaters and the permanent release of the French society. Upon the advise of Hilverding, Angiolini accepted the post of ballet master offered to him by Catherine II of Russia, in effect to replace Hilverding. Early in 1766 Angiolini travelled to the court in St. Petersburg. He arrived with a first-rate reputation as a fine, expressive dancer, a successful composer and as an innovator. Angiolini's imaginative qualities were put to work very soon in Russia. One of the earliest works that we know of this period of seven years in Russia is a pantomimic choreography for an entire opera by Baldassare Galuppi (1706-1785) (Angiolini had become enthused by Galuppi after seeing a performance of Galuppi's earlier work *Il Re Pastore*) *Didone abbandonata.* We have already seen that Angiolini also wrote his own *Sinfonia* for the work. Galuppi had been invited to St. Petersburg in the same year as Angiolini; the favourable impression made by *Didone abbandonata* (first presented in Modena in 1741) was no doubt greatly enhanced by Angiolini's pantomime, — though the spectacle of the burning of the city of Carthage upon the Russian stages may have had some effect!

In 1767 Angiolini went with the court to Moscow. There he continued to impress the Russians — and in effect (along with his predecessor there) to create what became the traditional romantic Russian style. Angiolini's next work, far from the idiom of Greek tragedy, was a strong work based on both old Russian dances and Russian folk tunes.[29] The following year the court returned once again to St. Petersburg, where Angiolini turned to allegory with a Russian programme in *The Prejudice Conquered*. The same year he supplied the ballet for another of Galuppi's works, *Ifegenia in Tauride*, and in 1769 for Tommaso Traetta's (1727-1779) *Olimpiade*.

During this period of Angiolini's sojourn in Russia, events in Vienna were leading to an eventual confrontation between Angiolini and Noverre, one in which Angiolini was to emerge much the worse for wear. After the period of mourning for the Emperor, Hilverding attempted to revive the ballet at the *Kärtnertörtheater*, but the departure of the best of the dancers and other members of the troupes led to his abandonment of the venture by February of 1767. The situation, then, in Vienna, was ripe for the invasion of new blood on the ballet stage, and for the beginning of a clearly new phase in the dramatic theater. On January 11, 1767 Gaetano Vestris, by then one of the grand old men of ballet in Europe, made a solo appearance. The news report stated that the famous dancer represented, "l'histoire de Medee en pantomime nach heuriger Art." The work was in fact a pantomime devised by Noverre in Stuttgart originally called *Medée et Jason*, with music by Johann Josef Rudolph — a work still unknown in Vienna in 1767.

What was probably the most important event of the end of the decade, however, took place later that year on September 10, 1767, the Viennese debut of Noverre, who came to Vienna and performed at the express invitation of the Archduchess Maria Josefa. He presented himself for inspection with a new work, another so-called "machine and pantomime" ballet, *L'Apotheose d'Hercule*, choreographed with the assistance of Vestris. In

---

29. Aside from the fact that the use of Russian folk tunes and dances were appropriate and to be expected considering Angiolini's situation, still, the incorporation of the folk element is consistent with the romantic trend in the dance theater.

December of that year Noverre had prepared a ballet for Gluck's *Alceste*, according to an anonymous report *(applouso)* "dans le goût grotesque." The Viennese critics, it seems, had still not attuned themselves to the developments of the past decade. Despite the narrow-mindedness of the critical reports, what there were of them, the theater of the dance was by this time dominated by the *ballet d'action* – the combination of what was to be the techniques of nineteenth century romantic ballet with, and at the service of, highly dramatic programmes. The nobleman nor the layman would no longer play the dual role of spectator and actor – that would call for a highly trained professional, able to act as well as dance. The other musical arts did not turn to professionalism, in our sense of the term, until the emergence of the keyboard and violin virtuosi of the first decades of the nineteenth century and the entrance of chamber music into the opera house and the concert hall (abandoning the courtly chamber); however, it is this aspect of the changes taking place, at the sociological level, in musical life that enabled the ballet-pantomime, the *ballet d'action*, to remain in the main stream of theatrical dance.

The period we have covered may, in effect, be said to close with the death of Hilverding at the end of May, 1768, but it is necessary to jump ahead some five years for a glimpse at the situation in Vienna upon the return of Angiolini in 1774, only in order to make a final juxtaposition of the aesthetics, work, and comparative success or failure in the eyes of history between Angiolini and Noverre.

Angiolini spent the year after leaving Russia in 1733 in Italy, at Venice and then at Padua, where he presented several new works (with his own music) and new productions of old works.[30] During this period, however, Noverre had been tremendously successful in Vienna, attaining a popularity with both the

30. Venice: *La pertenz d'Enco ossia Didone abbandonata* for *Merope* by Insanguine. *Ballo tragico in 5 atti.*
L'arte vintadalla natura for the same work by Merope.
Il re alla caccia for Hasse's *Solimano.*
Semiramis for Anfossi's *Antigono*, as well as the ballet pantomime *Il disertore francese* for the same opera. The music for all these ballets was by Angiolini.
Padua: *Ariana nell'isola di Nasso* for Naumann's *Armida*. One new work appeared in Milan before Angiolini returned to Vienna: *Solimano II* for Guglielmi's opera *Le Pazzie di Orlando*. The ballet music was by Angiolini.

audiences and the critical review that Angiolini had never experienced. In 1774, despite the solidity of his position, Noverre left Vienna for Milan, taking with him the best dancers in the city, which made things a bit difficult for those left behind. As well, Noverre certainly left a difficult atmosphere for Angiolini to return to, as Noverre had produced in December of 1773 a ballet in a deliberately satirical caricature of Angiolini's style. Noverre left the city ostensibly after a public falling out with Calzabigi, though not before the production of one of his most famous works *Les Horaces et les Curiaces, Ballet tragique en cinq actes.* The music was by Josef Starzer. Noverre then left Vienna, as though in anticipation of the arrival of Angiolini, taking with him the city's favorite *prima ballerina*, Mlle. Vigano.

Angiolini, then, was to have an impossible task ahead of him. The *Gothaer Theaterkalender* for 1775 indicates that Angiolini was not having any success with the Viennese audiences. Two letters from Maria Theresa to Archduke Ferdinand, one dated April 12, 1774, the second August 11, 1774, provide evidence of Angiolini's precarious position in Vienna. The general tone of the letters is that of complaint against Angiolini and the attempts to persuade Noverre to return to the court. The letter written in April states: "Angiolini nous a régalés de deux très mauvaise ballets; on les a siffles; je n'approve pas cette impertinance, peut-être fera-t-on autant à Noverre à Milan." and in August: "Je suis bien aise que Noverre ait reussi à Milan; on a débité le contraire ici, et on faisait comparaison, qu'Angiolini etait tant regretté là-bas que Noverre ici. Le premier donne des ballets abominables ici, et Madame se donne le plus grand airs. Je ne dit pas que Noverre soit dans le reste aussi parfait; il est insoutenible, surtout s'il a un peu de vin, ce qui lui arrive souvent mais je ne trouve inique dans son art, et à tirer parti des plus mauvais sujets."

The two ballets by Angiolini that failed so abysmally in the eyes of Maria Theresa were *L'Orphelin de la Chine*, again labelled in the press as a cold pantomime without any vestige of dance, and the second ballet, which though only conjecture, could have been *Alessandro*.[31] Coincidentally, or not, Noverre also wrote a major

31. The *Gotha Theater Calender*, edited by Reichard, for 1775, prints the scenario on page 43, and states expressly that the ballet was finished in Vienna, and not in Russia, though it may have been started in St. Petersburg. There has been a considerable amount

ballet with Alexander as the main character, *Alexandre et Campaspe de Larisse, ou le triomphe d'Alexandre sur soi même. Ballet heroi-pantomime*, (1774). In 1774 there were two more ballets given by Angiolini, *Le Cid* and *Le Roi et le fermier. Le Cid* was a large, tragic pantomime in five acts, and got only very little better reception than the previous works, with the solo role particularly chosen for harsh words about its cold and monotonous effect. *Le Roi et le fermier, ballet heroi-comique*, a three act work, was performed in April of 1774, with the music by Angiolini, though with several numbers taken directly from the French opera-comique of the same name.

Müllers Geschichte und Tagbuch der Wiener Schaubühne (Vienna, 1776), provides us with the information needed to follow the activity of Angiolini's last year in Vienna. *Orphelin* was presented only once more in February of 1775 at the Kärntnertortheater, *Le Cid* six times, and another work, *König und Pächter* five times. Aside from these there is only mention of a series of other ballets by Angiolini, though with no mention as to their relative successes: *Der Dorfeulenspiegel, Sidney and Silly, Il ritorno opportuno, Les Nymphes, Theseus in Kreta, Montezuma oder die Eroberungs Mexikos* (this work was choreographed and completely wirtten by Angiolini, and seems to have been his most successful work of the period, with more than the usual repeat performances), *Der Engländer ünter den Sclafern, Die ländlichen Unterhaltung, Die unnütze Vorsicht, Die Savojarden, Die Schnitter,*[32] *Der Wahrsager*, and in November of 1775 *Die von Amor beschützen Schäfer.*[33]

However, none of these works, generally successful or not, seemed to gain the approval of his superiors. In September of 1775 Maria Theresa sent for the dancer H. Gallet to perform in

of argument as to the dates for both the choreography and the music, which is most likely by Gluck (would the criticism have been so strong if Gluck's name had been writ large on the performances?). See Alfred Orel's, "Eine Bemerkungen zu Tanzdramen Ch. W. Glucks," *O. E. Deutsch Festschrift* p. 82-89. The work is, however, inconclusive.

32. Starzer's music is in manuscript (keyboard reduction) in the Archiv der Gesellschaft der Musikfreunde in Vienna. Angiolini's programme for the ballet was printed in the *Gotha Theater Calendar* for 1776.

33. The music is again by Starzer. The score was at one time in the Berlin State Library.

another presentation of Noverre's *Horacio*, which certainly meant the end of Angiolini's career in Vienna. In any case, Noverre made the next move in returning to Vienna at just about the time Angiolini was leaving.

The next fifteen years are merely a record of the wanderings of Angiolini in Italy: Pavia (1775), Bologna (1778), Verona and Milan (1780), Venice again (1782), Naples (1789), Turin (1790), and in 1791 he returned to Milan, where he at one point adopted Republican sympathies and was expelled in 1800; he was re-admitted into the city in mid-1801 however, and died in Milan 1803.

To conclude, then, it is only fair to take one last look at the relationship between Angiolini and Noverre. Noverre published in 1776 in Vienna a work called *Recuil de Programmes de Ballets*, the first piece of which was, "Introduction au Ballet des Horaces ou petite reponse aux grandes Lettres du Sr. Angiolini." Here Noverre attempts to stamp Angiolini as no more than a mere imitator of his own style. Noverre "remembers" that Angiolini had been in Stuttgart, seen his work, and had been completely overwhelmed by Noverre's tragic art. Angiolini, then, attempted to use the "new" style in his *Semiramis*, but without the superb dancing of Noverre's own pupil, the ballet could not succeed. Noverre is not only completely silent about the work of Hilverding, of whose work he probably knew nothing, but also concerning *Don Juan*, a work which certainly does not suit his purposes.

The fact is, that Noverre could not possibly have shown any development of the tragic idiom nor the *ballet d'action* prior to 1761, not even an attempt. It becomes apparent if one compares the description of his new style in the 14th and 15th "Lettres sur le Danse. . ." (1760) with the works of that year and earlier. As pointed out at the beginning of this paper, Noverre's first exposure to a new attitude was through his association with Garrick. It was only after the further influence of the "reform" operas of Traëtta that Noverre's first great works appeared – and that, only shortly before *Don Juan*. Noverre's peak doesn't come about until his stay in Vienna.

The importance of both Noverre and Angiolini has not

received the balanced evaluation of objective history. The period in Vienna to the end of the 1760s was a focal point for the shift from social dance, done in a virtuosic manner, to that of expression, with technical virtuosity at its command. The period saw the removal of masks for dancers and the continual addition of steps to the technique. More and more virtuoso dancers were adding to the possibilities for expression. Though Angiolini is the least known, and the most ignored, of the Gluck circle, further evaluation of the mid-century reforms in the theater will continue to add to his stature.

Programme for the Ballet Don Juan or
Festin de Pierre
(Paris Concervatory, Ms. N. 20)
Programm du Ballet de Don-juan, ou bien, du festin du pierre, pour l'intelligence de la musique, que le Sr. Gluck a faite à Vienne sur ce sujet.

La scene representé une place publique de Madrid. Ou voit d'un côté la maison du Commandeur et de l'autre coté une promenade.

Dom-juan avec son valet precedent une troupe de musiciens, que ce dernier place sous les fenetres de la niece du Commandeur. Les musiciens commencement leur serenade avec des guitares, sans autre instrument; la nièce du Commandeur paroit à la fenetre, et fait ouvrir la porte à Dom-juan, qui entre dans la maison du Commandeur tandis que la serenade se continue.

Le Commandeur surprend Dom-juan avec sa niece, et veut le tuer. Celui-ci met l'épée à la main dans la maison du Commandeur pour défendre sa vie. On entend le cliqueti des épées dans la rue. La porte du Commandeur s'ouvre, les musiciens le voyent l'épée à la main à la poursuite de Dom-juan, se sauvent. Le combat entre le Commandeur et Dom-juan est continue dans la rue. Le Commandeur est blessé, et se retire du coté opposé à sa maison, en tombant a chaque pas, et s'apuyant sur son épée pour se relever.

La scene change et represente une salle de la maison de Dom-juan, où l'on voit tous les aprêts d'une fête. Les amis de Dom-juan la célèbrent par leur danses tandisque l'on prépare le festin. Il y a un pas de deux entre Dom-juan et la nièce du Commandeur. Le valet de Dom-juan avertit que l'on est servi; comme on se met à table, on entend fraper fortement à la porte. Le valet de Dom-juan prend une Bongie pour aller toir qui c'est; il est epouvanté en apercevant la statue du Commandeur qui s'avance gravement vers Dom-juan jusqu'auprès de la table.

Les amis de Dom-juan, et la nièce du Commandeur ainsi que le Valet de Dom-juan, épouvantées, prennant la fuite et laissent Dom-juan seul avec la statue. Il l'invité à sa mettre à table et à manger. La statue s'assesit; comme elle voit Dom-juan pret à la servir, elle se leve et invite Dom-juan à venir souper avec elle dans le mausolée du Commandeur. Dom-juan promet de s'y rendre et reconduit la statue, qui s'en retourne.

Pendant que Dom-juan l'accompagne ses amis reviennent, et expriment par leur gestes la crainte, dont ils sont encore saisis. Dom-juan reparoit triomphant; —a sa vue la terreur s'empare encore de tous ses amis, qui fuyent de nouveau et le laissent seul avec son valet, qu'il arrête comme il tâche de l'esquiver.

Dom-juan, qui veut sortir pour se rendre dans le mausolée où il doit souper avec la statue, fait signe à son Valet d'aller chercher son chapeau et son épée. Le Valet les apporte. Dom-juan lui fait signe de le suivre au mausolée. Le Valet refuse en alleguant sa peur. Dom-juan insiste, le valet souffre toutes sortes de violences sans ceder. Dom-juan prend le parti d'y aller seul. Le Valet le laisse sortir, et par ses démonstrations envoye à tous les diables un Maître, qui veut le forçer à participer au danger, auquel il va s'exposer de son propre mouvement.

La scene change et represente 'le mausolée du Commandeur. Dom-juan y arrive. A l'aspect de ce lieu, terrible par l'horreur du silence, qui y regne, Dom-juan chancelle sur le parti qu'il doit prendre; la peur paroit s'emparer de ses sens. La statue du Commandeur paroit; à sa vue, Dom-juan rapelle son courage, et la vanité le fait triompher de sa terreur.

La statue du Commandeur, qui semble lire dans l'âme de Dom-juan qu'il n'agit que par les mouvemens d'une fausse et vaine gloire, lui montre le ciel, et le serrant tendrement entre ses bras, lui met a differentes reprises la main sur son coeur, qu'elle cherche à toucher par ses remonstrances. Dom-juan les meprise. La statue fait des nouveaux efforts pour soustraire Dom-juan —a sa perte, que son obstination semble rendre inevitable. Tout cela est inutile, Dom-juan repond en haussant les epaules et regarde la statue d'un ar moqueur. Elle lui fait entendre les gemissements des ames qui subissent la peine due à leur impieté. Dom-juan n'en est point touché, ni meme emu. Le Commandeur entre en fureur; il saisit Dom-juan par le bras, et frape violemment du pied, en lui montrant la terre prete à s'ouvrir pour l'engloutir dans l'abime qui va se creuser sous ses pieds jusqu'aux Enfers. Dom-juan est toujours le meme. Enfin la statue du Commandeur voyant la mesure de impieté de Dom-juan comblée, le livre à son mauvais destin en le prècipitant dans le gouffre qui s'entrouve sous ses pieds.

La scene change et represente les Enfers, ou l'on voit Dom-juan se debattre au milieu des demons qui dansent autour de lui la torche à la main, et qui le poursuivent sans cesse. Dom-juan paroit enfin ouvrir les yeux sur l'horreur de sa situation. Il est au desespoir d'avoir causé lui meme sa perte par son entetèment. Il cherche une issue pour s'echaper des Enfers; comme il croit en evoir trouvé une, il est arreté dans la fuite par une troupe de furies, qui lui barrent le chemin, et font siffler autour de lui les serpens dont elles ont la tête environnée, et qu'Elles excitent avec leur flambeux.

Dom-juan ne se connait plus, il donne toutes les marques du plus affreux desespoir, et dans l'exces de sa rage il regarde comme son unique ressource la fureur des demons, auxquels il se livre et s'abandonne de lui meme pour decider enfin son sort.

Il est enchainé par les demons, et precipité par eux dans le plus profond des Enfers, d'ou l'on voit de temps en temps sortir des tourbillions de le flamme qui le consume.

*   *   *

Indications des endroits de la musique qui ont raport à l'action exprimée dans le Ballet.

N.B. Les endroits interessants, dans le milieu des morceaux, sont marqués sur la musique meme dans la 1re partie avec du crayon pour renvoyer ici.

Indications

La symphonie est l'ouverture du Ballet.
No. 1. Dom-juan et son valet arrivent à la tete des musiciens.
No. 2. La serenade donnée avec des guitarres.
No. 3. Combat du Commandeur et de Dom-juan commencé dans la maison meme.
    a) Il est continué dans la rue, après la fuit des musiciens.
    b) instant ou le Commandeur reçoit le coup l'épée de Dom-juan.
No. 4. La scene change et represente les aprets de la fête que Dom-juan donne à ses amis.
No. 5. Chaconne Espagnole.
No. 6. Pas de deux entre Dom-juan et sa maitresse.
No. 7. Danse generale.
No. 8. On entend fraper à la porte au moment de se mettre à table.
    c) Le valet de Dom-juan va voir qui c'est.
    d) Il aperçoit le spectre
    e) Les amis de Dom-juan fugent en tremblant.
No. 9. La statue s'avance vers Dom-juan resté seul

f) Dom-juan invite la statue à se mettre à table.

g) Elle s'asseoit.

h) Elle se leve pour invite Dom-juan à son tour.

i) il hésite

l) il promet

m) Le Commandeur en doute.

n) Dom-juan affirme qu'il viendra

o) La statue se leve pour s'en aller. Dom-juan l'accompagne.

No. 10. Les amis de Dom-juan reparoissent et expriment leur crainte en regardent de coté et d'autre pour voir si Dom-juan n'est pas sorti effectivement comme ils le pensent.

No. 11. Retour de Dom-juan.

No. 12. Crainte nouvelle de ses amis à sa vue.

No. 13. Dom-juan envoie chercher son chapeau et son épée pour aller au mausolée.

p) il fait signe à son valet de le suivre.

q) Menaces de Dom-juan pour determiner son valet.

r) Le valet le voyant partir le laisse aller seul et exprime par ses gestes qu'il aime mieux perdre ses gages, et meme etre tué s'il le faut que de suivre son maitre qui va à tous les diables.

No. 14. La scene change et represente la mausolée.

s) Dom-juan paroit effrayé à la vue de ce lieu, ou du moins inquiet.

t) La statue paroit et vient au devant de Dom-juan.

u) Dom-juan se rassure par l'effet de son orgueil.

v) Commencement de l'exhortation du Commandeur.

x) Dom-juan la méprise.

z) La statue redouble ses instances en mettant la main sur le coeur de Dom-juan.

a) Elle montre le ciel.

b) Dom-juan n'en fait point de compte

c) La statue entre en fureur.

d) Elle prend Dom-juan par le bras.

e) Elle frappe du pied en lui montrant le danger qui le menace.

f) Elle precipite Dom-juan.

No. 15. La scene represente les Enfers.

g) Dom-juan s'arrache les cheveux de desespoir.

h) Les Demons tourmentent Dom-juan.

i) il croit avoir trouvé une issue et se trouvé arreté dans sa fuite par une troupe de furies.

l) desespoir affreux de Dom-juan.

m) Il se livre lui meme au pouvoir des Démons.

n) Il est precipité avec eux dans le plus profond des Enfers.[34]

---

34. As in Angiolini's forward to *Don Juan*, whatever inconsistencies and irregularities there are in the French, are as in the original manuscript. The autograph of the full score has not survived. There may probably have been one more act than described here.

Ballets choreographed by Angiolini
after leaving Vienna, 1775-1790

1775-1777:
Padua: *L'orfano nella China* for Bianchi's *Eurione*
1778-1780:
Bologna: Ballet for Gluck's *Alceste.*
1780-1781:
Verona and Milan: *Alessandro trionfante nelle Indie*, for Salieri's *La scuola de gelosi*; also used for Rust's *Gli antiquari in Palmiri*
   La morte di Cleopatra, music by Angiolini
   L'amoree l'azzarado, music by Angiolini
1781:
Milan: *Attila, il castigo de honzi*, for *Antigono* by Anfossi and Gatti, ballet music by Angiolini
Venice: *L'orfano della China*, ballo tragico in 5 atti
Lauretia, ballo erocomico in 3 atti, ballet music by Angiolini both of these ballets were for the opera *Cajo Mario* by Bertoni.
1782:
Venice: *Il Suffie e lo schiavo* and Il diavolo a quattro, ossia la *doppia metamorfosi*, both for *Artemizia* by Calegari. The ballet music in each case was by Angiolini
Milan: *I geni reuniti, Il Solimano Secondo, il diavolo a quattro, Lauretta*: Balli da rappresentarsi alternativemente for Caruso's *Il matrimonio in commedia* and for Gassmann's *L'amore artigano*. The ballet music used for Gassmann's opera was by Angiolini in each case.
1784:
Naples: *Lauretta* for L'artemice by Tritto
Padua: *Il daivolo a quartro* for *Ezio* by Calvi, music by Angiolini *Il convitato* for *Ezio by Calvi, music by Gluck*.
1789:
Milan: Amore e Psiche for *Nilleti* by Bianchi, ballo eroico in 5 atti, music by Angiolini
Le nozze de' Sanniti, and *Dorina, e l'uomo selvatico* for *La disfatta di Dario* by Giordani, music by Angiolini.
Fedra and *Lorezzo*, both for *Antigona* by Coltellini, music by Angiolini.
1790:
Turin: *Sargine* and *Lorezzo, I vincitori de guiocchi olimpici* for *L'Olimpiade* by Federici. Music by Angiolini.
L'orfano, Il re alla caccia, and *Il tutore sorpreso* for *Gulio Sabino* by Tarchi. Music by Angiolini.
Venice: *Tito, ola partenza di beremico, ballo eroico pantomimo in 5 atti.*

Musica della stresso G. Angiolini, direttore di tutto lo spectacolo. for
L'apoteosi d'Ercole by Larchi.
*La vendetta ingegnosa o la satua di Condillac, favola boscareccia
pantomima. Musica dello stresso G. Angiolini.* For Hasse's Demefoönte.

BIBLIOGRAPHY

Abert, Hermann. "J. G. Noverre und seine Einfluss auf die dramatische
Balletkomposition." *Jarhbuch der Bibliothek Peters, 1907* 15 Leipzig;
Peters, 1908, pp. 29-45. This work doesn't concern itself with the work
being done in Vienna independently of Noverre. Abert at this point was
not aware of the importance of Angiolini.

Angiolini, Gaspar Maria. *Lettere di Gasp. Angiolini a Monsieur Noverre sopra
i Balli Pantomimi.* Milan: Giovanni Batista Bianchi, 1773.
Riflessioni sopra l'uso de Programmi ne' Balli Pantomimi. Milan:
Giovanni Batista Bianchi, 1773.

Arteaga, Stefan. *Le Rivoluzioni del Teatro Musicale Italiano.* Bologna, 1783.
Revised second edition, Venice, 1785. 3 volumes.

Cahusac, Luis de. *La Danse ancienne et moderne ou traite historique sur la
danse.* a La Haye, 1794.

Crüwell, G. A. *Die Wienerin.* Vienna: Amathea Verlag, 1927. Crüwell deals
with the ballerinas dancing in Vienna in mid-century.

Dictionaire de Musique. Paris: Bordas, 1970. Edited by Marc Honegger. Vol.
1. A small article concerning Angiolini, which doesn't apportion his true
importance. The article is much longer for Noverre. This is not only the
general trend in encyclopedias, but is in fact in proportion to the
chauvinistic intensity of the editors.

Enciclopedia della Musica. Milan: Ricordi, 1963. Vol. 1, p. 76. Certainly
considerably more space is given here to Angiolini than in the *Dictionaire
de Musique*, but the article still tends to be superficial.

Gottschalk, Louis. "A Plausible Interpretation of the French *Philosophes.*"
Studies in Eighteenth Century Culture, Volume 2 = *Irrationalism in the
Eighteenth Century*, edited by Harold E. Pagliaro. Cleveland and
London: The Press of the Case Western Reserve University, 1972, pp.
3-12.

Haas, Robert. *Gluck und Durazzo im Bürgtheater. (Opera Comique im Wien).*
Leipzig: Peters, 1925. One of the important works on the dramatic
ınusical theater ın the eighteenth century.
"Die Wiener Bühnentanz von 1740 bis 1767." *Jahrbuch der Bibliothek
Peters, 1937.* Leipzig: Peters, 1938. Pp. 77-93.
"Wiener Ballet-Pantomime im 18 Jahrhundert und Glucks Don Juan."

Studien zur Musikwissenschaft. Vol. 10, pp. 6-36. (Vienna: Universal Edition, 1923.)

Huizinga, Jan. Wege der Kulturgeschichte. Munich: Drei Masken Verlag, 1930. 405 pages.

Lazzeru, Ghino. La Vita e l'opera letteraria di Ranieri Calzabigi. Citta di Castella, 1907.

Lifar, Serge. Histoire du Ballet Russe. Paris, 1950. A book meant for the layman, ballet buff and the dancer; however, with some interesting material.

Lowenberg, Alfred. "Angiolini" Grove's Dictionary of Music and Musicians. Edited by Eric Blum. Vol. 1, p. 157. New York: St. Martin's Press, 1954. The dates are incorrect and the article is only one short paragraph. Lowenberg seems not to have read past Haas' article of 1923. The editors would have been better advised to have omitted an article altogether as does Musik in Geschichte und Gegenwart.

Lynham, D. The Chavalier Noverre. The Father of Modern Ballet. London, 1950. A useful book on its subject.

Michaut, Pierre. Histoire du Ballet. Paris, 1945. A general history, with limited material on the coterie in Vienna, but, obviously, copious material on Noverre.

Michel, Herta. "Ranieri Calabigi als Dichter von Musikdramen und als Kritiker." Gluck-Jarhbuch vol. 4, 1918, pp. 99-171. Still provides the best background for the reform movements of the period. She points out that Calzabigi to the end of his life quotes Diderot almost verbatim, while being careful never to mention Diderot's name (p. 149).

Mooser, R. A. Annales de la musique et des musiciens en Russie au XVIIIe Siècle. Geneva, 1951. A more scholarly work than Lifar's. Quoted generally for its material of a detailed nature.

Noverre, Jean-Georg. Lettres sur la Danse et les Ballets. Lyon et Stuttgart, 1790.

Sonnenfels, J. von. Briefe über die wiennerische Schaubühne. 4 volumes. Vienna, 1768. Contemporary commentary. Criticism in newsletters of the mid-century was typically brief and less than to the point.

Sulzer, Johann Georg. Allgemeine Theorie der Schönen Kunst. Leipzig: Wiedmann'sche Buchhandlung, 1771-1774; 1702-1794. 5 volumes = Mitglied der Königlichen Akademie in Berlin.

Tani, Gino. "Angiolini." Enciclopedia della Spettacolo. Volume 1. Rome: Casa editore La Maschere, 1954-62. colls. 619-627. This is the largest article on Angiolini in any work consulted (except perhaps for the incorporation of material on Angiolini in the articles by Haas) and the most thorough. The encyclopedia is a large, ten volume work dealing with all aspects of the stage and theatricalism.

Paul F. Marks

The Oboe Concerto
and the
Virtuosi of the 18th Century

The handy terminology that has been so convenient for us in describing certain periods of music has become quite useless as our study of the 18th century has advanced. Not long ago in surveying the history of music one could say that the Baroque concept was replaced by the Classical style, which was subsequently replaced by the Romantic, and so forth. Now, however, we have an abundance of historical subdivisions in music so that, in addition to the above designations, we refer to periods in the 18th century as middle and late Baroque, pre-Classical, post-Classical and pre-Romantic, all terms that have been used by various scholars in recent penetrating studies of these periods. The variety of these appellations serves to describe the 18th century for what it was in music, namely, a vast conglomeration of styles. Some forms, such as the concerto grosso, lasted throughout the entire century due to their popularity at concerts such as those sponsored in England by the Concert of Ancient Music, and some, like the rondo, enjoyed only a relatively short musical life.

It would seem that the almost pathological desire on the part of the 18th century public for constant newness was responsible for the continuous succession of new musical styles. It was also true that the travelling virtuoso brought new ideas in music to an eager public and whetted their appetites for more. Fanny Burney's comment regarding a concert, that "it pained me to hear Cramer and Fischer play so divinely, . . . and especially Fischer, for he is always new" is but one illustration of this attitude.[1]

1. *Thy Diary of Fanny Burney,* ed. by Christoper Lloyd, London, 1948, p. 114.

The solo oboe concerto displayed a principal compositional idea that held great favour among the listeners of the 18th century. It was the principle of contrast, both sonic and dynamic, a condition that the oboe is most admirable in expressing. Indeed, it was when the fashion for this musical idea faded that the oboe as a solo instrument finally fell into obsolescence, eventually to find its home in the orchestra of the 19th century. Entering the musical scene in the late 18th century and eclipsing the popularity of the concerto, in new vogue was the sonata form concept, a musical idea which had been coming for some time. Since this form principally involves the continuous development of a musical idea over a relatively long period, the incisive tone of the oboe was obviously not the ideal vehicle for the expression of this genre; the improved piano with its greater homogeneity of tone colour became the favourite instrument in sonata construction, and the new vehicle for concerti. One only needs to note that from the Classical period there are extant but one concerto for oboe by Mozart (also arranged by him for flute) and one attributed to Haydn (now thought to be by the young Beethoven); this is the total representation of oboe concerti by major composers of this period.

From its early development by Hotteterre in the late 17th century to the refinements made in the 19th century by Triebert, the oboe's development has been in the hands of French artists. It is this instrument, the "hoboy" as it was known in England, that probably made its first appearance in Lully's ballet *L'Amour Malade* in 1657. All European performers were eager to adopt the new instrument, with the exception of the Viennese players who, with minor additions such as extra keys, play to this day on instruments little changed from those in use in Vienna in the early 18th century. These have much larger dimensions and dynamic range than the French instruments.

It is a common misconception that the oboe is a direct development of the shawm. The oboe, however, is not a refined version of that instrument, but is an independent musical instrument developed to meet new requirements in 18th century music. In fact, the two instruments appear to have coexisted side by side for some years, each having a separate function. The oboe of the 18th century remained fairly unchanged until the final years of that century and is the instrument upon which the concerti mentioned here were performed. The oboe was used not only in the concerted music of polite society, but also in military bands where it occupied the role of the principal melodic instrument, a position now assumed by the clarinet. It may be because of this fact that it became traditional for the oboe to give the tuning A to the band, a custom surviving today in orchestras in every country even though most orchestras usually have only two or three oboes. As an outdoor instrument, there were attendant liabilities for the performers, according to Congreve who notes that, "The Hautboys who played to us last night had their breath froze in their instruments till it dripped of the end of 'em in icicles, by god this is true."[2]

Marin Mersenne observing the tone of the oboe in his *Harmonie universelle* of 1635 writes, "It is suited to large functions . . . because it makes a big noise and fine harmony. Indeed, excepting the trumpet, its tone is louder and more violent than that of any other instrument."[3] C. S. Terry quotes this passage in his work on Bach's orchestra and uses this observation to support his thesis that the oboe of Bach's orchestra, the one he would use in his cantatas and oratorios, was "not the plaintive, nervous voice of the modern orchestra, but an adaptable ripienist, convenient for yoking with instruments of every timbre and even as a competitor with the trumpets and horns not despicable."[4]

Terry's own words, written in the early part of the 20th century, point to the danger of attempting to characterize the tone of any wind instrument in a given historical period. The "nervous voice" Terry describes is the one common in his native England, cultivated for many years as the kind of tone favoured in that country. It is not an accurate description of the tonal qualities of the oboe in other countries, however, and this discrepancy, dramatic enough in our own day, was especially marked in the 18th century.

2. Philip Bate, *The Oboe*, New York, 1956, p. 40.
3. Marin Mersenne, *Harmonie universelle, contenant la theorie et la pratique de la musique*, Paris, 1636, Vol. 5, p. 303.
4. Charles Sanford Terry, *Bach's Orchestra*, London, 1932, p. 103.

Of all the orchestral instruments of the 18th century, the oboe seems to have provoked the most variety of opinions about the actual sound or tone of the instrument. An early writer, Peter Leycester, writing in 1650 distinguishes the shawm as "loud and shrill" and the "hooby" as "very deep and humming."[5] In England in the 18th century the bore of the oboe tended to be smaller than in French and German oboes, giving a smaller and more incisive quality to the sound, very much as that said to have been produced by Johann Christian Fischer. Power, or loudness, did not need to be separated from sweetness of tone, and, indeed, Fischer was said to have possessed both. Power, however, became more desirable later in the century as public concert halls increased in size.

While specific opinions of persons such as Charles Burney and Leopold Mozart concerning the tone of the oboe must be considered in the light of their particular aesthetic leanings, it would be reasonable to say that the tone of the 18th century instrument ranged from a quite harsh, shrill and trumpet-like quality to a soft, warm and flute-like one. Oboe virtuosi such as the Besozzis, Sammartini, and Fischer were able to produce all of these qualities. Perhaps one should not feel too sorry for Johann Sebastian Bach who, while he may not have had the opulent sounds of the modern orchestra at his disposal, did have several kinds of each wind instrument and especially, according to an account by François Raguenet in 1702, of "the Hautboys, which by their sounds equally mellow and piercing, have infinitely the advantage of the violins in all brisk, lively airs."[6]

The early recognition of the distinctiveness of the oboe's tone quality foreshadowed the principal reason for that instrument's popularity in the middle and late 18th century, namely, the public's desire for constant newness which created the perfect situation for the oboe's incisive, flexible, and often unpredictable propensity. And the kind of musical personality that was attracted to playing the instrument also happened to be the type of

5. Quoted by Walter L. Woodfill in *Musicians in English Society*, Princeton, 1953, p. 370.

6. François Raguenet, "Comparison Between the French and Italian Music," (1702), ed. Oliver Strunk, *Musical Quarterly* 32, 1946, p. 415.

performer that the public both adored and associated with the operatic personality. It is in this dimension that the oboe differs so greatly from its generic relatives, the flute, bassoon and clarinet, and why it must be considered, at least in solo performance, to have shared a common heritage with the virtuoso singer up until 1800. In some cases 18th century oboists, recognizing the influence of the operatic tradition on their playing, teamed up with singers, often their wives, and became touring virtuosi in England and on the continent. Such duos as Franziska and Ludwig Lebrun, and the Weichsels whose daughter was the famous Elizabeth Billington, were popular favourites at all public and private concerts. An interesting example of a reverse influence of the combination of singer and oboist is seen in the case of Mrs. Weichsel, who apparently attempted to imitate vocally the sound emitted from her husband's oboe, eventually to find her voice becoming quite reedy. The Weichsels' daughter, Mrs. Billington, happily avoided this by imitating the clarinet in her later years. The lexicographer Busby notes that Mrs. Weichsel could also render staccato passages that rivaled those of the best violinists of the day.[7] In America the most important singer-oboist team was the Graupners, Johann Christian and Catherine, who as English expatriates were popular in Charleston, South Carolina, in the last quarter of the 18th century. Mrs. Graupner was celebrated as the first white woman to sing a Negro ballad in a public concert in America, and her husband was noted as the founder of the Haydn and Handel Society of Boston which gave the first performance in America of Handel's Messiah.

One of the historian's most difficult problems in studying the wind concerto, and in particular the oboe concerto, is the location and discovery of concerti mentioned in the various sources as having been played, but for which no manuscript or printed source has been found. Thy problem of locating source material is not so acute in the case of the sonata for a wind instrument. Sonatas were often in the realm of the capability of the musical amateur, and there was consequently a heavy, constant public demand for them to be made available for public use.

7. For a further discussion of these vocal-instrumental relationships see *Queens of Song* ed. by E. C. Clayton, London, 1848, p. 230 et passim.

The solo wind concerto, however, was a different matter. Primarily composed by virtuosi for their own use, wind concerti were performed almost exclusively by them, since the average amateur was not capable of playing such inherently difficult music. It is natural to assume that the virtuoso oboist, desirous of protecting his own work, was not anxious to have his concerti published, or certainly not until he had performed them over a wide area. Then too, the persistent demand on the part of the public at that time to hear new ideas in concerti naturally caused the composer-virtuoso to be concerned about guarding his own fresh innovations lest they be pirated by another virtuoso who might pre-empt them before he had a chance to utilize them at his next place of performance. These innovations often led to a musical style which was interesting and exciting, and which had implications for the emergence of the symphony.

There seemed to be much public demand for virtuosi on solo instruments. Charles Burney in his *Present State of Music in Germany* (London, 1776) furnishes us with an example of the musical fare at Dresden during his visit there in 1776:

> The concert was opened by a symphony of Hasse; after which, a solo on the violin by M. Hunt . . . The next piece was a German flute concerto, played by M. Götsel . . . After this, Signor Bezozzi (Carlo) played an extremely difficult concerto on the hautbois . . .

This was the first part of the concert. The second part began with

> . . . an admirable symphony of Vanhall . . . After this, a solo of Nardini, by M. Hunt . . . This solo was succeeded by another concerto on the German flute, by M. Götsel . . . Signor Bezozzi performed, after this, a new concerto on the hautbois . . .[8]

That there should be a problem in locating copies of concerti for oboe mentioned in sources, but not extant, is perhaps understandable when one realizes that most editions of concerti were hand-copied, and that publishers such as Breitkopf actually

---

8. Pages 44-45.

printed very few works. In cities such as London and Paris the engraver succeeded in taking over the duties of the copyist more than he did in Germany, Italy, and Austria. Breitkopf and Härtel, who then engraved more music than any other firm, operated the largest copying establishment in Europe. The problem would seem to be further compounded by the fact that people generally ordered parts, and not scores, of works to be performed, and this even when they might have had no intention of performing from them. Of printing in Venice in 1764, Burney says that he was unable to find a single work printed in the manner of the English publishers because the rage for novelty was so great that it was not worth the expense of engraving plates for such short-lived works.[9]

The "Galant" style, introduced into English society in the middle of the 18th century and typified by the concerts of music promoted by J. C. Bach and C. F. Abel in the Hanover Square rooms in London, was the standard in England by 1770, and seemed to bring with it a new concept in musical expression that was antagonistic to the Baroque concerto concept. There was, to be sure, much complaining about the new style, that the symphonies were technically too difficult and that the bass lines were uninteresting, but on the whole the new and large middle-class audience seemed to lack the power of concentration necessary to sustain interest over a relatively long time expanse. As a result, the virtuoso-composer developed a technique of writing in which the listener was carried from one height of intensity to another, the music seemingly consisting of a series of "cells," each with its own climax; final movements with a set of variations expressed this concept precisely. How much more radical is this idea in comparison to the high Baroque concept, in which the emotional level is comparatively even throughout a movement. There is emotion, certainly, but it is encompassed by logic and form that results in a controlled and measured treatment of one or more ideas.

The reasons for the amazing vogue of the new style cannot be discussed in detail here, but it is certain that it was the result of a multiplicity of causes, not the least of which was the social climate

9. *Ibid.*, pp. 46-47.

of the time. The large crowds of people who attended public concerts in the middle of the 18th century were far different from the small, select gathering earlier in the century. As they had paid to hear, they could, in essence, control the repertoire, and as they were in the position to command, they had to be pleased over and over again by each successive piece of the composer. Musically, the bass line became less important than the top line, providing the middle class audiences with a simple melodiousness more to their immediate comprehension. One might say that it was from this point that the *basso continuo* began to decline, even though many instrumental pieces were still accompanied by continuo instruments well into the 19th century.

The liabilities for the musician, while not at first apparent, soon began to be appreciated as the new style emerged. As larger concerts given by free-lance professional orchestras became more frequent, the amateur societies and subscription concerts became fewer. Not only did the composers write more demanding music technically, but the situation seemed to eliminate the weaker amateur players who had made up the bulk of the string sections in the orchestral societies. In effect, then, what the new style of writing did was to remove the responsibility hitherto found in the *ripieno* section (with its collection of musicians of mixed proficiencies) and place it in the hands of the *concertino* group of professional musicians. One can see that, as the principle of contrast was weakened, the Baroque concerto began to lose its effectiveness as a viable form for the listener of that time. There is also some indication that tempi were in general becoming faster, eliminating even more amateurs unable to keep up with the professional performer.

This new concept, together with the rise in popularity of the transverse flute, or German flute as it was more commonly described at the time, and the emergence of the clarinet into the repertoire foreshadowed the demise of the oboe in popularity and usage. Woodwind instruction books give some indication of the decline, and, while tutors specifically for oboe had not, comparatively speaking, been particularly abundant even in the early 18th century, they soon became quite scarce; by 1800 almost the total production of instruction books for wind instruments seemed to be for flute, clarinet, or the flageolet.

Perhaps the single most important mission for the virtuoso at the beginning of a work in the 18th century was to capture the initial attention of the audience, whether in the concert hall or at the private concert. While at the private concert this was fairly easy, due to the fact that the performer would have socialized with the patrons and guests beforehand and would be treated with some deference and civility, at the public concert the feat was sometimes impossible. Many of the oboe concerti were performed between the sections of an oratorio or acts of an opera, such as the Handel concerto Opus 3, No. 4, which was played by Fischer during the great Handel Commemoration in 1754 at Westminster Abbey and which, according to Burney, so delighted the King that he expressed his satisfaction in a note on his book of words. One need only to see Paolo Pannini's painting of 1729 titled *A Night of Italian Opera*, with its depiction of the fruit and condiment sellers hawking their wares during the performance, to appreciate the general uproar that the performer had to silence before commencing and the necessity for his holding the public's attention once it was obtained. The situation became worse throughout the century as musical compositions became longer. The introduction and its ritornelli, for instance, took on such lengths that in at least one instance the soloist had to call attention to his entrance by jumping on the floor. In a letter to Wolfgang, Leopold Mozart writes of a concerto performance by Fischer, ". . . each ritornello lasts a quarter of an hour, and then our hero comes in, lifts up one leaden foot after the other, and stamps on the floor with each in turn."[10]

The oboe became less and less effective as the development sections in concerti were expanded. As this concept became fashionable, the piano, ideal for expressing lengthy development sections, assumed new proportions as a solo concerto instrument. The oboe had heretofore been most useful in delineating short phrases, roulades, and configurations that pleased the listener by their novelty. But there is a limit to these conditions, and by overuse they soon became clichés. Even Burney, the leading

---

10. Emily Anderson, *The Letters of Mozart and His Family*, London, 1938, Vol. II, p. 77.

musical conservative who was a supporter of the society known as the Concert of Ancient Music, notes at a performance that he "did not like the (concerto), there was noise in the chorusses (i.e. the ritornelli), and in the solo parts, there were repetitions of old and common passages."[11] The proportions in the new concerti, with the emphasis on long development of material, put the oboe at a decided disadvantage, as it was unable to sustain the endurance required, and the oboe sound, if heard overly long, becomes tiresome.

The oboist-virtuoso, however, continued to explore new ways of gaining the initial and continuing attention of the 18th century listener. One of these was a mannerism taken over from the Venetian opera aria, known now as the "motto beginning" or Devise. It was simply an incomplete statement of the opening solo melody by the oboe, occurring during the instrumental introduction, after which statement the player rested until his "true" entrance many measures later. Beginning as a mannerism to announce the presence of the soloist, it later became incorporated into the oboe concerto as a compositional device and was of particular value in the long opening introductions of the concerti composed toward the end of the century in that it allowed the oboist a chance to keep his instrument warmed up.

Another dramatic condition taken over by the oboist from the singer's arsenal of vocal tricks was the crescendo on a single note, known everywhere in the 18th century as the *messa da voce*. This mannerism is extremely felicitous on the oboe because of the minuscule opening of the reed, which permits the air to be prolonged over a longer period than any of the other wind instruments, rivalling the human voice in this respect. But this device, with its swelling and subsequent decreasing of volume on a single note, grew into a grotesque and bizarre mannerism and prompted one listener to note that it sounded like Dr. Franklin's musical glasses when applied to every note in a slow adagio movement. The reference was to Benjamin Franklin's glass harmonica which has a rapid tone decay factor on each note.

The effect of the opera singers' influence on the oboe concerto

11. Burney, pp. 44-45.

is nowhere better seen than in the concerti of Tomaso Albinoni. A colleague of both Vivaldi and the Marcellos, he incorporated the Devise into every first and third movement of his oboe concerti, and the *messa da voce* at the beginning of every second movement. In its most extravagant use, the *messa da voce* is known to have been used by the oboist Carlo Besozzi, when he apparently tempered his continued tone to accomodate the harmonic changes of the accompaniment.

The many references in this study to the 18th century oboist, Johann Christian Fischer, are indicative of this performer's immense popularity in the courts and concert halls in England. Fanny Burney mentions in a letter to her sister Susan on July 23, 1786, that at a concert on the evening of that day "the sweet-flowing, melting, celestial notes of Fischer's hautbois . . . made the evening pass so smoothingly, I could listen to nothing else."[12] Like his colleague Sir William Herschel, who while being the most celebrated observational astronomer of the 18th century began his career as an oboist in the Guard's Band at Durham, Fischer moved in the highest circles of English society, and even if he were not to become famous in posterity as a celebrated musician, he would be noted because of his relationship with Thomas Gainsborough, who painted the full length portrait of him that now hangs in Buckingham Palace. Gainsborough was a lover of music and had attempted to become familiar with several instruments, especially after hearing performances on them by celebrated artists. Such was the case after he had heard K. F. Abel play the gamba at a London concert. But Gainsborough soon became disenchanted with trying to master this instrument, and in the words of William Jackson of Exeter, London, in 1798,

> he . . . now had a fresh object — Fischer's hautboy — but I do not recollect that he deprived Fischer of his instrument; and though he procured a hautboy, I never heard him make the least attempt on it. Probably his ear was too delicate to bear the disagreeable sounds which necessarily attend the first beginnings on a wind instrument. He seemed to content himself with what he heard in public, and getting Fischer to

12. Fanny Burney, *Diary*, p. 114.

play to him in private — not on the hautboy, but the violin. But this was a profound secret, for Fischer knew that his reputation was in danger if he pretended to excell on two instruments.[13]

Fischer had a fear of being called a "doubler," despite the fact that, according to a belief long held by musicologists, most wind instrument players in the 18th century were proficient on more than one instrument and did, in fact, perform publicly on them as the occasion demanded. Such was certainly the case quite early in the century, particularly regarding the players of the court bands whose proficiency on more than one instrument was an economic necessity. In the 1770s less celebrated players sometimes performed on more than one instrument, a Mr. Mahon being mentioned as having performed in the Oxford Music Room in 1772 a concerto on the hautboy and a few days later one on the clarinet. It would seem, however, that this instance was somewhat a novelty, as the clarinet was relatively new and would generate some interest because of that fact. Certainly the celebrated performers on the oboe played that instrument exclusively in public, and there is no mention that the most notable 18th century oboists, Sammartini, Besozzi, or Fischer ever did otherwise.[14]

Burney mentions that Fischer "stood so well at his instrument that his figure had all the grace of a Tibian at the altar of Apollo,"[15] but even the sonic and visual impact of a Fischer could

13. William Jackson of Exeter, London, 1798; from "The Four Ages; Together with Essays on Various Subjects." Quoted by Walter Armstrong in *Gainsborough and His place in English Art*, London, 1904, p. 148.

14. See Plate No. 1. The violin resting on the chair probably had symbolic value known only at the time to Fischer and Gainsborough. The oboe in the picture is the plain, two-keyed model popular in England in the last half of the eighteenth century, having a slightly smaller bore than its French and German counterparts. Milhouse of London was a leading maker of such instruments. The square (actually oblong) piano in the picture is by Joseph Merlin of London, whose shop in Oxford Street was known as "Merlin's Cave." Fischer's relationship with Gainsborough seemed to end with the secret marriage of Fischer to Gainsborough's youngest daughter, Mary, in 1780. The marriage lasted only a year, Mary becoming mentally deranged, a condition not ameliorated by Fischer's eccentric behaviour and choleric disposition.

15. Written by Burney for Ree's *Cyclopaedia* of 1800. Plate No. 2 "The Sharp Family on the Thames at Fulham" by Zoffany is included here as further indication of the popularity of Fischer among the cultured class. One asks if the male figure holding

not stem the rising tide of public appreciation for the symphony popularized by Haydn during the latter part of the 18th century. The virtuoso oboist had to accept this emerging condition and take his place as the delineator of short musical phrases within a larger ensemble. It was from this time that the performer began to concentrate more on the sonic value of his playing and less on the bravura and technical aspects. The new keywork being added to the oboe, hitherto used only for purposes of performing embellishments, was now used to stabilize and refine the tone and intonation of the instrument as the demands for meticulous ensemble now required. This condition is present today, and our great modern orchestras, too often viewed as curators of symphonic music and proponents of sumptuous tone, provide no forum for the modern listener to hear the oboe as auditors did in the 1700s. One can only envy the 18th century listener who had at his disposal a whole army of performer-composers who, as Burney says, were "as fit to fight a battle as to plan it."[16]

Wilbert D. Jerome

the music for the harpsichord player in the center of the picture is Fischer. He seems to be holding two single flageolets but the instrument on the top of the harpsichord is an oboe.

16. Burney, p. 71.

Bentley Bid the Pencil

When Bentley bid the pencil it did wonderful things. His friend Horace Walpole thought so — considered Bentley a genius and urged him constantly to greater efforts, though his urgings had modest success with such a determined dilettante — and Thomas Grey thought so, as witnessed by his laudatory "Stanzas for Mr. Bentley" from which my title phrase is taken.

Richard Bentley was born in 1708, the son of a deeply learned and fearlessly contentious Cambridge classical scholar, for many years the Master of Trinity College. Young Richard seems to have inherited a good share of his father's intelligence and eccentricity, but almost none of his application. Yet he *did* do wonderful things, and chief among them is his exciting set of illustrations to Gray's poetry, commissioned by Walpole, praised by Gray, and published in 1753 in a handsome folio entitled *Designs by Mr. R. Bentley, for six Poems by Mr. T. Gray.*

Look at the title page (Plate I): you will notice at once that the two sister arts are given balanced prominence, for if "Poems" is written larger, nonetheless the designs are mentioned first. This balance reflects partly Gray's reticence — he insisted the book should be considered more Bentley's than his — but partly it simply reflects the facts of the edition: it is as engaging to look at as it is to read. Indeed Gray expressed himself in his "Stanzas" as hoping his own "tardy verses" might "catch a lustre" from Bentley's "genuine flame."

This modesty seems excessive; Gray was and is, of course, one of the foremost poets of his time. But even here, already on the title page, the illustrator emerges too as a lively independent spirit;

he looks out at us through the eyes of that alert little monkey who sits deferentially beneath barren branches even as his own pencil has drawn for the inspired bard a handsome, flourishing tree. Both figures are treated, perhaps, with light mockery — Bentley was good at mockery, and his comic designs remind us of how good Gray was at it too — but they also lead us directly into an elegant and imposing edition that stands as a landmark in English book design.

Let me briefly recall for you the format of the book, taking as our example its handling of Gray's "Elegy Written in a Country Churchyard": each poem was introduced by a full-page design, a sort of frontispiece that summarized its whole intent.[1] For the "Elegy," Bentley frames the churchyard with an elaborate arch that reflects Gray's framing comparison of the barrenness of pomp and power with the earthy richness of simple village life (Plate II); but through that doorway is still the deathshead, with the kindred spirit's own shadow cast across the grave he inquires about, movingly stressing by pictorial gesture the inevitable progression of life towards death which is a central theme of the poem. Then a headpiece and decorated initial begin the text (Plate II): here the brawny vigor of country life is again celebrated, with the pipe and tabor above suggesting its simple pleasures, though the initial "T" counters with a *memento mori* in the ivy-mantled tower and moping owl; this darker note is taken up in the tailpiece (Plate III), in which a funeral procession bears the coffin to its final resting place — one like the sepulcher pictured beneath, lit by a burning taper that will soon flicker out in analogy to man's brief and fragile life.

Each of the six poems in this edition is similarly embellished, though to quite different effects; in concert they form a book of great wit and style. A typescript bound into a British Museum copy of this work calls it "one of the most charming books produced in England during the 18th century, unique in its way," and adds, "Had this been produced in France it would now rank among those very expensive books whose pedigreed exemplaires

1. The one exception is the frontispiece to "Ode" on the Spring, which introduces and alludes to all six poems.

form the aristocrats of bibliophily. Surely one of the most undervalued of English books."

In what ways, then, is it unique? And how did it come to be undervalued? The questions are related, I think, and I would like to approach them first by examining some of the background, both in English book illustration and in fine engraving generally. English books of the early and middle eighteenth century have never been praised for their decorative interest. As Alfred Pollard remarked in his summary study of *Fine Books*, "How low book-illustration had fallen in England at the beginning of the eighteenth century may be seen by a glance at the wretched plates which disfigure Rowe's Shakespeare in 1709, the first edition on which an editor and an illustrator were allowed to work their wills."[2] Hard words: but a glance at that edition shows at once what Pollard means. The figures are stilted, the pages crowded, the details of decoration quite unrelated one to another. Hogarth, of course, contributed brief distinction to English book illustration in the 1720s — though it was more the power of his satiric intelligence than the beauty of his page or fine engraving that we recall him for — and even his pieces for *Tristram Shandy* some forty years later offer, as illustrations, little innovation in conception or technique.

One of the most important and innovative books that did appear in England in the first half of the century was Pine's *Horace*, in 1733. John Pine (1690-1756) was a friend of Hogarth and a pupil of the influential French engraver Bernard Picart, who taught him what the best of the French were doing. Pine was quick to recognize the social and commercial possibilities of fine book-making, and his *Horace* (Plates IV, V), is important both for its beauty and for its unity of style — it was entirely engraved on copperplates, both text and illustration, and dedicated piecemeal to various leading figures of the day, among them Pope and Robert Walpole, Horace's father. It epitomizes the neo-classical values it appealed to: an understated octavo, its designs chiefly imitate classical medals, gems, coins, and bas-reliefs with decorous restraint. Even the initial letter, you can see, might serve as a

2. London, 1912, p. 294.

model for a Robert Adam moulding. As it happens, the engraved lettering appears to have impressed and influenced Pine's contemporaries more than either the mode of illustration or the more important conception of the book as unified whole.[3] Nevertheless it is the only English work I have seen that prepares the eye at all for Bentley: how well it does that, I will return to consider a little later.

Meanwhile Englishmen who wanted lovely books turned for the most part to the continent. Even a book like Edward Moore's sumptuous and vapid *Fables for the Female Sex* (1744) with Francis Hayman's designs engraved by Grignion — one of Bentley's two engravers — though it has obvious pretentions, remains routine in almost every way. Right into the 1750s the illustrations in English books, where there were illustrations at all, were usually like those in the Rowe Shakespeare: rectangular pictures of poor quality set box-like into the page, quite irrelevant to the design of other pages or of the book as a whole.

But Bentley's illustrations are altogether something else. They are closely and often penetratingly particular in their textual references as well as in their sensitivity to nuances of tone and poetic posture. And as engravings they are fresh and open in design, sharing space with the text with easy assurance. What models, then, did Bentley have for his book? No direct models at all, that I have been able to find; no one anywhere — in England or on the continent — had done anything quite like it before. Sir John Summerson, in the only attempt I have seen to suggest a source, says "his illustrations to Gray's poems, 1753, derive perhaps from Jean Bérain."[4] Bérain's designs (see Plate VI) are of course not book illustrations, but rather independent decorative plates; nevertheless one can see parallels in certain of the details, such as the quasi-architectural setting, the comic grotesques, or the interlaced strapwork that borders the Bérain design and that frames (for example) the bottom half of Bentley's full-page design for Gray's "A Long Story" (Plate VII). But how different are the

3. David Bland, *A History of Book Illustration*, 2nd. ed., London, 1969, suggests that "Its lettering with its strong contrasts between thick and thin strokes may well have influenced Baskerville and Bodoni in their type design." (p. 216).
4. *Architecture in Britain: 1530-1830*, London, 1953, p. 240.

total effects! And this particular design shows Bentley at what might be considered his most "French." Yet even here one sees how much Bentley's emphasis is on physical realism — in this case comic: the well-dressed gentleman at the left is in danger of toppling off his perch; the heads of Queen Elizabeth and the Pope glare at each other with the snappishness of political cartoonery; the floating ladies have rather realistically rumpled dresses and ungainly postures; and the "closet" to which the frightened poet is being conveyed for hiding is visibly what Americans now call an outhouse. All this is a far cry from any *fête champètre* of Watteau, who truly is an inheritor of Bérain, as one can see from Plate XIII, a Watteau design engraved by Boucher and published in 1727. What Bentley *could* have gotten from Bérain, or perhaps even more directly from Watteau himself, is that airiness of design, the lacy, open edges in contrast to the rigidly enclosed boxes preferred by the English — or at least accepted by them.

Yet Bentley had no need to cross the channel for models of lacy, open design. He had only to leave the genre of book illustration and look at other kinds of engraving in his own country — for instance the humble tradesmen's cards distributed all over London. Plate IX shows an example roughly contemporary with Bentley, and it reveals in yet another way how behind the times was British book illustration, how tied to its own established precedents. English designers and engravers were clearly quite capable of conceiving the airy and open, and you might think that the step from that to an illustration like Bentley's frontispiece to "Ode" on the Spring (Plate X) would be often and easily made; but in fact in the area of literary illustration no one in England except Bentley seems to have made it for the next thirty or forty years, that is until the time of Blake and the Bewicks.

The step is indeed made elsewhere with ease and authority, as in the sample books of furniture design, of which the most famous is Thomas Chippendale's *The Gentleman and Cabinet-Maker's Director* of 1754. There is, for example, a set of Pier glass frames (Plate XI) that defy all notion of squared-off blocks and stiff borders. And the English furniture designer Thomas Johnson even turned the tables — if that's the phrase I want — by incorporating little figures from Aesop's Fables, popularized by Francis Barlow's

17th-century illustrations, into the rococo fancy-work of some of his furniture pieces.[5]

I should mention that the mid-century reader might expect to find in his books pretty little printer's decorations — usually floral engravings — used to designate chapter divisions or to fill out a page. (The Rowe Shakespeare offers crude ones as headpieces.) In France these were often quite elaborate and elegant, including figures such as swans and putti as well as flowers, but such decorations were in any case not really illustration, as they had nothing to do with any particular text. The handsome 1734 Paris edition of Molière's *Oeuvres* offers some fine examples in this genre: each play in the series has one real illustration (by Boucher) as a frontispiece, but the decorative head and tailpieces and initial letters are used repeatedly throughout the six volumes, obviously without regard to the particular works they decorate. Again, they are much closer to Bérain than to Bentley.

By far the closest analogy to Bentley's book — both in format and in overall conception — is the celebrated Albrizzi edition of Tasso's *Jerusalem Delivered*, done in Venice, with engraved designs after Piazetta (Plate XII). When the book appeared in 1745 it was considered so daring that it made an immediate European sensation; when Goethe's father saw the proof sheets he "beheld them with astonishment and admiration." The novelty of the book lay in the series of vignette-shaped headpieces and tailpieces, "tossed on the page with a casual airiness that had never before been seen in book illustration," to quote A. Hyatt Mayer.[6] Albrizzi was so keenly aware of the importance of his new book that he took out a fifteen-year copyright on the copper plates. But of course what was really important about this work could not be copyrighted: it was no less than a fresh conception of the illustrated book, in which text and decoration are intertwined in

5. Another fine set of airy designs appears in *The Musical Entertainer (1737-1738)*, engraved by George Bickham the younger, with vignette headings to each song, after Watteau, Gravelot, etc.

6. For generalizations about the impact of the Albrizzi Tasso I am indebted to Anne Palms Chalmers, "Venetian Book Design in the Eighteenth Century," *The Metropolitan Museum of Art Bulletin*, January, 1971, pp. 226-235, and to A. Hyatt Mayor, "Italian XVIII Century Book Illustration," *The Metropolitan Museum of Art Bulletin* n.s. 8, 1950, pp. 136-44. The words quoted in my text appear in Mr. Mayor's article on p. 140.

ways that had not seemed possible since the days of handworked manuscripts. A rare modern approximation of such integrity in England had been Pine's *Horace*, in which both text and illustration were engraved, but with an overall effect that was neoclassically low-key.

Yet even the Albrizzi *Tasso* falls short of what Bentley was to do just a few years later — quite possibly without ever having seen the Tasso (surprisingly it was not in Walpole's library, though of course Bentley might have seen it elsewhere). The borders surrounding each of the fullpage illustrations in the Tasso are repeated throughout the work: two designs alternating in regular order. The decorated capitals are also repeated, and though the head and tailpieces generally differ with each canto (I found only one tailpiece repeated) their material is very broadly generalized. In short, aside from the frontispieces, most of the designs are more decoration than illustration.

With Bentley, however, every design is unique, and each is fitted in detail to the work it illustrates. I noted how the "ivy-mantled tow'r" and "moping owl" set off the initial "T" of the "Elegy Written in a Country Churchyard." In the same way Selima herself curls around the initial "T" of the "Ode on the Death of a Favourite Cat," and the headpiece of "A Long Story" shows the actual house in which the poet's "trial" took place. The headpiece to the "Ode" on the Spring depicts the "rosy-bosom'd Hours" and "Cool Zephyrs" in plump personification, and "Long-expecting flowers" twine about the decorated capital "L" as a moralizing fly climbs up the side of the letter itself.

In short, Bentley may have drawn on French rococo for modish decorative details such as the strapwork, festoons, canopies, and suggestions of the grotesque; on engraving in other fields than book illustration for the handling of vignette shapes and open edges; and perhaps on Venice for the way in which the open contours of decoration and lettering blend together in this particular format. But the sense of humor is as English as Hogarth, and the concept of illustration very much Bentley's own. As I have already suggested, his pencil showed marvelous sensitivity to the nuances of Gray's tone and language, a healthy respect for his detail, and a keen responsiveness to the social, artistic, and moral complexities among which poet and artist both worked. Let me leave for a while, then, the question of influence and demonstrate Bentley's own gift with a few examples.

Walpole was really grieved when his favorite cat, Selima, died, and so Gray undertook consolation in a witty "Ode on the Death of a Favorite Cat, Drowned in a Tub of Gold Fishes." The subject requires some delicacy, as any pet-owner will sense at once: the treatment must not be merely flippant, nor yet so earnest as to make the poem itself laughable. Gray's solution is brilliant, for he manages to compliment Selima with wry affection and still retain appropriate distance by drafting the story of her fall into the service of a gently mocking cautionary tale addressed to fashionable ladies — the whole connection turning, with perilous delicacy, on a punning split of the word "gold-fish." Selima lost her life in a plunge for fish; let not any lady lose that still more precious possession, her honour, in a similar plunge for gold.

These paired levels of application are underscored in the language, in juxtaposed levels of diction. An aristocratic "Hapless Nymph" is evoked with pompous circumlocution in such a line as "The slipp'ry verge her feet beguil'd," yet fast deflated in the next: "She tumbled headlong in."

But Bentley, coming to illustrate Gray's poem, though faced with all the same problems of tone, had to work with quite different tools. He might employ the cat-lady analogy in its bare outlines, but of course could not enrich it with Gray's subtly complex language. In fact what he did was something quite different. He recognized that Gray's achievement had been to offer Walpole's cat a setting that would honor her, yet keep appropriate perspective; so he worked to achieve in his own medium a perspective that would be comparable to Gray's — in both the literal and the figurative senses, and the result displays his triumphant gift for comedy (Plate XIII).

The literal perspective is obvious: we see Selima in her moment of peril from a good, healthy distance. But what a frame surrounds that rather gawky little cat! It is this frame that provides the figurative perspective, for Bentley has taken hints from Gray's language and created out of them a paradigm of the rich culture of fashionable eighteenth-century England, with its rococo elegance, its deference to classical tradition, its vogue of Chinoiserie. Gray's passing mentions of "Wat'ry God" and "Malignant Fate" bloom into robust imitations of classical architectural statuary supporting a massive pediment with earnest display of fine ornamental strapwork, festoon and swag, and a centerpiece of mousetraps. The little mice themselves frisk over the surface of this frame as if it were a solid physical object, an illusion reinforced by Bentley's careful representation of the shadows and the reflected light source – apparently the same source for inner picture as for outer frame. With no more to go on than that Selima had drowned in a vase decorated by "China's gayest art," Bentley further constructs an elaborate setting of Pagodas, costumed mandarin-cat, and elegant Chinese jars. The drama is emphasized by the piece of heavy drapery across the top, which suggests that at the proper moment it could drop across the opening and hide that painful scene soon to follow.

Finally, at the foot of the entire structure and displayed with conscious pomp are the signatures of Gray and his illustrator, the poet's initials inscribed on a lyre, the artist's on a palette. The whole design is thus gathered to its center: poet and painter have joined to celebrate poor Selima, to honor her in death with wryly fulsome elegy. Walpole was pleased.

Bentley was sensitive to social nuance again in response to Gray's "A Long Story," a topical poem so trivial, in its author's eyes, that he would not have allowed it to be published had it not been for Bentley's delightful designs to illustrate it.

In fact one of the illustrations – the headpiece – is virtually Gray's own anyway, for in order to guide Bentley's representation of the manor house at Stoke Poges, Gray himself made a sketch of the place, from which Bentley deviated very little. But the nicest clever twist in the designs is in the frontispiece, and seems to be Bentley's own, though a good deal of the point is lost in the engraved version (Plate VII). Gray had been visited, soon after he had moved to Stoke Poges, by two friends of the Dowager Viscountess Cobham whose father had bought the Manor House there. These friends, Lady Schaub and Miss Speed, finding Gray not at home, left a card for him and Gray returned the call. After they had all become friends, Gray wrote a fanciful account of the occasion, representing himself as "a wretched Imp they call a poet" and the two ladies as "a brace of Warriors" sent presumably to purge the countryside of such a nuisance. The Muses seek to protect him:

> On the first marching of the troops
> The Muses, hopeless of his pardon,
> Convey'd him underneath their hoops
> To a small closet in the garden.

But in vain, because the warriors have left a spell — the calling card — on his table, drawing him inexorably to the Peeress' house for trial. Instead of being condemned, the offending poet was of course invited to dinner — and the "long story" is tactfully curtailed by the announcement that "Here 500 stanzas are lost."

Bentley represents the initial scene of crisis: the warriors in search of the impish poet, the muses protectively hustling him into the "small closet" (that outhouse). But Bentley not only "illustrates" Gray's point, he wittily amplifies it by extending the compliment implicit in the poem's conception yet one step further, allowing the careful eye to observe that the muses who inspire and encourage the bashful poet are indeed no other than the "warriors" themselves, Lady Schaub and Miss Speed; they are in this guise sufficiently etherialized by harps and laurels to make the poet's compromising posture still no reflection on the real ladies, who are represented a bit more realistically at a safe distance in the clouds above, held aloft presumably by their billowing sleeves. Müller, the engraver of this plate, seems to have been aware of Bentley's point, though he has reproduced it only indirectly, by representing one of the ladies both times in profile, the other both times more nearly full face. Bentley makes the pairs much more obvious in his own drawing, and seems even to have essayed at portraiture. No contemporary portrait of either lady has come down to us, at least so far as I have been able to find; but a portrait of Miss Speed as she was some twenty years later shows a bright-eyed, sharp-chinned lady who answers well to Bentley's little drawing (she would be the one at left above, at right below) and to Gray's description of her as one whom "kind Heaven/ Had arm'd with spirit, wit, and satire."

But Bentley could be horrific as well as humorous. In his "Ode on a Distant Prospect of Eton College," (Plate XIV), Gray had reflected gloomily on the fate of the youngsters at a school like Eton, pursuing their studies and play in such happy ignorance of the agonies Gray believed maturity must inevitably bring. Turning to Father Thames, who has watched so many generations at Eton pass into manhood, Gray presents the bitter vision — and Bentley paints it.

> Alas, regardless of their doom,
> The little victims play!
> No sense have they of ills to come,
> Nor care beyond today:
> Yet see how all around 'em wait
> The Ministers of human fate,
> And black Misfortune's baleful train!
> Ah, shew them where in ambush stand
> To seize their prey the murth'rous band!
> Ah, tell them, they are men!

The ribbon below repeats the melancholy conclusion over a serpent, sword, and scorpion, tangled among toys and thorns: a visual synopsis of Gray's point.

Above, this synopsized point is given greater expansion in a full scene viewed through another architectural frame; at the side are terms representing Jealousy and Madness, two of the fury passions that will tear these children as they mature. Other passions are massed above, rather orgiastically enacting the terrors they represent, yet at the same time evidently ready to fall at any moment on their helpless prey below. Father Thames watches, but does not warn. What happiness they have — as Gray concludes in the poem — is the bliss of ignorance.

But in this picture, unlike the others, it seems to me that the appropriateness of Bentley's response might be questioned. Does Gray's poem really support the vigor and relish of Bentley's scene — all that plump flesh and hectic punishment? Father Thames here seems almost a voyeur. I hedge my language because I am aware how much such matters are up to individual perception; yet there is something in the sensuality of the children and the frenzied abandon of those "passions, misfortunes, and diseases" above them that invites speculation.

A fascinating connection that might help explain the confusing tone of Bentley's picture may be found in its literary and iconographical antecedents. Two of the poems in this group of six have important sources in Horace's first book of odes, namely "Ode" on the Spring and "Hymn to Adversity" (in Odes I, 4, and I, 35, respectively). Now this first book of Horace's Odes happens to comprise the section of Pine's *Horace* that was dedicated to Sir Robert Walpole; not surprisingly his son had a fine copy, which Gray and Bentley surely knew well both because of the aesthetic importance of the edition and because of the compliment to the Walpoles. I have already said that it is the only English work I have seen that prepares the eye for Bentley; but one of the illustrations does so especially, and appropriately it illustrates an ode from the first book — Ode I, 25, later called "Ad Lydiam" (Plate XV).

With the keen eye that was to make him seem in so many ways an early Romantic, Bentley has here fastened on the wildest thing Pine had to offer, borrowing each of these two main figures for use in his illustrations to Gray. The mourning figure appears, entitled "Melancholy," in Bentley's tailpiece to "Hymn to Adversity" (Plate XVI), a picture with which Walpole said Gray was "in love to distraction."[7] One can see how eloquently Bentley's illustration endorses Gray's view that the result of adversity is a kind of dignified human strength, here posed as romantic melancholy in pensive retreat. Years later, when Blake illustrated Gray, he parodied this picture savagely, feeling as he did that the notion that hardship is "good for you" is worse than sentimental — for one thing because it actually encourages oppression, even offers a rationalization for it. Gray's poem had addressed the "Stern, rugged Nurse," Adversity, whose job it was to form the infant mind of Virtue, Jove's "darling Child." Blake's nurse, modeled on Bentley's figure, holds a dead baby.

What Blake understood thoroughly, and what Pine gathered perhaps from his knowledge of classical imagery and iconography, is the close association between depression and rage: painful

7. *Walpole-Montagu Correspondence*, ed. W.S. Lewis, Yale Walpole edition, vol. 9, p. 143.

experiences elicit both emotions, and if they are not allowed reconstructive vent, they can become dangerous. Pine's engraving makes the connection visually. The lady below is bent with grief, but above her, and raging for redress, is the Fury who is equally "part of the picture." The ode this illustrates addresses a lady whose days are lengthening: "already less frequently" do her windows shake from the pebbles young men throw at them in the night, and the time will come, the poem says, when she will weep, rejected by her arrogant lovers as she stands abandoned in the street while the Thracian wind revels like a Maenad at the changes of the moon — when love and passion, flaming in her heart, "will rage not without lamentation." Rage above, lamentation below. The Latin diction evokes images appropriate to the furies, and connects them with the Thracian Maenads who, when repudiated by Orpheus, ran mad and tore him apart. The cause of Lydia's rage and grief is symbolized in that Priapic figure in the background, with his huge phallus and taunting leer. He represents the untrammeled male sexual instinct that will turn the young men heartlessly from Lydia as her beauty fades, and in this role he is re-enforced by the satyr masks at the sides, below.

The Fury who dominates this picture appears, as I said, in Bentley — not in any illustration to the "Hymn to Adversity," but rather in that frontispiece to the Eton College Ode (Plate XIV) — a poem that, like "Ad Lydiam," treats of the pain that comes with ageing. Regarding the Eton boys at play, Gray looks to their future:

> These shall the fury Passions tear,
> The vultures of the mind,
> Disdainful Anger, pallid Fear
> And Shame that sculks behind,
> Or pining Love shall waste their youth,
> Or Jealousy with rankling tooth . . .

Jealousy appears at the left, and at the right you see Pine's Fury, called "Madness" in the "Explanation of the Prints" that Walpole wrote to accompany this edition. Her wings are gone, but the traditional Gorgon hair and flaming torch of the Fury identify her for us: yet in this design the calm figure of Lamentation is missing, just as Blake was to complain that the *rage* was missing in the

"Hymn to Adversity." What Pine had recognized as two complementary sides to a full response — "rage not without lamentation" — Bentley had separated into lamentation alone (grieving yet dignified submission to Adversity), and rage alone (driven to madness by those "fury Passions" that will tear the Eton College boys).

Recall that Bentley's father was one of the great classicists of his time, and Gray was another. And Horace Walpole needed look no farther than his name to find his interests committed: "Horace" to the poet, of course, but even "Walpole" to Pine's dedication of these Odes to Sir Robert. Bentley's borrowings and allusions gather force from all this classicism, but they focus its light — tellingly — onto a scene that predicts some of the emotional disjunctions of what Mario Praz has termed "romantic agony."

We should see by now in what ways Bentley's Gray was unique, an aristocrat among books: it was a fresh departure in book design and at the same time an attentive and personal response to Gray's poetry, as well as to the social and intellectual milieu of Horace Walpole's special circle. If Bentley lacked the depth and tenacity of a specialist, his flighty eclecticism provided him with some surprising strengths. As an off-and-on writer himself and a friend of such men as Walpole and Gray, he was familiar with the avant-garde literary world and could sniff the winds of change. As a decorator-architect, working with Chute on Strawberry Hill, he was constantly exposed to the talents as well as the trade cards and design books of furniture makers, and in a period whose wealthy leaders regarded furniture as a most sensitive index of taste. Yet at the same time he remained the son of an eminent classical scholar. Thus, for example, his self-assured little monkey on the title page could derive with equally good arguments a pedigree from the singeries of Bérain and Watteau and their schools, or from the ancient and revered topos of the artist as the ape of God. Bentley doubtless had both in mind.

In short, this man came to eighteenth century book illustration with a fresh eye — not trained to assume, but widely acquainted and attentive to what lay directly to hand. I think his uniqueness really is the child of his eclecticism: since few of his individual elements of design were new, few contemporaries noticed that in putting them together as he did, he had created something utterly fresh. They saw and liked the work — even copied some of the designs — but they did not seem to grasp what Bentley's accomplishment might mean for them. So the native English tradition that should really have made a startling leap forward at his pencil's bidding, instead wandered unwittingly by, and took fully forty years to discover — by other means — the paths he had pointed to.

Irene Tayler

Blake's Initiation:
The Marriage of Heaven and Hell

Not long after William Butler Yeats had finished "Sailing to Byzantium," some spirit voices, speaking through a medium named Cooper, directed him to another special place: the bottom shelf of his study, third book from the right, page 48 or 84. The book turned out to be Blake's designs for Dante's *Comedy*, and the pages two images of Holy Fire (Plates I and II).[1] On Plate 48 the bite of a serpent sparks a fire that consumes Vanni Fucci, "a man of blood and rage"; though immediately he will rise from his ashes like the phoenix. As Dante, Blake, and Yeats agree, the "temporal fire" is merely a delusion. Vanni Fucci, twisting like a Laocoon bowed down to mimic his creeping earthly oppressors — mere transparent worms, as drawn by Blake — turns to the left, away from the pent-up sun, the true spiritual fire that could cure him. On Plate 84 (*Purgatorio* 27) an angel invites Dante to enter the wall of fire that surrounds Eden, the Earthly Paradise. Though encouraged by Statius and Virgil, Dante hesitates, clasping his hands, "gazing at the fire and strongly imagining bodies I once saw burned." Meanwhile the angel, placed by the text outside the flames but by Blake within, sings "Beati mundo corde": "blessed are the pure in heart," but here, more accurately, "the refined in spirit." At length, the thought of Beatrice's eyes will make the pilgrim risk the fire. In Blake's drawing, the tremendous vertical thrust of aspiration is balanced by a horizontal block of waters capped by a setting sun. As Dante has reminded us at the

1. *Illustrations to the Divine Comedy of Dante by William Blake*, London, 1922, a portfolio published by the National Art-Collections Fund. Albert Roe, *Blake's Illustrations to the Divine Comedy*, Princeton, 1953, supplies a fine commentary.

beginning of the canto and Blake reaffirms, in this earthly kingdom, with its earthly fire, the spiritual sun is partially obscured; yet in another kingdom on the other side of the earth — Jerusalem — it has just begun to rise.[2]

These plates can carry us deep into the poetic worlds of Dante and Blake. But for Yeats the crucial matter — the insight that made him shake with excitement — was not his reading of other poets but his sudden knowledge that the designs supplied a key to "Sailing to Byzantium." In the sensual blood and rage of Vanni Fucci, reduced to a caricature of a dying animal by his short-sighted entrapment in the world that is begotten, born, and dies, Yeats recognized his own torture in "that country." In the angel who stands amid the fire, whose singing instructs the pilgrim to be consumed, he recognized those "sages standing in God's holy fire," those "singing-masters" of his soul, to whom he prayed to be gathered "Into the artifice of eternity." Yet most of all he realized that the two plates, whose numbers mirrored each other, were mirror images of a single action. "Certainly," he wrote to Olivia Shakespear, "the knowledge was not in my head." Yet how well "it puts my own mood between spiritual excitement, and the sexual torture and the knowledge that they are somehow inseparable!"[3] Sexual torture and spiritual excitement — Vanni Fucci's hot blood and Dante's yearning for Beatrice — are seen by Yeats as one: the old man's rage at his body, the old man's passage through fire and time to be reborn in Eden.

Yeats had been sent a message. A few hours before he looked at the plates, he told Mrs. Shakespear, he had revised his early lyric, "A Dream of a Blessed Spirit," into the poem called "The Countess Cathleen in Paradise," whose revisions immerse the lady in holy fire. "Bathed in flaming founts of duty," she stands amid the angels of heaven, "Flame to flame and wing to wing." An amazing anticipation of Plate 84! "After this and all that has gone before I must capitulate if the dark mind lets me."[4] Was Yeats tinkering a little with the sequence of events? Was it Cooper, or his

2. The relevant passages are *Inferno*, XXIX, 97-129; *Purgatorio*, XXVII, 1-18.
3. 27 October 1927: *The Letters of W. B. Yeats*, ed. Allan Wade, New York, 1955, p. 731.
4. *Ibid.*

own memory, that sent him to that special place, that special book? It does not matter. Whether the images floated up out of Anima Hominis or Anima Mundi, Yeats was right to conclude that Dante and Blake, "his people," had sent him "Sailing to Byzantium." Indeed, a further clue exists. So far as I know, no one has previously noticed that the fullest and most compelling single anticipation of "Sailing to Byzantium" — that poem so rich in sources — is a passage in Yeats' early essay on "William Blake and his Illustrations to the *Divine Comedy*"; an essay to which Yeats had added a postscript as recently as 1924. Here is Blake as Yeats envisioned and remembered him.

> The kingdom that was passing was, he held, the kingdom of the Tree of Knowledge; the kingdom that was coming was the kingdom of the Tree of Life; men who ate from the Tree of Knowledge wasted their days in anger against one another, and in taking one another captive in great nets; men who sought their food among the green leaves of the Tree of Life condemned none but the unimaginative and the idle, and those who forget that even love and death and old age are an imaginative art.[5]

In the contrast of these two kingdoms — one passing, one to come; each sustained by its own tree; one inhabited by the unimaginative and idle, men who waste their days in anger and sensual captivity; the other, by men who know that love and death and old age are an imaginative art, since "True art is the flame of the Last Day, which begins for every man when he is first moved by beauty, and which seeks to burn all things until they become 'infinite and holy' "[6] — Yeats speaks with the voice of Blake to prophesy a poem. But thirty years would have to pass before he learned what his own words meant: the coordinates of "Sailing to Byzantium." For Yeats, like most creative artists, goes on a circular voyage; never so excited as when the poem he discovers in a flash of critical insight is his own.

My subject is not Yeats but Blake; not "Sailing to Byzantium"'

---

5. *Essays and Introductions*, New York, 1961, p. 130. The essay, dated 1897, had appeared in *Ideas of Good and Evil*.
6. *Ibid.*, p. 140.

but *The Marriage of Heaven and Hell.* Yet no understanding of Blake's book will be adequate, I think, without a similar context: the hazardous passage through fire, the poet or pilgrim's radical discovery of what he has meant all along. In the absence of such a context, the *Marriage* can seem — as to most readers it still seems — infinitely mysterious. Indeed, a way of dispelling the mysteries is very much needed. Despite the thousands of critical pages that have been devoted to the book, one searches in vain for a satisfactory reply to the most basic questions one can ask: what sort of work do we have here? what principles motivate the *Marriage* as a whole? We are told, by the best critics, that the book may be defined as an *anatomy*, or Menippean satire, like the *Anatomy of Melancholy, A Tale of a Tub*, or — conveniently — that brilliant parody of systematic thought known as *Anatomy of Criticism.* I admire the wit of this definition; and indeed it appears very judicious (Frye himself cites, in this connection, the Brobdingnagians' wise decision that Gulliver was a *lusus naturae*).[7] But it does not appear very enlightening. Like many literary definitions, it attempts to make sense of a protean form by describing some fluctuating surface features rather than the meaning, or the search for meaning, that gives the form its integrity. Yet the *Marriage* cannot be grasped by its surface. It burns surfaces away; it requires us to look for a life within. And the reader who would make sense of the work must become protean himself; not anatomizing the *Marriage*, but allowing himself to be instructed by it in ways of finding something more.

Must we say, then, that the *Marriage* is indeed a sport of nature, a work anomalous and unique? I wish to propose the opposite: to insist that it belongs, in fact, to a distinct literary kind; a kind with a long and honorable history, at which many great writers have tried their hands; though a kind as yet, unfortunately, without a name. Examples of this sort of work include, to return to the conjunction with which we began, Dante's *Vita Nuova* and Yeats' *Per Amica Silentia Lunae*; and

---

7. *Anatomy of Criticism*, Princeton, 1957, p. 313. In spite of this quarrel over terms, I am sure that my own debt to Frye will be apparent. "Anatomy," in any case, seems to me preferable to Foster Damon's more pretentious word for the *Marriage*, a "*Principia*" (*A Blake Dictionary*, Providence, 1965, p. 262).

other examples (for instance, certain portraits of artists as young men) should occur to every reader. But let me begin by christening it with a name: The Initiation.[8] Like the word "initiation," works of this kind imply both a beginning, the dawn of a whole new world of possibilities, and a ceremony or rite of instruction. First they undergo a trial by fire where understanding is refined, then they pass to a stage of higher knowledge where past experience is radically reinterpreted. All initiations draw upon this pattern; and for all their superficial differences, there is much else that they share.

They share, most obviously of all, an extraordinary mixture of verse and prose. In each case part of the work consists of an imaginative vision, often challenging and obscure, and part of prose commentary, often rather direct and explicit. The combination troubles many modern readers; Rossetti, for instance, would have preferred to omit Dante's prose divisions from *La Vita Nuova*. Similarly, it is hard to know which aspect of *The Marriage of Heaven and Hell* is more disconcerting: its dark enigmatic fancies, or its frank exegesis. Blake alternates the knotty poems with which he begins and ends, his poetic proverbs, his "memorable fancies," with sections of exposition so straightforward that a simple-minded commentator can find little to add. "From these contraries spring what the religious call Good & Evil. Good is the passive that obeys Reason. Evil is the active springing from Energy. Good is Heaven. Evil is Hell."[9] Can such blank and direct prose coexist with poetry?

The fact is that it can. For every initiation, whatever its dualities and disproportions, comes in the end emphatically to one thing: a book. The very notion of a book — its textual authority, its coherence, even its physical appearance — furnishes Dante and Yeats, like Blake, with a controlling metaphor and a structural design. The poet collects the members of his poems into a greater whole. No one has ever carried this principle further than Blake. From first to last he supervises the making of the *Marriage* at every

8. Since "initiation," in the specific technical sense used here, may easily be confused with the ordinary sense of the word, I might propose (should the term gain any currency) the alternative "inition," a rare older form of the same word. But I must confess that I do not like the sound of the latter.

9. Plate 3.

stage, from the first vision through the process of etching and printing (described on Plate 15),[10] until he binds it together — a book to reimagine the Bibles of the past and transmit them to future generations. We cannot say that book-making is a *metaphor* for the *Marriage*, since the work is actually, physically, the book it makes; but we can say that to be a book constitutes its highest and proudest claim. Within a little space, Blake recapitulates and captures all the books that have gone before, the microcosm of an infinitely grander creation. The nine surviving copies of the *Marriage* are a library for modern times; a parody Bible, complete with proverbs and commandments; a complete sacred code in fiercely concentrated form.

Sacred codes, however, need priests to interpret them. Perhaps the center of each initiation, that on which all the rest depends, is its effort to initiate the reader into its own way of meaning. The poems the book contains cannot be understood by ordinary methods, ordinary acts of attention. Rather, the reader must enter the book as if it were an antechamber to certain mysteries, a place where secret ceremonies of reading will be taught. Like the lovers in *The Magic Flute* (another strange eighteenth-century mixture of poetry and prose), someone who undergoes this rite of passage is promised a new mode of seeing.

Indeed, the very title-page of the *Marriage* — initiating us with a vengeance — seems intended to disorient the reader, to shake him out of trust in his senses (Plate VII).[11] What landscape is this? To what place have we come? A preliminary answer might be that

10. There is no fully satisfactory account of the "Printing house in Hell," but David V. Erdman's note, "The Cave in the Chambers," in *William Blake: Essays for S. Foster Damon*, ed. Alvin Rosenfeld, Providence, 1969, pp. 410-13, is a useful preliminary attempt to tie it to Blake's own practice of printing.

11. The following analysis proceeds on the assumption (demonstrated in recent years by a host of scholars) that Blake's illuminated works can only be understood through a careful study of the plates, pictures as well as text. The recent effort at "Reading the Illuminations of Blake's *Marriage of Heaven and Hell*" by David V. Erdman, with Tom Dargan and Marlene Deverell-Van Meter, published in the *festschrift* for Sir Geoffrey Keynes, pp. 162-207, is by far the most detailed and perceptive look at the "surface particulars" of the book. Its discussion of significant emblematic variants in all nine copies of the *Marriage* makes it especially valuable (I have touched on only a few variants below). Though I disagree with some of Erdman's interpretations, and in general I lack his confidence that every stroke of Blake's burin can be assigned a definitive meaning or pictorial intention, I owe him a great deal.

we have been raised one level above the scene on Plate 84 of the Dante designs. We now look *down* upon the purgatorial fires, through which pilgrims who have risked the refining wall of flame ascend to the earthly paradise above; presumably driven by love, like Dante in search of Beatrice, or like the embracing couple at the bottom of the page. Yet Blake has not made his plate so easy to read. It projects, rather, an ordeal for the imagination, a series of visual and mental paradoxes. The fires, though clearly they induce joy rather than torment (as we shall be told on Plate 6), are firmly labeled HELL; and the Eden above, whose large block letters squarely pronounce it HEAVEN, seems blighted and almost leafless. What is the underworld and what the firmament? Beneath the trees on the right, huge boulders sink down the page, passed by flying spirits; yet the base of the cliff turns into clouds on which an angel couches — kissing a devil. The greatest difficulty in reading the page, however, is kinetic: its paradox of motion. As W. J. T. Mitchell has pointed out, "the whole kinesis of the composition . . . produces an axis which goes from the lower left corner to the upper right."[12] An aspiring, ascending diagonal, stretching from flames below to birds above, tips the balance to the right, "in favor of the 'Devil's Party.'" Yet another impulse works against it, conditioned by our habits of reading: the title itself. "The Marriage of Heaven and Hell," proceeding stiffly downward one word at a time, drags against the upward flow; drags us down, in a re-enactment of the fall, to the lovers and their fire. Blake deliberately works the picture and text against each other — contraries from which progression will emerge.

Is there any way out of this ordeal, this Purgatorial no-man's-land between the lines of Heaven and Hell? A sign has been left, perhaps, for the initiated eye. The block letters of HEAVEN and HELL, childishly captioning the two opposing kingdoms, italicize their own rigid solemnity. Meanwhile, above, the curlicues of "Marriage" indicate a more generous, vital way of lettering and life. Entwining with the branches of trees and offering birds a perch in the sky, they dance along the artist's wiry, bounding line.

---

12. "Blake's Composite Art," *Blake's Visionary Forms Dramatic*, ed. David Erdman and John Grant, Princeton. 1970, p. 65.

Most remarkable of all, the final letter E ends in a long, expansive loop or scroll: Blake's image of his book itself. Note, at the bottom of the page, that the bodies of the embracing devil and angel, reading from left to right, also twist through a complete, serpentine curl; and that the cloud-bank on which the angel rests might also be a scroll. Even amid this chaos of warring motives, I suspect, Blake is hinting that we will find our way by following his winding path; by reading on. The old stories, the old associations of Heaven and Hell, should not confine our visions. The *Marriage* will teach us better.

Many later pages of the book present a similar theme in iconography that is far more clear. At the bottom of Plate 10, for instance, the last of the Proverbs of Hell (Plate IV), a devil unwinds a scroll of proverbs to be copied by a pair of scribes — the one at the right, alert and eager, suspiciously like the poet himself. Just above them, punctuating the appropriate proverb, "Truth can never be told so as to be understood, and not be believ'd," a bird (winged like the devil) holds another kind of loop or scroll, presumably a serpent. Apostles of liberty like Blake, the bird and devil transmit their knowledge through a twisting line. Later, on Plate 15, Blake specifically describes the manufacture of his book: "the method in which knowledge is transmitted from generation to generation"; and once again a drawn-out loop visually represents that method. Below, once more, a mighty winged creature grasps a lengthy serpent. Contra Laocoon and Vanni Fucci, this emblem of the prophetic spirit lifts its head, stamping itself in books, into the winding trail of history.

Perhaps, with the help of such icons, we can begin to consider ourselves among the initiate. But true initiation, of course, cannot be copied from another's scroll. Instead, Blake plunges his reader into the refining fire itself. The history of this process is writ on Page 14 (Plate V). Here, amid a bath of flames intended to consume the whole creation, a woman hovers over a man in suspended animation, calling him awake (in some copies she is blindfolded; in others, shouting). In George Cumberland's copy, the picture is titled "The Body of Hector"; and it is tempting, surely, to see a kind of Valkyrie reviving a hero — a complement to Siegfried's awakening Brünnhilde, with a kiss, from amid her encircling flames. But the definitive interpretation, certainly, belongs to Blake himself, who tells us that the picture is an image of his book.

> But first the notion that man has a body distinct from his soul, is to be expunged; this I shall do, by printing in the infernal method, by corrosives, which in Hell are salutary and medicinal, melting apparent surfaces away, and displaying the infinite which was hid.
>
> If the doors of perception were cleansed every thing would appear to man as it is, infinite.
>
> For man has closed himself up, till he sees all things thro' narrow chinks of his cavern.

Blake refers specifically to his printing process, the new acid-bath he had invented, the "infernal method."[13] Yet the material with which he works, clearly enough, is not only his copper plate, but we ourselves: those bodies, those caverns, which mask our infinite, and which fire must consume. With every means at his disposal — sensual enjoyment, hellfire, or even loving and explicit prose — Blake strives to loose us from our mind-forged sleep. As a famous American work of initiation would have it: "I do not propose to write an ode to dejection, but to brag as lustily as chanticleer in the morning, standing upon his roost, if only to wake my neighbors up."

In so far as it is successful, therefore, *The Marriage of Heaven and Hell* will effect a conversion; or rather, usher the reader into a state of hermeneutic maturity where he sees all texts plain. After the ordeal comes understanding. Northrop Frye has commented, on more than one occasion, that "learning to read Blake was a step, and for me a necessary step, in learning to read poetry and to write criticism."[14] Every initiation, given a proper reader, is capable of achieving the same result. Helpfully, insistently, it tells us to open our eyes, to change our lives.

But the true initiate, in every case, is the poet himself. Dante, Blake, and Yeats do not transmit a knowledge already learned and

---

13. On Blake's method, see Anthony Blunt, *The Art of William Blake*, New York, 1959, Ch. IV.
14. "The Keys to the Gates," 1966, *The Stubborn Structure*. Ithaca. 1970, p. 176.

codified. Instead, their books of initiation crackle with the excitement of new readings that unfold before them. In almost all initiations, moreover, the excitement derives from the same source: the poet realizes that his own personal history, reflected in his poems, coincides with the universal spiritual history of mankind. Dante recognizes Beatrice as the emissary of Christ on earth, Yeats discovers in his dreams a vision of *Anima Mundi*. And Blake, most remarkably of all, perceives that in this year of our Lord 1790 another age begins: Year One of Blake. The harbinger, Plate 3, is alive with images of regeneration (Plate VI). It welcomes the new age everywhere with open arms. On high a female devil, content amid transforming flames, stretches invitingly wide to greet Eternal Hell. Below, on the left, an actual birth is in progress; not, apparently, with labor pains, but with a kind of joy that prompts both mother and infant to cast their arms apart in an ecstasy of salutation. On the right, meanwhile, a contrary couple – he races while she reclines – open themselves to the meeting of active and passive, energy and reason. Even the tiny interlinear figures that flit among the text – again we shall see a bird, a serpent, a scroll, a plume of writing – stretch out their arms; note the happy fliers over "new" and "Adam," and the couple that greet each other (l. 9) in recognition that contraries are necessary.

The cause of such regeneration, and Blake's excitement, is stated in the text. "As a new heaven is begun, and it is now thirty-three years since its advent: the Eternal Hell revives. And lo! Swedenborg is the Angel sitting at the tomb; his writings are the linen clothes folded up. Now is the dominion of Edom, & the return of Adam into Paradise." A complete explication of these lines, especially with reference to Swedenborg and Isaiah, would require another Bible.[15] But we shall not understand the *Marriage* at all unless we understand that it represents, for Blake, one of the most significant "coincidences" in the history of the world. In 1757, the year of Blake's birth, Emanuel Swedenborg had announced the advent of the New Jerusalem. Now, thirty-three years later, Blake and the "new heaven" have reached their

---

15. Harold Bloom, *Blake's Apocalypse*, New York, 1963, pp. 67-76, sketches Blake's reactions to Swedenborg and Isaiah.

Christological age together. Moreover, in this year 1790 the flames of revolution fill the air. The time has come to die, to be reborn; the tomb is opened, Adam mounts to Paradise. In this rich atmosphere Blake repudiates Swedenborg himself — much of the *Marriage* is a dynamic parody of the static doctrines espoused in Swedenborg's *Heaven and its Wonders and Hell*, especially section XL, "Marriages in Heaven."[16] Now Swedenborg must be consumed, and the revival movement learn that a new Christ is arising to oppose the old. We shall be changed; by contraries, as in marriage. The Eternal Hell revives, and this time Heaven will be harrowed.

Yet none of these relations would have been decisive, perhaps, had Blake not been given a sign: the new printing process that he himself had manufactured. The technique of illuminated printing, perfected the previous year as a result of experiments with *Songs of Innocence*, allowed the artist for the first time to present his vision whole. In the *Marriage*, with terrific excitement, Blake perceives the spiritual implications of his new corrosive method, his trial by (acid) fire. The process itself abolishes the false dichotomy between vision and execution, form and content, technique and meaning, heaven and hell; spirit grasps matter tightly as an eagle holds a serpent. This discovery, I think, marks the decisive moment of Blake's career. All that he had done and thought — the poems and sketches, the apprenticeship in engraving, the early prophecies, the sympathy for revolution, the embattled struggle for survival, above all the visions — suddenly came together. He knew why he had been born: to make a book. And the proof of Blake's own prophetic spirit must be a book alive with vision in every part.

A spirit of prophecy, indeed, inspires the *Marriage*. John Grant has plausibly said that the book "is about the education of the Prophetic Character";[17] but the word "about" needs qualification.

16. "I heard an angel describing true marriage love and its heavenly delights in this manner: That it is the Lord's Divine in the heavens, which is Divine good and Divine truth so united in two persons, that they are not as two but as one. . . . the delight of the love of falsity conjoined to evil . . . is infernal delight, because it is the direct opposite of the delight of heaven" (XL, 374). If contraries could be perfectly united, in Blake's view, there could be no progression.

17. In a note to Mitchell's article (see note 12 above), p. 64.

The *Marriage* is not *about* the education of a prophet; it *is* that education, and that prophecy, it celebrates. Just as the Bible does not so much report as constitute the word of God, and identifies the immanent meaning of history with the chronicle of events, so Blake weds vision and interpretation. Poetic Genius, the same genius that inspired the Hebrew prophets, is at once his subject and his object; he sets out to transmit not only the history of biblical inspiration but its nature. Nor will he accept a division between the human and the divine. The Bible contains all proper human history, since man reveals himself above all in his bibles. The *Marriage* aims at nothing less than renewing the partial Testaments we inherit, converting them through fire to the present moment. Outrageously, with fearful energy, Blake grasps the Bible in his hand.

We open *The Marriage of Heaven and Hell*, in fact, to a page where all Bibles are comprehended (Plate VII). "The Argument," in six brief stanzas, recapitulates and progresses upon the Old Testament and the New, summarizing them with a peculiar Blakean twist. Failing to see this, much intelligent and sensitive criticism of the poem has missed its essential point.[18] Blake wastes no time on preliminaries; he starts, as all Bibles start, at the Beginning.

> Rintrah roars & shakes his fires in the burdend air;
> Hungry clouds swag on the deep.

In the midst of a primal chaos, a stew of elements where clouds lurch into and pillage the deep, and the air convulses with fire and earth, a Giant roars: Rintrah, "the Wrath of Prophecy." The moment is Genesis, or immediately preceding; and Rintrah, a force either creative or destructive, here seems identified with Jehovah; "the Jehovah of the Bible," we shall be told on Plate 6, "being no other than he who dwells in flaming fire." Clearly Blake is retelling the myth of Creation. Yet this version, unlike the Hebrew Bible, pays little respect to Jehovah. Rintrah, Titanic wrath without reason, seems more a part of chaos than its master — cousin to

18. For an outline of "The Argument" that anticipates my own in some respects, see the appendix to Morton Paley's *Energy and the Imagination: A Study of the Development of Blake's Thought*, Oxford, 1970.

those imprisoned Giants we see huddled and muddled together on Plate 16, "who formed this world into its sensual existence." The vision remains undefined. Though prophetic in its rhythms (that is, reminiscent of Hebraic poetry as described by Bishop Lowth), the very language is "burdend," clotted with multiple groups of consonants that retard the speed of the verse. Can such a jumble prepare the way for Genesis?. Blake's answer, of course, is that it can; not because, at some past hour, a superior being spoke a word in the darkness, but because at every moment the human imagination bears the light of its own vision. For that reason, Blake's parody of Genesis adopts the present tense. The moment of creation, he implies, is always at hand. It persists at every moment when the prophetic spirit within man sees primal chaos, the mere "withness" of matter or sensual existence, as the illusion that it is. In Blake's own Bible, freed from illusions, Jehovah becomes Rintrah, and the Poetic Genius, no longer dependent on myths of nature, creates perpetual Genesis in its own image.

Historically, however, the first incarnation of prophecy belongs to a Chosen People, and to their Book.

> Once meek, and in a perilous path,
> The just man kept his course along
> The vale of death.
> Roses are planted where thorns grow.
> And on the barren heath
> Sing the honey bees.

Here Blake summarizes, as he sees it, the essence of the Old Testament: "the fruit/ Of that forbidden tree whose mortal taste/ Brought death into the world, and all our woe,/ With loss of Eden." The Jewish Bible, in this version, tells the story of mankind after the Fall: the way that Adam, Eve, and their descendants learned to take strength from their sentence, and to build a world amid death and exile by the sweat of the brow. The theme of this story is justice. Man sinned, was rightly punished, and henceforth earned some stay of execution by hewing to the perilous and mortal path of the straight and narrow. Nor does Blake underestimate the virtue of such straitened labor. The just man, though meek before his God, knows how to fight, to work;

from thorns he makes roses, and draws honey from the barren heath. Even Blake's language, simple and strong (some of it taken from Exodus, and all of it biblical), reveals his admiration for the Jewish Testament, those men of law who built Jerusalem.

Moreover, the etching of the Argument offers remarkable pictorial support for labor. At the bottom of the plate, a naked languid couple (presumably Adam and Eve) lie stretched at their ease — prone and horizontal like worms upon a leaf — in that repose of Eden where nothing ever happens. But the right margin bursts with an opposing version of Eden: an energetic figure, high in a tree, hands down something hidden — is it fruit? — to a woman who reaches upward. Verticality, the line of power and aspiration, pronounces this the Tree of Life. Is the scene a fortunate Fall?[19] Not entirely, perhaps; the upward motion is arrested by the handing down, the legs of the girl below are crossed, the action itself seems furtive. Yet the striving and energy at the right are surely preferable to the torpor below. Compare the Tree of Life with the stunted little tree on the other side of the girl, a tree all loops and veerings from the upward path. The Tree of Knowledge, as Yeats maintained, belongs only to the unimaginative and idle. The couple at the right, on the other hand, need hardly fear their punishment: their very act of sin exerts the energy they will require to make a life in exile; they will have force to plant a rose. Indeed, the moral vigor of the Old Testament can energize its readers still. The Hebrew people (we are told by the text) followed righteousness "Once," in that time consecrated by their Book; but their spirit of prophecy continues to live wherever men engage in mental fight. Roses are planted, honey bees sing in the present, the present tense. Jerusalem might yet be built again, in the twinkling of an eye, by modern prophets.

Nevertheless, the Old Testament is flawed, in Blake's eyes, by paying too much regard to death. The just man labors under an illusion; he thinks himself bound by mortal flesh. To awaken him from this dream, another Book is needed.

19. John Grant makes the case for such a reading in a note on "Regeneration in *The Marriage of Heaven and Hell*," in *William Blake*, ed. Rosenfeld, Providence, 1969, pp. 366-67. As Erdman points out, however, the figure above seems to have the breasts of a girl, and therefore cannot be identified as Adam without some qualifications.

> Then the perilous path was planted:
> And a river, and a spring
> On every cliff and tomb;
> And on the bleached bones
> Red clay brought forth.

With the aid of conventional Christian typology, Blake rereads some episodes from the Old Testament – the creation of Adam, and Ezekiel's vision of the valley of bones – in the light of the New. The classic of death makes way for the classic of resurrection; springs flow from the tomb. The final line of the stanza bears its thematic seed. In Hebrew, Adam means "red clay," the earth from which man was made. Yet the second Adam, who came to redeem the first, was Christ; and this Adam, though a man of flesh, was also the Creator. The peculiar grammar of "Red clay brought forth" – is clay the subject or object? – emphasizes that new life is generated, in the New Testament, not through an external agent but through humanity itself, the irrepressible flowering of Genius in man. Of itself clay brings forth life, Christ-Adam rises of himself. Prophetic spirits learned, from the new Book, that they need not wander in the wilderness of death. Wherever man has vision, Eden may yet be resurrected.

Unfortunately, once a Bible gains authority vision may stagnate. The spirit of prophecy is kept alive in the human mind; by definition, it cannot dwell in an established Church, codified for unthinking passive men.

> Till the villain left the paths of ease,
> To walk in perilous paths, and drive
> The just man into barren climes.

The great tragedy of history, Blake argues, is the theft of the Bible by men with no prophetic inspiration in themselves. After Christ, every charlatan with a memory can pretend to possess the Word. True Christianity, founded on Jesus who "acted from impulse, not from rules," knows no greater enemy than the Christian Church; within the mother Church even perilous paths are shorn of terror, and invite the villain to stroll without risk. Thus the just man, Blake's prophet, must enter exile once more. Forced to choose between the Bible and the Poetic Genius from which all bibles are derived, he must choose the latter, whatever the cost. Nor is the cost small: barren climes, heresy, willfulness, death – the catalogue of ills that Milton assigned to rebels in *Paradise Lost*. Such is post-Biblical history; the nightmare from which Blake strives to wake.

> What of the present?
> Now the sneaking serpent walks
> In mild humility.
> And the just man rages in the wilds
> Where lions roam.

Far from being alleviated, the tragic theft of the Bible by its enemies has set the world awry. The priesthood walks – as well as a snake can walk – the path of the straight and narrow, the prophet roars like Rintrah in a wilderness where justice comes from tooth and claw. The time, of course, is 1790, *now*; revolution is in the air, and there can be no doubt where Blake's sympathies lie.[20] Nor should one underestimate his indignation. With savage irony he travesties the "Eden" of today. *Now* the serpent, an upright parody of a human being, has usurped the place of man, while the true man rages in an exile he has not deserved. Woe to the false lords of the earth! Surely some Second Coming is at hand.

> Rintrah roars & shakes his fires in the burdend air;
> Hungry clouds swag on the deep.

No, no Second Coming; only a repetition of that primal moment before creation. "The Argument" comes full circle by restating its premise. Yet this time the refrain carries the burden of all human history. No longer identified with Jehovah, Rintrah now seems a harbinger of the wrath of modern life, all those sounds of rage that seek an outlet amid confusion: the cannons firing in America, the cries of France (a wounded Giant), the frustrated prophetic fire in Blake's own heart. Who can see a clear way through such turmoil?

20. For a political reading of "The Argument," see David Erdman, *Blake: Prophet against Empire*, Princeton, 1969, pp. 189-92.

But the time of prophecy was not *then*, frozen in the past. Creation has not failed; rather, it has not yet been tried. The day when every man speaks the truth of his own Poetic Genius might dawn at any moment, for we all live at the dawn of creation. That is the argument of Blake's *Marriage*.

After so comprehensive an argument, however, embodying all human history and spiritual insight, what possibly can follow? The answer, of course, is that no parable immediately reveals all its meaning. As votaries, first we and Blake must learn to read. The greater part of *The Marriage of Heaven and Hell* is devoted to explaining its moment of revelation in the most explicit way Poetic Genius can find: not only by rational persuasion but by tangible acts of vision. Like a medieval illuminated manuscript, the book would strike even the illiterate as holy writ; but its shocking humor stings and taunts us into literacy. Blake makes a primer of prophecy. Every step of his little book is meant to be looked at, weighed in the hand, argued with, imagined. Layer upon layer, it draws the orthodox reader into an abyss of the five senses where even the profession of faith conceals a serpent. On Plate 20, for instance, Leviathan himself proves to be just another worm, if our spirits have it so; Blake redraws the terrors and torments of the Bible into his own great looping line of knowledge. At length, learning to distrust his senses, the reader will learn to trust himself. The *Marriage* offers initiation into a great teacher's mode of vision; it shows us how to see with the eyes of Genius. (The deepest irony of Blake's career, perhaps, is that he was born to teach, though few were born to study with him.)

Nowhere does the *Marriage* state its creed more clearly than on its fourth page (Plate VIII): "The voice of the Devil," heralded on either side by trumpets, played by cherubs whose robes trail off into the unfurling, looping banners of knowledge. Here the contrast of body-energy-evil with soul-reason-good, and their ultimate marriage, is firmly illustrated both by text and picture. At the bottom of the page, many of the images we have looked at are juxtaposed once more. Reversing Plate 84 of the Dante designs, fire consumes the right side of the page, the sun hovers over the sea on the left. Nor is the iconography obscure. The man at the right, who lives amid the flames, yearns and stretches toward the woman at the left, as Dante yearns for Beatrice; but he is restrained by a chain on his right foot. The woman and child at the left seem similarly restrained, apparently (to judge by their gestures) by fear. Although the scene is potent with such emblems of regeneration as the refining fire, the sun, the child, marriage will not as yet take place. Bibles and sacred codes — bibles like Dante's, Milton's, Swedenborg's — have come between the contraries, the illusion of eternal torment chains energy from eternal delight; body and soul still stand apart.

Can another kind of sacred code exist? With a blare of trumpets, Devil-Blake announces his truth: a code that contradicts all others. If the essence of the *Marriage* appears in its Argument — as the Argument itself, for instance, tells us that the essence of the Old Testament is contained in its first few pages — then the rest of the book must be concerned with doctrine; proper interpretation of the human story. But this doctrine, antagonistic to all codes, refuses to rigidify. We need, the Devil says, a counter-Bible, a profane code that will give the lie to pious half-truths. Body and soul, vision and word, must be reunited through opposition; the Bible must be redesigned. "Every thing possible to be believ'd is an image of truth." The *Marriage* sets out to break the chain of error by burdening it with excess images.

The form of the book, in fact, makes sense at once when we perceive how thoroughly it re-enacts and contradicts the Bible. Like the Old Testament, the *Marriage* is an anthology of literary kinds: the parable on Plate 2; the series of propositions on Plate 4; the literary criticism on Plates 5 and 6; the proverbs on Plates 7 through 10; the historical analysis on Plate 11; the symposium with other prophets on Plates 12 and 13;[21] and a host of "fancies," aphorisms, debates, and demonstrations. The logical culmination of this process occurs near the end, on Plates 23 and 24, when a Devil "proves" to an Angel that Jesus Christ broke every single one of the Commandments: "I tell you, no virtue can

21. The symposium, in which Blake interviews Isaiah and Ezekiel, may be taken as an example of his method. The prophets not only argue that imagination has dominion over the earth, but prove it by abolishing time and space; they dine in the artist's imagination, where his firm persuasion of their presence makes them plainly manifest. Moreover, Blake turns the form against itself. Ordinarily a symposium balances one speaker against another, creating a dialectic in which many sides of truth are exposed; but all the speakers in Blake's interview, being true prophets, sound just alike.

exist without breaking these ten commandments: Jesus was all virtue, and acted from impulse, not from rules." Here the Devil's party finally breaks the most sacred of codes, and wins its day. The Old Testament and the New, brought to violent confrontation, produce from their mutual destruction a fiery marriage: the new Bible before us.

The Old and New Testaments, however, constitute only two among many sacred codes. Poetic wisdom, Blake believes, descends from every great imaginer, whatever his race or mode of art. Indeed, nothing strikes Blake as more blasphemous than the notion that one people, one text, could ever possess exclusive rights to the word of God. His notes to the Bishop of Landaff's *Apology for the Bible* hurl mockery upon such notions. "That the Jews assumed a right Exclusively to the benefits of God will be a lasting witness against them. & the same will it be against Christians. . . . If historical facts can be written by inspiration Miltons Paradise Lost is as true as Genesis or Exodus."[22] The world of the imagination, the *Marriage* insists, is a democracy; the Bible belongs to every man's Genius, and its time is now. In making his Testament, therefore, Blake must revise all Bibles that have gone before: not only Moses's and Christ's, but Homer's, Dante's, Milton's, Swedenborg's. All religions are one, for better or worse, in the *Marriage*. It incorporates and parodies every authentic genius, every heaven and hell, that history preserves.

Page 5, for instance, turns *Paradise Lost* upside down (Plate IX). The prophet of restrained desire, Milton has reversed his own artistic wisdom and preached the fall of energy. Blake's comic genius turns the descent of the Archangel into prat-fall; not only Satan but Pegasus comes crashing down, with sword and broken chariot-wheel and − in later editions − sun and moon ("If the Sun & Moon should doubt/ Theyd immediately Go out").[23] In a marvelous satiric stroke, the picture makes fun not only of Milton's version of the fall but of Milton's habitual combination of

22. *The Poetry and Prose of William Blake*, ed. Erdman and Bloom, New York, 1965, pp. 605, 607. The whole set of annotations, written in 1798, is relevant to the *Marriage*; *e.g.*, p. 605: "The Bible or Peculiar Word of God, Exclusive of Conscience or the Word of God Universal, is that Abomination which like the Jewish ceremonies is for ever removed & henceforth every man may converse with God & be a King & Priest in his own house."

23. "Auguries of Innocence," 11. Lines 109-10.

classical myths with Christian images; as well as Satan, the chariot-wheel and horse tell us, the falling figure represents Phaëton, deluded by the sun. To set matters straight, we should have to turn the picture upright again by reversing the page. Now, standing on our heads, we can see the Devil's version of the story: another pilgrim, mounting with arms outstretched to Holy Fire.

A different Bible, still more ancient, is repossessed and corrected on Page 11: the animating stories of the ancient Poets, or Bards (Plate X). With child-like charm, the picture quickens objects into life. The sun-god-sunflower on the left, the bearded oak in which we see a bearded Druid's face, the naiad mother with a bud-like infant joy, all proclaim a time when gods and geniuses dwelt in woods and in poetic tales. Yet later versions of the Plate portray a crueler truth: the whole scene is perceived through the opening in a cave.[24] As Plato, that "wise ancient," knew, "man has closed himself up, till he sees all things thro' narrow chinks of his cavern," The cloistered vision of modern times has misconstrued the ancient poets. Their stories, Blake sees, are beautiful; but they must not lead us to forget that "All deities reside in the human breast." Abstraction will follow next – "thus began Priesthood" – and eventually the priesthood will issue forth the Bibles of systematic reasoning: Angels enclosed, like Swedenborg on Page 21, within a pyramid of geometric forms.

Thus Blake reviews the history of error. But no true Bible, however contradicted, ever loses its visionary power; a firm persuasion that a thing is so, the mock-symposium tells us, makes it so. Two contrary persuasions, two opposing Bibles, merely bring forth progression. *The Marriage of Heaven and Hell* does not destroy its enemies but regenerates them; and for all its hazards, it transports us to a happy end. The last two "Memorable Fancies" (pages 17-24) both depict cosmic conflicts resolved in favor of the Devil's party. In the first, Blake opposes his vision to that of a scholastic Angel, one who would reduce the Bible to moral codes and "Analytics": "The man who never alters his opinion is like standing water, & breeds reptiles of the mind." At length the poet

24. Blake revised this plate more thoroughly than any other in the *Marriage*; the mother, for instance, grew the long tail of a mermaid. For a detailed study of revisions, see Erdman (note 11 above), pp. 185-88.

succeeds in imposing his fantasy upon that analytic reptile, and makes Leviathan his own. The final "Memorable Fancy" records a still more decisive victory: a Devil and Angel confront each other on ultimate grounds — the Tablets of the Law or Ten Commandments — and the Devil's reading wins the last word.

A marriage of contraries ensues. On Page 24 (Plate XI) the Angel is converted; he leaves his cloud of mystery and joins the Devil in his flames. "I beheld the Angel who stretched out his arms embracing the flame of fire & he was consumed and arose as Elijah." Here Blake discloses the promised end for which the reader has been urged to risk initiation. Elijah, according to *A Vision of the Last Judgment*, "comprehends all the Prophetic Characters";[25] the reader who has committed himself to Blake's fire is now set free to read truth from his own prophetic spirit. At the top of the page, as impulse triumphs over rules, a tiny sketch shows us "before" and "after": Before squats or cringes on a heavy line, turned upon himself, while After dances like a sprite upon the waves. The conversion of the Angel into Elijah is followed by a line which Erdman calls "a seminar of five prophets"[26] — at last we have learned to read — and all the rest of the text bursts with flourishes and squiggles. The joy and energy of the artist fill every rift with ore. Visibly and spiritually the prophetic spirit has won its day; initiation has been achieved. With the sweetness of that victory, soon to be celebrated in "A Song of Liberty," our instruction properly ends, except for two postscripts: Blake's promise to continue to read the Bible "in its infernal or diabolical sense"; and the closing proverb that vanquishes the brutal image of Nebuchadnezzar.

Formally, Blake's "Note" is hardly an afterthought: those later Bibles he promises to write will authenticate his vision. How else can an initiation end but with a resolution to put the new mode of understanding to use? "The sun is but a morning star." Indeed, the most remarkable single trait shared by every literary initiation is that each ends with a prophecy of a greater work to

---

25. "If the Spectator could Enter into these Images in his Imagination approaching them on the Fiery Chariot of his Contemplative Thought ... then would he meet the Lord in the Air & then he would be happy." *Poetry and Prose of William Blake*, p. 550.

26. "Reading the Illuminations. ..." p. 200.

come. At the close of *La Vita Nuova*, Dante announces a marvelous vision that has determined him to write of Beatrice "that which has never before been written of any woman" — a prediction, it is generally agreed, of the *Commedia*. At the end of *Per Amica Silentia Lunae*, Yeats suggests that he may become a medium for Anima Mundi; and the voice that soon began to speak mysterious tidings through Yeats' wife, took its theme from *Per Amica*. "Sometimes," Yeats wrote more than a decade later, in the Introduction to *A Vision*, "when my mind strays back to those first days I remember that Browning's Paracelsus did not obtain the secret until he had written his spiritual history at the bidding of his Byzantine teacher, that before initiation Wilhelm Meister read his own history written by another, and I compare my *Per Amica* to those histories."[27] And Joyce's *Portrait of the Artist* ends not only with a reminiscence of Dante meeting Beatrice, but with glimmerings of *Ulysses*. Within this context, nothing could seem more predestined than Blake's promise, or threat, to give the world a future infernal Bible. Blessed with new life, he sights to his own greater prophecies, where the techniques of interpretation developed in the *Marriage* will reach their apotheosis. "I have also: The Bible of Hell: which the world shall have whether they will or no."

But our reading does not end here. Below, crouching on all fours like an ox, though with a lion's or druid's mane, the tyrant Nebuchadnezzar displays the essence of what tyrants come to: cramped boxes in a box; geometers whose rigid right angles, resisting the serpent's line of knowledge, reduce them to subhuman caricature. If the Angel embracing the flame of fire may be seen as a culmination of Plate 84 of Blake's Dante designs — a pilgrim who enters the fire not with reluctance, but with confidence that he shall arise as Elijah — then Nebuchadnezzar may be seen as a culmination of Plate 48: a Vanni Fucci whose blood and rage have brought him to his knees, subjected to the mad sensual despair that comes from having trusted nothing but the senses. "One law for the Lion & Ox is Oppression," a rallying cry for revolution, clearly expresses Blake's hatred for all

27. *A Vision*, New York, 1956, p. 9.

tyrannies, the "natural" laws that constrict most men — the uninitiate — in bondage.

The context of the motto points also to another reading. If no one law has the right to constrain everyone, then everyone had best make a law for himself according to his own kind. "I must Create a System, or be enslav'd by another Mans." Thus Moses made a law in tablets, Christ by breaking the commandments (on the previous page), the French by revolution — and Blake by inverting the Book of Law with a Bible of Hell. The codicil of the *Marriage* fulfills the prophecy of its "Argument": another Testament, a new Law, has been created. Blake does not claim that his Bible invalidates those of the past; any book touched by the Poetic Genius is infinitely persuasive. Indeed, if the creeping serpents of the establishment had seized control of Hell, he would doubtless have spoken for Heaven. Perhaps Blake, like Yeats, sees Plates 48 and 84, sexual torture and spiritual excitement, Nebuchadnezzar and Elijah, as finally one: twin perspectives on the single human voyage. Yet Oppression, the stultified and cautious interpretations of prophecy that insist on the letter of the text, has now been overthrown; each man is free to follow his own spirit. And Blake hopes that every reader will enter the Bible with him, like the Angel-Elijah embracing the flame of fire, and learn from him how to read it.

Our ability to read is immediately tested by "A Song of Liberty." Without a pause, the prophet launches into an apocalyptic story that anticipates all the major prophecies to come: the Eternal Female begets a new born son of fire, whom a starry king tries to stifle with war in heaven and commandments, but who finally triumphs, stamping "the stony law to dust, . . . crying Empire is no more!" Since internal evidence dates the "Song" a few years later than the rest of the *Marriage* (political references seem to indicate 1792-93), it has often been considered a separate work. But most scholars now consider them one,[28] for several good reasons: thematically, the "Song" incorporates many ideas and images from the *Marriage*; formally, it draws the work full circle by returning to a poetic "argument," now appealing

28. The first to make the case strongly was Max Plowman, in a note to his facsimile edition of the *Marriage*, London, 1927, p. 16.

prophetically to the future rather than the past; most important of all, Blake always bound the two together as a single book. The Biblical context of the *Marriage* as a whole, however, implies a still more striking reason for including the "Song": it constitutes nothing less than Blake's Book of Revelation. Just as the Bible itself ends in Revelation, a mode of pure prophecy that opens and reads the wonders of a book with seven seals, so the *Marriage* ends by rereading the wonders of John. Lest anyone should miss the point, Blake numbers his verses as in a Biblical chapter. The "Song" draws all its narrative from Revelation, especially from its famous twelfth chapter, where there appear successively, as in Blake, the groaning woman who brings forth a wonderful son, the opposition of a jealous dragon-king, a war in heaven, the casting-out of the rebellious cohort to earth, and at last (Revelation 12:10) a triumphant founding of Christ's kingdom to be. Blake shares that triumph. He has read the Bible from first to last, and shown anew how it must end.

The Song, however, is Revelation interpreted with *liberty*. At his close, as so often throughout the *Marriage*, Blake turns the Bible on its head. Indeed, the upside-down picture on Page 5 (Plate IX above) might stand as an emblem for much of the "Song." Pages 25 and 26 represent a motion of constant ungovernable falling. "5. Cast thy keys O Rome into the deep down falling, even to eternity down falling. . ,. 10. The speary hand . . . hurl'd the new born wonder thro' the starry night. 11. The fire, the fire, is falling! . . . 13. The fiery limbs, the flaming hair, shot like the sinking sun into the western sea. . . . 15. Down rushd beating his wings in vain the jealous king. . . 16. Falling, rushing, ruining!" The starry, gloomy king who falls is not Satan but Jehovah (in the Devil's version), and with him fall the new born sun-god (both Christ and Phaëton) and the keys of the Church of Rome. All mysteries, all constraints, must be cast into ruin, before Blake's liberty can dawn.

The specific liberty claimed by Blake, plate 27 makes plain, is liberty to read Revelation as he likes. Above all, he attacks a particular *mis*reading of the apocalypse, one given currency by the angel's proclamation in the ultimate chapter of Revelation.

14. Blessed are they that do his commandments, that they may have right to the tree of life, and may enter in through the gates into the city.

15. For without are dogs, and sorcerers, and whore-mongers, and murderers, and idolaters, and whosoever loveth and maketh a lie.

16. I Jesus have sent mine angel to testify unto you these things in the churches.

Jesus, according to these lines, has come to enforce the command-ments, strict rules interpreted by an established Church; and the penalty for disobedience is exclusion from the heavenly city. The nineteenth verse supports this interpretation with a threat or curse: "if any man shall take away from the words of the book of this prophecy, God shall take away his part out of the book of life, and out of the holy city, and from the things which are written in this book." But all Blake's protestant heart rebels. *His* Jesus, we have seen, broke every rule; though priestly eyes may view Him as a setting sun, He yet shall rise, "Spurning the clouds written with curses, stamps the stony law to dust." Against the Priests of the Raven of dawn, Blake raises the sons of joy; against the rules of the tyrant church, the impulse of the free; against exclusion, liberty.[29] No one, no dog or lover, shall be barred from Blake's own heavenly city: "For every thing that lives is Holy." The final "y" of the "Song," curling up and outward from the page, affirms that no period can be set to Revelation. All things are married, and the book of life may yet be opened and renewed.

At the end of *The Marriage of Heaven and Hell* Blake's way is clear. At once the prophet of initiation and its votary, he will carry the light of his new understanding to every dark corner of

29. Cf. "The Everlasting Gospel":
  The Vision of Christ that thou dost see
  Is my Visions Greatest Enemy . . .
  Thine is the friend of All Mankind
  Mine speaks in parables to the Blind
  Thine loves the same world that mine hates
  Thy Heaven doors are my Hell Gates . .,.
  Both read the Bible day & night
  But thou readst black where I read white.
    Poetry and Prose of William Blake, p. 516.

contemporary life; he will build his holy city. The later prophecies fulfill that promise. "A Song of Liberty" holds the seeds of many harvests to come. Its "new born fire" would soon be christened Orc, its "starry king," ruined "on Urthonas dens," Urizen; its giant forms, Albion, France, Atlantis, would be given bodies to express their revolutionary throes. And at the center of revelation, making sense of his own life, would be the spiritual form of William Blake. Like Dante and Yeats after initiation, Blake sets out to walk through the whole world of time and space, interpreting its secret history and meaning. Nor, since "every thing that lives is Holy," can any particle of life be excluded. Like the ideal cities of the *Commedia* and *A Vision*, the city of *Jerusalem* must make a place for every soul. It would be work enough for a lifetime.

Yet the way to Jerusalem proved more difficult, perhaps, than it had seemed at the time of the *Marriage*. One more brief emblem, one more comparison, may illustrate the problem. In section 24 of *La Vita Nuova*, Dante recounts a crucial vision: he sees two ladies approaching in single file, the first named Giovanna, the other Beatrice. To the poet, the meaning seems manifest: "the name Giovanna comes from the name of that Giovanni [John the Baptist] who preceded the True Light, saying [in Latin]: 'I am the voice of one crying in the wilderness: prepare ye the way of the Lord.'"[30] For Dante, thereafter, the authority of Beatrice is absolute. She must be, in fact, the type of Christ; the guide of all guides; the intercessor and goal whose force of love will draw the pilgrim upward, out of this wilderness which is human life on earth, until he reaches paradise.

On the frontispiece of *All Religions are One*, the tiny set of plates which, with its companion *There is No Natural Religion*, represents Blake's first experiment with illuminated printing, we meet the same familiar motto: "The Voice of one crying in the Wilderness" (Plate XII). Sitting on a stone, the youthful John the Baptist (his face, some scholars say, resembles Blake's) points both arms left. Yet no Christ follows him. Indeed, as we learn from the

30. The reference, of course, is Matthew 3:3; as well as Mark 1:2, Luke 3:4, John 1:23. Since Dante identifies Giovanna with the lady of his friend, the poet Cavalcanti, the vision "proves" that Beatrice, who surpasses all other ladies in kind as well as degree, must be celebrated by a new kind of poetry, fit for a savior. Blake, however, always seems to associate John's message with its original prophetic source in Isaiah.

text and from the *Marriage*, the priest-ridden England he preaches to may be a wilderness of the spirit — the just man's vale of death — but none can restore Eden except the man with prophecy in his heart. The savior whose way Blake prepares is Blake himself — or each of us. "The true Man is the source he being the Poetic Genius." Blake can be guided only by his own spirit. Nor can he follow others' ways. John had announced, "the paths of the Lord are straight"; but we have seen that Blake adopted a more curving, serpentine line: that of the Devil who unfurls a scroll for modern scribes to read. And on that same design (Plate IV above), over the Devil's scroll, another proverb tells us how the author travels: "Improve[me]nt makes strait roads, but the crooked roads without Improvement, are roads of Genius."

Dante knew Beatrice, Yeats heard a spirit voice. For Blake there was no master. The law he forged, the ceremony of initiation he performed, could not constrain a single soul; the lion and the ox must take their ways apart. Blake can trust no one; and that aloneness, though a source of strength, fills the major prophecies with repeated moments of crisis and torment. Nor can he pass *through* the fire. Corrosion, not purification, is his element; contraries progress, the burning of their marriage never ends. Without Statius, Virgil, or Beatrice for companion, Blake mounts into the flames. Alone, he casts himself into refining fire where he must live forever.

Lawrence Lipking

Flaxman's Drawings
for Pilgrim's Progress

Part I

John Flaxman (1755-1826) is chiefly known today as one of England's greatest sculptors, the first Professor of Sculpture at the Royal Academy, creator of funeral monuments in churches throughout Southern England, and, incidentally, friend of the then obscure William Blake. He was even better known to his contemporaries, particularly those on the Continent such as Goethe and Canova and David, as the author of outline designs to *The Iliad* (1793), *The Odyssey* (1793), Dante's *Divine Comedy* (1793), Aeschylus's *Tragedies* (1795), and Hesiod's *Works* (1817), which were persistently reprinted during the 19th Century and copied in Italy, France, and Germany.[1] These designs were enormously influential throughout Western Europe in creating, or at least in decisively confirming,[2] a technique of retelling a familiar story in a series of simple, graceful outlines without text (other than captions for the designs), derived from Classical models, particularly Greek and Etruscan vase paintings.[3] As Flaxman wrote in a letter of 26 October 1793: with the Homer, Dante, and Aeschylus designs,

1. See G. E. Bentley, Jr., *The Early Engravings of Flaxman's Classical Designs*, 1964.
2. See Robert Rosenblum, *Transformations in Late Eighteenth Century Art*, 1967, or, more appropriately, the dissertation on which it was based, "The International Style of 1800," New York University, 1956.
3. When he was working on these designs in Rome, Flaxman wrote an undated letter to Sir William Hamilton in Naples asking him "to indulge me with some few particulars of the Greek stories represented in those beautiful Etruscan vases which you have added to your collection since I was at Naples & which I have so great a longing to see" (*The Collection of Autographs and Historical Documents formed by Alfred Morrison*, Second Series, 1882-1893: The Hamilton & Nelson Papers, 1893, I, p. 188).

my intention is to shew how any story may be represented in a series of compositions on principles of the Antient. . . .[4]

Most of these designs were created and engraved during a brief and extraordinarily fertile period (1792-94) while Flaxman was living in Rome. His wife Nancy explained to her sister-in-law in London on 15 December 1792 that John worked on sculpture during the day but is

> at home in the Evenings — he is employ'd & *that closely too* — in making a compleat set of drawings from Dante. . . . from which engravings are Making . . . after these (or rather going on at the same time) are a set of drawings from Homer's Iliad & Odyssey — consisting of 60 most beautiful Subjects & as beautifully treated . . . the which are also Engraving here. . . . I have already named 2 hundred & thirty drawings which employ your Brothers time & attention in the Evenings

but besides these he was making other (unidentified) sketches in the evenings.[5]

In addition to the more than two hundred designs for Homer, Aeschylus, and Dante which were engraved in Rome at the time, in 1793-94, Flaxman was making other illustrations which did not reach publication and which, as a consequence, are little known. Probably the most extensive series is the forty-some designs he made for *Pilgrim's Progress*, three of which (No. 4A, 5, 14A) are carefully dated "June 1792." As Flaxman's early biographer Alan Cunningham wrote in 1830, "it was his chief delight to make designs from the poets, from the Bible, and from the Pilgrim's Progress," for which he made many illustrations.[6] Only a few of these Bunyan designs have been reproduced, and they have never been discussed as a series or analysed.

Before Flaxman's time, the history of the illustrations to *Pilgrim's Progress* had been complex but unenterprizing.[7] The first

4. Quoted from the MS in The Fitzwilliam Museum, Cambridge.

5. British Museum Add. MSS 39, 780, f. 197.

6. Alan Cunningham, *The Lives of the Most Distinguished Painters, Sculptors, and Architects*, 1830, III, pp. 289, 351. Flaxman's Bunyan designs are numbered according to the order in the catalogue below.

7. See John Brown, *John Bunyan (1628-1688): His Life, Times, and Works*, Rev. Frank Mott Harrison, 1928, Chapter xix, "Editions, Versions, Illustrations, and

editions of *Pilgrim's Progress* Part I (1678) and of Part II (1684) had no plates, but the publisher, Nathaniel Ponder, soon observed "that many persons desired to have it illustrated with Pictures," and, as he explained in an advertisement accompanying the 1680 edition of Part I, he therefore "hath provided Thirteen Copper Cutts curiously Engraven" by an anonymous engraver.[8] Under each of the thirteen plates were four lines of yeomanlike verse, presumably by Bunyan,[9] and these designs, or the verses they apparently illustrated, were the inspiration of many of the plates in succeeding editions. Indeed, in editions of 1688 and later which were illustrated with woodcuts set into the type-set text, the quatrains became, as it were, part of the text, and some editions lost the woodcuts but preserved the verses. Thus the early designs had a reciprocal effect on the text through the quotations, and doubtless some later artists illustrated the quatrains without knowing that they had been originally created to elucidate the first designs. These verses had a powerful effect upon controlling the designs to *Pilgrim's Progress*, for they seemed to give Bunyan's authority to the subjects. Most of the hundreds of later editions of *Pilgrim's Progress* were illustrated, and for a century many editions had some of their designs derived from this first illustrated edition of 1680.

More satisfactory plates than those commissioned by Ponder were engraved by Jan Luyken and issued by John (Joannes, Jean) Bockholt in Amsterdam with a translation of *Pilgrim's Progress* into Walloon French (1685), and seven of these Dutch designs were substituted for corresponding English ones in English editions from 1695 onwards.

Imitations of *The Pilgrim's Progress*," pp. 438-86; Harrison, "Some Illustrators of *The Pilgrim's Progress* (Part One): John Bunyan," *Library*, 4 S, XVII, 1936, pp. 241-63 (there is no similar account of illustrations for Part II); F. M. Harrison, "Editions of *The Pilgrim's Progress* [Part I]": *Library*, 4 S, XXII, 1942, pp. 73-81 (which records over 1,300 editions and reprints, not counting alterations in verse, as plays, and for children; there were 160 editions by 1792); John Bunyan, *The Pilgrim's Progress*, ed. James Blanton Wharey, Oxford, 1928, with a history of editions of *Pilgrim's Progress* (xx-cx); and F. M. Harrison, *A Bibliography of the Works of John Bunyan*, 1932.

    8. See Wharey, p. xlii.

    9. Wharey, Harrison, and Roger Sharrock (rev. ed. of Wharey's *Pilgrim's Progress*, 1960) are silent on the subject, but Wharey (p. xciii) assumes that some at least of the similar added marginal glosses are Bunyan's. Certainly the trudging quality of Bunyan's other verse is like that below the designs.

The next important illustrations were the designs by John Clark (frequently imitating Luyken's) which were engraved by John Sturt for the 22nd edition of Pilgrim's Progress in 1727-1728.

Thereafter many illustrated editions simply copied the designs of Ponder-and-Luyken or of Sturt, either in woodcuts, which were customarily of execrable quality in cheap and vulgar editions, or in copperplates in dearer and more elegant editions. From the first illustrated edition in 1680 to Flaxman's designs in 1792, the vast majority of the printed illustrations for Pilgrim's Progress were essentially those of the Ponder-Luyken-Sturt editions.

Beginning in the 1770s, a surge of vitality manifested itself in English book illustrations of all kinds. Many more books were illustrated, and the quality of both designing and engraving increased enormously, until, by the time of the French Revolution in 1789, England no longer had to import the best engravings, such as Luyken's for Pilgrim's Progress, or even the best artists like Holbein and Van Dyke, but had a substantial surplus of exports over imports of engravings. The effect was felt in Pilgrim's Progress in ambitious designs by Flaxman and his friends and contemporaries Thomas Stothard (1788-91), George Cruikshank (1813), William Blake (c. 1824), and John Martin (1830).

Each of these designers virtually ignored the previous published illustrations to Bunyan and chose the elements in the book which spoke most strongly to him. Stothard's folk, for example, are distinctly domesticated contemporaries, with children sitting before a fire in one and a family gathered round to listen to a tale in another. Indeed, it is no surprise that Stothard is the first designer of quality to devote much attention to Christiana and her children in Part II.[10] Stothard's designs are apparently the first series of illustrations to Pilgrim's Progress to stand aside from the iconographical tradition and to make an entirely fresh start, particularly in Part II.

10. Stothard's 16 designs stippled by Joseph Strutt were issued separately, without text, by John Thane in 1788-91; a few of his designs were used to illustrate other editions (e.g., one of 1796 with 3 designs and another of 1840); and then 20 were reproduced in chromo-lithography by C. Schecher in The Select Works of John Bunyan, With a Life by George Cheever and an Introductory Essay by James Montgomery, 1865 — the edition also has 104 woodcuts, some by E. & G. Dalziel.

Even more independent were the designs made by Stothard's friend William Blake about 1824, for Blake seems to add in significant ways to Bunyan's story. Blake's extraordinary Apollyon seems to be making an explicitly sexual attack upon Christian, and the architecture of Blake's City of Destruction is certainly not Bunyan's.[11] Nevertheless, his designs are remarkably faithful to the spirit, and even to the minutiae, of Bunyan's book. Some of Blake's Bunyan illustrations are minor masterpieces and deserve more attention than they have yet received.

Finally, John Martin's heroic designs of 1830 of course ignore poor Pilgrim with his head bowed to the ground by the weight of his Burden and depict instead an endless celestial city built upon clouds in God's everlasting sky.[12] Martin illustrates Pilgrim's Progress as if it were *Paradise Lost*, with majestic vistas which reduce mankind to microscopic dimensions. With Martin, everything is background — indeed, the background is the subject — whereas with Flaxman there is no background and only the human figures are important.

In each case, the artist has transformed Bunyan's book into his own eternal truths. The designs tend to take on an importance independent of the text, and sometimes *Pilgrim's Progress* seems to be the occasion rather than the subject of the illustration. Flaxman's generation had come to accept illustrations of literary texts as important ends in themselves, justifying the publication of sets of engravings without the texts they illustrate, as in Flaxman's Homer, Aeschylus, and Dante designs of 1793, in Stothard's Bunyan designs of 1788-91, in the Boydell illustrations to Shakespeare of 1803, and in the plates for Hume's *History of England* in 1806. Engravings from Flaxman Bunyan illustrations would, I am sure, have been welcomed by his contemporaries.

Most of what has been said about *Pilgrim's Progress* thus far applies primarily to the illustrations for Christian's long, lonely journey in Part I. The sequel in Part II, narrating Christiana's tardy

11. Blake made a few pencil sketches, plus 24 watercolours on paper watermarked 1824 which were first published in an edition of *Pilgrim's Progress* With a new Introduction by Geoffrey Keynes, 1941. Mr. James T. Wills, who is presently preparing a study of them, has given me friendly advice about the history of Bunyan illustrations.

12. Martin's two splendid plates appeared in *Pilgrim's Progress*, With a Life by Robert Southey, 1830.

and contrite journey with her children to join her husband, was of course far less popular than Part I.[13] It is therefore interesting that half of Stothard's designs are for Part II, as are four-fifths of Flaxman's. Christiana's adventures are less extravagant and harrowing than Christian's — she is threatened but not harmed, her battles are fought by others for her, and she is supported throughout by her children and by a growing host of friends. Poor Pilgrim struggled by himself in heroic isolation, whereas Christiana moves more surely in a Christian society. For these or other reasons, Flaxman and Stothard chose to devote much or most of their attention to Christiana and became the first important illustrators to Part II, a century after it was first published in 1684.

Flaxman made at least forty-one drawings for *Pilgrim's Progress*, of which I have traced all but one in half a dozen different collections. They vary markedly in degree of finish, from the merest sketches to very precise outlines similar in completeness to those for Homer or Aeschylus prepared for the engraver, with a few showing extensive washes in the background. Unfortunately, the proportion of highly finished ones is low, for only about fourteen are very complete (No. 2, 4A-B, 5, 7-9, 10?, 12?, 14, 16A?, 18?, 19, 23B), and many of these are for scenes which come early in the book. Further, though there are forty-four designs, there are only thirty-two scenes represented. Twenty-six of the sketches (No. 4A-C, 14A-B, 15A-C, 16A-C, 17A-D, 18, 20A-B, 21A-B, 22, 23A-B, 25A-B, 29A-B, 30) are variants of only twelve designs, and twelve pages (No. 1, 11, 13, 14A, 15B-C, 16B, 20A-B, 22, 25A, 26) have designs for more than one scene on the same page.

Inscriptions:

Most of the designs are inscribed with a quotation from Bunyan (No. 1, 4A, 5, 7-15B, 16A-17A, 17C-20A, 21B-23A, 25, 28A, 29). Where there is more than one version of a design, at least one of them has an identifying inscription. Indeed, the

---

13. A spurious Part III appeared in 1693 and was vigorously denounced in the genuine 13th edition of Part I (1693), but went through 59 editions by the end of the eighteenth century (Wharey, p. cx). So far as I know, no important illustrations were made for it.

inscription is often the clearest indication that the design belongs with the *Pilgrim's Progress* series, and some of the uninscribed sketches (e.g., No. 4C, 17B, 20B, 21A) probably could not be associated with the series except for their similarity to inscribed drawings.

Date:

Flaxman's designs for *Pilgrim's Progress* were at least begun by 1792, when he was living in Rome and making the great series of outline illustrations for Homer, Aeschylus, and Dante; for three of the drawings (No. 4A, 5, 14) are inscribed "J Flaxman f[*ecit*]. June 1792." Each of these drawings is highly finished, and apparently Flaxman added his name and the date to indicate that they were complete.[14] The style is in line only, almost entirely in outline, with shading indicated only by straight lines, chiefly on flat surfaces. This technique of shading is peculiarly characteristic of Flaxman, and is intended, I think, for direct and minutely faithful transfer to copper. In style, these Bunyan designs are very like those for Homer, Aeschylus, and Dante which Flaxman prepared for the engraver in 1792-1794, and it is not implausible to suppose that he intended to publish his designs for Bunyan as well.

However, Bunyan is of far more parochial interest than Homer, Aeschylus, and Dante, being little known or translated in Italy in the 18th Century, and it is scarcely likely that Flaxman would have found a market for engravings illustrating Bunyan before he left Rome in 1794.

All the Bunyan drawings dated 1792 exhibit the same method of shading by straight lines, and we may tentatively associate all the drawings using this straight-line shading with 1792 — drawings 1-5, 11, 13-15B, 16A-17A, 17D, 19-20A, 21A-23A, 25A, 26-27, 29A-30. If we add to these the drawings which have no shading at all (No. 10, 12, 15C, 17B-C, 20B), some of which are demonstrably first thoughts of early drafts of designs later manifesting the straight-line manner of shading,[15] we find that we have

14. Only two other drawings in the series exhibit the same kind of finish (No. 2 and 4B), and the second of these is a duplicate of a signed design.

15. No. 10 is an exception, for it is quite finished, and no other version is known.

associated with the period 1792-94 most of the Flaxman designs for Bunyan which have been traced. Perhaps most of the surviving designs were made about 1792-94 in Rome in the hope that they could be engraved in outline, perhaps by Piroli, as those for Homer, Aeschylus, and Dante were.

The only other clear date associated with the composition of Flaxman's designs for *Pilgrim's Progress* is the watermark of 1795 in Nos. 7-9. These three designs have apparently always remained together, and they differ strikingly from most of the others in that they are highly finished, with shadows and contours indicated by extensive wash. No. 7 seems to have been drafted in No. 22 with straight-line shading. Only three other drawings have similar wash shadows, No. 18-19, and 23B, and each is highly finished as well; one of them (No. 23B) is a polished version of a design drafted earlier with straight-line shading (No. 23A). There is, then, a clear progression from the straight-line shading to the wash shading, and it is plausible also to associate all the drawings using wash shading (No. 7-9, 18-19, 23B) with 1795.

1795 is an important year in Flaxman's life. Late in 1794 he had returned from Rome to begin his professional career in London as a sculptor; he became an Associate member of the Royal Academy (1797); he organized the publication by his aunt Jane Matthews of his *Odyssey* and Aeschylus designs in London in 1795; and he set out to consolidate the reputation as a promising sculptor which he had forged during his seven years in Italy. It must have been an extraordinarily busy period for him, and he can have had little time to devote to entirely new publications — indeed, his next independent series of illustrations to literature, the designs for Hesiod engraved by William Blake, were not published until 1817, twenty-two years later.

There was, however, one way of turning the Bunyan designs to account, and that was by selling individual drawings to private patrons. This, I suspect, is the origin of No. 7-9, which have evidently always stayed together as a group, and of No. 18-19 and 23B, the last of which is a highly finished version of an earlier design. Some confirmation of this hypothesis may be seen in the fact that these drawings with wash shading would not have been suitable for transfer to copper in this form; the engraver would have had to copy them again, translating the wash-shadows and contours into a form which he could reproduce in line-engraving on copper. Probably all the drawings with wash shading were made in or after 1795, after Flaxman's return from Rome to London, and were made for private patrons with no thought of publication.

This very tentative evidence suggests, then, that the bulk of Flaxman's drawings for Bunyan were made in Rome about 1792 and were intended for publication, but that the plan was abandoned on his return to London in 1794, and thereafter he made Bunyan designs with wash shadows chiefly for his own amusement and for his friends and patrons.

Numbers:

Many of Flaxman's Bunyan designs are numbered, and the numbers on the designs are as follows:

Design:	7	8-9	14A	15A	16B,17A,C-D		19	20A,21'	22	30
Number:	6	7	18	25	28		34	44	54	139
Sharrock Page:	284	284	292	296	299		302	309	315	374

Only drawings for *Pilgrim's Progress* Part II are numbered; there are no numbers on Flaxman's designs for Part I. There is a stable relationship between the numbers on Flaxman's Bunyan designs and the *Pilgrim's Progress* pages (in the Sharrock edition) which they illustrate, with a ratio of about three in the Bunyan numbers for every two Sharrock pages. Remark that when there is more than one design for a page (as with No. 16-17, 20-21), the different designs bear the same number. I conclude, therefore, that the numbers on Flaxman's Bunyan designs refer to the page of an edition of *Pilgrim's Progress* published before 1793 in which Part II is bound in a separate volume, or at least separately paginated, that the text in it occupies about 177 pages (150 per cent of Sharrock's 118 pages), and that the preliminary poem, "The Author's Way of Sending Forth his Second Part of the Pilgrim" (Sharrock pp. 273-280), is separately paginated in the edition Flaxman used.[16] Note also that the numbers appear on both the

16. The description fits the illustrated edition of Part II, ed. W. Mason (n.d., bound, in my copy, with Part I of London, 1778), except that five of the eleven page

early designs with straight-line shading of about 1792-94 (No. 13, 15-17, 20-22, 29) and on the later ones with the wash-shading of 1795 and after (No. 7, 9, 19), suggesting that Flaxman brought his edition of *Pilgrim's Progress* with him from Rome to London.

Relationship to Other Designs:

One of the most striking characteristics of the new illustrations of *Pilgrim's Progress* which began to appear in the 1790s was their independence of the long tradition of designs for Bunyan. Men like Stothard, Blake, and Flaxman either scarcely looked at previous illustrations to *Pilgrim's Progress*, or, more probably, they looked but found little there corresponding to their vision of Bunyan's story. They sometimes illustrate the same scenes — for example, the account of the Muckraker was a favourite — but, when they do repeat a scene, their versions differ radically from the earlier ones.

I have looked at scores of editions of *Pilgrim's Progress*, including, I believe, all the important illustrated ones, but I have found no designs which Flaxman seems to be echoing closely.[17] What Flaxman wanted to say about *Pilgrim's Progress* differed substantially from the conclusions of his predecessors.

I have, however, found two instances in which another artist seems to have repeated Flaxman's unpublished designs. The first is the most puzzling. Blake's design for pl. 16 of his own poem called *Europe* (1794), showing a giant naked jailor climbing a stairway at the right leading up from a dungeon cell, is strikingly similar to Flaxman's *Pilgrim's Progress* design of Giant Despair leaving Christian and Hopeful in the dungeon of Doubting Castle (No. 5). The relationship seems so close, particularly in that strange back view of the powerful giant, that I, at least, should say confidently that one artist was consciously echoing the design of the other, were it not for the plaguy chronology. Flaxman's design is plainly

references (for No. 15, 19, 21-22, 29) are wrong by one to four pages — the differences caused by the amount of footnote matter.

17. Flaxman's design (c. 1792) of Christian at the Cross with Three Shining Ones (No. 2) is distinctly related to one by Sturt (1727-28, repeatedly repeated, e.g., in 1791), which in turn was echoed in one by Stothard (1788–, and Blake illustrates (c. 1824) the same scene. Flaxman's Christian and the Sleepies (No. 3) is much like Luyken's of the same scene (1685), one of the designs which was *not* incorporated in the Ponder-Sturt series.

dated "June 1792," indicating that it was made during his stay in Rome from 1787 to late 1794, while Blake's *Europe* is equally plainly dated in London in 1794. Unless we are prepared to perform some persuasive sleight-of-hand with these dates and places, we must subside into the conclusion that the relationship between these two strikingly similar designs is merely coincidental.

However, Blake's own design for Christian in the prison of Despair for *Pilgrim's Progress* also shows a strange, naked giant seen from behind. Surely, in 1824 when this watercolour was made, Blake had seen and admired Flaxman's design. Such a relationship is entirely to be expected, for we know that Flaxman borrowed from Blake,[18] and we know that Blake admired Flaxman, whom he called "My Dearest Friend."[19] Flaxman's Bunyan designs seem, then, to have had an effect upon subsequent artists even though they were not published.

Characteristics of Flaxman's Designs:

Flaxman's designs for *Pilgrim's Progress* form a very strong contrast with previous illustrations for the work. In the first place, they are very spare, with few details, and those details indicated only in outline, not in rounded contours. Everything is focused upon the persons, and there are scarcely any buildings or scenery at all — by contrast, John Martin's later illustrations are *all* vistas and palaces. In the second place, where Flaxman's predecessors had preserved only a somewhat approximate relationship to the text, Flaxman, like Blake later, was minutely faithful to Bunyan's words. I have found no instance in which Flaxman significantly departs from Bunyan; indeed, I think practically every visual detail may be found in Bunyan's text. It is true that Flaxman's lion (No. 24) is rather shrunken from the monster one imagines in reading Bunyan's book, and the tail on Flaxman's Ill-Favoured Ones is an extension of Bunyan's meaning rather than a literal illustration of it, but these exceptions are rare and are matters of emphasis. Flaxman clearly respected Bunyan's text and tried to illustrate it faithfully.

Flaxman seems to stress the passive nature of humanity, to

18. See *Blake Records*, 1969, pl. vi.
19. Letter of 12 September 1800.

show men submitting to spiritual forces, indeed attacked and protected by spiritual forces, rather than controlling their own destinies. Partly this is due to the fact that most of Flaxman's designs illustrate Part II, in which Christiana plays a much more passive role than Christian did in Part I, but Flaxman's own spiritual understanding is also revealed clearly here. In Bunyan's Part I, Christian by himself struggles through the Slough of Despond (though Help lifts him out), he fights with and defeats Apollyon by himself, he climbs the Delectable Mountains, but none of these popular scenes does Flaxman illustrate. Instead, in Part I he shows Christian with the Three Shining Ones, or Christian Received into the House Beautiful, or Christian and Hopeful in Prison. Even in Part I, Flaxman shows man as the subject of great spiritual forces, rather than as an independent being controlling, or at least directing, his own destiny by his own efforts.

Instead, in Part II Flaxman concentrates on Christiana's graceful humility, on her trusting dependence upon others, and on the spiritual strength she lends to her children and to Mercie. Christiana's trials are manifested as inward ones, and she triumphs through her humility as a mother and as a follower of Christ.[20]

The theme of man's dependence on superior powers is stressed by the frequent presence of children in the designs (in No. 1, 7-10, 12-14, 16, 18, 20-26). In this respect, Flaxman's designs for *Pilgrim's Progress* are very reminiscent of Stothard, and indeed some of his designs for Bunyan have been persistently catalogued as Stothard's.[21] Children appear in Flaxman's designs even for Part I (No. 1), where they are only of incidental importance to Bunyan's narrative. The children there become of retrospective significance later in Flaxman's series, however, because in Part II they appear in *most* of Flaxman's designs and are of course of great importance in the text. The presence of young children

20. I think W. G. Constable, *John Flaxman 1755-1826*, 1927, p. 52, misses the point when he writes:: "The homeliness and simplicity of Bunyan gave him opportunity; but he was rarely able to express the grandeur and pathos of *The Pilgrim's Progress*. Christiana and her companions . . . become transformed into the very every-day young women of Flaxman's family circle." Surely the contemporary, every-day nature of Christiana, the homeliness and simplicity of her family and friends in Flaxman's designs show his profound understanding of Bunyan's story.

21. Those now in the Folkestone Public Library and Museum.

clinging to their mother's skirts in Flaxman's design at the beginning of Part I suggests that he even then intended to illustrate Part II as well.[22]

Numbers of other features of Flaxman's designs emphasize man's dependence upon higher powers. The series is notable for the frequent opportunities Flaxman has created to depict maternal tenderness or feminine grace (No. 4, 7-14, 16, 18, 20-26) to illustrate simple, unpretentious beauty in contexts where Bunyan's text seems rather to stress merely simplicity and humility. These may be only neighbour women whom we see, but their unaffected attitudes and gestures are frequently mutely beautiful.

Flaxman's designs portray Christiana in most of the scenes of Part II, as is appropriate to the text, but they consciously stress the presence of a Christian community round Christiana by showing her with her friends and helpers such as Mercie, the Reliever (No. 17A-D), Old Honest (No. 26), Goodwill (No. 14A-B), the Old Saints (No. 18), The Interpreter (No. 21), and especially the warrior-guide Mr Greatheart (No. 15B, 23-27, 29). Christiana and her boys are almost always surrounded and borne up by others. In Flaxman's designs, as in Bunyan's text, Christiana wins through not by her own efforts but by the assistance of others more powerful than she. Spirits of good appear repeatedly (No. 2, 4, 13-15, 19, 21, 23, 25, 28), some of whom are explicitly angelic (No. 2, 14A, 19). In Flaxman's designs, Christiana's most important acts are acts of will and humility; most of the important corporeal acts are performed by others.

There is a good deal of violence in Bunyan's text, but comparatively little in Flaxman's designs, though he does show violence in No. 15-17, 25, 28-30. Most earlier illustrations of *Pilgrim's Progress* had shown Christian's Fight with Apollyon, Faithful's Martyrdom in flames, Christian's passage between the Lions and so on, but Flaxman eschews all this. He is concerned rather to show the demonic origins of corporeal evil, for example, rape (see No. 5, 8, 15-17, 25-26, 29), so that the Evil-Ones have elongated ears and tails (No. 8),[23] and his figures of Giant Despair (No. 5, 15B, 30), Giant Grim (No. 25-26), Giant Slaygood (No.

---

22. The sizes and ages of the children change oddly.
23. It is only in the later wash-drawings that the tails appear.

29), and Giant Maul (No. 28), and of the Ill-Favoured Ones (No. 8, 16)[24] are all shown as naked and brutish. Indeed, in general men shown in action are naked, except for the armour of Greatheart, while men in repose are clothed. There are classical precedents for such a distinction, with naked Greek warriors and clothed Greek philosophers, but they have little to do with Bunyan's narrative. Apparently Flaxman is trying to distinguish between merely corporeal action on the one hand and acts of will and mind deriving from spirit on the other hand. For such a theme, of course, Part II of *Pilgrim's Progress* is wonderfully appropriate.

There is a cool, uncluttered elegance about Christiana and her friends, an absence of props or background, which would have surprised Bunyan, though it seems artistically faithful to his text in most respects. The appearance and dress of the different figures are consistent as they reappear from design to design. The costumes are generally classical (except for No. 26), the gowns flowing in long straight folds (e.g., No. 4), the women's hair often piled on top of their heads, the men often of heroic proportions and either naked or wearing only symbolic clothes such as a belt or sandals (e.g., No. 5). Some of the men even wear a kind of toga, for example Goodwill in No. 14, and Old Honest in No. 25A.

Christian's costume is fairly consistent; he wears a flat-brimmed, flat-topped hat (No. 2-4), a jacket extending to his knees (No. 1, 3) or once to his hips (No. 2), with a round wallet at his hip (No. 2). Sometimes he has a long cloak (No. 3-5) or once a short cape (No. 2), and he carries a long pilgrim's staff (No. 2-4). Greatheart wears an elaborate suit of armour (No. 23, 25-28),[25] he carries a sword but apparently has no scabbard for it (No. 15B, 23, 25-26, 28), and once his helmet has a surprising Cromwellian visor (No. 26), appropriate to Bunyan's character but out of keeping with the other costumes.

All the women wear long dresses unmarked by ornaments, patterns, or gatherings, of a very Greek simplicity. Christiana usually wears a loose headdress like a head-shawl (No. 7, 9, 107, 12-13, 16, 18, 20, 22-23, 25A?, 26), which helps to identify her and to distinguish her from her constant companion Mercie, whose

24. It is not possible to be clear about such details in No. 15, 17.
25. In the latest version (No. 23B), it shows a cross on the chest.

hair is long, flowing, and unrestricted (No. 10?, 12?, 13-14, 16, 18, 20, 23, 25). It is curious, however, that Christiana's costume does not change after she is arrayed in fine linen by the Interpreter (No. 21A-B); apparently heavenly garments are not different in style from earthly ones.

Flaxman's designs for *Pilgrim's Progress* are thus a self-sufficient series, probably the most extensive set of designs he made which are still unpublished, and one of the most important in the long and crowded history of illustrations to Bunyan's masterpiece. They mark a striking departure from the strong tradition of Bunyan illustration persisting before 1790 and are notably independent in conception and execution. Flaxman's designs are far less concerned with Christian's corporeal adventures in Part I than had been most previous illustrations. His stress upon spiritual humility and upon the omnipresence of spiritual forces is novel in Bunyan tradition, accords strikingly well with Flaxman's own Swedenborgian bliefs, and is particularly appropriate to Part II of *Pilgrim's Progress*, which the majority of his designs illustrate. I think the spiritual impetus of Flaxman's designs, their independence of previous tradition and simultaneous faithfulness to Bunyan's text, and their chaste beauty make them one of the most interesting and important series illustrating *Pilgrim's Progress*. Bunyan's heroes of humility suited Flaxman's spiritual temper, and his designs for *Pilgrim's Progress* show, it seems to me, a major promise and a satisfying accomplishment.

Reproductions

Nos. 7-9 were reproduced and described in *Drawings by John Flaxman in the Huntington Collection*, ed. Robert R. Wark, 1970, No. 20-22, and No. 4B, 10, 12, 16A, 17C-D, 18, 29A-B are reproduced (in small size in pale sepia, often very hard to make out) and described summarily in *The Drawings of Flaxman in the Gallery of University College London*: Autotype Reproductions from the Original Frames in Thirty-Two Plates, ed. Sidney Colvin, 1876, pl. vii (No. 29A-B), viii (No. 17C-D), xx (No. 4B), xxv (No. 10, 12, 16A, 18).

Provenance

The very fragmentary history of Flaxman's drawings for *Pilgrim's Progress* before about 1870 is set out below:

1830. May 21 Christie sale of the First Part of the Sir Thomas Lawrence

Collection of Original Drawings by Modern Artists, lot 171 was two Flaxman drawings, one for *Pilgrim's Progress*, "Ann. 1792" (No. 4A, 5, 14A are dated 1792), soled to Kennedy for £1.18*s*.

1846. July, No. 14A was acquired by The British Museum Print Room.

1862. April 10-11, Christie sale of the property of John Flaxman, included No. 3, 4C, 11, 13, 14B, 17A-E, 22, 25B-26, according to Sidney Colvin (ed., Flaxman, *Drawings*, 1876, 2), and all but 4A went to University College, London, as part of the Flaxman Gallery given by Flaxman's sister-in-law and adopted daughter Maria Denman with the assistance of Henry Crabb Robinson.

No. 4A passed from Denman (?i.e., the Flax an sale above) to William Russell; Frederick Locker[-Lampson];[26] The Right Hon. G. L. Lampson; Old Hall Gallery, Rye 1961; Mr. Paul Mellon (ex Nickelson's Inc., Oct. 1962) — exhibited at the Royal Academy in 1881 and the Burlington Fine Arts Club in 1934. William Russell owned No. 2, 4A, 5-6; T. J. Denman had some, Col. [Gould] Weston had "two or three," and F. T. Palgrave had several others, according to Colvin (*op. cit.*, 44).

Locations

British Museum Print Room, twenty: No. 2-3, 4C-5, 11, 13-15C, 17A-B, 20-21B, 25B-28.

University College, London, eight: No. 4B, 10, 12, 16A, 17C-18, 29A-B.

Folkestone Public Library and Museum, six: No. 14B, 16B, 22, 24, 25A, 30.

Henry E. Huntington Art Gallery, three: No. 7-9.

Mr. Christopher Powney, three: No. 19, 23A-B.

Ashmolean Museum, one: No. 1

Mr. Paul Mellon, one: No. 4A

Untraced, one: No. 6.

26. It is inscribed on the verso: "This drawing was all I got for a bad debt of £120./F. Locker." The information about No. 4A derives from two complementary sets of notes, one on a photography of the drawing in the Witt Library of the Courtauld Institute of London University, and one with the photograph generously sent me by Mr. Paul Mellon.

PART II
CATALOGUE OF FLAXMAN'S ILLUSTRATIONS TO
PILGRIM'S PROGRESS

The designs are in pencil, or ink, or wash applied with the tip of the brush, occasionally with a little broad wash in the background.

Pilgrim's Progress Part I

1 a) Christian Explains their Danger to his Wife and Children (p. 146)[1] and
b) Christian Derided by his Wordly-Minded Friends (p. 147)
Description: There are two clear outline sketches, one (a) above the other (b). Shading is with straight lines.

a) Christian stands at right with his arms spread in an emphatic gesture, a book (Bible) shown open in his left hand, expostulating with Christiana who stands facing him at the left, holding her youngest son (aged about three) in her arms, while her three other sons, aged about five to eight, cluster around her skirts looking at their father.

b) Christian sits at the left on a cube reading intently in his Bible, while at the right stand three men, "his Relations," the two closest to him apparently naked, the third in a long cloak. The left hand man faces Christian with a gesture like Christian's above in a), the second turns away with extended left arm and a shrug of the shoulders, and the third man seems also to be turning away, looking over his left shoulder; perhaps they represent the words "sometimes they would deride, sometimes they would chide, and sometimes they would neglect him" (p. 147).

Inscriptions: a) "Explains their mutual danger to his wife" (a paraphrase of p. 146, not a quotation).

b) "derided by his worldly minded friends —" (also a paraphrase).
Number: None.
Size: 4 1/2 in. x 8 1/4 in.
Watermark: None.
Collection: ASHMOLEAN MUSEUM.

1. The page references at the ends of the titles refer to John Bunyan, *Grace Abounding to the Chief of Sinners* and *The Pilgrim's Progress*, ed. R. Sharrock (1966).

2) *Christian at the Cross with Three Shining Ones (p. 169)*

Description: A finished sketch depicts a man at the right with a long staff in his right hand and a flat hat in his left, a tunic with attached cape, and a round wallet at his belt, facing left toward three women with wings standing before a large cross. Shading is with straight lines.
Inscription: None.
Number: None.
Size: 6 5/8 in. x 7 1/8 in.
Watermark:
Collection: BRITISH MUSEUM PRINT ROOM, Binyon 48b2

3) *Christian Trying to Awaken Simple, Sloth, and Presumption (p. 170)*

Description: A fairly finished sketch represents Christian in a long coat and a wide-brimmed hat holding in his right hand a long staff with a knob at the top (the hat and staff like Christian's in No. 2) as he bends forward to touch with his left hand the belt of one of three prone figures (Simple, Sloth, and Presumption). The figure nearest Christian has his feet toward Christian, to the right is another sleeping on his arms with his head toward Christian, and in the background is a third with his head away from Christian. The two nearest sleepers (the only ones whose feet we can see) have fetters on their ankles. Shading is with straight lines.
Inscription: None.
Number: None.
Size: 7 1/8 in. x 4 in.
Watermark:
Collection: BRITISH MUSEUM PRINT ROOM, Binyon 49a.

4A) *Christian Welcomed to the House Beautiful (p. 177)*

Description: A finished drawing of a man ("Christian") with a cross-headed staff and a hat in his hands walking left toward the steps on which stand seven women with their hands outstreched in greeting to him, while behind him stand four more women ("Discretion," "Charity," "Piety," and "Prudence"). Shading is with straight lines.
Inscription: "And many of them meeting him at the threshold of the house, said Come in Thou Blessed of the Lord;/ Pilgrim's Progress/ J Flaxman f. June 1792".
Number: None.
Size: 8 3/4 in. x 10 5/8 in.
Watermark:
Collection: MR. PAUL MELLON

2. Lawrence Binyon, *Catalogue of Drawings by British Artists and Artists of Foreign Origin Working in Great Britain*, Preserved in the Department of Prints and Drawings in the British Museum (1900), II, 145-147.

4B) Christian Welcomed to the House Beautiful (p. 177)

Description: A finished drawing like 4A except that Christian's staff has a fleur-de-lis at the top and he has a kind of epaulette. The heads of the women behind Christian are somewhat different. Shading is with straight lines.
Inscription: None.
Number: None.
Size:
Watermark: Invisible (pasted down).
Collection: UNIVERSITY COLLEGE, LONDON.

4C) Christian Welcomed to the House Beautiful (p. 177)

Description: A clear sketch of Christian as in 2b but lacking the staff and epaulette: the other figures are indicated only very roughly. There is no shading.
Inscription: None.
Number: None.
Size: 6 5/8 in. x 4 3/8 in.
Watermark:
Collection: BRITISH MUSEUM PRINT ROOM, Binyon 48a.

5) Giant Despair Leaving Christian and Hopeful in Prison (p. 233).

Description: A finished drawing shows Giant Despair, apparently wearing only sandals and a belt, seen from behind, as he mounts a dark stairway to the right. Behind him in an unfurnished room Christian and Hopeful sit disconsolately against the wall at the left, Christian with his head back and mouth open, Hopeful with his head bowed and his hands in his lap. A large block of stone in the wall facing them has hooks from which hang neck(?) and wrist manacles. Shading is with straight lines.
Inscriptions: "Christian," "Hopeful," "Giant Despair"; "At this they trembled greatly, & I think that Christian fell into a Swoon;/ Pilgrim's Progress'; "J. Flaxman f. June 1792."
Number: None.
Size: 9 1/8 in. x 7 1/2 in.
Watermark:
Collection: BRITISH MUSEUM PRINT ROOM, Binyon 50.

6) The Fight of Christian with [the Brothers] Guilt, Mistrust, Faint Heart, and their Master [the King of the Bottomless Pit] (p. 244).
Description: Unknown.
Inscription: Unknown.
Number: Unknown.
Size: Unknown.

Watermark: Unknown.
Collection: UNTRACED. My only information about the drawing beyond the descriptive-title above is that about 1875 it belonged to William Russell (*The Drawings of Flaxman in the Gallery of University College London*, ed. Sidney Colvin [1876], 45).

7) Christiana Confessing to her Four Sons (p. 284)

Description: A finished drawing, with Brown wash shading in the immediate background and on the figures, represents Christiana kneeling with her arms spread over three small boys (about 7-10 years old) who are hugging her, while to her left (our right) facing her and us, a fourth boy looks at her in anguish.[3] Here, as in all the designs, Christiana wears a vague long dress with a kind of snood on the back of her head.
Inscription: "Then said she to her Children, Sons we are all undone, I have sinned [against *del*] away your Father and he is gone; he would have had us go with him, but I would not go myself, I have also hindered You of life."
Size: 7 3/8 in. x i 7/8 in.
Watermark: I TAYLOR 1795.
Collection: HENRY E. HUNTINGTON ART GALLERY.

8) Two Ill-Favoured Ones Plotting by the Bed of Christiana and her Children (p. 284).

Description: A finished drawing, with Brown wash chiefly on the Ill-Favoured Ones and the background, represents two demonic naked men, bald, with tails and elongated ears, who kneel ominously and talk with faces and gestures beside the bed in which sleep Christiana and two of her sons (aged about 1 year).
Inscription: ". . . she thought She saw two very ill-favored ones Standing by her bedside & saying what shall we do with this woman —."
Number: "7."
Size: 7 3/8 in. x 8 7/8 in.
Watermark: I Taylor 1795.
Collection: HENRY E. HUNTINGTON ART GALLERY.

9) Christiana with her Four Sons Opens the Door to Secret (p. 285)

Description: A finished drawing, with Brown wash on Secret and for shadows, shows Christiana, with three sons (aged about 3, 5, and 6) in front

---

3. A rough sketch in the British Museum Print Room (Binyon 57a), without inscription or number, 5 1/2 in. x 3 3/4 in., seems to represent a seated woman(?) with her head resting on her left hand, while four or more children clutch her waist. The faint plinth and vague monumental standing figures in the background suggest to me that this is a design for a funeral effigy and not for *Pilgrim's Progress*, despite the similarity to No. 7 above.

of her and the fourth behind her (aged c. 9) opening the door to Secret, who enters with a sealed letter ["from thy Husbands King"] in her hand.[4]

Inscription: "- - to whom She Spake out, saying, if thou comest in God's name, come in. So he Said amen, & opened the door."

Number: "7."

Size: 7 3/8 in. x 8 7/8 in.

Watermark: I. TAYLOR 1795.

Collection: HENRY E. HUNTINGTON ART GALLERY.

10) Christiana's Neighbours Find her Preparing to Depart (p. 287).

Description: A fairly finished sketch represents two women at the left (Timorous and Mercie) bending over Christiana, who is kneeling on the floor looking up over her shoulder at her visitors. On her lap are clothes which two children of about 6 are making into bundles, while a third child of the same age is carrying such a bundle on his head. There is no shading.

Inscription: "Behold they found the good Woman preparing to be gone from her house."

Number: None.

Size: 6 7/8 in. x 6 1/2 in.

Watermark: Invisible (pasted down)

Collection: UNIVERSITY COLLEGE, LONDON.

11) Timorous Acquaints her Friends what the Good Christiana Intends to Do (p. 289), with two other slight sketches.

Description: There are three sketches on the sheet, one at the left fairly finished (a), one at the right in outline (b), and one at the bottom right very rough (c).

(a) A group of five women, two on the left (the central one with talking hands) facing three on the right, evidently represent Mrs Timorous indignantly telling her neighbours Mrs Bats-eyes, Mrs Inconsiderate, Mrs Lightmind, and Mrs Know-nothing "the story of *Christiana*, and of her intended Journey."[5] Shading is with straight lines.

(b) A more faintly outlined woman at the right seems to be for Mrs Timorous with her hands in a different position.

(c) At the bottom right is a faint sketch of an old(?) man on the ground,

---

4. I do not see the resemblance of this drawing to no. 20A [Binyon 51a], which Work (*op. cit*) says is "preparatory" to it.

5. Binyon calls it The Neighbours expostulating with Christiana (see p. 287), but this seems implausible, for there are only three women in the scene (Christiana, Mercy, and Mrs Timorous), and one of the women here (No. 11) looks much like Christiana. The two women at left wear their hair up in buns, but the three figures at right have cropped hair and look rather masculine.

apparently in distress, perhaps for the death of Giant Despair (below, no. 14B[b]).

Inscription: "P.P."
Number: None.
Size: 6 7/8 in. x 6 in.
Watermark:
Collection: BRITISH MUSEUM PRINT ROOM, Binyon 51b.

12) Christiana, Mercie, and the Four Children Setting Out (p. 291)

Description: A clear sketch shows a procession of persons walking to the right. At the left, Mercie puts her hand to her forehead. Beside her, Christiana, with a bundle under her left arm and holding the left hand of the smallest child (aged about 3) in her right hand, turns anxiously to Mercie. Before them walk two boys, of about 7 and 9, with bundles on their shoulders, and before them walks a boy of about 6 with a bundle under his arm. (A virtually identical scene is sketched in 18A[c]." There is no shading.

Inscription: "and Mercy began to weep."
Number: None.
Size: 6 3/4 in. x 6 5/6 in.
Watermark: Invisible (pasted down).
Collection: UNIVERSITY COLLEGE, LONDON.

13) a) Christiana, Mercie, and the Children at the Slough of Despond (p. 292) and b) The Trumpeter at the Wicket Gate (p. 294).

Description: There are two fairly clear and quite distinct sketches, one (a) above the other (b). Shading in each is with straight lines.

a) Seven persons walk to the right. A child of about 5 holds the arm of a boy of about 10, who in turns holds the right hand of Christiana; between the last two is a child of three, and on Christiana's left are two boys of about 6 and 7. In front Mercie fearfully lifts up her dress, perhaps as she steps into the water.

b) In a break(?) in a high wall, a man leans toward us with a trumpet to his lips. Below him, the long-haired gate-keeper gestures up toward him with both(?) hands, while behind him stands Christiana with her four boys, aged 3 to 9, clustered round her.

Inscriptions: a) "But Said Mercy come let us venture only let us be wary"; b) "he called to a Trumpeter."
Number: a) "18."
Size: 5 3/4 in. x 8 1/8 in.
Watermark:
Collection: BRITISH MUSEUM PRINT ROOM, Binyon 53b.

14A) Goodwill Opens the Wicket Gate and Finds Mercie Fainted (p. 294).

Description: A finished drawing with a few straight lines for shading represents Goodwill in a long loose robe passing towards us through a doorway, with an inscribed lintel and a door with a circular knocker, and looking down at Mercie stretched to the right on the ground. (Another version may be sketched in 20A[b].)

Inscriptions: "Knock and it shall be opened unto you," "Goodwill," "Mercy," "So he opened the Gate & looked out but Mercy was fallen down without in a Swoon/ Pilgrims Progress," "J. Flaxman f. June 1792."

Number: None.

Size: 9 1/2 in. x 8 in.

Watermark:

Collection: BRITISH MUSEUM PRINT ROOM, Binyon 54.

14B) a) Christiana's Entry into the Celestial City(?) (pp. 393-395); b-c-d) Goodwill Finds Mercie Fainted (p. 294)

Description: There are at least four sketches on three levels.

a) At the top middle, two winged women(?) in long dresses, watched by a smaller standing figure at the right, mount left up steep steps toward five floating winged figures. (No such scene seems to be described in *The Pilgrim's Progress*, but perhaps it represents the entry of Christiana into the Celestial City [pp. 393-395], where the inhabitants are winged [see p. 270].) Shading is with straight lines.

b) At the top right is a sketch (partly cut off) of the same scene as in c below, except that Mercie's head is raised.

c) In the middle is a sketch of a man (Goodwill) in a doorway, with a long staff in his right hand, who leans over as "he took her [*Mercie*] by the hand" (p. 294); the scene is later than that in 14A, Mercie now lies on her back, and her head is to the left (not the right). To the right is an apparently confused mass of figures, perhaps children backed by adults looking on in anxiety. To the left is a very faint pencil sketch which I cannot make out.

d) At the bottom are several rough groups of figures, evidently adults and children, perhaps trials for the onlookers in the scene above.

Inscription: None.

Number: None.

Watermark: Crowned crest without letters or date.

Size: 6 5/8 in. x 9 in. no. 14B is on the verse of no. 22.

Collection: FOLKESTONE PUBLIC LIBRARY AND MUSEUM.

15A) The Devil's Dog Worrying the Pilgrims (p. 296).

Description: A rough but clear sketch shows an enormous dog of the boxer type, apparently with a huge spiked collar, who bestrides a pilgrim fallen on his side and hauls another who flees to the rear towards a winged man (the Lord's "timely Help") who is about to strike the dog with a sword(?). Straight lines are used for shading.

Inscription: "he has broken out & has worried some that I loved; but I take all at present patiently. I also give my Pilgrim timely Help."

Number: "25."

Size: 6 in. x 4 in.

Watermark:

Collection: BRITISH MUSEUM PRINT ROOM, Binyon 55c.

15B) a) *The Devil's Dog Worrying Pilgrims (p. 296)* b) *Despair's Death (p. 374), and four others.*

Descriptions: There is a fairly clear sketch at the top (a) and another quite distinct one at the bottom (b);[6] in addition, there are: a very distinct sketch at the top right (c), a somewhat clearer sketch (d) to the left between a and b, and a very faint sketch (e) to its right, and a confused sketch (f) at bottom right.

a) The scene is very like that for 15A, except that the fallen pilgrim is now on his back, the fleeing man looks towards the angel, not toward the dog, and the angel, whose wings are now much vaguer, desparately holds the dog's leash.

b) A huge Giant Despair struggles to lift himself from the ground with his left hand in order to swing a huge club with his right hand; his Cap of Steel is on the ground beneath his head. Three men[7] drive great spears into him from before, while behind him a fourth (Greatheart) is about to sever his head from his shoulders with a sword. (The design is repeated in No. 30.)

c) I can make out no details of c.

d) Two men at left beat down a large figure to the ground (Giant Despair or "*Diffidence*, the *Gyantess*" whom "old Mr. *Honest* cut down" [p. 373]); to the right is another fallen figure.

e) A very faint sketch seems to represent figures struggling.

f) A somewhat clearer sketch also seems to represent figures struggling.

Inscription: b) "Dispair's Death."

Number: None.

Size: 6 1/4 in. x 8 3/4 in.

Watermark:

Collection: BRITISH MUSEUM PRINT ROOM, Binyon 49b (17A is on the recto).

15C) a) *A Cat and* b) *The Devil's Dog (p. 296).*

Descriptions: Two moderately clear, unrelated sketches represent a) at the left, the unfinished head of a cat, and b) at the right, a profile of a

---

6. In both, shading is indicated by straight lines.
7. Binyon erroneously describes them as "Christiana's sons."

barking dog, like the Devil's even to the spiked collar, except that his tail is curved over his back and is bushy.

Inscription: None.
Number: None.
Size: 5 5/8 in. x 2 1/4 in.
Watermark:
Collection: BRITISH MUSEUM PRINT ROOM, Binyon 55b.

16A) Two Ill-Favoured Ones Scuffle with Christiana and Mercie (p. 299)

Description: A fairly clear sketch represents, at left, Christiana in her customary head-scarf, pushing away the head of a naked man; Mercie, with flowing hair, grasps the waist of Christiana while her breasts are grasped from behind by a similar naked cat(?)-faced man. Behind them, to the right, four naked boys, aged about 3 to 7, clasp or raise their hands and cry out. There are a very few straight lines for shadows.

Inscription: "The Women were in a very great Scuffle/ the children also stood crying by."
Number: None.
Size: 6 7/8 in. x 6 7/16 in.
Watermark: Invisible (pasted down).
Collection: UNIVERSITY COLLEGE, LONDON.

16B) a-d, f-i) Two Ill-Favoured Ones Scuffle with Christiana and Mercie (p. 299) and e) The Old Saints' Kind Reception of Christiana and her Children (p. 302)

Description: There are nine rough pencil-sketches on four levels of the page, the most detailed one in the centre (b). All but one (e) represent the Two Ill-Favoured Ones Scuffling with Christiana and Mercie. The ones in the top row and the centre (a-b) are very like 16A, and the central one has these details confirmed in ink. Those in the middle right (c), lower middle-left and right (d, f), and the bottom (g-i) are much like 16C. In none are there any children. These appear to be the first drafts.

In the centre of the lower-middle is a small faint sketch very like No. 18 of The Old Saints' Kind Reception of Christiana and her Children.

Inscription: None.
Number: None.
Size:
Watermark:
Collection: FOLKESTONE PUBLIC LIBRARY AND MUSEUM.

16C) Two Ill-Favoured Ones Scuffle with Christiana and Mercie (p. 299).

Description: One woman stands facing us and another kneels with her left arm round the first, while behind them are two men with fierce expressions, perhaps bald but entirely human. To the left two children clutch the dress of the standing woman. Shading is with straight lines. The scene seems to be a moment after no. 16A, which is clearer.

Inscription: "The women were in a great Scuffle the Children also stood crying by."

Number: "28."

Size: 4 in. x 6 1/2 in.

Watermark: None.

Collection: FOLKESTONE PUBLIC LIBRARY AND MUSEUM

17A) The Two Ill-Favoured Ones Escaping from the Reliever (p. 299).

Description: A clear sketch shows two dark, naked(?) men with indistinguishable features (the Ill-favoured Ones) who plunge headlong over a low wall into a bushy garden [of the Devil], pursued with outstretched arms by the naked(?) Reliever. Straight lines indicate shadows.

Inscription: "He also attempted to take them but they did make their escape over the wall."

Number: "28."

Size: 5 3/4 in. x 4 1/4 in.

Watermark:

Collection: BRITISH MUSEUM PRINT ROOM, Binyon 56b (15B is on the verso).

17B) The Two Ill-Favoured Ones Escape from the Reliever (p. 299).

Description: A much rougher sketch of the same subject as 17A.

Inscription: None.

Number: None.

Size: 4 7/8 in. x 4 in.

Watermark:

Collection: BRITISH MUSEUM PRINT ROOM, Binyon 56a.

17C) The Two Ill-Favoured Ones Escape from the Reliever (p. 299).

Description: A somewhat firmer sketch of the scene in 17A-B, but without the wall.

Inscription: "He also attempted to take them."

Number: "28."

Size: 4 3/16 in. x 3 7/8 in.

Watermark: Invisible (pasted down).

Collection: UNIVERSITY COLLEGE, LONDON.

17D) The Two Ill-Favoured Ones Escape from the Reliever (p. 299)

Description: A sketch, about as complete as 17A, shows the same figures, but the pale Reliever runs towards us and the two dark Ill-Favoured Ones run on either side past him toward the wall. Shadows are indicated by straight lines.

Inscription: "He also attempted to take them, but they make their [escape] over the wall."

Number: "28."

Size: 4 7/8 in. x 3 13/16 in.

Watermark: Invisible (pasted down).

Collection: UNIVERSITY COLLEGE, LONDON.

18) The Old Saints' Kind Reception of Christiana and her Children (p. 302).

Description: A fairly finished sketch with a few wash shadows, of Mercie, with loose-flowing hair, and Christiana with her hair-shawl sitting at the right, while a child of about 6 hides his face in Christiana's lap. On the left two women (called the *"Old Saints"* in Bunyan's marginal gloss) look right toward a woman who holds up her long dress and bends to caress the face of the tallest of the three boys aged about 3 to 9 standing by Christiana's knees. (A rough sketch is on no. 16B.)

Inscription: "They stroaked them over their faces."

Number: None.

Size: 6 7/16 in. x 6 3/8 in.

Watermark: Invisible (pasted down).

Collection: UNIVERSITY COLLEGE, LONDON.

19) The Muck Raker and the Angel (p. 302)

Description: A finished sketch in Grey wash with straight lines and touches of pale Brown wash in the background represents a bearded, naked(?) man, with his left knee on the ground and his right knee raised, bending forward as he draws toward him a rake with long teeth and a very short handle. Above him, apparently unseen by him, hovers horizontally in air a figure in a flowing gown and long tresses, holding to the left a chaplet of stars.

Inscription: "There was a Man with a Much Rake and one stood over him proffering a Celestial Crown — but he did not observe him" (close paraphrase). Below is an ink inscription, mostly cut off, apparently of the same words.

Number: "34."

Size: 6 1/2 in. x 6 7/8 in.

Watermark:

Collection: Mr CHRISTOPHER POWNEY.

20A) Christiana, Mercie, and the Boys Entering the Bath (p. 309) and four others.

Description: There are at least five sketches on the page: a) The clearest one, almost finished, at thy middle right; b) A faint one at middle left; c) A clear one at bottom left; d) a very faint vague one at bottom right; e) A very faint one at top left.

a) From a doorway at the right, Mercie, with her hair in a bun, and her four boys aged 3 to 9 descend two steps, on the bottom of which Christiana with her hair-shawl sits washing her foot in the water.

b) A dim prostrate person raising himself on his left elbow looks up and left at a yet dimmer standing man in a doorway, perhaps another version of No. 14.

c) The scene is virtually identical with No. 12.

d) I cannot make out the confused scene in front of the pedestrians of c.

e) Christiana and Mercie stand or walk with the four boys; perhaps it is another version of 12, 13 or 20A (a).

Inscription: 1) "Then they went in and the[y] washed Yea & the boys & all."

Number: a) "44."

Size: 6 1/8 in. x 8 3/8 in.

Watermark:

Collection: BRITISH MUSEUM PRINT ROOM, Binyon 51a.

20B) Christiana, Mercie, and the Boys Entering the Bath (p. 309) and several others.

Description: There are four somewhat faintly outlined sketches on the page: a) The central design, above; b) Two figures at the left; c) The same two figures at the right; d) The same two figures at top right.

a) The central design is virtually identical with 20A, except that the doorway is invisible, the figure of Mercie being clearest.

b-d) The virtually-identical designs of two figures in b-d, one sitting facing us and the other to the right kneeling in profile reaching to the right, do not seem to be repeated in Flaxman's other Bunyan designs. The top right kneeling woman (d) may be leaning over a step to the water.

Inscription: None.

Number: None.

Size: 6 1/2 in. x 4 1/4 in.

Watermark:

Collection: BRITISH MUSEUM PRINT ROOM, Binyon 52c.

21A) The Interpreter Arraying Christiana and her Children in Fine Linen (pp. 309-310).

Description: A fairly rough outline shows the Interpreter holding a garment over the head of Christiana who reaches up toward it, while two(?) children beside her dress themselves.

Inscription: None.

Number: "44."

Size: 2 1/4 in. x 4 1/4 in.

Watermark:

Collection: BRITISH MUSEUM PRINT ROOM, Binyon 52a.

21B) The Interpreter Arraying Christiana and her Children in Fine Linen (pp. 309-310)

Description: The design is almost identical to 19A, except that the Interpreter's head is more finished, the bottom left child's head is less finished, and the head of a second man(?) with a halo(?) is visible at the top right by Christiana's elbow.

Inscription: "So he commanded them to put it on. It was fine linnen white & clean."

Number: None.

Size: 2 1/8 in. x 4 1/4 in.

Watermark:

Collection: BRITISH MUSEUM PRINT ROOM, Binyon 52b.

22) Getting Water from the Spring (p. 315).

Descriptions: There are two scenes, one (a) at the top and one (b) at the bottom.

a) Christiana Confessing to her Four Sons (p. 284); b-c) Getting Water from the Spring (p. 315).

There are three designs on three levels of the page, one below the other.

a) At the top, an earlier draft of no. 7, a clear sketch with straight-line shading but no background, shows Christiana kneeling with three children hiding at her breasts and a fourth sheltering behind her.

b) Below it is a more finished sketch with horizontal shading of two women kneeling before bushes (beside a stream?); between them is a very large pot, which the woman on the left seems to be filling with a pan or dipper in her right hand.

c) At the bottom is a faint pencil sketch which seems to represent the two women in the same positions.

Inscription: b) "They took it up & put it into an Earthen pot."

Number: "54."

Size: 9 in. x 6 5/8 in. No. 14A is on the verso of No. 22.

Watermark: Crowned crest without letters or date.

Collection: FOLKESTONE PUBLIC LIBRARY AND MUSEUM.

23A) Greatheart Helps the Pilgrims Descend into the Valley of Humiliation (p. 333).[8]

Description: A clear, fairly finished drawing shows Greatheart, armed cap-à-pied, leans his left hand on his great broadsword as he turns back to give his right hand to help Christiana (with her head shawl) descend a steep hill. Christiana is holding with her right hand the right hand of a child of about 6 who is taking a great step down, behind them are two other boys of about 7

8. The inscription does not identify a precise scene, but the text (pp. 333-334) describes the descent into the Valley of Humiliation in terms very like those depicted here, while there is no description of the descent into the Valley of the Shadow of Death (pp. 337-338).

and 9, and between Christiana and Greatheart but in the background are two adults with bobbed hair, evidently Prudence and Mercie. (Perhaps Christiana's fourth son is standing behind Greatheart helping down the middle woman; at any rate there is an apparently extra pair of legs and a hand which are most easily explained thus.) Some shading, especially behind Greatheart, is shown by straight lines.

Inscription: "Christiana & Knight Pilgrims progress."
Number: None.
Size: 7 in. x 8 3/4 in.
Watermark:
Collection: Mr CHRISTOPHER POWNEY.

23B) Greatheart Helps the Pilgrims Descend into the VAlley of Humiliation (p. 333).

Description: A highly finished drawing, with extensive pale Brown wash in the background, represents a scene virtually identical with 23A, except there are many more minor details, Greatheart has a cross on his breastplate, and his breastplate lacks the dagger-like protuberances from flat circular plates over his breasts, and Mercie and Prudence are seen in full, rather than three-quarter, profile.

Inscription: None.
Number: None.
Size: 5 7/8 in. x 6 1/4 in.
Watermark:
Collection: Mr CHRISTOPHER POWNEY.

24) James Falls Sick (p. 338)

Description: Four women (Mercie, Christiana, and probably Prudence and Piety) crouch over a young man (James) lying contorted on the ground as he "began to be Sick" from "Fear" (p. 338).

Inscription: "James falls sick," "PP[?]."
Number: None.
Watermark: None.
Size: 6 1/4 in. x 3 1/8 in.
Collection: FOLKESTONE PUBLIC LIBRARY AND MUSEUM.

25A) a) Christiana, Mercie, and the Children with Old Honest (c. p. 344); b-c, e) Christiana, Mercie, and the Children Led by Mr Greatheart (c. p. 333);[1] d) Greatheart Attacks Giant Grim and his Two Lions (pp. 318-319)

Description: There are five sketches on three levels, two (a-b) at the top,

---

1. Perhaps it illustrates: "they went forward until they were come to the Brow of the Hill" (p. 333). If so, Prudence and Piety should be with them.

two (c-d) in the middle, and one (e) at the bottom left.

a) At the top left, two women bend down with their hands on the shoulders of two(?) standing children looking down to the right at a duckling and a duck, while to the right watching them stands an old man clad like Old Honest in 25(b).[1]

b) At the top right is a very faint pencil sketch evidently representing Greatheart in c below, holding one child in his left hand and perhaps one or two others to his right.

c) In the middle left, Mercie and Christiana follow three children, aged 6 to 10, up a slight hill behind Greatheart, who holds in his left hand the right hand of another child and in his right carries his naked sword over his shoulder, as he does in No. 25B.

d) The most elaborate sketch on the page, with straightline shading, occupies the right of the middle and bottom of the page. In it, Greatheart, apparently in armour, climbs a steep hill and threatens with his drawn sword in his right hand Giant Grim, bearded, naked, and unarmed, who lowers above him between two lions.

e) At the bottom right is a confused pencil sketch perhaps representing Greatheart leading the Pilgrims, as in c above.

Inscription: None.

Number: None.

Watermark: None.

Size: 6 3/8 in. x 9 in.

Collection: FOLKESTONE PUBLIC LIBRARY AND MUSEUM

25B) Christiana, Mercie, and the Children Led by Mr. Greatheart and Followed by a Lion (p. 338).

Description: A clear but unfinished outline sketch represents Christiana walking to the right holding the hand of the youngest of three children, aged about 5 to 9. She is preceded by Mr Greatheart, with a sword over his right shoulder, to her left is a large, vague figure (rather too large to be her eldest son), and behind her is Mercie, the clearest figure of all, who raises her hands in fear as she looks over her right shoulder at a lion, about the size of a sheep, who marches fiercely behind them.

Inscription: None.

Number: None.

Size: 5 7/8 in. x 4 1/4 in.

Watermark:

Collection: BRITISH MUSEUM PRINT ROOM, Binyon 57b.

---

1. I find no such incident in *The Pilgrim's Progress*. The man also recommends Goodwill in No. 14A.

26) a) *Grim the Giant (p. 340) and b) Old Honest's Blessing (p. 344).*

Description: There are two quite distinct designs, one (a) above the other (b). Shading is with straight lines.

a) Grim the Giant crawls out from a cave(?)[9] and glowers to the right at Greatheart, wearing a helmet and with a sword over his right shoulder, who looks over his left shoulder and walks away from him behind three(?) other figures.

b) Old Honest, with a cloak hanging from, and a long staff leaning on, his left shoulder, puts his hands on the heads of the two smallest of four boys, aged about 4 to 15, who stand before Christiana with her head-shawl, who has her arms round the shoulders of the two larger boys. To her right is Mercie, and behind her is Greatheart, in dark armour, with a visored Cromwellian helmet, leaning on his broadsword. Below Honest and in the bottom right corner are very faint, indecipherable sketches, perhaps unrelated to those above.

Inscriptions: a) "Grim the Giant"; b) "old Honests Blessing."
Number: None.
Size: 5 5/8 in. x 7 1/4 in.
Watermark:
Collection: BRITISH MUSEUM PRINT ROOM, Binyon 53a.

27) *Great-heart Struck Down by Giant Maul (p. 341)*

Description: A somewhat rough sketch, with straight lines for shadows, represents an almost prone man in armour who has one knee on the ground as he tries to raise himself. (The identification is somewhat uncertain; the design is connected to *Pilgrim's Progress* chiefly by the similarity of the armour to that of Great-heart in no. 23A-B, 25B and 28 — though it has elaborate knee-guards not visible elsewhere — and by its correspondence to the text: "the *Giant* stroke Mr. *Great-heart* down upon one of his knees.")

Inscription: None.
Number:None.
Size: 4 in. x 2 5/8 in.
Watermark:
Collection: BRITISH MUSEUM PRINT ROOM, Binyon 55a.

28) *The fight of Great-heart and Giant Maul (p. 341).*

Description: A clear though rough ink sketch shows Christiana, Mercie, and the four(?) boys cowering behind Greatheart, armed cap à pied, who holds a great broadsword over his right shoulder with the knuckles of both hands uppermost (i.e., in a way making it impossible to swing it) threatening a naked figure (Giant Maul) leaping past him and turning with arms extended backward from the expected blow.

---

9. It looks rather like the ribs of an overturned boat or the skeleton of a great animal. Bunyan calls it a "Cave."

A pencil sketch beneath that in ink shows the victim shrinking from Greatheart with his arms forward rather than back, and in the bottom right corner the same figure is sketched again. In the top right corner, a vague pencil sketch may be a study of Christiana, Mercie, and the boys cowering, seen from a front.

Inscription: None.
Number: None.
Size: 5 7/8 in. x 3 1/2 in.
Watermark:
Collection: BRITISH MUSEUM PRINT ROOM, Binyon 57c.

29A) *Slaygood Rifling Feeble-mind (p. 360).*

Description: A rough sketch shows a kneeling giant ("Slaygood") at left reaching toward a roughly sketched figure ("Feeble mind") on the ground at right, while in the background, seen between them, two other kneeling(?) figures raise their hands in alarm. Over all is an arch shadowed in straight lines, to represent Slaygood's cave.

Inscriptions: "Slay good," "Feeble mind."
Number: None.
Size: 3 3/8 in. x 2 5/8 in.
Watermark: Invisible (pasted down).
Collection: UNIVERSITY COLLEGE, LONDON.

29B) *Slaygood Rifling Feeble-mind (p. 360).*

Description: A sketch very similar to 29A but considerably clearer, especially in Slaygood (it is now clear that he has a wide belt) and Feeble-mind (whose human features are now plain). The watchers are moved from the central background to behind Slaygood, at the left, the nearer one seems to have a sword over his right shoulder, held by the blade, and the further one seems to have a helmet, suggesting that they are Great-heart (who kills Slaygood four paragraphs later) and perhaps Gaius or Honest, though their roughly-sketched features are reminiscent of the Ill-Favoured ones. The shading is in straight lines.

Inscription: None.
Number: None.
Size: 3 1/4 in. x 2 5/8 in.
Watermark: Invisible (pasted down).
Collection: UNIVERSITY COLLEGE, LONDON.

29C) *Slaygood Rifling Feeble-mind (pp. 360, 368)*

Description: A grey-wash sketch similar to 29A represents Slaygood on his knees at the left as he drags Feeble-mind towards him on his back. The background, chiefly in straight-line shading, is very dark, apparently to represent Slaygood's cave. Vague swirls behind the figures may represent other people.

Inscription: "Slay-good/ The many [that] thou has slain [of the Pilgrims] when thou hast/ dragged them out of the King's high-way" (p. 360) in ink; "he had dragged by mere force into [his Net *partly cut off*]" (p. 368) in pencil; above, a later hand has written hopefully "W Blake."

Number: None.

Size: 6 1/2 in. x 2 1/2 in.

Collection: Mr CHRISTOPHER POWNEY.

30) Despair Surrounded (p. 373)

Description: A clear grey-wash sketch with straight-line shading represents Giant Despair in the centre beset by "six men" (Greatheart, old Honest, and Christian's four Sons). Despair, naked except for his Cap of Steel and conspicuously lacking his Brestplate of Fire and Iron Shoos, swings with both hands from behind his back his great Club. To our left are three naked young men (one in shadow only in'back), one in front driving a sword into Despair's right breast, one further left swinging his sword over his head. To our right are three more naked men, the two nearest being young men who are driving spears into Despair's left breast, while behind an older man (Great-heart) swings his sword over his head.

Inscription: "Despair Surrounded" and, cheerfully in a later hand, "W Blake."

Number: None.

Size: 6 1/2 in. x 5 in, both bottom corners cut off.

Collection: Mr CHRISTOPHER POWNEY.

31) The Death of Giant Despair (p. 374)

Description: In the centre a) is a clear, bold drawing of the fight with straight-line shading, while to the right b) is a confused sketch which seems to represent Despair's head.

a) Giant Despair, lying on the ground with his head apparently resting on his Cap of Steel, feebly tries to swing his great Club over his shoulder, while two naked young men at the left drive spears into his breast and behind him Great-heart swings his sword over his head to sever Despair's head from his shoulders.

Inscription: "and Giant Despair was brought down to the ground but was very loth to die."

Number: "139."

Size: 4 1/4 in. x 6 1/2 in.

Watermark: None.

Collection: FOLKESTONE PUBLIC LIBRARY AND MUSEUM

G. E. Bentley, Jr.

Ut Pictura Poesis and the Problem Of Pictorial Statement in William Blake

It is my intention to discuss Blake against the background of the humanistic theory of painting (as it is sometimes called) and to examine some of the difficulties of interpreting his mute response to literary subjects. It would serve no purpose to review in detail the development and centuries long history of the influential and subtly changing doctrine of *ut pictura poesis* because that has already been done by several fine critics and historians;[1] however, I should like to mention briefly here and there some of the philosophical influences on that doctrine. It is not easy to place Blake in the history of *ut pictura poesis*,[2] but his opinions and attitudes on painting have a certain relevance to several of the many phases discernible in its long history, influenced as it was by complicated and developing formulas and theories extrapolated from the aphorisms of Simonides and Horace. In many ways, Blake is out-of-step with the eighteenth century — not because he belonged mainly to the future but rather because he also belonged, at least in part, to the past.

In his argument with Reynolds, Rubens, Rembrandt, and the direction in which pictorial art was developing, Blake takes an essentially anti-modernistic albeit radical stance, because he seeks to maintain or revive an earlier kind of pictorial art. His commitment to Michelangelo, Raphael, and Poussin is matched by

1. See, for example, Rensselaer W. Lee, *Ut Pictura Poesis: The Humanistic Theory of Painting*, New York, 1967.
2. For the most recent attempt, see Jean Hagstrum, "Blake and the Sister-Arts Tradition," *Blake's Visionary Forms Dramatic*, eds., D. V. Erdman and J. E. Grant, Princeton, N.J., 1970, pp. 82-91.

the intensity of his disapproval of Rubens and Rembrandt. He simply ignores or is unaware of Poussin's Cartesian mentality. Actually it is Reynolds rather than Blake who is the more sensitive to the anti-formalistic tendencies of the Romantic movement and its celebration of *"la belle Nature,"* for Blake, even while Turner was already well-launched on his career, remained a non-empirical, non-impressionistic, and very literary painter who sought to copy the idea of beauty, or the idea of anything else, that he believed existed *a priori* in his imagination. His antagonism to "Nature" as a subject for painters (or poets and philosophers for that matter), his predilection for biblical and various literary subjects, and his belief in the ideal and in mental life, not to mention his admiration for what he calls the lost art of the Greeks, which he says he shall attempt to restore, make Blake the painter an anti-modernist. In short, he was a history painter, but a history painter of a very special kind. Although his view was tempered by his eighteenth-century Longinian enthusiasm and the emphasis he placed on independent and original genius, his commitment to the manner of the energetic Michelangelo or the learned Poussin and his bread-and-butter occupation as an illustrator only reinforced that anti-modernism. Blake not only believed that the artist should paint the idea or the forms of the mind but that he ought *not* to let "this world" interfere with his efforts to see through and beyond it. His scorn for much of European art from Rubens to Reynolds identifies him with fashions in painting and illustrating that were already well out of date by the end of the eighteenth century. Of course, such a statement does not ignore the many innovations in art for which he is responsible and the dynamic influence he has had in the twentieth century as a poet, an artist or a revolutionary.[3]

Blake is very much attracted by the symbolism of light that predominates in Christian and Hebraic art and which belongs, in part, to a long established anti-pictorialist tradition. He admires the fully lit picture and abhors chiaroscuro. He shares with the Middle Ages a theoretical Christianized neoplatonic bias very

3. See Herbert Read, *The Meaning of Art*, London, 1931; 1972, pp. 171-74, for an important perspective on Blake which while not altogether correct is worth careful consideration.

different from the doctrinaire mysticism that some of his literary critics have found in this work. This bias is complicated by his need as a painter much more than as a poet to invent *visibilia* in order to express his meaning;[4] hence his allegory and symbolism are quite complex, traditional, and very personal because they are related to the demands of pictorial statement as much as they are to the demands of literary expression. Blake's divided allegiances to pictorial and literary statement are further complicated by his twofold commitment to the two very different kinds of motives that are behind the pictorial thrust in each of the two arts. He often paints like a poet, but he rarely writes like a painter, even though his conception of metaphor and symbol is deeply influenced by his highly developed visual sense.

In a general summing up of the developing sister arts, Hagstrum remarks on the two "profoundly antithetical" ways of "making verbal images during the long history of poetry." "One of them, the roots of which lay in the naturalism of antiquity and the Renaissance," he says, "may be exemplified by the rhetorical and critical notion of *energeia*, or lifelike vividness. The other, peculiarly characteristic of the medieval centuries and of the baroque seventeenth century, tended to remove the pictorial from the external and natural and associate it with the internal and supernatural."[5] Blake admired certain major visual artists in antiquity and the Renaissance, but his concern for man's mental life is comparable to the "internal and supernatural" preoccupations of the medieval centuries and the baroque seventeenth century because while he desired to create in the fashion of Apelles, Raphael, Michelangelo, and Poussin, he nevertheless associated that activity with the internal rather than the external world. In a word, he sought to paint mental life by making pictorial images that had lifelike vividness but portrayed the internal. (As a poet he also concentrated on the inside narrative.) If he can be said to have any commitment to naturalism, it is to be found in his negative view of Rubens whose men, he says, are of

4. See, for example, my article, "Visionary Forms Dramatic: Grammatical and Iconographical Movement in Blake's Verse and Designs," *Criticism* 8:2, Spring, 1966, pp. 111-25.

5. Jean Hagstrum, *The Sister Arts*, Chicago, 1958, p. 129.

leather and whose women are like chalk. Indeed, they come off badly when he compares them to his own healthy, naked ancient Britons. Although his naturalism is reminiscent of Michelangelo's, the great Italian master was not confronted directly by the problem of having to illustrate on the page of a book. Both artists share strong Manneristic and literary qualities,[6] some of which are forced on Blake by severely confined or broken space like the page of a book.

Blake does not belong to the *ut pictora poesis* tradition as it was preached and practiced in the eighteenth century, but rather to an earlier stage in that tradition before it was gradually transformed by Newtonian mechanism and Lockean empiricism. And even in that earlier stage Blake could only be said to belong to the *ut pictura poesis* tradition when it was most under the influence of Platonism, platonized Aristotelianism, or Neoplatonism, when the object to be copied was neither nature according to Descartes and the non-platonized Aristotle nor nature according to Hobbes and Locke. This is not to say that Blake would have shared all the platonizing opinions of such a Manneristic theorist as Lomazzo or the influential Ficino,[7] but there are obvious similarities to be found in the works of each of these writers. Nevertheless, for Blake the imagination is not a mirror or even a storehouse of generalized archetypes, but instead the energetic process of mental forming. And it is this idealizing creativity even more than the ideal itself that Blake the artist sought to copy and then to make visible. So far as the inter-relation of painting and poetry are concerned, Blake as a painter and poet remained forever committed to the portrayal of mental life whether in pictures or words. And it is this commitment to mental life that troubles art and literary critics alike, even when they try to examine his pictures or his verse exclusive of one another.

Because Blake disliked Reynolds for personal and professional reasons, his annotations to the first eight of Reynolds's *Discourses* are more vigorous than they would likely have been, had the pronounced and frequent disagreements that Blake recorded been

6. Anthony Blunt, *William Blake*, New York, 1959, pp. 72-73.
7. Anthony Blunt, *Artistic Theory in Italy 1450-1600*, Oxford, 1940; 1968, pp. 20-22; 138-44.

confined only to matters of artistic theory and practice. Despite these disagreements, however, there are some obvious areas of agreement, perhaps more than is at first apparent. In fact, the same can also be said in part but perhaps with less confidence of Burke and Blake. We can never forget that Blake includes Burke in his scathing indictment of Reynolds, because he believes them to be of the same party. Blake attacks Burke and Reynolds for promulgating ideas and opinions that are politically, philosophically, and aesthetically in error. In his heated reaction to Malone's preface to the *Discourses*, which quotes Burke, Blake writes, "This Whole Book was Written to Serve Political Purposes" (*ARD*, civ: E 630).[8] Blake's main thrust at Burke comes, however, at a later point in the Annotations when, in another sweeping comment, he identifies Burke and Reynolds with Bacon, Newton, and Locke: "Burke's Treatise on the Sublime and Beautiful is founded on the Opinions of Newton & Locke on this Treatise Reynolds has grounded many of his assertions. in all his Discourses I read Burkes Treatise when very Young at the same time I read Locke on Human Understanding & Bacons Advancement of Learning on Every one of these Books I wrote my Opinions & on looking them over find that my Notes on Reynolds in this Book are exactly Similar." (*ARD* VIII, 244: E 650) Blake is certainly accurate in searching out those philosophical and psychological influences that most profoundly influenced Reynolds's *Discourses*, although others might not have made of them what Blake did. Whatever in Reynolds he found attractive came from Sir Joshua's recognition of developments in art and art theory that took place well before mechanistic materialism and empirical idealism forever changed the humanistic theory of painting, effects that may well have prepared *ut pictura poesis* for its demise in the Romantic reaction which Blake, especially as a poet, certainly anticipated. After its own fashion the Romantic Movement, like the eighteenth century, celebrated *la belle Nature*, but Blake held fast to a major tenet of the high Renaissance and of Antiquity, a tenet that dominated the naturalism of those periods in the history of western art. That

---

8. All quotations are from *The Complete Poetry and Prose of William Blake*, ed., David V. Erdman, New York, 1970: E. *ARD* is Annotations to Reynolds's *Discourses*; *MHH* is *The Marriage of Heaven and Hell*; *PA* is *Public Address*.

tenet is best expressed in Blake's work by one of the "Proverbs of Hell": "where man is not nature is barren" (*MHH* 9: E 37). A more devoted history painter than Reynolds (had he read it), would have understood the force of Blake's aphorism. It goes some way to explain why Blake turned to the Bible and Michelangelo for pictorial inspiration, and why he admired Poussin and could not abide Rubens, whose Luxemborg Gallery with its flattery of the Medici family he characterized as "Bloated Gods Mercury Juno Venus & the rattle traps of Mythology & the lumber of an awkward French Palace . . . thrown together around Clumsy & Ricketty Princes & Princesses higgledy piggledy" (*PA* 18: E 568). Blake believed in man and understood deeply the painter's compulsion to idealize him. He certainly would have responded to Michelangelo's rebuke of his critics when they criticized him for not making his statues of the Medici brothers lifelike resemblances. Michelangelo is supposed to have replied that in two hundred years nobody will remember what they looked like.

Together with subject, invention, and execution in painting, Blake also emphasized the bounding line, drawing, and expression. Having no sympathy with the politics or the emotional naturalism of Rubens, he was continually drawn, as I have said, to the platonizing tendencies of early Christian thought which emphasized the inner world of the imagination and associated that inner world and the mind of man with the mind of God. Such an emphasis and such a view was not likely to find much in Reynolds or Rubens that was satisfying. It is hard to believe that he would have been any happier with Hazlitt and the distant object or the paintings of Monet. In fact, he is more likely to have responded with glee to Mark Twain's description of one of Turner's paintings, which the irreverent American said looked like a tabby cat having a fit in a bowl of milk.

No sensible critic can evaluate Blake well without emphasizing the inter-relationship of the two arts that Blake employed to make a total and unified statement. However, while this complicated problem in criticism may be approached with a certain kind of freedom when Blake as a painter and a poet is making this single statement in his own illuminated poems, it is another matter when he speaks only as a painter. How free, after all, can the critic be to verbalize the mute responses of Blake the painter. If Hagstrum is correct, and I think he is, when he says Blake's "manner of proceeding can be called a version of picture-gallery form, in which the reader moves like a spectator from tableau to tableau,"[9] then the reader-spectator-critic must approach Blake's pictorial statements with care. He must see the tableau as something more than simply disguised Blakean verse, for while the painted tableau before him may be literary in origin *his original insight into the literary form itself may well have been pictorial.* Whatever our opinion may be of Michelangelo as a poet or of his success in versifying problems in pictorial art, we would not try to translate Michelangelo's pictures into his verse or try to see *his* verse in his paintings.[10]

I have called attention elsewhere to the non-linear and non-sequential structure of Blake's poems and the unity of his work according to pictorial and mental form.[11] However, unlike Hagstrum I do not believe that Blake was altogether happy with personification as it is usually employed because his strong biblical leanings undercut his pictorial objectives by substituting metaphysical and value imagery for lifelike vividness or natural verisimilitudinous pictures. He was made captive, in a sense, by non-pictorial similes like the well-known comparison of the beloved's nose with the temple of Lebanon facing Damascus in the Song of Songs, a typically non-pictorial biblical image.

While perhaps ironic, considering Blake's opinions of Burke, it was not particularly unusual that Blake should choose to paint the one scene that Burke specifically praised as an example of the sublime in *Paradise Lost* (Plate I). Fuseli, Barry, and others had portrayed Satan, Sin, and Death. The incident of their meeting at the gates of Hell in *Paradise Lost* was assumed, in keeping with Burke, to be sublime; however, neither Satan nor Sin nor Death

9. "Blake and the Sister-Arts Tradition," in *Blake's Visionary Forms Dramatic*, p. 85.

10. In *Artistic Theory in Italy*, pp. 58-81, Anthony Blunt relates Michelangelo's pictures to his theory of art as expressed in his verse, which, I hasten to add, is not to relate, of course, verbal with visual iconographical figures on the broad scale current in Blake criticism.

11. See, for example, my article, "Blake's *Milton*: The Poet as Poem," *Blake Studies* 1:1, Fall, 1968, pp. 16-38.

are really personifiable as a human form, especially as "human form" was understood by Blake. They represent ideas and events of psycho-philosophical, spiritual, and mental import, while personifications are designed for the weak vegetative eye.

Interestingly enough both Blake and Burke were drawn for different reasons to the ancient architectural marvel of Stonehenge because of its sublimity. But Stonehenge represents not the past alone, but the idea the eighteenth century had of a specific kind of past, a point that Blake's illustrations make clearly (Plates II & III).

Blake strives throughout his work to make his so-called personifications resistant to personifying critics — to make them sublime. When confronted with the verse of poets other than himself, he continues in the same fashion. He must make their words into pictures, but he clearly reveals that he wants to make them into much more than pictures. He is a history painter whose history is man's mental life. His paintings executed on paper were conceived for walls. He needed a space sixteen by thirteen feet, not sixteen by thirteen inches. His pictorial so-called allegory, like his own sublime allegory, is addressed to the intellectual powers.

No illustrator ever burdened himself more heavily than William Blake did and neither the verse of the greater Milton nor the lesser Young could relieve him of that burden. By making the invisible visions of other poets visible in pictorial forms, Blake in the act of translating words into pictures translated pictures into visions. He does this in such an energetic way that his own views shine through the *visibilia* he employs to illustrate verse not his own. For Blake the act of illustration was a selfless act, the kind of self-sacrifice Los encourages in *Jerusalem*. In giving himself up to the vision of the poet that he sought to illustrate, he seems to the uninitiated only to have egoistically replaced or modified the original import of the poet's verse with the pictorial equivalents of his own verse, but what he has tried to do, instead, is to transmit to the imagination of the spectator what the poet may well have seen in his mind before he wrote. In this way Blake went beyond the goal of the painters of the high Renaissance. He chose to portray as an illustrator not simply an idealized or a grandiose literary form, but the idea of that form in the creative imagination, hence the giant forms which abound even in the *Night Thoughts* designs. I realize that it is not easy to prove this contention to everyone's satisfaction. Furthermore, I also realize that it is not demonstrable in every one of Blake's pictures. As an illustrator of his own work, he oftentimes could not translate his own verbal visions into an equally powerful pictorial statement. His illustration for "The Tyger" is an obvious example (Plate IV).

Blake admired Raphael, Michelangelo, and Poussin for many of the characteristics that Reynolds, in fact, enumerates in the *Discourses*, since Sir Joshua praises what he considers are the best qualities of each of these painters. Reynolds, in fact, writes admiringly in Discourse IV of Michelangelo and Poussin, emphasizing their draftsmanship and portrayal of the ideal form. Blake may well have rejected Poussin's Cartesian affinities, had he been fully aware of them, but Reynolds's elucidation of Poussin's antique style, which is discussed in discourses that Blake annotated and others that he did not annotate, interested him just as much as did Reynolds's comparison of Poussin and Rubens or Rembrandt. What Blake sensed in Poussin's work was the quality Reynolds was later to single out in Discourse XIV. Reynolds says indirectly that Poussin possessed a "mind thrown back two thousand years, and as it were naturalized in antiquity." What Blake admired in the way of pictorial statement was the kind of painting that was produced by a mind "naturalized in antiquity." Art produced by such a mind has for Blake the timeless quality of the *eternal* imagination. Its effect is to restore the lost art of the ancients. He certainly responded to that very quality in Raphael and Michelangelo. One of the main reasons that Raphael, Michelangelo, and Poussin could paint ancient and biblical subjects as if they were poets (Reynolds often uses the word "poetical" to describe certain paintings), was presumably because they could throw their minds back. I have suggested elsewhere that *Jerusalem* is also an attempt to throw the mind back.[12]

Reynolds and his contemporaries admired the highly imaginative character of the so-called "poetical" painter. And although

<hr />

12. "The Structure of Blake's *Jerusalem*," *Bucknell Review* 11:3, May, 1963, pp. 35-54.

Blake also valued immensely a highly imaginative genius, it is not altogether clear that he and Reynolds understood "poetical" or the imagination in the same way. Nevertheless, it is characteristic of anyone influenced by the tradition of *ut pictura poesis* to believe that the best painters were indeed poets. Blake sought to paint, however, not only like a poet, but like a poet with the vision of a prophet.

It is possible to demonstrate Blake's devotion to "poetical" or, as Blake might prefer, visionary painting in many ways. Geoffrey Keynes and Anthony Blunt have called attention to Blake's seeming intention to paint the Bible from Creation to Revelation.[13] I should like to make a few observations on the paintings Blake made for chapters twelve, thirteen, and seventeen in the Book of Revelation. That these chapters were of continuing interest to him as a painter cannot be denied, since many years before he painted his well-known watercolors, he resorted to the same chapters of Revelation for two of the nine title page designs he made for Young's *Night Thoughts*. Many of Blake's illustrations for the Bible are highly original simply because no painter before him chose to paint many of the subjects that moved him. Indeed, there are in Medieval, Renaissance, and Baroque painting many madonnas, crucifixions, last suppers, and repeated attempts at traditional and familiar subjects, like the Israelites gathering the manna in the wilderness, but few sevenheaded beasts, Babylonian whores, red dragons, and apocalyptic queens.[14] While Blake belonged to the brotherhood of allegorical painters whose imaginations were kindled by literary sources, it must be remembered that very few, if any, of that brotherhood were English. As Fuseli remarked, there is "little hope of Poetical painting finding encouragement in England. The People are not prepared for it. Portrait with them is everything. Their taste and feelings all go to realities."[15]

In commenting on the later Mannerists in *Artistic Theory in Italy 1450-1600*, Anthony Blunt says of Lomazzo and Zuccaro,

13. Blunt, *William Blake*, pp. 104-14.
14. Bosch or the School of Bosch is, perhaps, the exception.
15. Quoted in Nikolaus Pevsner, *The Englishness of English Art*, Harmondsworth, Middlesex, 1956; 1964, p. 31.

"Whereas for the writers of the Early and High Renaissance nature was the source from which all beauty was ultimately derived, however much it might be transformed by the artist's imagination, for these Mannerists beauty was something which was directly infused into the mind of man from the mind of God, and existed there independent of any sense-impressions."[16] It is not necessary to know much about Blake to realize how central to his views of the artist's mental life this opinion is or to realize how much in keeping with the theological basis of the New and Old Testament such an opinion of the artist's relation to the Divine is, especially if that artist is committed to making pictorial statements about and illustrations of the *words* of writers inspired by God or of God himself. Since the "idea in the artist's mind was the source of all the beauty in the works which he created, and his ability to give a picture of the outside world was of no importance, except insofar as it helped him to give visible expression to his idea,"[17] the task of illustrating visionary literature was not impeded by the demands of naturalism. Blake's illustrations for a book like Revelation, where the demands of naturalism are comparatively slight, are devoted, therefore, not to what is normally called lifelike vividness but instead to the rendering of an accurate visible expression of vision. He is free in these illustrations more than elsewhere in his biblical designs to do justice both to the verbal transcription of the vision of John of Patmos and his own visionary interpretation.

There are four separate designs which may be said to be devoted to Revelation 12:1-6, two of which appear recto-verso on the title page of Night the Third in Blake's series of 537 watercolour drawings made for Young's *Night Thoughts*. The two *Night Thoughts* designs, numbers 78 and 79 (Plates V & VI), were made roughly about ten years before the two later watercolours, one now in the Rosenwald Collection of the Library of Congress and the other in the Brooklyn Museum. The two later watercolours illustrate Revelation 12:1-6 (Plates VII & VIII) directly whereas *Night Thoughts* 78 and 79 are intended to illustrate

16. *Artistic Theory in Italy*, pp. 140-41.
17. *Ibid.*, p. 141.

Young's poem by alluding to Revelation pictorially; a difference in primary intention that makes a side-by-side discussion of the four designs interesting because the purport of the two *Night Thoughts* designs affects the way in which the details of John's account are rendered and the way in which the pictorial motifs are modulated through the symbolic figures of Young's poem. In all four designs we see the woman as she is described in Revelation 12:1-2: "And there appeared a great wonder in heaven: a woman clothed with the sun, and the moon under her feet, and upon her head a crown of twelve stars. And she being with child cried, travailing in birth, and pained to be delivered." The signs of pregnancy in all four illustrations are not pronounced, but her identity is unmistakable and the moon and crown of stars are clearly although differently present in *Night Thoughts* 78 and the two watercolours. The sequence of the two *Night Thoughts* designs, moreover, redirects the events of Revelation while also picturing a python-like serpent similar to the one in *Europe* but wholly unlike the humanoid dragon-serpent of Revelation 12:3-4, who is portrayed in the two later watercolours with his seven heads and ten horns: "And there appeared another wonder in heaven: and behold a great red dragon, having seven heads and ten horns, and seven crowns upon his heads. And his tail drew the third part of the stars of heaven, and did cast them to the earth: and the dragon stood before the woman which was ready to be delivered, for to devour her child as soon as it was born." In *Night Thoughts* 79 it is the woman herself we see devoured, at least figuratively, since she is encircled by and manacled to the serpent and while in great discomfort seems to be vegetating or giving birth to vegetation. She is very much in contrast to her previous state of crowned and golden splendour. Her apparent plea for aid or mercy in that design seems to have gone unanswered, an interesting departure from the events recorded in Revelation 12:5-6 where she as the apocalyptic mother of God gives birth to a man-child who is caught up by God. In Revelation she is not caught by the ouroboros but instead flees into the wilderness "where she hath a place prepared of God." The confrontation in the two later watercolours is less obviously resolved than in the two designs for the *Night Thoughts*. There we see the winged, red, and humanoid dragon-serpent hovering above and around the distressed apocalyptic queen who is below him. His seven heads and ten horns are easily visible in the Rosenwald design and he seems to hang in the air above a dominated world. The familiar Blakean zig-zag lightning bolts frame in the equally familiar and demonic batwings, his serpent spiraled or coiled tail echoes the lightning bolts. Together they remind the spectator of the lightning bolts and whirlwind of the last design in Blake illustrations for *Paradise Lost*. The dragon's batwings in the Rosenwald design are set against the woman's butterfly wings while his angelic pinions carry the horizontal lines of the outstretched arms of each figure to the highest plane of the picture. In *Night Thoughts* 78, the crescent moon upon which the woman stands neatly encloses the serpent's head, a situation quickly reversed in *Night Thoughts* 79 where the lady is enclosed by the serpent. In the two later watercolours the crescent moon is inverted and serves as a kind of throne or vehicle for her. In the two later watercolours as in the profile view in *Night Thoughts* 78, the woman is bathed in sunlight, but the golden glow of *Night Thoughts* 78 is unrivaled in that design by the red of the dragon in the two watercolours. In surveying the four pictures we see Blake probing his verbal source for pictorial possibilities. His attempts at a faithful visible expression of Revelation 12:1-6 are modified by indirection (especially in the context of pictorial allusion in the *Night Thoughts* designs) and by his efforts to make a pictorial statement that will represent the spirit as well as the letter of his text.

Blake's interest in the dramatic encounter in Revelation 12:1-6, which he first exploits in the *Night Thoughts* illustrations where he universalizes Young's "Narcissa," the poet's allegorical name for his daughter, Mrs. Temple, whose death is the main subject of Night the Third, is reaffirmed not only in the two later watercolours but also in *A Vision of the Last Judgment* where the apocalyptic queen of heaven is identified with the Church Universal. In *Night Thoughts* 78 and 79, the seeming "Christian Triumph" portrayed in the first of the two designs is reversed in the second design. The woman is clearly imprisoned by the Serpent. By introducing the apocalyptic queen of Revelation into the illustrations for Young's poem, a poem in which she is not mentioned, Blake reinforces the contrast between the biblical symbolism and iconography that is much more pronounced in his own work than in Young's and the stilted and conventional classical imagery of the *Night Thoughts*, which goes on at length about Cynthia whom Blake places in the moon in several of the designs (Plate IX). The fact that the serpent encircles the textbox as well as crushing the woman gives us a clue as to Blake's essential opinion of Young's accomplishment as a poet. It is interesting to note, however, that whereas Blake capitalizes on zodiacal and Egyptian symbolism here and there in his work, there is little or no hint that he understood that the apocalyptic queen of Revelation was the zodiacal sign of Virgo or that the dragon-serpent may have had something to do with the sign of Draco, the myth of Typhon, and the serpentine Nile in flood, a flood that according to Revelation issues forth from the serpent but from which the woman is saved when the waters are swallowed by the earth.

The recognizable and naturalistic serpent of the *Night Thoughts* illustrations, who seems to be victorious in *Night Thoughts* 79, modulates in the watercolours into the creature described by John of Patmos, and while Blake more often than not includes his seven heads and ten horns he does not do so always. The beast seems to have interested Blake greatly as a pictorial subject, and I have included in this discussion five different versions of him with his many heads and horns in addition to those four I have already cited. In the first two of these five designs for Revelation, chapters thirteen and seventeen, the dragon-serpent appears as a kind of double-beast (Plate X and XI). In the three remaining designs he is ridden upon by the scarlet whore. The double-beast, as I have called him, is really two more aspects of the demonic power described initially in Revelation chapter twelve as a dragon and then as a serpent: "And I stood upon the sand of the sea, and saw a beast rise up out of the sea, having seven heads and ten horns, and upon his heads ten crowns, and upon his heads the name of blasphemy. And the beast which I saw was like unto a leopard, and his feet were as the feet of a bear, and his mouth as the mouth of a lion: and the dragon gave him his power, and his seat, and great authority . . . And I beheld another beast coming up out of the earth; and he had two horns like a lamb, and he spoke as a dragon. And he exerciseth all the power of the first beast before him, and causeth the earth and them which dwell therein to worship the first beast, . . . And I saw a woman sit upon a scarlet coloured beast, full of names of blasphemy, having seven heads and ten horns. And the woman was arrayed in purple and scarlet colour, and decked with gold and precious stones and pearls, having a golden cup in her hand full of abominations and filthiness of her fornication: and upon her forehead was a name written, MYSTERY, BABYLON THE GREAT, THE MOTHER OF HARLOTS AND ABOMINATIONS OF THE EARTH." (Rev. 13:1-3; 11-12; 17:3-5).

The two illustrations featuring the double-beast carry forward the red, ram-horned, multi-headed and horned dragon-serpent whom we saw hovering over the apocalyptic queen in the watercolours for Revelation 12. He continues to occupy the same portion of the picture, his wings bearing suggestively a number of the "one-third" of the stars of heaven enumerated in Revelation. In these two pictures the "wild beast" occupies that portion of the picture previously assigned to the apocalyptic queen. In the first design (now in the Rosenwald Collection, Library of Congress), the beast rises out of the sea a shadow but slightly different many-headed image of the dragon above him. In the second design (now in the Collection of the Philip and A.S.W. Rosenbach Foundation), the beast with his back to the spectator (recalling the perspective in the Brooklyn Museum design) converses with the dragon as he ascends out of the earth, the multitudes bowed down before him as he sits upon a red throne-like promontory. In the previous design he had raised in either hand the sword and sceptre, signs that authority over the earth had been given him. In the second design, the sword has disappeared and instead the beast now points accusingly in typical Blakean fashion with his left hand. In this design, also, Blake has tried to include the composite animal forms of the leopard, bear, and lion described in Revelation 13:1-3. This animalistic triune form reinforces the mocking parody of God the Father and God the Son acted out by the dragon-serpent and the "double-beast" who are joined in chapter seventeen by the Whore of Babylon who is a demonic version of the apocalyptic queen. These two pictures attempt to establish with pictorial clarity the chain of command and interrelated power of the demonic forces that are described verbally in Revelation.

The three designs devoted to the Whore that I have included span a considerable period in Blake's career and in each she is seen riding on the compound seven-headed and ten-horned Beast of Revelation 17:3-5. The first design is the title page to Night the Eighth of the *Night Thoughts* (Plate XII). The second design is a separate watercolour done roughly ten years later, perhaps about the same time Blake did the Red Dragon and Beast designs (Plate XIII). The third design is on plate 75 of *Jerusalem* (Plate XIV). The last design done very much in the manner of the *Jerusalem* style, in which nakedness is pronounced, returns in part to the manner of *Night Thoughts* 78 because the Dragon-Beast's heads are once again serpentine. Riding in the Dragon-Beast's coils, the whore seems to have become almost one with the Beast. Cheek to cheek with one of the heads she caresses him in the manner of Satan and the serpent in the *Paradise Lost* designs (Plate XV). The earliest design of the three, the striking illustration for Young, includes the cup and inscriptions. The heads of the Beast have a carnival masquerade quality to them and seem a mixture of beasts, clerics, kings, magicians, knights, and soldiers. The second design again includes the cup from which various spirits issue. The heads of Beast are human but animalistic. He bears some resemblance to Blake's Nebuchadnezzar and on all fours devours the multitudes. Thus, as Blake writes on plate 75 of *Jerusalem*:

> . . . Rahab is reveald
> Mystery Babylon the Great: the Abomination of Desolation
> Religion hid in War: a Dragon red, & hidden Harlot

There is in this series of Revelation designs for chapters twelve, thirteen, and seventeen one design I have left until now even though that is to remove it from the order of the events as they are recorded in John's vision. It is the well-known picture of Michael and the Dragon (Plate XVI) now in the collection of the Fogg Museum, Harvard University, which illustrates Revelation

12:7-9: "And there was war in heaven. Michael and his angels fought aginst the dragon; and the dragon fought the angels, and prevailed not; neither was their place found any more in heaven. And the great dragon was cast out, that old serpent, called the Devil, and Satan, which deceiveth the whole world. . . ." Inveterate Blake critics see Los as Michael and inveterate students of composition see ying and yang. Both observations are justified, but we should note that Blake forsakes the seven heads and ten horns. It would seem that in order to control his subject pictorially and to ensure that the composition had the proper symmetry, Blake forsook the seven heads and ten horns. The Dragon, like Rahab, in Blake's verse and designs for his own works, can appear with one or several heads at will — even so the mighty Hand.[18] What Blake is illustrating is a spiritual or mental vision based upon a verbal version subject itself to interpretative exegesis; it is a mental form adapted to the needs of the vegetable eye and the demands of pictorial forms or visible expression but dependent for its full impact upon the visionary eye of the spectator who follows Blake's advice on how to see a picture by entering into it rather than looking at it.

In the absence of Blake's verse, however, and relying only on his pictorial statements, how do we account for the variations in his illustrations of Revelation 12 or the Beast or the Whore, especially when we know how much wider the variations can be in the illustrations of less homogenous symbolic books than Revelation? In the absence of any fixed traditional iconographical motifs, like that of Father Time (Plate XVII) who appears conventionally in the *Night Thoughts* illustrations,[19] is it adequate to judge Blake on either his faithfulness to his literary source (he is more often than not exceedingly faithful, even in minor details, to the literature he illustrates)[20] or his faithfulness to the pictorial

18. See my article, "Blake's Hand: Symbol and Design in *Jerusalem*," *Texas Studies in Literature and Language*, 6:1, Spring, 1964, pp. 47-58.

19. See Erwin Panofsky, "Father Time," in *Studies in Iconology*, New York, 1962, pp. 69-94. See, also, p. 6 for Panofsky's opinion of Rubens' "Galerie de Medicis" which would have infuriated Blake. See my article, "'A Most Outrageous Demon': Blake's Case Against Rubens," *Bucknell Review* 17:1, March, 1969, pp. 35-54.

20. See, for example, Blake's notes for his illustrations to *L'Allegro* and *Il Penseroso*, E pp. 663-67.

figures that he employs when he illustrates his own verse? If either the lapse of time or experimentation or both are responsible for differences, then with what confidence can the interpreters of Blake's iconography relate his pictorial statements to one another when they appear in different contexts? Answers to these questions depend on how completely we believe Blake was influenced by the *ut pictura poesis* tradition. As a literary or history painter and as a working book illustrator, he was obviously heir to a tradition with which he had considerable sympathy but only partial knowledge or familiarity. Blake criticism has proven that his critics and interpreters can rarely divorce his literary statements from his pictorial statements, yet a true appreciation of Blake's pictorial accomplishments will not occur until we can understand his pictorial statements in terms of his pictorial intentions and execution, one reason why the intentional fallacy has no place in Blake criticism since it is purely a literary chimera that no art critic or historian normally fears. Blake's illustrations for chapters 12, 13, and 17 of Revelation or his use of iconographical motifs, drawn from these chapters in Revelation in illustrations not immediately or directly concerned with the Book of Revelation itself, like many of his biblical illustrations, arise from an exegetical biblical tradition that was only intermittently and self-consciously pictorial.

The problem of pictorial statement in Blake's work is rooted in his individual originality and in his unique inventions. He forces his spectators, critics, and interpreters to become acquainted with his own personal pictorial tradition that as often as not is committed as much as his poetry and prose to recounting an inside narrative or to spinning out his own philosophy and history of literature and the pictorial arts. Blake turned away from the sense impressions of this world more completely than any Mannerist theorist by reinforcing his pictorial prejudices against naturalism with his spiritual and literary commitment to the prophetic and religious exaltation of that which can be seen only with the inner eye. For Blake, as for Coleridge, "the decline of painting since the Renaissance is related directly to the growth of empiricism since the time of Bacon."[21] As Roy Park also points out, "Once the

21. Roy Park, "'Ut Pictura Poesis': The Nineteenth-Century Aftermath," *Journal of Aesthetics and Art Criticism*, 28:2, Winter, 1969, p. 159.

transition from the general to the particular had been successfully effected, the doctrine of *ut pictura poesis*, which had previously served to cloak the new emphasis in eighteenth-century critical thought, could be discarded."[22] Of Blake more than anyone else, it can be said with confidence that "In the transition effected by the literary critics and theorists of the late eighteenth century from the ideal theory of art to a theory of art as essentially individual, painting was perhaps literature's most potent ally."[23] Devoted as he was to Michelangelo and Raphael, Blake fused aristocratic and Renaissance forms to democratic and Romantic hopes and adapted an ideal theory of art to the particular and the individual rather than, as Reynolds often implies, the general or, to use Blake's perjorative term, "bloated" form. Unlike Hazlitt or Coleridge, Blake was both a painter and a poet. Like Barry whom he often admired and certainly took pains to defend, Blake saw that "both arts were essentially twin facets of a unified poetic experience."[24] In his own terms, he was probably as devoted to the humanistic theory of painting as any eighteenth-century artist could be.

22. *Ibid.*, p. 163.
23. *Ibid.*, p. 163.
24. *Ibid.*, p. 156.

APPENDIX:
Additional Notes to the Illustrations

So far as pictorial statement is concerned, it is obvious that Blake's approach to the visualization of Revelation is affected by whether or not he is alluding to Revelation through the screen of another work of art or whether he is illustrating it directly. This difference in the degree of immediacy obviously changes the character of his pictorial statement. Blake's pictorial statements are affected not only by subject and intention but by problems in composition and design with which, like many pictorial artists, he often grapples mainly because of his interest in the problems themselves. He will often resort, too, to favorite iconographical elements that seem but do not always imply in a given picture the import they may have in another picture. Many designs could also be cited to demonstrate that Blake makes broad and specific pictorial statements on philosophy and the history of literature or classical myth while at the time illustrating other subjects.

Plate I

I have always found Blake's approach to the problem of making invisible-death visible in this design intriguing. In the *Night Thoughts* designs where Death is an important and frequently seen figure, he abandons such a difficult attempt.

Because Blake pictures Sin as one with the Cerberus-serpent, Sin in the *Paradise Lost* designs bears a pictorial relation to the Whore of Revelation we see in figures 12, 13, and 14.

Plates II & III:

The exaggerated proportions of Stonehenge in Blake's designs make the ancient shapes many times larger than life and reduce the human form framed in them to a size suitable to Blake's mythic view of the fate of man under the eye of Moloch.

Plate IV:

Despite whatever can be said about the varying ferocity of the tyger in different copies of the poem, the illustration is clearly overpowered by the poem. Much the same can be said of the verse of "The Blossom" on that page of the *Songs of Innocence and of Experience* because it is overpowered by the illustration. The delicate balance of verse and picture is difficult to maintain.

Plates V & VI:

The sexual implications are heightened by the woman's nakedness in the "swallowing" design.

Plates VII & VIII:

The tail of the dragon in figure 8 is wound suggestively around the loins of the lady, but he is clearly conceived after the same mental form pictured hovering over the lady in Plate VII. His tail and his position in both designs implies a sexual assault.

Plate IX:

Several designs in Night the Third are devoted to Cynthia in her moon. The iconographical contrast between the *classical* figure of virginity and constancy and the *biblical* bride is striking, especially in light of the assaults of the serpent-dragon.

Plates X & XI:

This pictorial rendition of the demonic *doppelgänger* of Revelation is certainly an exceptional and original invention for which Blake has not been, I believe, sufficiently praised.

Plates XII, XIII, & XIV:

These different treatments of the same subject in different contexts and at different times in Blake's career reveal a constancy to subject but a flexibility of invention not always recognized in Blake's work.

Plate XV:

Because of the presence of the phallic serpent, the sexual and perhaps homosexual implications in this design are witty to the point of being Melvillesque.

Plate XVI:

The single human but somewhat bestial head may be looked upon as a pictorial resolution of the two (Plate XV) or the seven heads seen elsewhere.

Plate XVII:

Father Time, while not the youthful and energetic Los of *Milton* and *Jerusalem*, does reflect in the *Night Thoughts* designs the dilemma cited by Blake in *A Vision of the Last Judgment*: "The Greeks represent Chronos or Time as a very Aged Man this is Fable but the Real Vision of Time is in Eternal Youth I have however somewhat accomodated my Figure of Time to the Common opinion as I myself am also infected with it & my Visions also infected & I see Time Aged alas too much so."

This page also shows us Blake's pictorial conception of Death in 1795-1797 which while similar in appearance to Blake's portraits of Urizen is very different from his visualization of Death in the *Paradise Lost* designs (Plate I).

Hume's Account of Personal Identity

Hume's account of personal identity is superior to most other accounts because it is more penetrating. It is given in two parts. First, there is the reductive theory set out in the main body of the *Treatise*, and then in the Appendix there is the recantation of that theory. Since the two parts cancel out, it is unrealistic to ask whether the whole account contains more truth, or less error, than other accounts. But we can assess it in another way. We can ask whether the trip was a good one, and whether we learned anything from the arguments which Hume uses, first against rival theories, and then against his own. When his discussion is assessed in this way, it should get high praise. It made a permanent difference to the subject.

The theory offered in the body of the *Treatise* was intended to explain the fact that a person is a single unified being, persisting through time. It is a theory based on several axioms, and Hume builds it up on this basis very carefully and very scrupulously, never allowing himself to slip extra material into the structure, or extra assumptions. But in the end he finds that the theory does not fit the fact which it was designed to explain. So he is faced with a dilemma: either he must argue that the fact is not really what he had taken it to be, or else he must abandon the theory. He chose to abandon the theory, and he confessed that he was unable to find a better one to put in its place.

That is a summary description of an investigation which is lengthy and complex. I shall now go back to the starting-point and explain the axioms on which Hume based his supposedly unsuccessful theory. These may be divided into two groups. The first group is concerned with the conditions of perfect identity; and the second group is concerned with the nature of the connection between the components of a composite thing.

The axioms in the first group are the following:

(1) An incomposite thing enjoys perfect identity as long as it lasts.

(2) A composite thing enjoys perfect identity so long as there is no change in the identity of its incomposite components.

(3) There is no third way of achieving perfect identity through time.

Axiom (3) is directed against any third way that might be suggested. But the suggestion which Hume had chiefly in mind, and on which he spends a lot of argument, is the suggestion that a composite thing might achieve perfect identity through a constant substrate. This substrate would be a substance in one sense of that word, but not in the sense in which Hume allows that an incomposite thing would be a substance. That is a different use of the word. An incomposite thing would be a detectable substance, but a substrate would be an undetectable substance, and so, according to Hume, even if its nature were intelligible, its existence would be dubious. An incomposite thing is a kind of substance which avoids these disadvantages, but has another disadvantage instead; it selfishly refuses to extend perfect identity to anything other than itself.

Let us now look at the axioms in the other group, which is concerned with the nature of the connection between the components of a composite thing. I give these in Hume's words:

(4) "All our distinct perceptions are distinct existences." ("*Treatise*": Appendix; Fontana edition, p. 331).

(5) "The mind never perceives any real connection among distinct existences." (*Ibid.*)

These two axioms are stated for the special case in which the composite thing is a person's mind. But Hume really subscribes to generalised versions of them, which apply to composite material objects as well as to minds.

The next thing is to ask how he proceeds to build up his supposedly unsuccessful theory on the basis provided by these axioms. But before tackling that question I want to divide his discussion of personal identity into two layers, in order to make it more manageable. On the surface there is his elaborate argument about identity, diversity and change, leading to the conclusion that persons do not enjoy perfect identity through time. Let us call this "the surface plot," meaning not that it is superficial or unimportant, but only that it is explicit. Beneath the surface plot, and largely hidden by it, there is what I shall call "the underplot."

This division of Hume's discussion may be pictured as a horizontal line, whereas the other division that I mentioned, between the theory itself and the recantation of it, would be drawn as a vertical line. Above the horizontal line the surface plot is played out. The distinctive mark of the surface plot is that it treats persons like ordinary composite material objects. I do not mean that Hume treats persons *as* material objects. Far from it. After a few allusions to human bodies, he turns his back on them, and addresses himself to the narrower task of explaining the unity of human minds rather than human beings. What I mean is that, having restricted himself to human minds, he treats them *like* ordinary material objects, e.g., when he asks whether the impressions and ideas, which go to form a mind persisting through time, are organised in a way that confers perfect identity on that mind, he construes this question like the question posed by William James in his discussion of this subject: Are the individual beasts in a herd of cattle persisting through time organised in a way that confers perfect identity on that herd? (*Principles of Psychology*, Vol. I, p. 333A.). Both these questions get a negative answer based on Axioms (2) and (3), according to which, whenever there is any change in the identity of the components of a composite thing, physical or mental, it loses its title to perfect identity through time.

I am not yet in a position to give a detailed characterisation of the underplot. But what can be said in general is that it takes account of factors which are peculiar to persons and certain other animals, and perhaps some machines. This, of course, is only a schema for describing the underplot, and different people will fill in the details in different ways. My way of filling them in will be based on Hume's text. I am interested only in those peculiarities of embodied minds which almost break the surface of his discussion of personal identity, but which do not quite succeed in breaking it. It would, of course, be possible to broaden the scope of the inquiry, so as to bring in factors such as intentions and actions which lie entirely outside the drama as Hume presents it in Book I of the *"Treatise"* and in the Appendix. But I prefer to keep the inquiry more narrowly focussed on to those two texts, because I want to exhibit the tensions between his surface plot and his underplot.

I shall not say much about the surface plot, because the general pattern of it is tolerably clear. It is important to notice that right from the start Hume turns his back on the human body, and concentrates on the unity of the human mind. He easily shows that a mind does not satisfy either of the two conditions of perfect identity laid down in Axioms (1) and (2). Then he dismisses the third suggestion, that it might achieve perfect identity through a substrate. This is dismissed by an appeal to Axiom (3). Anyone who claims to have a distinct impression of his self as a distinct entity is guilty of "a manifest contradiction and absurdity" (*loc.cit.*, p. 301). I take it that the absurdity that he means is the absurdity of identifying an enduring substrate with any of the components which go to make up the composite thing whose substrate it is. At least, that is how the absurdity is presented in the surface plot. Just as the substrate of a lump of rock cannot be identified with any of its physical components, so too the substrate of a mind cannot be identified with any of its mental components.

But here I must interrupt the exposition of the surface plot in order to glance at the underplot. For the surface plot does not exhaust the richness of the absurdity which Hume is trying to expose. In the case of a material object, such as a table or chair, it is absurd to identify the suggested substrate with any detectable component. But in the case of a mind there is an extra dimension to the absurdity. There is, first, the parallel absurdity of identifying the substrate with any detectable component of the mind, *i.e.* with any impression or idea. Then there is the additional complication that, if we did make such an identification, the impression of the self would be an impression of another impression, and, therefore, in Hume's terminology, an impression of reflection. Now this complication is not enough, in itself, to lead to any further absurdity. For it would have been possible to argue, as William James did later, that consciousness simply consists in the fact that one component of the mind reflects another (*loc.cit.*, p. 342). But Hume's adversaries required the self to be a single subject, and such a subject could hardly get an impression of itself. James' theory that the subject is the passing thought, which apprehends earlier thoughts but not itself, avoids the absurdity, but only by abandoning the requirement for a single subject. Thus something which is simple enough in the surface plot carries richer implications in the underplot.

Let me return to the surface plot. The next step in its development concerns the relations between the mental components which go to form a single mind enduring through time. According to Hume, these relations are resemblance and causation. As demonstrated, they do not produce perfect identity, but they do produce the inferior substitute with which we have to rest content when we leave the philosopher's study. In other words, when Hume wrote the text of the "*Treatise*," he believed that his theory of personal identity founded on resemblance and causation, was an adequate theory, in spite of the fact that it does not satisfy philosophers' dreams about perfect identity. He believed, as we say nowadays, that his analysis of the concept of personal identity was correct.

Since he had ceased to believe this by the time that he wrote the Appendix, it might be a good thing to mention two relations which have a strong claim to be included on his list, but which are not included in it. Contiguity is not included, in spite of the importance of temporal contiguity in the mental life of a person, and in spite of the fact that causation, which he does include, is said by him to involve contiguity. Another equally striking exclusion is the memory relation. This is the relation which holds between a memory impression and the earlier mental component of which it is a memory impression. When I say that he excludes the memory relation from his list, I mean only that he does not treat this relation as part of the basis of personal identity. Naturally, he thinks that memory is indispensable, but only as a means of acquiring knowledge of one's own identity. For without memory, how could anyone discover that a series of mental items really were related by resemblance and causation, which, according to the theory, are the two basic relations? How could he even discover the existence of the mental items? But this does not make the memory relation into a third basic relation. It is true that he allows it a minor role in producing personal identity, as opposed to discovering it. Because he thinks that memory impressions are replicas, the memory relates and multiplies resemblances and so helps to produce personal identity as a sort of side effect. But this work is done through resemblance, and resemblance is a basic relation already on the list, and so the memory relation does not acquire a title to a place of its own on the list.

It might be argued that Hume was right to refuse to put the memory relation on the list of relations that constitute personal identity. Perhaps memory does only discover personal identity. This is a difficult matter to settle, and the difficulty can be exhibited in the following way. Suppose that he had said that the memory relation also helps to produce personal identity by multiplying causal connections between mental items. This would have been a much more important point than his suggestion that it multiplies resemblances. As far as I know, he never says that memory helps to produce personal identity in this way. But if he had made this point, he could have argued very plausibly that it locates the most important thing that memory contributes to constituting personal identity. But would this give the memory relation a title to a place of its own on the list of basic relations? Probably not. For if he had made the point about memory and causality, he could still have defended his refusal to give the memory relation a place of its own on the list. Memory would play its further role only through causation, which is already on the list. So perhaps his refusal to add the memory relation to the other two is not wrong, and the only fault in this part of his argument is that he does not offer a full justification of his refusal.

What then is the *dénouement* of the surface plot? If we do not include the Appendix, the story ends with Hume's acceptance of a reductive theory. A human mind is composed of impressions and ideas related by resemblance and causality. He argues that there is no real alternative to this theory. Those who say that a human mind enjoys a tidier type of identity have simply made a mistake about the nature of the scale of better and worse types of identity. When we place various kinds of things on this scale, we are merely applying axioms (1), (2) and (3) to the empirical phenomena. If the result is that a physical atom exhibits perfect identity through time, while cabbages and kings do not, that is a final result, and there is no appeal beyond it. Of course, someone might challenge Hume's account of the empirical phenomena, and claim that the identity of a physical atom, or of a cabbage, is not as he describes it. Or someone might make the more radical suggestion that we should not use the three axioms to define perfect identity; or even that we ought to give up talking about perfect identity altogether, because each kind of thing has its own appropriate criterion of identity, and there is no competition between them. But if we do construct the scale in the way sketched by Hume, and if we cannot find any mistake in his description of the empirical phenomena, then that result is final. It is a misunderstanding of the nature of the scale to bring in the unempirical concept "substrate," and to try to use it as the basis for a third type of perfect identity, which would be a sort of consolation prize for those who fail in the empirical competition.

So Hume is satisfied with his reductive theory, and he has an explanation of his adversaries' dissatisfaction with it. His adversaries are obsessed with perfect identity, and try to find it where it does not exist. But when we follow the surface plot into the Appendix, there is a dramatic change. All his satisfaction with his theory vanishes. He still refuses to accept the suggestion that we have an unempirical concept of substance. But when he reviews his account of the connections between the impressions and ideas of a single person, he finds it defective. Since philosophers' recantations are not too common, let me quote some of this one: "If perceptions [*i.e. impressions and ideas*] are distinct existences, they form a whole only by being connected together. But no connections among distinct existences are ever discoverable by human understanding. We only *feel* a connection or determination of the thought to pass from one object to another. It follows, therefore, that the thought alone feels personal identity, when reflecting on the train of past perceptions that compose a mind;

the ideas of them are felt to be connected together, and naturally introduce each other. . . . But all my hopes vanish when I come to explain the principles that unite our successive perceptions in our thought or consciousness. I cannot discover any theory which gives me satisfaction on this head." (*loc.cit.*, p. 331).

This really is a recantation. It is not just a case of Hume's common flirting with his adversaries' feelings. His treatment of causal necessity contains several examples of this kind of insincerity; or, it may be, irony. I am thinking of the passages in which he expresses the fear that his reductive account of causal necessity may not only look too sceptical, but actually be too sceptical. But on the whole he is satisfied that that theory is adequate because it covers everything that is empirically accessible. So his settled conclusion about that matter is that his adversaries are misled by the mind's "great propensity to spread itself on external objects, and to conjoin with them any internal impressions which they occasion" (*loc.cit.*, p. 218).

Why, then, is he not equally satisfied with his reductive theory of personal identity? We may suspect that he must be influenced by something in the underplot. For example, minds are self-reflexive, and so, though it may be a good explanation of causal necessity to say that the mind spreads itself on external objects, it does not sound so good an explanation of personal identity to say that it spreads itself on internal objects. However, Hume does not explicitly bring in the underplot at this point. He sums up his reasons for rejecting his theory of personal identity in the following words: "In short, there are two principles which I cannot render consistent, nor is it in my power to renounce either of them, viz. *that all our distinct perceptions are distinct existences*; and *that the mind never perceives any real connection among distinct existences*. Did our perceptions either inhere in something simple and individual, or did the mind perceive some real connection among them, there would be no difficulty in the case. For my part, I must plead the privilege of a sceptic, and confess that this difficulty is too hard for my understanding." (*Ibid.*).

This is not irony. Hume was a subtle writer, capable of irony which often passes undetected. So it could have been irony. But it is not in fact irony, and the proof of this is that it is entirely different from his later reaction to his reductive theory of causal necessity, which is given in his "Abstract" of the *Treatise*.

Why, then, did he recant about personal identity? In the remainder of this paper I shall go through the underplot trying to show that his real reasons for recanting are to be found there. But, naturally, I shall start from the reasons that he himself gives in the Appendix.

The explicit reasons, given in the Appendix, belong to the surface plot. He does not say anything that is not also true of ordinary material objects, and his argument could equally well be applied to the identity of cabbages. This is a very striking fact. An even more striking feature of his recantation is that he sums it up by repeating Axioms (4) and (5) and saying that he cannot renounce either of them and yet that he is unable to render them consistent. Now Axioms (4) and (5) belong to the second group that I distinguished at the beginning of this paper. They are concerned with the nature of the connections between the components of composite things, and they stipulate that these connections are always contingent. What then can he mean when he says that he cannot render them consistent? They do not even look inconsistent with one another. In fact, it would be plausible to argue that (5) merely gives the definition of the word "distinct" as it is used in (4) (See Von Wright: *The Logical Problem of Induction*, Ch. II). If this is correct, Hume's point is that there are *a priori* connections between ideas, and associational connections between ideas produced, *e.g.*, by constant conjunctions of impressions, but no third kind of connection called "real connection."

I think that the solution to this problem of interpretation is that Hume means not that the two axioms are inconsistent with one another, but only that taken together they are inconsistent with the fact that a person is a single unified being persisting through time. In other words, he takes this fact to imply a greater degree of unity than the two axioms allow. If he had been prepared to revise his interpretation of the fact, he would not have had to recant. But he found himself unable to accept a more reductive interpretation of the fact, and so he recanted.

As far as the text goes, this interpretation fits the whole tenor of the passage. Moreover, he never says that the two axioms are inconsistent with one another, but only that they are inconsistent. But I must admit that even this is an odd way of expressing the view that I am attributing to him, and possibly his manuscript omits some part of what he intended to write at this point.

In any case, this interpretation will be convincing only if it can be explained why the lack of a real connection between the components of a mind left Hume disatisfied. After all, the two axioms only require the connections to hold contingently. So if I have a taste impression followed by a memory idea of Paris, it will only be a contingent fact that the second followed the first. But what is wrong with that? He can hardly have supposed that such a connection ought to be non-contingent. Admittedly, in this example the connection happens to be causal, but then his main thesis about causal connections is that they only hold contingently. In any case, non-causal examples could easily be found.

It seems that the only way to answer this objection and to give an intelligible reconstruction of his reasoning is to draw on the underplot. Minds differ from ordinary composite material objects in more than one way, and it is likely that some of those differences will provide clues to his line of thought.

For example, the ownership of impressions and ideas has several well known peculiarities. If I have a sense impression, there is no room for any question about its owner — the owner must be myself. Nor can I speculate that the sense impression might have been yours instead of mine, or that it might have existed on its own, not belonging to anybody. Such speculations lack sense. Now these peculiarities of the ownership of mental objects have to be accommodated in any viable theory of personal identity. But how was Hume to accommodate them in his theory? How was he to weave these threads from the underplot into a surface plot whose dominant pattern was set by the analogy between mental objects and ordinary material objects?

One would expect that there would be some distortion at this point, and in fact there is. Instead of saying that, if I have an impression it must be mine, could not have belonged to anyone else, and could not have existed on its own, he wants to be able to say that, if I have an impression, it could not have failed to occur in the series that is myself. But that would not be the same thing. I think that it seemed to him to be the same thing because he pushed the analogy between mental objects and material objects too far. If a cow belongs to a particular herd, it need not have belonged to it, and it — the very same cow — might have belonged to a different herd, or even lived on its own. This may have suggested to him that, if he had allowed that a certain sense impression which occurs in the series that is myself might not have done so, then he would have been forced to allow that it — the very same sense impression — might have occurred in a series that is someone else, or even existed on its own. In fact no such concession would have been forced from him. He could have pointed out that there is a limit to the analogy between mental objects and material objects. But because he failed to see thy limit, he thought that the only way to accommodate the peculiar features of the ownership of mental objects would be to say that, when a series contains a particular mental object, it could not have failed to contain it. In short, he confused the following two modal propositions:

   (i) This series might not have included S.

   (ii) S might have occurred outside this series.

   The thesis, that Hume is here exaggerating the analogy between mental objects and material objects, must not be taken to imply that all types of material object have criteria which make their numerical identities independent of the numerical identities of any other type of material object. That is not so. Although most types of material object are not identity-dependent in this way, some types are. For example, a particular brick is not dependent for its identity on the wall in which it has been incorporated, and it could have been incorporated in a different wall. But suppose that I point to the branch of a tree, and say that it — the very same branch — might have grown on a different tree. Here we have a material example of identity-dependence, and my speculation would lack sense. All that I can imagine is that another tree might have grown a branch exactly like this one, and that, at the same time, this tree might not have grown this one. So this kind of identity-dependence is not confined to mental objects.

However, it does seem to extend to all types of mental object, and it is, perhaps, especially puzzling in this area. Its puzzling character may be brought out through a contrast between a branch of a tree and a sense impression. An explanation of the identity-dependence of the branch would go something like this. In the case of a branch we could always adopt a new criterion, according to which its numerical identity would be tied to the matter out of which it is formed. Then the speculation that lacked a sense could immediately be given one. It would mean that that matter might have been absorbed by a different tree, and might have come out of it in the form of a similar branch. Of course, someone might object that this would still not be a case of the very same branch growing on a different tree, because he might persist in treating the numerical identity of the tree as a necessary condition of the numerical identity of the branch. But there would be no mystery about this. We would have three discernible things to juggle with, the matter of the branch, its form, and its relation to a particular tree. These three things could be used in various ways to produce alternative criteria of numerical identity for branches. The relation to a particular tree is only one thing, and it is easy to see what is going on when someone refuses to allow the numerical identity of a branch to be independent of this relation.

But the whole affair is more mysterious in the case of a sense impression. For though two of the things ae used in this case – the form, or quality of the sense impression and its relation to a particular person – the third thing – its matter – is not used. Consequently, we do not have such a clear idea of what we would have to do in order to give a sense to the senseless speculation. Would we merely collapse the concept of the numerical identity of a sense impression into exact similarity? Or would we have to wait until we were in a position to base a new criterion of numerical identity on the matter of the nervous system?

To return to Hume – it may seem hard to believe that he could have exaggerated the similarity between sense impressions and material objects, such as bricks, to quite such an extent. For the facts about the ownership of mental objects are familiar, and so they might seem to be less malleable than this. But half thought out analogies are very powerful in philosophy, and there is ample evidence in the *Treatise* for this account of what was going on in his mind. For example, in the chapter on the Immateriality of the Soul, he says ". . . since all our perceptions are different from each other, and from everything else in the universe, they are also distinct and separable, and may be considered as separately existent, and may exist separately, and have no need of anything else to support their existence. They are, therefore, substances, as far as this definition explains substance" (*loc.cit.*, pp. 283-84). This is not an isolated passage, and it sets out a line of thought which Hume was prepared to follow in the text of the *Treatise*, but not in the Appendix. The analogy with bricks, or perhaps with physical atoms, is being openly pushed to the extreme. In this way sense impressions acquire a degree of independence which seems to make it impossible to explain the fact that one of mine could not have been one of yours.

This strange way of treating mental objects is connected with his account of the way in which memory helps a person to answer a question about his own earlier identity. He says that memory discovers, but does not constitute personal identity, except in so far as it multiplies resemblances between a person's mental objects. This suggests that my memory puts me in touch with a number of mental objects, about which I then ask whether they belong to the series that terminates on myself on the present moment, and that I am supposed to answer this question by applying the criteria of resemblance and causation. But this description of my procedure presupposes that memory is an impersonal way of collecting data, which are then examined and assigned to myself or some other person. Did Hume then deliberately use "memory" to signify a faculty which puts me in direct touch with earlier mental objects that belong to any person, myself or another? Apparently not. For there is no evidence to support the view that in his discussion of personal identity he is intentionally presupposing a predicament that is not ours. Of course, he allows for errors of memory, but not for what Shoemaker calls "quasi-memory" ("Persons and their Pasts," *American Philosophical Quarterly*, 1967). On the other hand, in this discussion, he does not even mention any of the ordinary ways in which we discover the objects in other people's minds. So there really is a presupposition that memory is an impersonal way of collecting data. How should we interpret it?

It should probably be connected not with any carefully thought out theory about the way that the data are, or might be, acquired, but, rather, with his general picture of the world of mental objects. When he pushed the analogy between mental and material objects too far, it was natural for him to write as if we could establish the existence of mental objects without prejudice to the question of their ownership, as can be done with cattle. Then, if he retained his uncritical assumption that memory is the only source of the relevant data, it would be assigned a role which it could not possibly perform. For how could I rely on my memory for the existence of an earlier mental object, while rejecting the inference that it was mine?

Only too easily, it might be retorted, if the concept of memory is changed. But since there is no evidence that Hume was deliberately changing the concept in the required way, it is more likely that he slipped into the impersonal treatment of memory because he exaggerated the analogy between mental and material objects without fully realising the consequences.

So much for the second of the two possibilities whose unrealisability he laments in the Appendix — "did the mind perceive some real connection among them [our perceptions]. . . ." The first one still remains to be considered — "did our perceptions . . . inhere in something simple and individual. . . ." Why did he say that, if this possibility were realised, "there would be no difficulty in the case"? What made him wish that he had been able to accept this kind of theory?

This question is unlikely to be answerable in as straightforward a way as the question about his other wish. The theory that a mind is "something simple and individual" is such a panacea that the wish for it is likely to be overdetermined. Nevertheless it is surprising to find how very general Hume's stated reasons are. The considerations that he adduces apply not only to minds but also to composite material things. According to him, the only kind of identity enjoyed by all these composite things is the inferior, fictional kind. But if the problem is so widespread, why does he confess his inability to solve it only in the case of minds? Here too there must be something at work in the underplot. But what?

It would be too simple to suggest that he felt that, if the impressions and ideas of a person were not presented to something, consciousness would remain unexplained. For he did not need, and did not think that he needed, to point to a single subject in order to explain the phenomenon of consciousness. He took it for granted that one component of a mind can be reflected by another, and his course appeared to be set towards the kind of theory that was later developed by William James. He allowed himself to make use of intentionality, without trying to explain it, and he seems to have felt no doubts about its range, and so to be unaware that there might be a problem about the synthetic unity of consciousness.

However, he certainly did feel the need for a single subject. If his reason was not purely phenomenological, the only plausible alternative seems to be that he felt it because he had detached the mind from the physical world. If he had used the fact that the mind has a physical basis, he could have explained its knowledge of the world and of its place in it, without requiring it to be "simple and individual." All that would have been required was a careful account of the causal mechanism of memory, and of our method of checking it. But when he detached the mind from its physical basis, he deprived himself of the material that he needed for such a reconstruction of empirical knowledge. It therefore seemed to him that he had to fall back on a single simple subject persisting through time. But that, he realised, is a philosopher's dream.

This interpretation, like that of his other wish, is necessarily conjectural. But there are strong reasons for accepting it. The alternative suggestion, that his problem was purely phenomenological, is implausible, and the idea that the subject needs a para-mechanical vehicle fits his Newtonian conception of psychology very well.

First, consider how he explains consciousness. I pointed out earlier that, if he had identified the self with any detectable component of a mind, the impression of the self would have been an impression of that component, and so it would have been an impression of reflection. Now there were two reasons why he did not treat the self in this way. In general, it is absurd to identify a composite thing with any of its components, and a single subject could hardly get an impression of itself in this way. Of course, this does not explain why he thought that the demand for a single subjet is legitimate, if unfulfillable. But in his critique óf the theory that there is an impression of the self, he gives no hint of any purely phenomenological problem. He simply takes the fact of intentionality for granted.

So, if he had not felt the need for a single subject, he could have given a coherent account of the idea of the self without violating the principles of his empiricism. That idea would not be an idea of a single mental component. It would be an idea of an expanding series of mental components. These components would be identified not only through their contents, but also through their positions in the series. But the idea of the self would have a special kind of content, which increased as the series expanded. It is evident that this theory would depend on impression of reflection and impressions of memory. But Hume felt no phenomenological difficulties about these two types of impression.

His difficulty begins when he has to explain how a mind acquires any knowledge of the world and of its place in it. For how can he explain the working of memory in his system? If I wonder whether a man sitting opposite me in a train is the one who sat opposite me yesterday, I would take my own identity for granted. But if he questioned whether I was the man who had occupied the same seat on yesterday's journey, I would have to verify my claim that I was, perhaps by producing memory impressions which could be checked. Similarly, the identity of a star could be established through a photograph taken by a rocket-borne camera, or the identity of the camera could be established through the images on its film. In both cases it is necessary that we should be able to argue either from the identity of the recorder to the identity of what it records, or in the reverse direction. This evidently requires that there should be general agreement between the record and the recorder's independently established history. But how could memory meet this requirement in Hume's system?

That depends on how literally his system is constructed. He occasionally speculates about the physical basis of the mind, and, if he had allowed himself to use that kind of material in his discussion of personal identity, he might have given an adequate account of memory. But in fact he does not use it, and the implication is that he can solve the problem entirely from the resources of the mind. This restriction puts memory in an impossible position. Just as I, body and mind, am related to the two appearances of the man in the train, so too I, the remembering subject, ought to be related to any sense impressions that occur in my mind. But this will not work. For in the example, there were independent ways of checking my identity, but there are no independent ways of checking the identity of the remembering subject in his restricted system. His wish that the subject were single is merely the wish that this did not matter. Another reason why the analogy does not work is that there is no material left over for incorporation in an account of the causal mechanism of the remembering subject. His wish that the subject were simple is merely the wish that this too did not matter. However, it does matter that his picture of the mind impels him towards a theory which makes the subject independent of any checks and independent of any mechanism. He knows that such a theory is a philosopher's dream, but he does not retrace his steps in order to find out which of them led him into the impasse.

David Pears

Scepticism and Anti-scepticism in the Latter Part of the 18th Century

In the twenty-five years that I have been examining the course of modern scepticism, I have rarely ventured beyond Hume. In this paper I shall offer some tentative views about the development of scepticism and anti-scepticism in the latter part of the eighteenth century. In these decades the conflict between two views seems to have been crucial for the future course of Western thought. The way in which the conflict unfolded revealed the end of the Grand Illusion that had dominated European man from ancient Greece until the Enlightenment, that human rational activity could comprehend the cosmos.

In an early study on "Scepticism in the Enlightenment"[1] I contended that philosophical scepticism, that is the questioning of whether there can be adequate or sufficient evidence to support knowledge claims about areas of human concern, pretty much died out during the Enlightenment. The sort of questioning posed by the sceptical tradition, primarily French, in the seventeenth century, seems to have ended with Pierre Bayle and Bishop Pierre-Daniel Huet, along with its attendant avowal of fideism. The optimism of the Enlightenment, with its conviction that human reason properly freed and illuminated, could find and was finding the truth, made scepticism part of the dark pre-Newtonian, pre-Lockean age. Histories of scepticism, as a now defunct movement, could be written, diagnosing why such a strange aberration had flourished in by-gone ages.[2] This is not to deny that

1. Richard H. Popkin, "Scepticism in the Enlightenment," in *Studies on Voltaire and the Eighteenth Century* 24-27, 1963, pp. 1321-45.
2. Cf. Abbé Etienne Bonnot de Condillac, *Cours d''etudes pour l'instruction du*

some occasional, mediocre versions of past glories of doubting did reappear on the scene in France and Germany.[3] But for all practical or serious purposes, sceptism, as a living or vital movement was dead by the middle of the eighteenth century, save in the person and thoughts of David Hume. Hume, raised in the glories of the Newtonian epoch, and privately nurtured on the doubts of Pierre Bayle, senses a deeper and more modern sceptical crisis than his predecessors had perceived. In his youth he had ventured on "a new scene of thought" and collapsed into a nervous breakdown.[4] He went to France in 1734, a youth of 23, armed with his folio volumes of Bayle's *Dictionary* and *Oeuvres diverses*, to compose his *Treatise of Human Nature*, a Newtonian attempt to introduce the method of experimental reasoning into moral subjects.[5] The schizophrenic result, of an optimistic psychologism that would explain all of man's intellectual endeavours and a desperate scepticism about whether anything could be explained, ended in the utter dismay of the author in the conclusion of the first book. He could only alternate between being a positive Newtonian social scientist and a complete sceptic, undermining everything including his own scientific achievements. He could find no peace in a fideistic solution, but could only rely on Nature. "Philosophy would render us completely Pyrrhonian, were not Nature too strong for it" he wrote in his own review of his efforts.[6] When Hume came to sum up his achievement, he seemed to recognize the hopelessness of modern man, shorn of Divine Guidance and help, to find any answers to what he was, what his world was, or why it was. He was fully aware of his ability to doubt everything, and of his inability to justify any of his beliefs. "Nature by an absolute and uncontrolable necessity has

Prince de Parme, III, xxii, in *Oeuvres philosophiques de Condillac*, ed. Georges Le Roy, Paris, 1948, Vol. II, pp. 73-76; J. H. S. Formey, *Histoire abregée de la philosophie*, Amsterdam, 1760, pp. 243-48; and Jacob Brucker, *Historia critica philosophiae*, 2nd ed., Leipzig, 1767, sections on scepticism in vols. I and IV.

3. Some of these are discussed in my article cited in n. 1. See also the detailed treatment of minor sceptical writers in Pierre Rétat, *Le Dictionnaire de Bayle et la lutte philosophique au XVIIIe siècle*, Paris, 1971; and Giorgio Tonelli, "Kant und die antiken Skeptiker," in *Studien zu Kants philosophischer Entwicklung*, pp. 93-123, plus Tonelli's forthcoming study on some of the little known French sceptics of the period.

4. See Hume's letter of March or April 1734, in *The Letters of David Hume*, ed. by J. Y. T. Greig, Oxford, 1932, Vol. I, letter no. 3, pp. 12-18. The letter is listed as to (Dr. George Cheyne). However, Ernest C. Mossner in his *The Life of David Hume*,

required us to judge as well as to breathe and feel."[7] But Nature has not provided us with any justifications for the beliefs we have to accept, and reason undermines whatever evidence we think we have for the beliefs. We are torn between an inescapable and irrefutable scepticism and a natural, forced dogmatism. We can rest our cause only in an animal rather than a supernatural faith. Hume's dilemma at the end of Book I of the *Treatise* seems that of modern man, questing for knowledge and truth about the world, but cut off from it by the force of scepticism, having to believe, but unable to justify what he believes.

Hume alone of his time seems to have recognized that Enlightened man was man without hope of assurance and man without the ability to achieve the solace of complete doubt. He had to believe, but his beliefs were unfounded, as Hume's brilliant analyses had shown. Hume managed to go through life in fairly good cheer, mainly by avoiding philosophizing on man's state. Most of his life he spent in other public or literary pursuits, but each time he returned to philosophy, he saw and portrayed the abyss. When he was accused of being an arrant sceptic, Hume replied in 1745 (in the recently discovered *Letter from a Gentleman*),

> As to the *Scepticism* with which the Author is charged, I must observe, that the Doctrine of the *Pyrrhonians* or *Scepticks* have been regarded in all Ages as Principles of mere Curiosity, or a Kind of *Jeux d'Esprit*, without any Influence on a Man's steady Principles or Conduct of Life. In Reality, a Philosopher who affects to doubt of the Maxims of *common Reason*, and even of his *Senses*, declares sufficiently that he is

Austin, 1954, p. 84, indicates it is to Dr. John Arbuthnot. On Hume's nervous breakdown, see Mossner, chap. 6, "Disease of the Learned" and chap. 7, "Recovery through Catharsis."

5. On Hume's use of Bayle, see R. H. Popkin, "Bayle and Hume," *International Congress of Philosophy*, XIII, Mexico, 1963, pp. 317-27. The title of Hume's first book is *A Treatise of Human Nature: being an Attempt to introduce the experimental Method of Reasoning into Moral Subjects*.

6. David Hume, *An Abstract of a Treatise of Human Nature*, Cambridge, 1938, p. 24.

7. Hume, *A Treatise of Human Nature*, Selby-Bigge ed., Oxford, 1951, p. 183. See also, R. H. Popkin, "Hume and Jurieu: Possible Calvinist Origins of Hume's Theory of Belief," *Rivista Critica di Storia della Filosofia*, 1967 (fasc. IV), pp. 400-17.

not in earnest, and that he intends not to advance an Opinion which he would recommend as Standards of Judgment and Action. All he means by these Scruples is to abate the Pride of *mere human* Reasoners, by showing them, that even with regard to Principles which seem the clearest, and which they are necessitated from the strongest Instincts of Nature to embrace, they are not able to attain full Consistence and absolute Certainty. *Modesty* then, and *Humility*, with regard to the Operations of our natural Faculties, is the Result of *Scepticism*; not an universal Doubt, which it is impossible for any Man to support, and which the first and most trivial Accident in Life must immediately disconcert and destroy."[8]

At the end of his life, in perhaps his last philosophical statement, in a footnote he added to the *Dialogues Concerning Natural Religion* to 1776, he described his and man's situation as follows:

it seems evident, that the dispute between the sceptics and dogmatists is entirely verbal, or at least regards only the degrees of doubt and assurance, which we ought to indulge with regard to all reasoning: And such disputes are commonly at the bottom, verbal, and admit not of any precise determination. No philosophical dogmatist denies, that there are difficulties both with regard to the senses and to all science; and that these difficulties are in a regular, logical method, absolutely insolveable. No sceptic denies, that we lie under an absolute necessity, notwithstanding these difficulties, of thinking, and believing, and reasoning with regard to all of subjects, and even of frequently assenting with confidence and security. The only difference, then, between these sects, if they merit that name, is, that the sceptic, from habit, caprice, or inclination, insists most on the difficulties; the dogmatists, for like reasons, on the necessity.[9]

Hume's recognition of the human situation hardly impressed his contemporaries. As Hume said sadly, of his work, "Never

8. David Hume, *Letter from a Gentleman to his friend in Edinburgh*, 1745, ed. by E. C. Mossner and John V. Price, Edinburgh, 1967.
9. Hume, *Dialogues concerning Natural Religion*, ed. by Norman Kemp Smith, London, 1947, p. 219 n.

literary Attempt was more unfortunate than my Treatis of human Nature. It fell *dead-born from the Press*; without reaching such distinctions as even to excite a Murmer among the Zealots."[10] In the mid-eighteenth century, Hume was the *only* living sceptic; on the one hand an anachronism, and on the other, the man who was most aware of the new predicament created by the Enlightenment — that there was no faith left to guide men. He was at first ignored by his countrymen. However, his effect on the three major Enlightenment cultures in France, England and Germany was to set the pattern and the path for much of modern thought.

Scepticism in the second half of the eighteenth century was, I believe, mainly Hume's views and their influence. Anti-scepticism was primarily the growing realization of Hume's accomplishment and the reaction to it. In choosing to discuss France, England and Germany in this order, I think I am reflecting both the order in which the reactions occurred and the increasing importance of these reactions.

Hume's first signs of success appeared in France in the 1750s when his *Political Discourses, Moral Essays*, and *History of England* appeared in French. He quickly became the darling of the French Enlightenment, the monumental example of how Newtonian social science and social criticism could be applied to the *ancien regime* and religious orthodoxy. This Humeaphoria continued into the 1760s when Hume served as a diplomat in Paris, and became a central figure in the *salons*, and in the club of the Enlightenment leaders. But, as Laurence Bongie has shown, Hume was admired not for his epistemological scepticism but for his social criticism.[11] Turgot diagnosed the case first, and saw that Hume was not one of the *illuminati* who saw science as the new truth, and science as the way to the infinite perfectibility of mankind.[12] D'Holbach discovered to his dismay that Hume was

10. Hume, "My Own Life," published in *The Letters of David Hume*, Vol. I, p. 2. Mossner, in his *Life of David Hume*, pp. 116-32, shows that Hume overstated the lack of interest in his work.

11. Laurence Bongie, "Hume, 'Philosophe' and Philosopher in Eighteenth Century France," *French Studies* 15, 1961, pp. 213-27.

12. See J. H. Burton, editor, *Letters of Eminent Persons addressed to David Hume*, Edinburgh, 1849, Turgot's letters of 25 March 1767 and 3 July 1768, pp. 150-52 and p. 163; and Hume's letter of 16 June 1768 in Hume, *Letters*, Vol. II, p. 180. Turgot's dispute with Hume is discussed in Laurence Bongie, *David Hume, Prophet of the Counter-Revolution*, Oxford, 1965, pp. 47-52.

not an atheist.[13] Diderot wrote him off as an anti-scientic sceptic.[14] As Hume was being deserted by the Enlightenment Establishment as not with it, the right wing discovered him. Various abbés found that the essay "Of Miracles" was a defense of the faith against Enlightenment atheism.[15] The *History of England* became the model against the revolutionists, in terms of Hume's picture of the pitfalls and disasters of the English Revolution of Cromwell's time. Louis XVI became a Humean and read Hume's account of Charles I just before his own execution.[16] By the time of the Revolution, Hume had become anathema to the radicals, his scepticism a stumbling-block to their assurance that they had found the way to the Millenium. His legacy had passed to the reactionaries. DeMaistre and Bonald found in his scepticism a road to their own conservativism and orthodoxy. DeMaistre, in fact, wrote a work called *Reflections on the French Revolution* made up entirely of quotes from Hume, who had died just at the outbreak of the earlier American Revolution.[17] The theory of orthodoxy of DeMaistre and Bonald (and later of Lamennais) builds out of aspects of Humean scepticism, insisting on the inability of individual reason to find a way to truth, and therefore the need to rely on tradition and revelation, especially in the form of the infallible pronouncement of the Church and the Pope. Lamennais, in his rebellion against the Church may have seen the full implications of this fideism, based on pure scepticism (as he cried out from jail in his *Paroles d'un Croyant*) and seen that it must be the faith of the believers alone that can survive. Hume became the prophet of the Counter-Revolution and the Counter-Enlightenment in France.[18] And this may account for his lack of

13. Cf. Mossner, *Life of Hume*, pp. 483-86.

14. Denis Diderot, "Pyrrhonienne ou sceptique philosophie," *Encyclopédie*, Vol. XIII, p. 613b-614a, seems to be a rejection of Hume's scepticism on these grounds. See Popkin, "Scepticism in the Enlightenment," pp. 1336-38.

15. Bongie, *David Hume, Prophet of the Counter-Revolution*, pp. 34-39.

16. *Ibid.*, esp. chap. IV.

17. On De Maistre's and Bonald's use of Hume's ideas, see the references to them in Bongie, *David Hume, Prophet of the Counter-Revolution*, esp. pp. 159-62. The last chapter of De Maistre's *Considerations sur la France* (1796) is entitled, "Fragment d'une historie de la revolution française par David Hume."

18. See the discussions of scepticism in Hughes Félicité Robert de Lamennais in his *Paroles d'un croyant* and *Essai sur l'indifference*. Rétat, in *Le Dictionnaire de Bayle*, shows that the same happened with Bayle's ideas. See especially pp. 445-48.

influence in French thought thereafter and for the lack of sceptical thought in the culture that had spawned modern scepticism until well into the twentieth century.

The sole sign I have found of a left-wing Hume in French (but not in France) in the late eighteenth century, is the preface to the translation of the *Dialogues*. The title page says the work was published in Edinburgh in 1780, but T. E. Jessop seems to believe that it is more likely from Amsterdam.[19] The author of the preface is unknown. He spoke of Hume's almost unique ability to present the force and precision of ideas, and then says "David Hume is one of the greatest geniuses of the eighteenth century."[20] The *Dialogues* are presented as showing the necessity to turn to revelation because of the limits and uncertainty of human knowledge. But this is then made out to be not traditional orthodoxy, as Bonald, DeMaistre and Hamann saw it, but what religion ought to be, in opposition to the superstitious, intolerant actual religion. (What this is is not indicated, but from the critical remarks it certainly is not Catholicism).[21] The author asserted, in contrast to the Enlightenment atheists, who could only see the *Dialogues* as wishy-washy agnosticism, that "One ought to regard this work, as small as it is, as the most complete theology and metaphysics that has yet appeared,"[22] a view definitely not shared by the dogmatic atheists or religious bigots in France. It would be interesting to find out who this French-speaking admirer of the sceptical anti-institutional religion Hume was, and whether he was a unique case. He said that he had received a copy of the *Dialogues* several months before publication in English from one of Hume's friends, so he may have been in contact with Adam Smith, or

19. "Avertissement du traducteur," *Dialogues sur la religion naturelle*, Ouvrage posthume de David Hume, Ecuyer, Edimbourg, 1780, pp. 43-46. T. E. Jessop lists this edition as, "Despite the imprint, probably printed and publ. in France or Holland." *A Bibliography of David Hume and of Scottish Philosophy*, New York, 1966, p. 41.

20. *Dialogues sur la religion naturelle?*, p. 3. "DAVID HUME est un des plus grandes génies du dix-huitième siècle."

21. Catholicism is attacked on p. 6. "Il pourra même arriver que la sainte Inquisition, plus habile à bruler qu'à raisonner, s'avise de regarder toute cette production comme un persifflage impie. Mais quel bon ouvrage la superstition n'a-t-elle pas devoué aux flammes." Then the Inquisitors of Lisbon and Rome are criticized for their hypocrisy.

22. *Ibid.*, p. 5. "On doit regarder cet ouvrage tout petit qu'il est, comme le traité le plus complet de Théologie & de metaphysique qui ait encore paru."

someone like that. The prevailing attitude to Hume in France is shown by the fact that except for his *History of England*, his other works did not come out in France or in French for about 100 years after the Revolution, although they had been extremely popular earlier in the century. His *Treatise on Human Nature* did not, in fact, appear in French until the 1950s.[23] Hence concern with Hume and his scepticism left the mainstream of French thought as the Enlightenment came to realize that he did not shed conservatism and reaction for progress and the new dogmatism of science.

In the British Isles, Hume's impact had a very different history. His views at first were not as ignored as the author claimed, but whatever positive interest there was seemed to come mainly from French Protestant refugees like Demaizeaux and Maty, familiar with Bayle's scepticism, and from Scottish intellectuals like Kames.[24] Criticism started in the 1740s mainly from ministers charging Hume with irreligion, scepticism, and with denying the existence of causal connections in the world. In the early 1750s serious arguments against Hume's theory of knowledge began to be propounded, and it is in this period that one can begin to speak of the development in England of an anti-scepticism resulting from Hume's efforts.

Henry Home, Lord Kames, Hume's relative and friend, is probably the first serious critic. Kames, and the critics who were to follow up to Thomas Reid and his commonsense school, seem to have just been continuing a traditional English way of dealing with the sceptical crisis. Throughout the seventeenth century, the great Anglican divines. William Chillingworth, Archbishop John Tillotson, Bishop John Wilkins (the founder of the Royal Society of England) and Bishop William Stillingfleet, had propounded a commonsensical answer to the scepticism being raised against

23. Hume, *Traité de la nature humaine*, trans. by André Leroy, Paris, 1946.

A translation of Book I, done by Chas. Renouvier and F. Pillon appeared in Paris in 1878.

24. See the review of Hume's *Treatise* by Desmaizeaux in the *Bibliothèque raisonnée des ouvrages des savans de l'Europe*, 1740, Vol. XXIV, pp. 324-55, Vol. XXVI, 1741, pp. 411-27, and the review of Hume's *Political Discourses* by Maty in the *Journal britannique*, 1752, VII, pp. 243-67, and 387-411.

Henry Home, Lord Kames, discussed Hume's views, mainly critically, in his *Essays on the Principles of Morality and Natural Religion*, Edinburgh, 1751.

them by their Catholic opponents, and to the scepticism they saw coming out of the Cartesian revolution in philosophy. They had all admitted that in a fundamental sense, the sceptical challenge to human knowledge could not be refuted; that it could not be established that any human knowledge claims might not be false, or that human beings possessed any infallible knowledge. However, in spite of this, the Anglican theologians insisted, people are not in fact in doubt about everything, and they do seem to possess adequate principles and information for the affairs of life, sufficiently adequate for the development of sciences, the defense of religion and the erection of legal standards. If one examines why 'reasonable' men are not in complete doubt, one can find the bases of a kind of philosophy — not one that would satisfy a Descartes, a Spinoza, a Leibniz or a Malebranche, in that it did not claim to be based upon self-evident first principles, and it did not claim to answer the fundamental sceptical problems. But it would be a philosophy that represented the belief's people live by. The Anglican divines were not driven by the need for consistency or ultimate certainty, but would settle for plausibility and as much certainty as the case admits of. They found in the examination of commonsense beliefs about the character of the world, sufficient guides for the solutions of human problems. While passionate seekers like Pascal were driven to fideism and myticism in order to satisfy their craving for complete certainty, the Anglicans developed a tepid middle ground between scepticism and dogmatism, and tried to hold on to their latitudinarian version of Christianity on the basis of commonsense evidence and scientific findings, and to show that their reasonable man would not be tempted into Catholic infallibility, dogmatic deism or Spinozistic atheism.[25]

Perhaps the very best of these thinkers was Bishop Stillingfleet, who in fifty years of his intellectual activity challenged the

25. On this Anglican tradition see Henry Van Leeuwen, *The Problem of Certainty in English Thought, 1630-1690*, The Hague, 1963; Van Leeuwen's introduction to John Wilkins, *Of the Principles and Duties of Natural Religion*, photoreproduction edition, New York, 1969; R. H. Popkin, "The Philosophy of Bishop Stillingfleet," *Journal of the History of Philosophy* 9, 1971, pp. 303-19; and Robert T. Carroll, *The Philosophy of Bishop Edward Stillingfleet in its Seventeenth Century Context*, Ph.D. dissertation at the University of California, San Diego, forthcoming as a publication of the *International Archives of the History of Ideas*.

emergence of irreligious scepticism, Catholic dogmatism, the new rationalist metaphysical systems, and the empiricism of John Locke, all in terms of his commonsense views. In his debate with Locke, he saw what Reid was later to report, that the 'way of ideas' was the highroad to Pyrrhonism — complete scepticism.[26] As Locke pointed out to Stillingfleet, the Bishop really was not making any counterclaims as to how one could gain true knowledge of reality. Their difference was that Locke insisted that though we had no evidence in the matter, we had to believe there were substances in the world, and the Bishop insisted that this was not just a psychological fact about us, but a basic feature of our thought, a principle we had to start from.[27] The difference turns out to be, as we will see with Hume and Reid, primarily one of emphasis, and not of philosophical evidence or argument.

While the French world was struggling throughout the seventeenth century with the sceptical crisis engendered by the Reformation and the Renaissance, the English world was taking the matter rather calmly. They were in fact accepting a kind of semi-scepticism and stating it as if it were an answer to scepticism. They were conceding without a fight the basic epistemological issues, and insisting on the merits of what was found to basic beliefs of mankind, regardless of their lack of philosophical support. The depths of the sceptical challenge were ignored, and the Anglican divines and their scientific friends placidly and contentedly lived through the century hoping to hang onto man's commonsense beliefs and the core of his religious ones in the face of the colossal upheavals going on around them. Their reasonable religion, which they thought was being buttressed and confirmed

26. See Edward Stillingfleet, *A Discourse in Vindication of the Doctrine of the Trinity*, London, 1696, last chapter; *The Bishop of Worcester's Answer to Mr. Locke's Letter*, London, 1697; and *The Bishop of Worcester's Answer to Mr. Locke's Second Letter*, London, 1698.

In Stillingfleet's answer to Locke's first letter, he declared "in an age wherein the Mysteries of Faith are so much exposed by the Promoters of *Scepticism* and *Infidelity*, it is a thing of dangerous consequence to start such new methods of *Certainty* as are apt to leave men's minds more doubtfull than before." Pp. 38-39.

27. See John Locke's three answers, *A Letter to the Rt. Rev. Edward, Lord Bishop of Worcester*, 1697; *Mr. Locke's Reply to the Right Reverend the Lord Bishop of Worcester's Answer to his Letter*, 1697; and *Mr. Locke's Reply to the Right Reverand the Lord Bishop of Worcester's Answer to his Second Letter* (1699). These three works comprise Vol. IV of the 1801 edition of Locke's *Works*.

by modern science, the voyages of discovery, ancient learning, etc., seems to have provided a sufficient shield.

In this context, I think Hume's views were, and were intended to be, the decimation of this kind of optimism. Hume's earliest philosophical writing, the essay "Of Miracles," started off as a comment on a claim of Archibishop Tillotson, but seems to me to be a refutation, by *reductio ad absurdum* of the theory propounded in Stillingfleet's major work, the *Origines Sacrae*.[28] Using the empirical and commonsense standards that Stillingfleet had set forth as the bases of reasonable religion, Hume showed it would take a miracle for the reasonable man to believe in Judeo-Christianity, a miracle that would subvert all understanding and make one believe something contrary to all custom and experience.[29] As Hume developed his scepticism, he showed that the 'reasonable' beliefs not only rest on no foundation other than human psychology, original instincts of human nature, but that they provide no knowledge of what the world may be like, and even worse that they provide no consistent believable picture of the world. We believe what we have to, when we have to, but it gives us no intelligible information about reality.

Hume's undermining of the English solution to scepticism led to a 'new' anti-scepticism, a reassertion that we *must* believe various things about our situation. However, this coupled with an

---

28. Stillingfleet, in his *Origines Sacrae*, London, 1662, contended that there was sufficient, if not complete evidence, that God exists, and that Scripture is His Word and provides the most plausible picture of what the world is like. A reasonable man, according to Stillingfleet, would find it more likely that the Biblical view is true than that it is false.

29. Hume, *An Enquiry Concerning Human Understanding*, Selby-Bigge edition, Oxford, 1961, pp. 130-31. Hume, after giving his own rendition of the content of the *Pentateuch*, then offered Stillingfleet's criterion for accepting it as true, "I desire any one to lay his hand upon his heart, and after a serious consideration declare, whether he thinks that the falsehood of such a book, supported by such a testimony, would be more extraordinary and miraculous than all the miracles it relates; which is, however, necessary to make it be received, according to the measures of probability above established." Hume then concluded that since a reasonable man could not believe Christianity on this standard, "that the *Chrsitian Religion* not only was at first attended with miracles, but even at this day cannot be believed by any reasonable person without one. Mere reason is insufficient to convince us of its veracity: And whoever is moved by *Faith* to assent to it, is conscious of a continued miracle in his own person, which subverts all the principles of his understanding, and gives him a determination to believe what is most contrary to custom and experience."

inability to cope with Hume's sceptical challenge, revealed the bankruptcy of this kind of response to scepticism. Kames first asserted that a sane man could not believe what Hume appeared to be saying. He told this to Hume when they went over the text of the *Treatise* together.[30] He said this in his *Essays on the Principles of Morality and Natural Religion* (1751) as an answer to both Berkeley and Hume. He offered as an answer to Hume's analysis of causality the contention

> That nothing can happen without a cause, is a principle embraced by all men, the illiterate and ignorant as well as the learned. Nothing that happens is conceived as happening of itself, but as an *effect produced by some other thing*. However, ignorant of the cause, we notwithstanding conclude, that every event must have a cause. We should perhaps be at a loss to deduce this principle, from any premises, by a chain of reasoning; but feeling affords conviction, where reason leaves us in the dark.[31]

Hume would have agreed with all of this, but saw it as man's tragic situation, not some kind of commonsense solution. Kames with his naturalistic outlook might feel secure if belief in causality was natural. Bt the question still remained as to whether it gave us any true knowledge of reality.

The most extensive early criticism of Hume was by John Leland, in the second edition of his *A View of the Principal Deistical Writers of the Last and Present Century*, (1755).[32] This work, which was reprinted well into the nineteenth century, and which was translated into German right away, has hardly been studied.[33] Leland was very impressed by Hume's anti-Christianity

30. Cf. Kames' report to Boswell about going over the *Treatise* with Hume right after it came out, cited in Mossner, *Life of Hume*, p. 118. The copy Hume gave to Lord Kames is apparently the one in the Gomperz collection at the University of Southern California.

31. Henry Home, Lord Kames, *Essays on the Principles of Morality and Natural Religion*, p. 156.

32. John Leland, D.D., *A View of the Principal Deistical Writers of the Last and Present Century*, London, 1755. The second volume "containing Observations on Mr. Hume's Philosophical Essays" as well as an answer to Bolingbroke. I have used the third edition of 1757, since it was the only one presently available to me for citations.

33. There is an edition, apparently the sixth, in London in 1838. The work came out in German in 1755, translating the second edition with the criticism of Hume

and his subtlety and metaphysical genius. "But it is obvious to every judicious reader, that he had in many instances carried scepticism to an unreasonable height."[34] As a prime example of this, Leland took up Hume's analysis of causality. He outlined Hume's case, pointed out the far-reaching sceptical implications of Hume's theory, and then, like the bulk of Hume's critics, just insisted that one could not accept the Humean sceptical conclusion, though no evidence or argument was offered against it. "You will scarce expect, that I should enter upon a laborious confutation of so whimsical a scheme, though proposed to the world with great pomp and represented by the author himself as of *vast importance*."[35] All Leland did was to make some general observations to the effect that one cannot believe Hume's view, and that Hume's negative arguments do not rule out the possibility that unbeknownst to us there are real causal connections in the world.[36] (This view was earlier propounded by Hume's patron, the Chevalier Ramsay, who may be Hume's source for the causal argument. Ramsay had shown that we could not discover causal relations by rational or empirical means, but insisted that this did not mean that they were not there. He also claimed that we could learn about them through mystical contact with God.)[37]

Edmund Burke, in his *A Philosophical Enquiry into the Origin of our Ideas of the Sublime and Beautiful* briefly raised another form of anti-scepticism, namely that if we entertained the sceptical possibilities, no knowledge would be possible. "If we suffer ourselves to images of things, this sceptical proceeding will make every sort of reasoning on every subject vain and frivolous, even that sceptical reasoning itself, which had persuaded us to entertain a doubt concerning the agreement of our perceptions."[38]

(covering 187 pages), entitled *Abriss der vornenisten Deistischen Schriften, die in dem vorigen und gegenwärtigen Jahrhunderte in England bekant geworden sind. Es werden in demselben Hrn. Humes Philosophische Versuche gepruft* . . . (Hannover, 1755).

34. Leland, *View of the Principal Deistical Writers*, 3rd ed., London, 1757, Vol. I, p. 258.

35. *Ibid.*, p. 262.

36. *Ibid.*, pp. 261-62.

37. Andrew Michael Ramsay, *Voyages de Cyrus*, Paris, 1807, Book VI, pp. 229-35. Cf. R. H. Popkin, "The Sceptical Precursors of David Hume," *Philosophy and Phenomenological Research* 16, 1955-56, p. 69.

38. Edmund Burke, *A Philosophical Enquiry into the Origin of our Ideas of the Sublime and Beautiful*, ed. by J. T. Boulton, London & New York, p. 13.

Four ingredients appear in the early criticisms of Hume, which seem to me to comprise the main features of anti-scepticism in the late eighteenth century. These are to point out the irreligious consequences of Hume's views, the sceptical implications of them, the incredibility of these implications, and the natural human need to believe various things. These claims might have had more force before Hume, but post Hume they hardly constituted an answer to his sceptical arguments and analyses. The critics also assumed, or acted as if, Hume himself, or the mythical 'sceptic' *believed* the sceptical conclusions, and hence could be disposed of by pointing out the sorts of mad behaviour that would ensue.

The particular form of anti-scepticism that dominated Scottish and British thought in the latter part of the eighteenth century was that stemming from the commonsense philosophy of Thomas Reid. Reid's version was more elegant than that of the earlier critics and less vituperative than that of most of the religious zealots and bigots. It builds on the traditional English way of dealing with scepticism, and more immediately, David Norton, has shown, on Lord Kames' adaptation of the moral sense theory into a commonsense theory.[39]

Reid reported that it was the appearance of Hume's *Treatise* in 1739 that led him to re-examine the bases of all of modern philosophy. "The ingenious author ... hath built a system of scepticism which leaves no ground to believe any one thing rather than its contrary. His reasoning appeared to me to be just; there was, therefore a necessity to call in question the principles upon which it was founded, or to admit the conclusion."[40] Reid worked on finding an answer for twenty-five years, and finally in 1764 produced his *Inquiry into the Human Mind*. In this he elaborately showed that Hume's sceptical results were the logical conclusions of modern philosophy based upon the assumptions introduced by Descartes and Locke. Once one had decided to try to know the world by 'the way of ideas,' one was doomed to Humean

---

39. David Fate Norton, *From Moral Sense to Common Sense: An Essay on the Development of Scottish Common Sense Philosophy, 1700-1765*, Ph.D. Dissertation, University of California, San Diego, 1966.

40. Thomas Reid, *An Inquiry into the Human Mind on the Principles of Common Sense*, in Wm. Hamilton edition of Reid, *Philosophical Works*, with introduction by Harry M. Bracken, Hildesheim, 1967, p. 95.

scepticism about the possibility of knowing anything at all. But, Reid also contended, no one, including Hume himself could in fact be that sceptical.

> It seems to be a peculiar strain of humour in this author, to set out in his introduction by promising, with a grave face, no less than a complete system of the sciences, upon a foundation entirely new — to wit, that of human nature — when the intention of the whole work is to show, that there is neither human nature nor science in the world. It may perhaps be unreasonable to complain of this conduct in an author who neither believes his own existence nor that of his reader; and therefore could not mean to disappoint him, or to laugh at his credulity. Yet I cannot imagine that the author of the 'treatise of Human Nature' is so sceptical as to plead this apology. He believed, against his principles, that he should be read, and that he should retain his personal identity, till he reaped honour and reputation justly due to his metaphysical *acumen*. Indeed, he ingeniously acknowledges, that it was only in solitude and retirement that he could yield any assent to his own philosophy; society, like daylight dispelled the darkness and fogs of scepticism, and made him yield to the dominion of common sense. Nor did I ever hear him charged with doing anything, even in solitude, that argued such a degree of scepticism as his principles maintain. Surely if his friends apprehended this, they would have the charity never to leave him alone."[41]

The stories about Pyrrho of Elis, Reid, like Hume before him, regarded as fantastic. Nobody could be that dubious and yet remain sane. There is nothing he could do that would not belie his alleged complete scepticism. And if he did not act, he would either go mad, or be destroyed by the course of natural events.[42]

The incredibility of scepticism as a way of life Reid then took as a 'justification' for his own commonsense realism. The examination of what sane, reasonable, commonsense people did in fact believe, and could not be led to disbelieve by any amount of

41. *Ibid.*, p. 102.
42. *Ibid.*, p. 102.

argumentation or evidence, then came to constitute an anti-sceptical philosophy that people could live by, whose truth ultimately rested on a conviction of God's veracity.

Hume was definitely unimpressed at first, as his letter to Reid of 1763 shows. Reid had sent Hume the manuscript. After studying it, Hume came to the conclusion that Reid had really perceived the problem, but had found no other solution than the one that Hume had already presented, namely that Nature prevents us from being actual living sceptics, even though we are unable to resolve the sceptical difficulties. Besides a minor disagreement over a technical point, Hume's only criticism was that there was a Scotticism in the book.[43] Reid, in reply, tried to explain to Hume that Hume's system was solid and destroyed modern philosophy. Because of this, Reid had questioned the very assumptions of modern philosophy, and offered an answer to its sceptical debacle.[44] But Hume seems to have seen that it was not really an answer, but just another way of saying what Hume had already asserted, only with a different emphasis. Perhaps Hume had noticed what Thomas Brown (who started as a Reidian and ended up a Humean) later saw.

> Sir J. Mackintosh relates that he once observed to Dr. Thomas Brown that he thought that Reid and Hume differed more in words than opinions; Brown answered, 'Yes Reid bawled out we must believe in an outward world; but added, in a whisper, we can give no reason for our belief.' Hume cries out we can give no reason for such a notion; and whispers, I own we cannot get rid of it.[45]

Reid's anti-scepticism blossomed into a school of philosophy that was to continue in the British Isles and America for another century. The tone of Reid's disciples got to be more abusive against Hume, and came to stress the irreligious aspects of Hume's scepticism, especially after the *Dialogues* appeared in 1779. One of

---

43. See Hume's letter to Reid, 25 Feb. 1763, in *Letters*, Vol. I, pp. 375-76.
44. Thomas Reid's letter to Hume, 18 March 1763, cited in Hume, *Letters*, Vol. I, pp. 376 n. -77 n.
45. Cited in George Henry Lewes, *The History of Philosophy from Thales to Comte*, London, 1867, Vol. II, p. 383.

the most notorious of the anti-sceptics, James Beattie, in his *An Essay on the Nature and Immutability of Truth, in Opposition to Sophistry and Scepticism*, emphasized that

> Mr. Hume, more subtle, and less reserved, than any of his predecessors, hath gone still greater lengths in the demolition of common sense; and reared in its place a most tremendous fabric of doctrine; upon which, if it were not for the flimsiness of its materials, engines might easily be erected, sufficient to overturn all belief, science, religion, virtue, and society, from the very foundation.[46]

Beattie scoffed at Hume, ridiculed what would happen if one psychologically adhered to the doubts of Hume's scepticism, pointed out what good and true people believe, but he never came to grips with Hume's epistemological arguments.[47]

As anti-Humeanism became a national industry in Scotland, Hume became annoyed at the abuse and misguided attention, and wrote an "Advertisement" in 1775 "a compleat Answer to Dr. Reid and to that bigotted silly Fellow, Beattie." His response was not to argue the case, but to disown the battlefield, Hume's *Treatise*, as a juvenile work, and to insist they take his later works as the ones to fight about.[48]

Joseph Priestley, in his *An Examination of Dr. Reid's Inquiry into the Human Mind on the Principles of Common Sense, Dr. Beattie's Essay on the Nature and Immutability of Truth and Dr. Oswald's Appeal to Common Sense in Behalf of Religion*, 1774, seems to have diagnosed the case quite well. Reid and his followers claimed to be saving the world from scepticism by rejecting the principles of modern philosophy.

This solid foundation, however, had lately been attempted to

46. James Beattie, *An Essay on the Nature and Immutability of Truth, in Opposition to Sophistry and Scepticism*, Edinburgh, 1770, p. 200.

47. Beattie's criticisms have not been given serious study. He does raise many interesting points, and I have pointed out in my article, "The Philosophical Bases of Modern Racism," in *Essays in Honor of Herbert W. Schneider*, forthcoming, he sharply and forcefully attacked Hume's racist views in Part III, chap. i of the *Essays*.

48. The "Advertisement" appears in all editions of Hume's *Essays and Treatises* after 1775. It is described in Hume's letter to William Strahan, 26 October 1775, *Letters of Hume*, Vol. II, p. 301.

be overturned by a set of pretended philosophers, of whom the most conspicuous and assuming is Dr. Reid, professor of moral philosophy in the university of Glasgow, who, in order to combat Bishop Berkley, and the scepticism of Mr. Hume, has himself introduced almost universal scepticism and confusion; denying all the connections which had before been supposed to subsist between the several phenomena, powers, and operations of the mind, and substituting such a number of *independent, arbitrary, instinctive principles*, that the very enumeration of them is really tiresome.[49]

The new commonsense school Priestley saw as themselves just sceptics, but even worse than the ancient ones, "the ancients professed neither to *understand* or *believe* anything, whereas these moderns believe everything, though they profess to understanding nothing. And the former, I think, are the more consistent of the two."[50]

Priestley observed that Reid and his followers could not give any explanation or justification of our knowledge, but could only insist that we believed we had some. They accepted Hume's arguments, could not answer them, and then tried to ignore them. What in fact they had accomplished was to accept a thoroughgoing scepticism. Priestley proposed instead sticking by good old Locke and Hartley, insisting that what Kant called "the physiology of the understand" gave an account of what we know and what the world is like, even though we may not be able to justify this account.[51] Priestley's psychologism, like Hartley's before him tried to turn truth into scientific findings, without realizing or caring about the sceptical difficulties in justifying such information as revealing the true nature of things. (There is an interesting somewhat sceptical work written against Priestley and the Scottish commonsense realists, *An Essay on the Nature and Existence of a*

49. Joseph Priestly, *An Examination of Dr. Reid's Inquiry into the Human Mind on the Principles of Common Sense, Dr. Beattie's Essay on the Nature and Immutability of Truth and Dr. Oswald's Appeal to Common Sense in Behalf of Religion*, London, 1774, pp. 5-6.

50. *Ibid.*, p. xxi.

51. David Hartley presented this position in his *Observations on Man, His Frame, His Duty and His Expectations*, London, 1749, Vol. I, chap. iii, "Of Propositions and the Nature of Assent."

Material World, London 1781. The work is anonymous, and is attributed to someone named Russell by the British Museum. It indicates some sceptical opposition existed to the prevailing anti-Humean treands.)[52]

The anti-Humean literature in England from 1750 to 1800 needs thorough investigation. In my own work so far I have only studied samples of it. It appears to me, from these soundings, to have failed fundamentally to come to grips with the basic challenge raised by Hume. In readapting the standard English response to the modern sceptical crisis, it tried to rest on a weak middle ground, not answering the sceptics, but insisting on the importance of what people have to believe. Post-Hume this position was even weaker than pre-Hume, in that Hume had undermined the irrationality of the situation in which our only way of making any sense or order out of our world resulted from unjustifiable and inexplicable qualities of human nature that could not be reconciled into any consistent pattern. Our beliefs could only be sustained by an animal faith, if one no longer was willing or able to make the religious leap into faith to resolve the sceptical crisis.

In the post-Humean era to appeal to our need to believe and our will to believe no longer constituted a genuine answer to scepticism, since Hume had absorbed these into modern scepticism. To get beyond Hume would require some basis for guaranteeing or justifying our knowledge that showed that we could somehow know the nature of reality. The British answer, in failing to come to grips with the basic epistemological issues, has left British philosophy adrift ever since, vascillating between reporting what we have to believe, how we speak, etc., and making a virtue of Humeanism in the form of positivism. Occasionally, and only occasionally, as in the case of the later Russell, in his *Human Knowledge, Its Scope and Limits,*[53] does the force of scepticism come to the fore, only to retreat into scientism, psychologism and naturalism. Those, including myself, who find most Anglo-American philosophy trivial, find it so, I believe,

52. I have been unable to find out any more about this work than is recorded by the British Museum. Coleridge is the only one I know of who mentions having read it.
53. Bertrand Russell, *Human Knowledge, Its Scope and Limits,* New York, 1948.

because of its failure from the seventeenth century onwards to recognize the problem involved in the sceptical crisis, its far-reaching implications for modern man, and the situation left after Hume's analysis. The anti-scepticism that pervaded England and Scotland in the late eighteenth century represented refusal to face up to the implications of Hume's work, and a refusal to deal with it. The reasonable man, like the ordinary man described by Hume, would be saved from the horrors of the sceptical crisis by stupidity and inattention, and would get through life with his beliefs. Hume, so sensitive to the abyss he had revealed, would have to struggle alternating between sceptical despair and being a normal man believing what came naturally.

If the English and Scottish reaction to Hume was tepid, uninspiring, and unsatisfactory, the monumental reaction to ultimate scepticism occurred in Germany, and has affected metaphysics ever since. In the middle of the eighteenth century there were many signs that scepticism was being taken very seriously. From the 1660s onward there were a stream of German dissertations dealing with the refutation of scepticism. My favourite of 1706 treated of the problem of whether Job or Solomon was the founder of scepticism, and concluded that it was the devil, since he made our first parents doubt the word of God himself.[54] From the time Hume appeared on the European scene, it was the leaders of the Prussian Academy who translated and commented upon his views. Formey and Mérian, who did the French translation, and Sulzer, who did the German, have not been studied. They recognized the tremendous importance of Hume's arguments, and tried to rebut him. Along with their work, translations of portions of Sextus Empiricus appeared, as well as the aphorisms of a genuine total sceptic, Platner (who later translated Hume's *Dialogues.*)[55] The insipid English answers to Hume were also translated into German.[56] In this atmosphere, it is

54. Q.D.B.V. de Scepticorum Praecipuis Hypothesibus, secundum constitutionem Fridericianum, Praeside Georgio Paschio, Kiloni, 1706, p. 4.
55. For information of this, see Popkin, "Scepticism in the Enlightenment," pp. 1341-42; and Tonelli, "Kant und die Antiken Skeptiker." Platner's translation, Gespräche uber naturliche Religion von David Hume, Leipzig, 1781, appears with a lengthy essay by Platner, "Ein Gesprach über Atheismus," pp. 255-396, dealing with Hume, Sextus, Pyrrhonism, fideism and atheism.
56. Leland as well as major and minor Scottish opponents of Hume were quickly translated into German.

not surprising that Kant became aware of what was afoot. The climax of the German Enlightenment came, of course, when Kant was awakened from his dogmatic slumbers by realizing what Hume had accomplished. As Kant pointed out in his original preface, the sceptics had previously been a small and ineffectual group, Locke had seemed to put an end to all disputes, until Hume came on the scene, and *really* raised the problem of whether it was possible to have any knowledge.[57]

Like Reid and the leaders of the Prussian Academy, Kant realized that Hume had raised a fundamental problem. Unlike them, he was aware that the problem could not be dealt with by evasions, but only by a revolutionary new programme. Kant's copernican Revolution in philosophy had the effect of simultaneously raising Hume's points to a transcendental status, while purporting to offer a way of dealing with them. Kant claimed to find a compromise between an unvanquishable scepticism about the possibility of any knowledge of the nature of reality and a universal and necessary certainty (constituting genuine knowledge) about the conditions of all possible experiences. Kant could see that Hume had eliminated any hope of finding universal and necessary knowledge by the experimental method of philosophizing, that had so impressed the *philosophes*. Kant transformed the issue by asking not "Is Knowledge possible?" but "How is Knowledge possible?" In this way, one did not have to argue with the sceptics, but instead one only had to explain the way in which we actually overcame scepticism. And, in Kant's rendition, we overcame it by conceding that it was unconquerable with regard to knowledge of external or internal reality, but could be conquered in terms of our knowledge of the form, and conditions of experience.[58] The Kantian system, it seems to me, embedded scepticism at such a fundamental level, that it made philosophy in its traditional sense impossible. It purported to get beyond scepticism, to, in fact, become an anti-scepticism, opening the way to a genuine appreciation of the character and evaluation of what knowledge was possible. One of Kant's disciples, Friedrich Staudlin, wrote a work in 1794, with the title of the *History and*

57. Immanuel Kant, *Kritik der reinen Vernunft*, ed. Adickes, Berlin, 1889, "Vorrede zur ersten Auflage vom Jahre 1781," p. 6.
58. Kant, *Kritik*, Einleitung and Der transendentalen Elementarlehre.

Spirit of Scepticism. It traced the history of scepticism from Pyrrho onward. On the title page were portraits of the two main characters, Hume and Kant. The second volume deals with them. Kant was portrayed as the thinker who had finally emerged triumphant in the life and death struggle between scepticism and dogmatism by finding a new way to accept the unanswerable arguments of the sceptics about the knowledge of reality without denying the existence of genuine knowledge about human experience.[59]

Kant, in raising the sceptical arguments to a transcendental level, made them central to all future metaphysics. His own claims to have gotten beyond scepticism spawned new forms of scepticism and in turn radical new means to escape the sceptical crisis. The intellectual battles fought in the last two decades of the eighteenth century in Germany over the status and import of Kant's critical philosophy have shaped the course of metaphysical theories ever since. Kant was assaulted from all sides. What interests us here is those attacks relating to the sceptical struggles. On the right wing was the criticism of his friend, the religious fanatic, J. G. Hamann. Hamann was immersed in Hume, read English, translated portions of the *Dialogues*, and found in Hume, "the greatest voice of orthodoxy."[60] Hume had seen that belief-faith was at the root of any human comprehension of the world. Hamann pressed Kant to see the fideistic core of any view of the world. Kant's second preface to the 1st *Critique*, where he claimed he had eliminated knowledge to make room for faith in the practical sphere, may have been an attempt to conciliate Hamann.[61] Hamann, as a result of confronting Hume's scepticism, rejected the Enlightenment, lock, stock and barrel, and opted for faith, pure Biblical faith. He saw Kant as weak-kneed in his reaction to Hume, refusing to follow the implications of total scepticism. Hamann translated the first and last of Hume's

59. Carl Fridrich Stäudlin, *Geschichte und Geist des Skepticismus*, Leipzig, 1794.

60. Hamann, commenting on the conclusion of Hume's essay, "Of miracles" said, "so ist diess allemal Orthodoxie, und ein Zeugniss der Wahrheit in dem Munde eines Feindes und Verfolgers derselben." Johann G. Hamann, *Schriften*, Theil I, Berlin, 1821, p. 406.

61. Kant, *Kritik*, "Vorrede zur zweiten Auflage," B.XXX, "Ich musste also das Wissen aufheben, um zum Glauben Platz zu bekommen."

Dialogues to try to bring Kant to his senses or to his faith.[62] Hamann's irrationalist fideistic response was to open the road to Kierkegaard and then to modern Neo-Orthodoxy. Hume had closed the door on reason, and thereby, made it possible to appreciate the need to return to pure faith. It was in fact Hamann's Humeanism that converted Kierkegaard.[63]

If irrationalism-fideism was one kind of sceptical response to Kant, another was the stark drawing of the sceptical implications of Kantian thought, as was done by G. E. Schulze-Aenisedemus. Schulze chose the name "Aenisedemus" to indicate what he was trying to show, namely that Kantian philosophy, whatever its assertions to the contrary, could not justify any knowledge-claims whatsoever. Schulze-Aenisedemus insisted that Kant's introduction of the "thing-in-itself" was illegitimate and that all his elegant system only dealt with the world of appearance. If Kant were consistent, Schulze-Aenesidemus insisted, he would be reduced to the ancient sceptical position.[64]

While Hamann tried to drag Kant off to religion, and Schulze-Aenesidemus to complete doubt, the most interesting development, at least to me, appeared in the writings of the strange Jewish philosopher, Solomon Maimon, the man whom Kant considered his most worthy opponent, the only one who had really understood him. Maimon had come from his Talmudic studies in Lithuania into Enlightenment Germany. A friend of Kant's Jewish friends, Moses Mendelsohn, Marcus Herz and Lazarus Ben David, Maimon showed them his criticisms of Kant's *Critique*. Herz sent these to Kant, who wrote "but a glance at the manuscript soon enabled me to recognize its merits and to see not only that none of my opponents had understood me and the main problem so well, but that very few could claim so much penetration and sublety of mind in profound inquiries of this sort

62. Cf. Philip Merlan, "Hamann et les Dialogues de Hume," *Revue de Métaphysique et de Morale* 59, 1954, pp. 285-89; and "Hume and Hamann," *Personalist* 32, 1951, pp. 111-18. See also R. H. Popkin, "Kierkegaard and Scepticism" in *Kierkegaard. A Collection of Critical Essays*, ed. by Josiah Thompson, Garden City, N.Y. 1972, pp. 361-72.

63. Cf. Walter Lowrie, *Kierkegaard*, London, 1938, pp. 165-67.

64. Gottlob Ernst Schulze, *Aenesidemus oder über die Fundamente der von dem Herrn Reinhold in Jena gelieferten Elementarphilosophie. Nebst einen Vertheidigung des Skepticismus gegen die Anmassungen der Vernuftkritik*, n.p., 1792.

as Herr Maimon."[65] In his brief philosophical career ending in 1800, Maimon tried to show the weaknesses of Kant's attempt to overcome scepticism, and the opening of a new road beyond scepticism, that was to usher in the next metaphysical era with Fichte's subjective idealism, set forth in his *Vocation of Man* (1800).[66] On the one hand Maimon argued that Kant could not establish the relevance of the categories to experience except *a postiori*, and hence that no synthetic *a priori* knowledge about experience was possible. On the other hand, he argued against Hume and Schulze that there had to be an *a priori* structure, otherwise nothing at all made any sense. Logic and mathematics indicated this was not the case. His position between Hume and Kant would amount to what later emerged as logical positivism, except for his indication that the creative power of the mind, its reflection of the power of infinite mind, opened a different door via intuition and feeling to an understanding of experience. This turn to non-rational factors as those constitutive of our knowledge began a road to romanticism, or metaphysical idealism. Johann Gottlieb Fichte developed this new avenue. Both Fichte and the young Hegel saw scepticism as the beginning moment of philosophizing. The recognition of the limits imposed on human rational efforts of previous philosophy then made one aware of the possibilities actually open to man. For Fichte, one only overcame scepticism by a deliberate act of the will.[67] One's ego, through its own actions, creates the knowledge of reality as well as relaity itself. It is no longer necessary to try to bridge the gulf between subject and object. One's own creative efforts provide the basis and structure of both.

The German reaction to Hume's scepticism was more fundamental than that that occurred in France or England. In the person of Kant, the Germans saw that traditional philosophy had reached a total impasse. It was not a question of developing

---

65. Cited in Samuel Atlas, *From Critical to Speculative Idealism. The Philosophy of Solomon Maimon*, (The Hague 1964), p. 5. On Maimon's career, see his *Solomon Maimons Lebensgeschichte*, (Munich 1911). On his scepticism, see chap. xiii of Atlas's book.

66. On Maimon's relation to Fichte, see Atlas, op. cit., pp. 316-24.

67. Cf. Johann Gotlieb Fichte's *Die Bestimmung des Menschen* and *Grundlage der gesamten Wissenschaftslehre*, erster Teil.

another, now hopeless, anti-scepticism, but rather a post-scepticism. The Grand Illusion, developed from Greek days onward, that human reason and science could gain knowledge of necessary essential features of reality, had been ended. All that could be done was either accept the situation and describe the characteristics of what people "know" as Kant and Husserl did, or to develop different avenues to knowledge as Hegel did. The march of reason developed to the sceptical impasse. The creative power of the mind, its immersion with universal reason could carry it beyond by processes beyond pure reason. Whether these have in fact revealed reality, or just more of the human predicament I do not know. Heidegger's rendition would seem to indicate the utter hopelessness of these means to penetrate the Mystery of Being.

Hume's scepticism produced, I believe, a monumental crisis for Western philosophical thought. The reactions to it in France, England and Germany indicate the range of philosophical attempts to deal with it. The anti-scepticisms of the latter part of the eighteenth century have shaped and formed the course of though ever since. We are now living in full realization of the consequences of this period in intellectual history. The serious study of it may reveal both the roots of our problems, and the possibilities for any further constructive discourse between us and our world.

Richard H. Popkin

Jerome – Plate I

rome – Plate II

DESIGNS

BY

Mr. R. BENTLEY,

FOR SIX

POEMS

BY

Mr. T. GRAY.

LONDON:

Printed for R. DODSLEY, in Pall-mall.

MDCCLIII.

ELEGY

Written in a Country Church Yard.

 HE Curfew tolls the knell of parting day,
The lowing herd wind flowly o'er the lea,
The plowman homeward plods his weary wa
And leaves the world to darkness and to me

No

The EPITAPH.

HERE rests his head upon the lap of Earth
   A Youth to Fortune and to Fame unknown,
ir Science frown'd not on his humble birth,
d Melancholy mark'd him for her own.

rge was his bounty, and his soul sincere,
av'n did a recompence as largely send:
  gave to Mis'ry all he had, a tear,
  gain'd from Heav'n ('twas all he wish'd) a friend.

farther seek his merits to disclose,
  draw his frailties from their dread abode,
here they alike in trembling hope repose)
e bosom of his Father and his God.

Taylor — Plate III

    Poplitibus, timidoque tergo.
Virtus, repulsae nescia sordidae,
Intaminatis fulget honoribus;
   Nec sumit aut ponit secures
    Arbitrio popularis aurae.   20
Virtus, recludens immeritis mori
Coelum, negata tentat iter via;
   Coetusque vulgares, et udam
    Spernit humum fugiente penna.
Est et fideli tuta silentio   25
Merces: vetabo, qui Cereris sacrum
   Vulgarit arcanae, sub iisdem
    Sit trabibus, fragilemque mecum
Solvat phaselum. saepe Diespiter
Neglectus incesto addidit integrum: 30
   Raro antecedentem scelestum
    Deseruit pede poena claudo.

Taylor — Plate IV

ODE XXII.

AD ARISTIVM FVSCVM.

INTEGER vitae, scelerisque purus
   Non eget Mauris jaculis, nequearcu,
   Nec venenatis gravida sagittis,
    Fusce, pharetra;
Sive per Syrtes iter aestuosas,   5
Sive facturus per inhospitalem
Caucasum, vel quae loca fabulosus
   Lambit Hydaspes.
Namque me silva lupus in Sabina,
Dum meam canto Lalagen, et ultra   10
Terminum curis vagor expeditis,
   Fugit inermem:
Quale portentum neque militaris
Daunia in latis alit esculetis;
Nec Iubae tellus generat, leonum   15
   Arida nutrix.

M

Taylor — Plate V

Taylor — Plate VI

A LONG STORY.

 N BRITAIN's Ifle, no matter where,
An ancient pile of building ftands :
The Huntingdons and Hattons there
Employ'd the power of Fairy hands

To raife the cieling's fretted height,
Each pannel in achievements cloathing,
Rich windows that exclude the light,
And paffages, that lead to nothing.

Full

Taylor – Plate VII

LE DENICHEUR DE MOINEAUX

Taylor – Plate VIII

Taylor — Plate IX

William Henshaw,
CABINET-MAKER,
To the Cabinet and Chair,
On the South Side of St Paul's Church Yard,
London
Makes and Sells all sorts of
Glass, Chair, and Cabinet Work
Where Gentlemen, Merchants, & Others
may depend upon being serv'd with
the very best Goods, at the most
Reasonable Prices.

SIZE OF ORIGINAL 8½" × 6½" *See page 83*

Taylor — Plate X

O D E.

 O! where the rosy-bosom'd Hours,
Fair VENUS' train appear;
Disclose the long-expecting flowers,
And wake the purple year!
The Attic warbler pours her throat,
Responsive to the cuckow's note,
The untaught harmony of spring:
While whisp'ring pleasure as they fly,
Cool Zephyrs thro' the clear blue sky
Their gather'd fragrance fling.

Where'er

Taylor — Plate XIII

O D E

On the Death of a Favourite CAT,

Drowned in a Tub of Gold Fishes.

WAS on a lofty vafe's fide,
Where China's gayeft art had dy'd
  The azure flowers, that blow;
Demureft of the tabby kind,
The penfive Selima reclin'd,
  Gazed on the lake below.

Her confcious tail her joy declar'd;
The fair round face, the fnowy beard,
  The velvet of her paws,
Her coat, that with the tortoife vies,
Her ears of jet, and emerald eyes,
  She faw; and purr'd applaufe

Still

Taylor — Plate XIV

O D E

On a Diftant Profpect of

ETON COLLEGE.

·E diftant fpires, ye antique towers,
    That crown the watry glade,
    Where grateful Science ftill adores
    Her HENRY's holy Shade;
And ye, that from the ftately brow
Of WINDSOR's heights th' expanfe below
Of grove, of lawn, of mead furvey,
Whofe turf, whofe fhade, whofe flowers among
Wanders the hoary Thames along
His filver-winding way.

Ah

Thy form benign, oh Goddefs, wear,
Thy milder influence impart,
Thy philofophic Train be there
To foften, not to wound my heart,
The gen'rous fpark extinct revive,
Teach me to love and to forgive,
Exact my own defects to fcan,
What others are, to feel, and know myfelf a Man.

Saeviet circa jecur ulcerofum; 15
  Non fine queftu,
Laeta quod pubes edera virenti
Gaudeat, pulla magis atque myrto;
Aridas frondes hiemis fodali
  Dedicet Hebro. 20

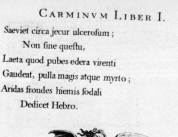

Taylor — Plate XV

Taylor — Plate XVI

Lipking — Plate I

Lipking – Plate II

Lipking – Plate III

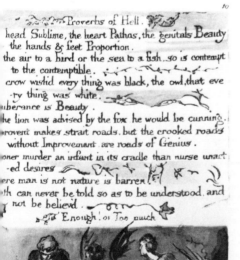

Lipking – Plate IV

Lipking – Plate V

As a new heaven is begun, and it is now thir-
ty-three years since its advent: the Eternal Hell
revives. And lo! Swedenborg is the Angel sitting
at the tomb: his writings are the linen clothes folded
up. Now is the dominion of Edom, & the return of
Adam into Paradise; see Isaiah XXXIV & XXXV Chap:
Without Contraries is no progression. Attraction
and Repulsion, Reason and Energy, Love and
Hate, are necessary to Human existence.
From these contraries spring what the religious call
Good & Evil. Good is the passive that obeys Reason.
Evil is the active springing from Energy.
Good is Heaven. Evil is Hell.

Lipking – Plate VI

The Argument.

Rintrah roars & shakes his fires in the burdend air
Hungry clouds swag on the deep

Once meek, and in a perilous path,
The just man kept his course along
The vale of death.
Roses are planted where thorns grow,
And on the barren heath
Sing the honey bees.

Then the perilous path was planted:
And a river, and a spring
On every cliff and tomb;
And on the bleached bones
Red clay brought forth.

Till the villain left the paths of ease,
To walk in perilous paths, and drive
The just man into barren climes.

Now the sneaking serpent walks
In mild humility,
And the just man rages in the wilds
Where lions roam.

Rintrah roars & shakes his fires in the
burdend air;
Hungry clouds swag on the deep.

Lipking – Plate VII

Those who restrain desire, do so because theirs
is weak enough to be restrained; and the restrainer or
reason usurps its place & governs the unwilling.
And being restraind it by degrees becomes passive
till it is only the shadow of desire.
The history of this is written in Paradise Lost, & the
Governor or Reason is calld Messiah.
And the original Archangel or possessor of the com-
mand of the heavenly host, is calld the Devil or Satan
and his children are calld Sin & Death
But in the Book of Job Miltons Messiah is calld
Satan.
For this history has been adopted by both parties
It indeed appeard to Reason as if Desire was
cast out, but the Devils account is that the Mess-

Lipking – Plate VIII

The ancient tradition that the world will be consumed in fire at the end of six thousand years
is true, as I have heard from Hell.
For the cherub with his flaming sword is
hereby commanded to leave his guard at tree
of life, and when he does, the whole creation will
be consumed, and appear infinite, and holy
whereas it now appears finite & corrupt.
This will come to pass by an improvement of
sensual enjoyment.
But first the notion that man has a body
distinct from his soul, is to be expunged; this
I shall do, by printing in the infernal method,
by corrosives, which in Hell are salutary and me-
dicinal, melting apparent surfaces away, and
displaying the infinite which was hid.
If the doors of perception were cleansed
every thing would appear to man as it is, infinite.
For man has closed himself up, till he sees
all things thro' narrow chinks of his cavern.

Lipking – Plate IX

The ancient Poets animated all sensible objects
Gods or Geniuses, calling them by the names and
ning them with the properties of woods, rivers,
ntains, lakes, cities, nations, and whatever their
d & numerous senses could perceive.
nd particularly they studied the genius of each
e country placing it under its mental deity.
ill a system was formed, which some took ad-
ge of & enslav'd the vulgar by attempting to
lize or abstract the mental deities from their
cts: thus began Priesthood.
hoosing forms of worship from poetic tales.
nd at length they pronounc'd that the Gods
I order'd such things.
hus men forgot that All deities reside in
the human breast.

Lipking – Plate X

pulse, not from rules.
    When he had so spoken: I beheld the Angel who
stretchd out his arms embracing the flame of fire
he was consumed and arose as Elijah.
    Note. This Angel, who is now become a Devil, is
my particular friend: we often read the Bible together in its infernal or diabolical sense which
the world shall have if they behave well.
    I have also: The Bible of Hell: which the world
shall have whether they will or no.

One Law for the Lion & Ox is Oppression

Lipking – Plate XI

Lipking – Plate XII

Bentley — 2

Bentley — 1 a (top), 1 b (bottom)

Bentley — 3

Bentley — 4A

Bentley — 4B

Bentley — 4C

Bentley — 5

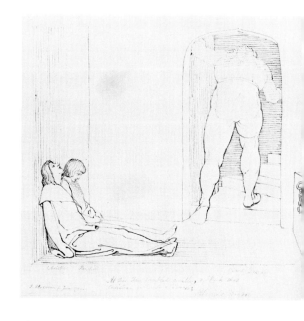

Then said she to her Children, Sons
we are all undone, I have sinned against away
Your father and he is gone; he would
have had us go with him, but I would
not go myself; I have also hindered
you of life;

Bentley — 7

... she thought she saw two very ill-favoured ones standing by her bedside, & saying what shall we do with this woman.

Bentley — 8

...to whom she spake out, saying, if thou comest in Gods name, come in. So he said amen, & opened the door

Bentley — 9

Behold, they build the good Woman preparing to be gone from her house.

Bentley — 10

Bentley — 1

and Mercy began to weep

Bentley — 12

Bentley — 13 a (top)
13 b (bottom)

Bentley — 14A

Bentley — 14B a (top) b-c-d (middle & bottom)   15B a 15B c

he has broken out & has worried some that I loved; but
I take all at present patiently. I also give my Pilgn
timely Help.

25

Bentley — 15A

Bentley — 16A

Bentley — 16B a-d, f-i

16B e (lower middle)

Bentley — 16C

He also attempted to take them
but they did make their escape over the wall.
28

..., attempted to take them
28

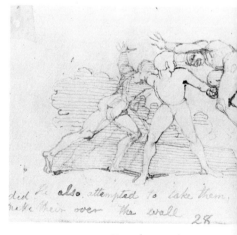

did he also attempted to take them,
make them over the wall 28

Bentley — 18

They stroaked them over their faces

Bentley — 19

Then they went in and they washed gently his legs & all

44

Bentley — 20A

Bentley — 20B

So he commanded them
ut it m. it was f
linnen white & cle

Bentley — 21A

Bentley — 21B

Bentley — 23A

Bentley — 22 a (top), 22 b (bottom)

Bentley — 24

Bentley — 23B

Bentley — 25A

Bentley — 26 a (top), 26 b (bottom)

Bentley — 25B

Bentley — 27

Bentley — 28

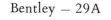

Slay good   Feeble mind

Bentley — 29A

Slay-good
The many thou hast slain when th
dragged them out of the King's h

Bentley — 29C

Bentley — 29B

Bentley — 30

and Giant Despair was brought down to the g
but was very loth to die   139

Bentley — 31

Rose – Plate I

Rose – Plate II

Rose – Plate III

Rose – Plate IV

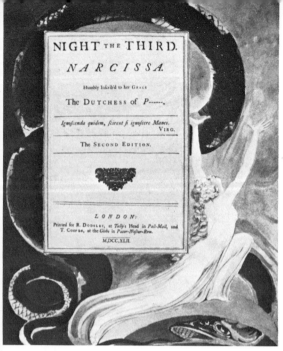

Rose — Plate VI

Rose — Plate V

Rose — Plate VII

Rose — Plate VIII

Rose – Plate IX

Rose – Plate X

Rose – Plate XI

Rose – Plate XII

Rose – Plate XIII

Rose – Plate XIV

Rose – Plate XV

Rose – Plate XVI

NIGHT THE SECOND.

ON

TIME, DEATH, FRIENDSHIP.

HUMBLY INSCRIB'D

To the RIGHT HONOURABLE
The EARL of *WILMINGTON.*

LONDON:

Printed for R. DODSLEY, at *Tully's* Head in *Pall-Mall,* and
T. COOPER, at the *Globe* in *Pater-Noster-Row.*

M,DCC,XLII.

Rose — Plate XVII